Ostromirovo Gospel (Ostromir's Gospel), 1056-57, the oldest dated East Slavic text.

DMITRIJ TSCHIZEWSKIJ

RUSSIAN INTELLECTUAL HISTORY

Translated by John C. Osborne
Edited by Martin P. Rice

Ardis / Ann Arbor

Russian Intellectual History

*Das heilige Russland. Russische Geistesgeschichte
I: 10.-17. Jahrhundert. Zwischen Ost und West.
Russische Geistesgeschichte II: 18.-20. Jahrhundert*
originally published by Rowohlt, Hamburg 1959
and 1961.

Published by Ardis, 2901 Heatherway, Ann Arbor,
Michigan, 48104.

ISBN 0-88233-219-8

CONTENTS

Part I: *Holy Russia, 900-1700*

Part II: *Russia between East and West, 1700-1905*

The Izbornik of 1073, a miscellany translated for Sviatoslav. Calendar notations and Zodiac signs are in the margins.

EDITOR'S NOTE

This translation presents Professor Tschizewskij's *Das heilige Russland. Russische Geistesgeschichte I: 10.-17. Jahrhundert* and *Zwischen Ost und West. Russische Geistesgeschichte II: 18.-20. Jahrhundert* (Hamburg: Rowohlt, 1959 and 1961). This new material, which reflects the latest scholarship in Russian intellectual history, replaces the former "Source Appendix" of the German edition. The bibiliography has been compiled by the editor; however, whenever English translations of works in Professor Tschizewskij's bibliography were available, they were included. The *Chronological Overview* of the original covered only the years treated in Part I and has been extended to cover the period until 1905. In addition, certain footnotes which were of significance only for a German reader have been deleted and a few supplemental footnotes have been added. These latter are indicated in brackets as "Editor's note."

Russian words have been transliterated according to System II in J. Thomas Shaw's *The Transliteration of Modern Russian for English-Language Publications* (Madison, Wis., 1967). However, proper names which are generally familiar to English-speaking readers—Dostoevsky, Tolstoy—have been retained in their usual form.

M.P.R.

Cathedral of St. Sophia. Kiev 1017-37. Detail of interior.

PART I: *HOLY RUSSIA, 900-1700*

St. Dmitrii Cathedral in Vladimir, 12th century.

INTRODUCTION

The Proper Concern of Intellectual History

What is the proper concern of intellectual history? This question can be answered tautologically: it is the historical development of man's "intellectual and spiritual character." We can presume that the meaning of "historical development" is generally known, but the term "intellectual and spiritual character" requires some explanation, and I shall attempt to define it as simply and as succinctly as possible. By "intellectual and spiritual character" we mean man's consciousness of the ultimate foundations of his existence. Every human being possesses such consciousness, be it ever so vague and ill-defined. There are two major aspects of this consciousness: first, man's conception of what place he occupies in his social environment, in the natural physical world, and in the supernatural realm (if he acknowledges that such exists); and second, his notion of how he is related to the past and to the future. Intellectual history can treat this consciousness of the individual only if it is formulated in concepts. Since the intellectual historian has at his disposal as source material primarily written documents (and less frequently oral traditions), he can hope to arrive at conceptual formulations through interpretations of the facts at his disposal. Even when he deals with *realia,* he can occasionally arrive at a conceptual comprehension of the human consciousness which produced them. In this book we shall be concerned almost exclusively with written documents.

When I referred above to the "place" of the individual human being in a given *environment*, I was actually indicating that intellectual character and spirit become manifest whenever a human being or group of human beings is confronted with *"something else,"* for it is only in this process of coming to grips with "something else" that a given cast of mind can arise.

Intellectual history, then, is concerned with the development of man's spiritual and intellectual character during a period of time, and through the course of time intellectual history can trace constant changes in the attitudes of "significant representatives," i.e., men and women in whom the intellectual and spiritual character of an age is manifest. We shall focus primarily on such individual figures, and we believe it our duty to emphasize primarily what in each of them is *typical of the era* in which he lived.

We should bear in mind that if we look for "typical" phenomena of intellectual history we shall usually be dealing with a limited number of documents. Every age has its "significant representatives," and it is their utterances—not the opinions, attitudes, and desires of the silent masses—to which the intellectual historian has access. It is possible that the statements made by

11

these "representatives" may go further or be more pointed than the opinions of the masses; it is therefore the scholar's task to determine as far as possible to what extent the ideas of a "representative" are in fact typical of his time and accurate reflections of the attitudes of the masses. The scholar, of course, can never be absolutely certain that his assessment is accurate, and in this respect intellectual history is similar to all disciplines which deal with intellectual and cultural phenomena—the history of philosophy, the history of literature, and, perhaps to an even greater degree, the history of politics.

I should emphasize that in dealing with Russian intellectual history in this book I have distinguished sharply between the Russian spiritual and intellectual character and "the Russian soul." I personally do not believe that it is possible to characterize "the Russian soul." The soul of an individual is unique, it cannot be duplicated, and it cannot be considered an inseparable part of an agglomerate. In my opinion, all attempts made thus far to characterize "the Russian soul" have proven to be completely arbitrary intellectual constructs which reveal less about the intangible "Russian soul" than they do about the soul of the person trying to characterize it. Moreover, in many instances characterizations of the "Russian soul" have been based on the study of Russians of different epochs and from different geographical areas and even on the study of "people presumed to be Russians," such as Ukrainians, and even Poles and Finns. I cannot go further into a criticism of the concept of the "soul of a people" here, but the above remarks should suffice to make clear my own point of view.

But can we not raise similar objections to the concept of "the intellectual and spiritual character of a given people at a given time in history?" I do not think so. Whereas experiences of the *soul* can be extraordinarily varied, and whereas we have no right to presume that members of the same people—often merely citizens of the same state—have identical souls, in *intellectual* history we are dealing with relationships of the human consciousness to its environment, and in every epoch this environment is essentially the same for everyone; that is, an entire group of human beings—a people, for instance—is confronted by the same temporally conditioned complex of events and must therefore find solutions for the same set of problems. This common "frame of reference" makes it possible for the intellectual historian to draw a uniform picture of intellectual and spiritual character and to conceptualize it.

It cannot be denied, of course, that contemporaries often give different answers to the same questions posed to them by their environment. I will even go so far as to assert that one of the essential characteristics of intellectual and spiritual development is that in a given "intellectual area" and at a given time the "significant representatives" tend to adopt opposing, perhaps even diametrically opposed points of view. When conservative and reactionary trends grow stronger, as a rule revolutionary and anarchistic attitudes and movements also grow stronger. The two opposing trends are faced with the same realities and therefore seem to us "hostile twin brothers." The same thing frequently occurs with intellectual trends of a non-political nature; often, though not always, literary, philosophical, and religious movements also evoke the movements which oppose them. Numerous examples of this can be cited. When one attributes to the French intellectual and spiritual character a particular inclination toward rationalism, one must not forget that simultaneous to the rationalism of the seventeenth century Pascal and Malebranche were advocating mystical thoughts and that Malebranche's mystical Augustinian system, although based on Cartesian philosophy, was paradoxically seeking to overcome Cartesian rationalism. And empiricism alone is by no means, as it often thought, characteristic of the English intellectual and spiritual character. For seventeenth-century England Platonism was no less significant, and in nineteenth-century England Hegelianism was almost as influential as empiricism and associationism. Moreover, elements which are not empirical but of quite a different sort are actually central to the thought of such "empiricists" as Locke and Berkeley. In the works of Locke we find "supra-empirical" thoughts which are related to Husserl's phenomenology, and Berkeley developed a metaphysical system akin to that of Plotinus.

The development of intellectual and spiritual character in polar opposites is especially characteristic of Russian intellectual history, as will be seen below. It may suffice for now to call attention to such parallel phenomena as "Slavophilism" and "Westernism" in the nineteenth century, or to the simultaneous existence, in our time, of a religious metaphysics which has been able to exert influence outside Russia and an atheistic, anti-metaphysical, Marxistic (or pseudo-Marxistic) philosophy which has also been influential beyond the borders of Russia.

Even though the intellectual character of a people during a given epoch may split into opposing intellectual trends locked in combat with each other, the trends themselves are nevertheless confronted with the same temporally conditioned complex of problems, and they therefore can and indeed must be considered in conjunction with each other. In such instances the result is a "dialectic" picture which, for all its lights and shadows, will nevertheless constitute a unity.

Source Material for Russian Intellectual History

For the time after the Christianization of Russia we possess a considerable number of written sources; one of the foremost experts on old Russian literary monuments estimates that about 100,000 manuscripts dating from the eleventh to the seventeenth century have been preserved and notes that the number increases from century to century in a geometric progression. Unfortunately, these sources express only infrequently and then not always clearly the *basic ideas* which inspired and motivated their authors. Often we simply must rely on our ability to interpret the sources, and interpretations, as is well known, are often disputed.

We also have at our disposal documents written by non-Russians. The oldest such works, those of the Byzantines and the Arabians, cannot be utilized without careful analysis. The ever larger number of reports written by people who traveled in Russia during the sixteenth and seventeenth centuries and later are also full of the sort of misunderstandings which so easily arise when persons who do not have a sufficient grasp of a foreign language make a conscious attempt to assess objectively the customs and attitudes of the people who speak that tongue.

Assessments of Russian antiquity which are based on documents written in recent times (primarily folk tales and works dealing with folk superstitions) can no longer be taken seriously. The romanticists of the nineteenth century and the scientific dilettantes of all ages believed that numerous elements from long-forgotten epochs could be found in the life of the common folk today; but since it can be proved that many of the customs and usages, songs and proverbs, etc., which were thought to be "as old as the hills" are actually of quite recent origin, we must exercise great caution whenever we use modern depictions of times gone by. Poems composed in the eighteenth and nineteenth centuries have been found among the most popular Russian "folk songs"—the famous "Volga Boatman's Song" did not appear until after 1870 —and numerous Russian proverbs turn out to be translations from the Greek and later the German, or borrowings from Polish, and therefore can by no means be considered manifestations of "Russian folk wisdom." This state of affairs forces the intellectual historian to be very skeptical and circumspect when investigating earlier ages and to prefer in cases of doubt to remain discreetly silent rather than to assert too much which cannot be proved.

The attempt is also often made to reconstruct some facts of Russian intellectual life in analogy to similar phenomena among other Slavic peoples or even among the Indo-Europeans, but these conclusions by analogy usually afford us only apparent insights and obstruct for us the path to further unprejudiced research. Moreover, the source material at our disposal is frequently quite limited. Our best sources often provide no answers to important questions, quite apart from the fact that we no longer have a completely clear understanding of many words, mainly technical terms, such as those which are used in old legal documents. Many details are not reported with sufficient thoroughness. For example, in Russia at legal proceedings, the so-called ordeals—trial by fire and water—and trial by combat were known. We would like to know more about them, of course, but our sources report on them only in rather general terms. Dare we employ the method of analogy and draw conclusions from old Polish law, for instance, which was reproduced in German in the thirteenth century in the so-called "Elbinger Buch"? Another example: in Russia the throwing down of the gauntlet to declare a feud was known, but only once, in an account of a saint's life, do we find a report of

14

this legal-symbolic act. Dare we assume that throwing down the gauntlet was generally widespread? There are a host of such unanswerable questions.

Even the concrete facts of a given historical event are not always clear to us today. For example, we do not even know whether a Greek metropolitan maintained a residence in Kiev from 988, the date of Christianization, until 1037. We are also unable to determine whether, as some sources assert, the first tsar of the new dynasty, Mikhail Romanov, accepted any restrictions of his autocracy when he acceded to the throne in 1613.

Another factor is the partisanship with which Russian history has been depicted since the earliest times. In many questions even the old Russian chronicles can be faulted on this score. Since the sixteenth century the dynastic point of view has dominated all historical portrayals. The theme "Holy Russia" is also treated in a crude and one-sided way, and recent Soviet Russian scholarship introduces even into popular literature several allegedly indisputable theses which in reality are not supported by sufficient reasons. Soviet scholars deny, for example, that the Normans (Varangians) played any decisive role in the establishment of the East Slavic states (some deny that they played any role at all). A second example: the significance of Byzantium for the development of the old Russian language and its literature is underestimated. And a third: Soviet scholars often find in the slightest intimations sufficient evidence to construe that in all ages the "oppressed classes" in old Russia engaged in "revolts." There are no facts whatsoever to support such assertions, which are in reality based either on exaggerated nationalism or on the theory of "the class struggle" now elevated to dogma. Regrettably, these tendentious statements are occasionally accepted as fact by scholars in the West. An even more pernicious distortion occurs when the scholar or popularizer arbitrarily evaluates or revaluates the facts of the past, as is sometimes the case in histories of literature, and especially in histories of the Church.

Naturally I cannot discuss all the points of view advanced in secondary literature, but the reader should not be surprised if he encounters in other works on Russian intellectual history, especially those which have appeared in Soviet Russia, different views on many questions.

Plan and Organization

This work will deal with neither the pre-Christian nor the post-Revolutionary period; it begins with the Christianization of the East Slavs and traces Russian intellectual history up to about 1905. The portrayal is divided into two parts: Volume I, "Holy Russia," begins with the tenth century and extends to the beginning of the seventeenth century; Volume II, "Russia Between East and West," treats the eighteenth, nineteenth, and early twentieth centuries. While the entire East Slavic area will be considered for the period from the tenth to the thirteenth century (the period during which the three

15

East Slavic peoples—the Great Russians, the Ukrainians, and the White Russians—began to take shape and become differentiated from each other), the portrayal of the remaining epochs will be restricted to the Great Russians. The Ukrainians and the White Russians not only belonged to a different state (Poland-Lithuania), they also underwent completely different intellectual-historical processes and in this respect had even less in common with the Great Russian than they did in respect to language, folklore, and politics. In the seventeenth century, it is true, strong Ukrainian and White Russian influence on the culture of Muscovy begins, but it seems to me that the origins of the great crisis of the seventeenth century are essentially Muscovite in character.

I have chosen to concentrate in Volume I on the two most important problems in older Russian intellectual history: political consciousness and religious experience.These problems sometimes overlap;in the sixteenth and seventeenth centuries they merge almost completely; at other times they develop independently of each other and in quite different ways. In Volume II, I have focused primarily on Russian attempts to come to grips with the West. These efforts are most intimately linked with the problems of political consciousness and religious experience and, more importantly, with questions concerning the future of Russia.

Volume I, "Holy Russia," begins with a portrayal of the Christianization of the East Slavs (Chapter I) and then deals with four complexes of problems which follow in chronological order. After Christianization was well under way in the tenth century we find in the religious literature of the eleventh and twelfth centuries controversies between two religious trends which are important for Russian intellectual history (Chapter II). With the invasion of the Tatars in the thirteenth century there begins an intellectual crisis which dominates the fourteenth and fifteenth centuries (Chapter III) and which leads in the sixteenth century to the consolidation of the Muscovite empire and also to new intellectual-historical conflicts (Chapter IV). The victory of Muscovite absolutism and of the notion of "Holy Russia" (beginning in the sixteenth century) is followed at the beginning of the seventeenth century by upheavals, by an initial and at first relatively modest "turn to the West," and by another religious crisis leading to the Church schism, which concludes the seventeenth century and the intellectual history of old Russia (Chapter V).

Volume II, "Russia Between East and West," begins with a retrospective survey of Russian relations with and attitudes toward its neighbors in Europe and in the Orient. The superficial and "external" Europeanization" of Russia was effected by Peter the Great during the first quarter of the eighteenth century (Chapter I), and during the reign of Catherine the Great (1762-1796) various attempts were made to establish a more meaningful and profound relationship to European intellectual life (Chapter II). After the defeat of Napoleon in 1815 there began the period of conflict between Slavophilism and Westernism (1815-1850), an era during which independent views on Russian culture and the relationship of Russia to the West emerged (Chapter III). The Russian Enlightenment which followed (1850-1880) witnessed the rise and spread of political radicalism (Chapter IV), and during the decade and a half before the Revolution of 1905 the Russian conception of culture changed and "modern" intellectual and political Russia arose (Chapter V).

It was impossible, of course, to pursue all lines of development. In fact, it is far more difficult to discuss the Russian intellectual history of the eighteenth and nineteenth centuries, from which a large number of documents are available, than it is to treat the older period. In my discussion of the modern period I have attempted to present a coherent picture and to pass over in silence only those phenomena which have exerted no lasting influence or are of no great significance for an understanding of developments in Russian intellectual history since the Revolution of 1905. It was therefore necessary to limit discussion to the most salient facts, even though in the process some significant personalities and movements had to be ignored completely or only mentioned in passing. We are fortunate in possessing in English a number of works devoted to specific problems, epochs, and aspects of Russian intellectual history; the most worthwhile of these are listed in the bibliography appended to this volume.

CHAPTER I. THE CHRISTIANIZATION OF THE EAST SLAVS

Date of Christianization

It is possible to give an exact date for the Christianization of the East Slavs: 988. To be sure, this designates only the year when Christianity was recognized as the offficial *state* religion and when the royal family was baptized. Our chief sources here are the old Russian *Chronicles,* the oldest of which was probably not written until some fifty years after Christianization. It is noteworthy that this Chronicle—the *Primary Chronicle,* or, as it is also called, after one of its compilers, the *Nestor Chronicle*—gives several versions of the events which led up to Christianization.[1] The only thing that is certain is that the Christian faith was introduced by Prince Vladimir the Saint after negotiations with Byzantium, and that the population of Kiev was baptized in 988.

The East Slavic Region and Its Population

At that time the East Slavic population was situated in Eastern Europe, mainly in lands along a line running from Lake Ladoga in the north to the Black Sea in the south. There were also, of course, settlements further to the northeast and to the south along the Sea of Azov. Artifacts from excavations have been analyzed by modern methods, and the results warrant the assumption that the major occupation of the East Slavs was agriculture—not hunting and fishing, as had been presumed until only a few decades ago. Numerous cities were scattered over this area. Some were real cities in which trade and industry prospered, but others were merely places of refuge surrounded by mighty earthworks, fortified spots to which the rural population would flee in times of danger. Two of the major cities of the first type were Novgorod, situated on the Volkhov River not far from Lake Ilmen, and Kiev, located on the middle course of the Dnieper. The Novgorod-Kiev trade route was the important one leading from Scandinavia to Byzantium, and the trade relationships made possible by this route were also the basis of the wealth of Eastern European trade centers, especially in the tenth and eleventh centuries. The route served for both transit and export trade, and the main exports were pelts, honey and wax, slaves, and perhaps also grain.

Trade also led to the rise and establishment of organized states. As early as the ninth century Slavs attempted to organize governments side by side with the organization which the Varangian princes had established, primarily for trading purposes. There is documentary evidence that toward the end of

18

the tenth century several lands were ruled by Varangian princes. Later tendentious histories—the chronicles of the eleventh century are perhaps the first—claim that there was only one Varangian royal dynasty, that of the semi-legendary Riurik (Roerek), but scattered reports in the chronicles betray the true state of affairs, namely that there were several Varangian dynasties, at least three of them, which reigned along side of the last Slavic chieftains and princes. The Varangian princes were served by Varangian warriors, and as late as the eleventh century new troops were occasionally imported from Scandinavia. Some Scandinavian knights, merchants and minstrels also still visited the land from time to time. By that time the dynasty had already been Slavicized to a considerable degree, and most of the military leaders bore Slavic names. It becomes clear that the cultural influence of the Varangians must not be overestimated when we consider the astonishing fact that there are only an insignificant number of Scandinavian borrowings in the East Slavic languages, which have several hundred Greek loan words and in earlier and later times borrowed numerous words from non-Scandinavian Germanic languages. Furthermore, there is no tangible evidence that the Varangians exerted any intellectual influence on the East Slavs. In the beginning the Varangians probably remained faithful to their Scandinavian gods and to certain legal symbols and the like, but it is highly questionable whether these Scandinavian relics were adopted by the Slavic population. Whether some parallels between Scandinavian and Slavic sagas may be considered proof that the Varangians influenced the Slavs is a moot question: the motifs which the sagas have in common are known throughout the world.

Prince Vladimir (actually Volodimer), like his father Sviatoslav, and one of his two brothers, Yaropolk, had Slavic names. The East Slavic tribes, however, were given the Scandinavian name "Rus'," probably the name of the tribe to which the semi-legendary Riurik and his historically documented successors belonged. Echoes of the name can still be heard today in the modern Swedish place name "Roslagen." It is possible that it somehow became fused with similar place names in Eastern Europe, but this is doubtful. In any event, both older and modern attempts to prove that the name "Rus' " is Slavic in origin can hardly be taken seriously. They are simply the product of nationalism, and nationalism is often misleading.

The Byzantine Influence and Christianization

The Scandinavians in Eastern Europe were warriors and merchants, and until the middle of the eleventh century (1043) their lively trade relations with Byzantium—and with the Orient via another route, the Volga—were often temporarily suspended because of military conflicts. All of the trade treaties which have come down to us are the result of these conflicts. The influence of the wealthy and culturally advanced Byzantine empire on the East

19

Slavs was incomparably stronger than that of the Scandinavian dynasty, and it is quite understandable that Byzantine Christianity was also brought to Eastern Europe. There had been Christians in the Khazar empire, which was situated on the Volga and on the lower course of the Don and was destroyed by the Slavs in the tenth century. The trade treaty of 945 mentions Christian representatives of the East Slavic lands (no mention of them occurs in the treaty of 912), and whether these representatives were Slavs or Varangians is immaterial.

Olga (Helga in Scandinavian), the grandmother of Prince Vladimir and reigning princess of Kiev from 945 until the early sixties, took an important step when she had herself baptized. According to the *Chronicle* she was baptized in 955, but whether her conversion took place in Kiev or on the occasion of her journey to Constantinople cannot be ascertained. She did not succeed, however, in converting others to Christianity; even her own son, Sviatoslav, refused baptism. The Byzantines either attributed no particular significance to the conversion of the princess or wanted to place the congregation directly under the Byzantine hierarchy, and so Olga requested the Western Church to send her a bishop. Bishop Adalbert of Magdeburg was sent, but he did not arrive in Kiev until after the death of the princess, and he returned to Germany without having accomplished anything.

Prince Sviatoslav, Olga's bellicose son, rejected his mother's request that he permit himself to be baptized. His warriors were probably all pagans, and the *Primary Chronicle* asserts that he believed that they would be against his conversion. There is some reason to believe that Sviatoslav's two older sons, Oleg and Yaropolk, or at least one of them, did convert to Christianity; his illegitimate youngest son, Vladimir, remained a pagan. After Oleg and Yaropolk had been killed in the feud which broke out among the three brothers, Vladimir became the "absolute monarch" of the entire territory along the great trade route.

According to the *Primary Chronicle* the first years of Vladimir's reign were times of "pagan reaction." He had images of the Slavic gods erected in Kiev, and while it is probably not true that human sacrifice was made to them, two Varangian Christians were killed by a mob because they refused to make sacrifices to the images. The *Primary Chronicle* gives various reasons for Vladimir's decision to become a Christian, and three or four different traditional versions exist. According to one version Mohammedan, Jewish, Roman, and Byzantine missionaries came to visit the prince, and after listening to their reports he decided in favor of Christianity. According to another, Vladimir sent ambassadors to various countries to visit religious services, and the ambassadors recommended that Eastern Christianity be adopted because the Byzantine church service had made a particularly strong esthetic impression on them: "We did not know whether we were in heaven or on earth, for on earth there is no such beauty and their—the Greeks'—religious service is better than that of all the other countries. We can nevermore forget this beauty, just as any man who has tasted of something sweet will never again want to partake of anything bitter." They also gave the following reason for their recommendation: "If Greek law were bad, your grandmother, who was the wisest of all human beings, would not have accepted it."

In addition to these versions, obviously the product of popular tradition, the *Primary Chronicle* reproduces a long sermon by a Greek missionary. The sermon cannot have had ecclesiastical sanction, for it contains several apocryphal motifs. Morever, there is reason to suspect that this sermon was simply borrowed from a story about Prince Boris, a Bulgarian who had been baptized a century earlier.

Yet another account of Vladimir's conversion reports that Vladimir sued for the hand of a Byzantine princess and that when her brothers, the emperors Basil and Constantine, refused to give their sister in marriage to a pagan, Vladimir launched a campaign against the Greek colony of Chersonesus in the Crimea, conquered the city, had himself baptized, and received the hand of the princess in marriage. In reality, Vladimir's marriage to a Byzantine princess was probably a reward for aid which he had given the two emperors in their struggle against a mutinous general. In the end, the *Primary Chronicle* has to admit that no one knows when and where Vladimir was baptized.

Later a tradition developed which makes no mention at all of the role of the Greeks in the prince's conversion to Christianity and portrays it as a purely religious experience. There can be no doubt, however, that Vladimir had political aims in mind when he converted to Christianity or that the Byzantines for their part expected to gain certain political advantages from his conversion. For Vladimir, conversion to Christianity meant a closer alliance with the culture of a mighty empire. By marrying a Byzantine princess he might expect to achieve a rank equal to that of the Byzantine emperors. Possibly the prince hoped that the Church would support his state policies, as it did those of the Byzantine rulers. The Byzantines expected that Christianization would "tame" their restless and dangerous neighbors and believed that when the country became Christian it would to some degree subordinate itself to Byzantium, the "center of Christendom." The expectations of both parties were fulfilled only in part, however.

In any event, a new era for the Slavs did begin, one which soon provided some insight into the intellectual develpment of the Russian people, particularly of the classes which were the cultural leaders; and the literary sources available to us from this time on do permit us to make some judgments about the "intellectual character of the time."

Vladimir "commanded that the idols be removed, that some of them be destroyed, that others be committed to the flames, but he commanded that the image of Perun be tied to a horse's tail and dragged from the mountain to the river . . . and that twelve men beat it with iron staves, not because the wood was able to feel anything, but so as to mock the devil, who in this form had led men astray . . . . While the idol was being dragged to the Dnieper the unbelievers, who had not received holy baptism, mourned . . . and the idol was thrown into the Dnieper." Vladimir "commanded that if the idol should float to the banks of the river his people should push it back into the river until it floated through the rapids . . . . And after passing through the rapids it was thrown onto a sand bank which is now [probably about 1035] called Perun's Sand Bank." According to the legend written down later, the pagans ran along the banks of the river behind the idol, begging it to climb out of the water. In Novgorod, the story continues, the idol hurled a staff which it held in its hand onto the bridge it was about to float under. Since that time this bridge has played a fateful role in the life of the city; during the turbulent "Novgorod Republic" it was the scene of veritable battles between opposing political parties.

The people, of course, were converted only gradually to Christianity. Whereas the population of Kiev was baptized in one day (on August 1, according to a fifteenth-century tradition)—in the Dnieper River, in fact—Novgorod was not converted until some time later, and in the countryside Christianization proceeded even more slowly. Novgorod is the only city in which resistance by the pagans is reported. The story that the people did not look on calmly when their idols were hurled into the river and that crowds of people walked along the river banks after the floating wooden idol, imploring it to climb out of the water, has the ring of truth to it. But the lack of any persistent and organized resistance to Christianization is rather astonishing. Did the masses, even then, stand mutely by, as they often did in later centuries when radical changes in Russian life occurred?

East Slavic Paganism

Unfortunately, very little is known about East Slavic paganism. In the framework of this study the pagan world of the East Slavs can hardly be considered a phenomenon of intellectual history. The names of a few gods have come down to us, and it is no longer necessary to view this tradition as sceptically as leading experts on the subject did only a few decades ago.[2] However, we can sketch the religious attitude of the pagan East Slavs only in very general terms, and this is all the more regrettable because for this reason it is impossible to ascertain why the East Slavs abandoned paganism with such alacrity and with so little resistance. Some of the West Slavs, by contrast, continued to cling quite tenaciously to pagan beliefs.

It is very probable that the paganism of the East Slavs had not reached the stage at which religions develop a system of dogma, no matter how primitive, and create a fixed group of gods, an Olympus. We know the names of some of their gods: *Perun,* who was probably connected with storms, thunder, and lightening; and *Veles* (or *Volos*), who was responsible for maintaining

22

the general welfare of the people and was linked in particular to animal breeding. The names of other gods cannot be connected unequivocally with any specific ideas, and the accuracy of the evidence we have about these gods is open to doubt, although in some cases it can be supported by etymological evidence. *Khors*, for example, was probably a personification of the sun; the name *Mokosh* does not sound Slavic, but it is probably connected with *mokrii-mokhnut'* (moist, to become moist); and *Stribog* may have been the "god of the winds" (In the *Lay of the Host of Igor,* which was written down between 1185 and 1187, the winds are called Stribog's "grandchildren"). Other names, such as *Dazhbog* and *Svarog,* cannot be interpreted with as much certainty. *Dazhbog* was perhaps "the giving god," the bestower of goods. The function of *Svarog* (or *Svarozhich*) is not clear, perhaps he was "the warrior" and thus the god of war, although according to another interpretation he was the god of fire or even, probably in contrast to *Perun*, the god of friendly skies. On the other hand, *Dazhbog* and *Svarog* may be merely different designations for gods we have already mentioned before. One thing is clear: all the gods we have mentioned are connected in some way with agriculture.

Only by analogy to the practices of other peoples can we draw any conclusions about the relationship between these gods and those who worshipped them. Whether there were temples or places of sacrifice or how many of these there were is not known. Were there such places of worship only in the cities or could they also be found in the countryside? What sort of sacrifices were made? The only story of human sacrifice which can be found in the *Primary Chronicle,* for the year 983, is clearly a later invention. Was there a special caste of priests? All these questions remain unanswered.

If it can be assumed with some measure of certainty, however, that at least one group of the East Slavic gods was agricultural in character, then it follows that the whole "agricultural year" was divided into "calendar festivals," each connected with a specific agricultural activity. Such agricultural calendar festivals are strictly observed, for they are meant to ensure that the farmer's labors proceed in proper sequence and, more importantly, meet with success; and it is only natural that an agricultural people would retain these calendar festivals much more stubbornly than they would their belief in gods who were, after all, quite removed from daily life. It is indeed a fact that until very recent times the "agricultural year" among the East Slavs had preserved numerous vestiges of this "lower stratum" of pagan belief and usage.

"Low" Mythology

As we have indicated above, much is known about the lower stratum of East Slavic pagan mythology and about the worship of various demons who in Christian time were frequently degraded to devils and evil spirits. One

23

example is the house spirit, *domovoi*, which continued to be considered a benevolent protector of home and hearth. Other "demons" also continued to be worshipped and often became identified with Christian saints. *Perun* was the only one of the "high gods" whose function, that of "thunder-lord," was taken over by a Christian figure, the prophet Elijah. In many instances we can only suspect that behind a Christian saint there lurks a demon about whom we no longer have any detailed knowledge.

It is thought that in "low" mythology there were a considerable number of spirits, ranging from benevolent ones who helped with childbirth (*rozhenitsy*) or protected life (*beregini*, perhaps from *berech'*, "to preserve," "to protect") to originally evil spirits like the water sprite (*vodianoi*) and probably also the wood sprite (*leshii*), who sought to lure mortals into their realm and enslave them. There are occasionally allusions to other spirits whose nature remains completely unclear. For example, the *Chronicle* notes that some ignorant people (*neveglasi*, which usually means "pagans") believe that during eclipses the sun and the moon are "eaten up." Eaten up by whom or by what? By a sun wolf, as is the case in Norse mythology? Or by a snake, as was believed in many parts of the Orient? *Karna* and *Zhlia* are mentioned in *The Lay of the Host of Igor;* they are possibly spirits which had something to do with the ceremony of mourning the dead. *The Lay of the Host of Igor* also mentions the prophet of doom, *Div,* whom some construe to be nothing more than a bird or a wildcat (*dik*).

Customs

A good deal is known about those customs and usages of pagan times which lived on, sometimes in changed form. There is evidence enough that the old East Slavs worshipped springs, rivers, and trees, but neither the felling of "holy trees" nor the destruction of "holy springs" and "groves" is mentioned, as is the case in other areas. This probably indicates that this worship was of no great importance. Various customs reveal, however, that nature was thought to be full of demons. In this respect some of the customs which later came under attack are of great significance, among them "praying under the grain wagon" (*ovin*) and the worship of the earth, "Mother Moist Earth," to whom "confession was made." These two customs are likewise connected with agriculture, but they were perhaps influenced by the Christian rules for prayer and confession. Whatever the case, "Mother Moist Earth" (*mat' syra zemlia*) was able to survive for a long time; its later variants, from the seventeenth through the nineteenth century, are more familiar to us. The idea of "Mother Earth" often blended with that of the Mother of God. The fact that the East Slavs addressed the stars (*tselovat' mesiats*) would be of interest, were it not for the fact that a report of this practice could just as well have been borrowed from the Bible.

The pagan burial customs, a funeral banquet (*trizna*) and jousting at the burial barrow, are probably not peculiar to the Slavs but to the Varangians, or to the Varangian princes alone (cf. *The Primary Chronicle* for the year 945). An Arabian report about the burial of a wealthy "Russian" probably concerns the funeral of a Scandinavian. In some cases it is not known whether certain customs were common to all East Slavs or were peculiar to the people of a limited area. The same holds true for some nature demons known only to the people of certain regions—the Ukrainian population of the Carpathians, for example. It should also be kept in mind that a considerable number of present-day Great Russians are Slavicized Finns and that their customs go back to the traditions of a Finnish and not a Slavic people or tribe.

One thing is certain: the world of the old East Slavs was a world full of demons and secret magic powers. These were presumably thought to be thoroughly tangible, "material," so to speak; and the existence of ancestors after death was also conceived of as a material existence. The *rusalki*, who are generally regarded today as water nymphs and whose name is derived from a foreign word, Latin *rosaria*, were in earlier times spirits of quite a different sort. In accounts written during the Christian era, most of them from later times, the *rusalki* are described as the "souls" of children who died without being baptized and of people who died suddenly and who were therefore deprived of the Christian sacraments. The *rusalki* dwelt not only in the water or by the water; they were everywhere, often in the forests, and they could be dangerous to human beings. Presumably it was believed that after death people existed as "revenants" and climbed out of the grave and led a life similar to life on earth. Burial sites confirm this: objects needed for everyday living were buried along with the dead. The revenant could even be a vampire (*upyr'*), and associated with this belief are several burial customs which were intended to protect the living from the dead. There were ways to make it difficult for the dead to return to the earth. To prevent the deceased from finding his way back to where he had lived, he was not carried out through the door of his house but instead was lifted out through an opening made in the roof; his eyes were closed; even in the summer he was borne on a sled which left easily eradicable tracks in the snow and almost no tracks at all on the ground. This custom still existed in the nineteenth century in some parts of the Ukraine. Baptism freed man from life after death as a revenant, and to rest in the grave until the day of resurrection must surely have been felt to be a "salvation."

Vestiges of Paganism

Much that was pagan persisted after the East Slavs had been Christianized. The "great gods" soon vanished from memory, and only seldom were their functions taken over by Christian saints. The figures from "low" mytho-

25

logy, by contrast, lived on for a long time, often as devils, evil demons with which it was nevertheless possible to live in peace; and sometimes the functions of these figures were assigned to Christian saints. The usages and customs which were most successfully preserved, however, were those which possessed the magic power to ensure the normal sequence of natural phenomena and of human life from the cradle to the grave. Sometimes elements of the new faith were able to prevail over these vestiges of paganism. The "sign of the cross," the act of crossing oneself, came to be considered a sure way to combat not only Christian devils but also malevolent pagan spirits and powers. In many instances Christian prayers served as models for superstitious "semi-pagan" prayers and incantations. Finally, the idea that one lived on after death as a revenant persisted, but now the only people who needed to fear such a life after death were those who had died without being baptized or receiving the sacraments.

In the past scholars have often spoken of the "double faith" (*dvoeverie*) of the Russians after Christianization, and in doing so they have assuredly overestimated the importance of *conscious* pagan psychology. The vestiges of paganism were not any stronger in Russia than in the West. The apparent absence of a caste of pagan priests among the East Slavs may have been one deciding factor here. We cannot assert unequivocally that there were no pagan priests, but it is a fact that no mention of them can be found in documents which have come down to us. The old monuments speak only of magicians and soothsayers (*volkhv, volshebnik, kudesnik, kobnik*). The Russian word for priest, *zhrets,* means "performer of sacrifices" and was so little associated with pagan practices that when the Bible was translated, the word was used immediately to render the Christian term "priest." The East Slav magicians were obviously unable to mount any resistance strong enough to attract the support of large numbers of followers, and in later times conjurers and healers (*znakhar*) remained active for a long time without ever wanting or being able to establish any independent *Weltanschauung* in opposition to Christianity.

Early East Slavic Christianity

"Christian life," whether life within the Church or Christian forms of life in the world, spread only very slowly. The East Slavs had an advantage, for they had at their disposal the rather extensive Christian literature which the South and West Slavs had developed earlier. These works included, but were by no means limited to, liturgical books and the Bible (from which, it is true, the historical books of the Old Testament were omitted). The first translations had been made in the ninth century, and in the tenth century Bulgaria had enjoyed a literary efflorescence. The East Slavs took over products of this flourishing literature, both translations and original works, as well as some works from Bohemia, where the Slavic liturgy was not forbidden until the end of the eleventh century. South and East Slavic works were written in Old Church Slavic, which was based on a Bulgarian dialect and contained some few lexical items from West Slavic. At that time this language was easily intelligible to the East Slavs, and when copying books from Old Church Slavic it was not difficult to adapt the orthography to East Slavic pronunciation. Thus the East Slavs possessed from the very beginning a comprehensive body of religious literature in a language which they could understand. Very soon original works began to appear. The oldest preserved manuscript, the *Ostromirovo Gospel,* dates from 1056/1057, but it can be stated with certainty that the first original East Slavic works were written as early as the tenth century. A short work, about the founding of the Kievan Church, probably written about 990, has been preserved in copies which were made at a later date.

Only the content of these writings is of interest to us. A few works, although composed somewhat later, in the middle of the eleventh century, reveal the way in which the East Slavs experienced Christianization. Christianity was probably not completely alien to them, for even earlier there had been Christian Greeks and Slavs in the large cities. The *Primary Chronicle* intimates that the people of Kiev already knew something about Christianity (*byli naucheny*). To the "new Christians" baptism seemed to be an entry into a better world, a guarantee of salvation. It is clear that they generally believed that those who were baptized were purged of their sins and assured everlasting bliss in the hereafter, and it is conceivable that the doctrine of resurrection, when compared to life after death as a revenant, was adopted with a feeling of particular relief and gratification.

Our sources supply no details of the early years of Christianity among the East Slavs, but even somewhat later, down to the end of the eleventh century, the same joyous tones are heard in various works of literature: "in the hour before death" the Christian was united with the entire Christian world; through baptism he was freed from the powers of evil, from both sin and malevolent demons; he could expect with certainty everlasting bliss in the hereafter. Combined with these thoughts were tones of esthetic enthusiasm which were awakened by the new Christian temples and by the church service.

Soon, to be sure, different tones could be heard. The new faith imposed heavy moral obligations on those who were baptized. From time to time the notion even arose that asceticism was perhaps the best way after all to achieve salvation for the soul. For more than a century, however, the voices we hear are those of Christian optimism.

The East Slavic Church

The history of the first decades of the East Slavic Church is still unclear in some respects. According to tradition, after Christianization the Rus immediately became members of the Greek Church, which was represented by the

27

Greek metropolitan of Kiev and by a few bishops. Questions of Church history cannot be examined here, but a brief discussion will show that the facts about the situation are not that cut and dried.

Up to 1037 nothing is known for sure about the Kievan metropolitan. In that year the Greek hierarchy in Kiev is mentioned for the first time. It seems unlikely that Greeks would have brought along Bulgarian and West Slavic books and would have preached in a Slavic language. All the chroniclers up to the beginning of the twelfth century were monks, and they would have had no reason to suppress the names of earlier Greek metropolitans. Furthermore, in 1037 the chronicler could hardly have forgotten the name of the man who served as metropolitan the year before. It therefore seems safe to assume that before 1037 the metropolitan was neither a Greek nor a "legitimate" Church dignitary. Various hypotheses have been advanced to explain the historical facts, but only the three most convincing ones will be mentioned here.

It is not inconceivable that Vladimir turned to the West when no bishop was supplied by Constantinople. The schism of the Eastern and Western Church had not yet taken place, and until well into the twelfth century there is no evidence that Russian royalty was overtly hostile toward Rome. On the contrary, on various occasions there were marriages with royal families of the West, that is, with "Latins." Even the Slavic clergy was at times conciliatory toward the Western Church. At the beginning of the twelfth century, for example, Daniil, an East Slavic abbot, journeyed to Palestine with King Baldwin, the leader of a crusade. As late as 1094 the relics of a Kievan saint were sent from Kiev to Bohemia. Moreover, various religious works translated from Latin into Slavic were received from the West, from Bohemia: two versions of the life of the Czech saint, St. Wenceslas; the life of another Czech saint, St. Ludmila; the life of St. Vitus, the patron saint of Prague; some prayers; the Roman *Patericon* of Pope Gregory; and many other works. It is possible that between 988 and 1037 a churchman from the Western Church, not necessarily a bishop, was called on to help organize the new East Slavic Christian Church.

The assumption that the East Slavic Church was originally subordinated to the archbishop of Bulgaria, who had independent status until 1037, seems even more probable. This would explain the rapid spread of Slavic books, and some details of clerical and secular life support such a thesis. In 1037, after the death of Archbishop John of Bulgaria, the autonomy of the Bulgarian church was terminated, and it was then that Grand Prince Yaroslav the Wise of Kiev probably succeeded in convincing Constantinople to assign to the East Slavs a metropolitan of their own. It is also possible that after the Greeks refused to establish a bishopric in the newly converted country, Vladimir appointed as head of the new East Slavic Church Anastasius (Nastas), a churchman taken prisoner during the conquest of Chersonesus.

No matter which hypothesis one believes to be correct, it must be admitted that almost nothing is really known about the first decades of the East Slavic Church. The history of the clerical hierarchy is not even fairly well known until after the middle of the eleventh century. When this fact is taken into consideration, it is evident that there is no reason to assert that the Byzantine Church was the unconditionally recognized leader in ecclesiastical matters in Russia. In the middle of the eleventh century and later in the middle of the twelfth century there were attempts to appoint Slavic metropolitans, but these were not recognized by the patriarch of Constantinople. Striking aspects of several documents are the deliberate silence about the role of Byzantium in Christianizing East Slavic lands and the derogatory remarks made about the Greeks, one of which even goes so far as to assert that "Greeks have always practiced deceit."

CHAPTER II. INTELLECTUAL LIFE IN THE ELEVENTH, TWELFTH, AND THIRTEENTH CENTURIES

The Rise of the State

Our sources, primarily the *Chronicles,* depict the rise of the East Slavic state in retrospect as the achievement of the Scandinavian princes, the Varangians. The *Primary Chronicle* for the year 862 reports that the East Slavs were unsuccessful in their attempts to create an independent political organization: "they began to rule themselves, but there was no justice, and the several tribes fought with one another, and there were feuds, fighting among themselves. And they said to themselves: 'Let us seek a prince who can rule over us and dispense justice to us.' And they went across the sea to the Varangians, and in fact to the Varangian tribe called the Rus', and said to them: 'Our land is great and rich, but there is no order (*nariad*) in it; come and rule us and be our masters.' " Riurik and his brothers responded to this request. At first they ruled in the three northern regions; then the power of their successors was extended over the southern regions, down the Dnieper to the Black Sea.

The *Chronicles* depict the expansion of the power of Riurik's dynasty as a natural process but are unable to conceal the fact that there were Varangian rulers in Kiev, Polotsk, and probably elsewhere who were not subject to Riurik and who were deposed by the "legitimate" Riurik dynasty only by cunning or by force of arms. The idyllic description of the "appeal to the Varangians" is without doubt a later interpretation of the actual events. The *Primary Chronicle* also reports that even earlier some Slavic tribes had been paying tribute to the Varangians, while the southern tribes paid tribute to the Khazar empire, which was situated on the Volga and the lower course of the Don. The story of the "appeal," a motif widely used in developing historical legends, begins with the report that the Varangians were "driven out" by the Slavs and that only then did the "disorders" arise which led to the dispatch of emissaries to Riurik. This means, however, that some sort of political organization already existed. If we accept as fact the "accession" of Riurik and his brothers (except for the date and even the names of the brothers, which remain uncertain), then this "accession to the throne" was probably the result of conquest. The term "appeal" may refer to a defensive treaty with the Varangians, and if the Varangians actually did come into the country as protectors and judges, they soon became as much the rulers of the land as if they had come as conquerers.

The Varangian princes, as depicted in the *Primary Chronicle,* devoted themselves to maintaining trade relations with Byzantium and with the Orient and to conducting military campaigns against these trading partners—trade and taking booty went hand in hand—and against other southern and south-eastern neighbors of the East Slavs. The battles with the Khazar empire and somewhat later with the nomadic Pechenegs in the southern steppes probably fall under the heading of "defensive actions," while the campaigns against Byzantium served to ensure continued trade relations. Since at least the tenth century the Slavs were also parties to this trade, as we can see from the fact that Slav names—only a few of them, to be sure—occur in the list of "Russian" representatives who signed the Russo-Byzantine trade treaty of 945.

The military campaigns were also motivated by the desire to take booty by force of arms. This is how Oriental and Byzantine sources depict the attacks of the "Russian" Varangians; and later the *Primary Chronicle* describes how the conquerors pillaged, murdered, and laid waste to the country in their victories over the Greeks in 866, 907, and 912. For the year 941 the *Primary Chronicle* reports: "They set fire to many holy churches, burned monasteries and villages, and took considerable goods back to their own country with them." According to the *Chronicle,* however, the Slavic subjects of the Varangians had a similarly low opinion of the way Prince Igor, the hero of the campaign of 941, collected tribute; the Prince, it says in the section devoted to the year 945, was "like a plundering and ravening wolf." Even the victorious campaigns of Prince Sviatoslav (d. 972), which crushed the Khazar empire and successfully defended the country against the Pechenegs, were viewed with disapproval by the Slavs. Sviatoslav's campaigns against Byzantium and into Bulgaria and the Caucasus and his intention to establish a residence on the Danube were felt to constitute neglect of "his own country": "He sought out a strange land and scorned his own." Even Prince Vladimir the Saint is portrayed, before his conversion to Christianity, as a fratricide, a tyrant, and a libertine, views which the chronicler surely took over from oral tradition.

There is no need to be concerned here with the thorny question of the part played by the Varangians and by the Slavs in establishing and developing the political life of the East Slavs. The fact remains that the first Varangian princes successfully defended their Slavic lands, brought the East Slavic tribes closer together, and through trade with Byzantium promoted material and cultural progress in the country. St. Vladimir (978-1015) united under his rule the principalities along the trade route from the Baltic to the Black Sea, and this territory remained to some extent a political entity until the death of Prince Mstislav the Saint of Tmutorokan and Chernigov in 1132. The dynasty played a decisive role in Christianizing the country and thus linking it to the culture of Europe. It is also quite significant that very soon the Varangian princes no longer considered themselves the "occupiers" of the East Slavic lands. As early as the tenth century Slavs were active as merchants, diplomats, public officials, and military leaders. The Varangian dynasty, for its part, was completely assimilated into the Slavic environment.

The authors of the *Primary Chronicle*, beginning with the first one, who wrote around 1035, attributed to the Christian state ruled after 988 by St. Vladimir rather peculiar characteristics which probably reflect in part the actual situation and in part an ideal which the chronicler had in mind. There are, of course, reports of the construction of churches and the organization of the Church, but the chroniclers do not fail to mention also the prince's state banquets—even the German chronicler, Dietmar of Merseburg, who in other respects took an unfavorable view of Vladimir, describes them. The *Chronicle* tells how Vladimir "came to love" the words of the Gospel: "Once when the Gospel was being read aloud he heard the words: 'Blessed are the merciful' [other quotations from the Old and New Testament follow]. He commanded that every beggar and every poor man come to the royal palace and receive there all he needed—food and drink and likewise money from the treasury." When Vladimir saw that "the weak and the sick could not come to his court he ordered his men to load bread, meat, fish, various vegetables, and barrels of mead and kvas onto wagons and to drive through the city asking 'which of the beggars and sick men here cannot walk?' and to distribute among these people whatever they needed." Dietmar speaks of special banquets for Christian prisoners-of-war whom Vladimir had ransomed, and the *Primary Chronicle* reports that banquets attended by Vladimir's vassals and boyars and by the "distinguished citizens" of the town were held every week in the royal vassals' hall. Even in the portrayals found in old Russian literature this picture of a happy "welfare state" is unique.

The chronicler also endows Vladimir's foreign and domestic policy with traits of a "Christian utopia." The foreign policy was one of peace. The prince lived in peace with the neighboring Poles, Hungarians and Bohemians. Vladimir's domestic policy, on the other hand, is elevated by the chronicler to the level of *Christian anarchism*: "Vladimir lived in fear of God. And crimes (*rozboeve*) increased greatly. And the bishops said to Vladimir: 'The number of criminals has increased. Why do you not punish them?' Vladimir, however, answered: 'I am afraid of committing a sin.' The bishops then said to him: 'You have been appointed by God to punish the wicked and to show mercy to the good; you should punish the criminals, after you have investigated their crimes, of course.' And Vladimir . . . began to punish the criminals." Even if this passage refers only to robbers and not to all criminals, and even if Vladimir was in danger of committing a sin if he sentenced the criminal to death and not to some other punishment, this is a very radical conception of the Christian state. It reminds one immediately of Leo Tolstoy's philosophy. The state, of course, cannot operate on Tolstoy's principle of "non-resistance to evil."

In reality the reign of the first Christian prince of the East Slavs was by no means so idyllic. Vladimir had to make war on the pagan nomads, the

32

Pechenegs; and even among members of the royal family relations were by no means peaceful. Vladimir died in 1015, just as he was preparing for a campaign against his oldest son, Yaroslav, who was prince of Novgorod. Yaroslav was already hiring mercenaries to defend himself against his father. At this time another of Vladimir's sons, Sviatopolk, was being held prisoner by his father.

The Royal Martyrs Boris and Gleb

Vladimir had several sons and daughters, and we do not know what Vladimir himself and his contemporaries conceived to be legitimate succession to the throne. In any event, after his father's death Sviatopolk, the imprisoned son, immediately eliminated his three brothers, who could have been considered pretenders to the throne. Two of them—Boris, whose name is Bulgarian, and Gleb, whose name is Scandinavian—became the first Russian saints, and their canonization is symptomatic of the political attitude of early East Slavic Christians.[3] Three works, all written before the end of the eleventh century, are devoted to the portrayal of their martyrdom. In only one of them, probably the latest of the three, is the pious and virtuous life of the two brothers mentioned; in the other two their deaths alone were apparently the decisive factor which made them worthy of veneration as saints. As "sufferers" (*strastoterptsy*) they were the first of a long line of Russian saints. In the eyes of the "new Christians" *innocent suffering* sufficed to purge man of his sins and indeed to sanctify him.

All three of the descriptions depict the death of the two princes as a passive acquiescence to menacing danger. Boris, who had just returned with his army from a campaign, dismissed his men and awaited his murderers with the serene knowledge that "if my blood is shed I shall become a martyr in the eyes of the Lord." These words, of course, express the views of the authors of this saint's life. Furthermore, Boris allegedly was reminded of the deaths of many holy martyrs and most of all of the crucifixion of Christ: "O Lord Jesus Christ . . . who has suffered death for our sins, find me worthy to endure suffering."

Another reason advanced for the actions of the two princes is characteristic of the age and reflects the mentality of the readers of the time: the two brothers, through their deaths, purchased *peace* for their people; they did not wish to stir up feuds by offering resistance. "See, O brothers, how highly the submission of the saints to their older brother is prized" are the words with which one of the authors concludes the life of the two saints. The memory of the death of the two holy brothers became "the voice of conscience of the princes," who were inclined to take up arms to defend their rights and their interests, legitimate or otherwise, as Fedotov so aptly puts it.

Paradoxically, the two peace-loving holy brothers later became the

33

Russian dioscuri, the patron saints who protected the Russian army and came to its aid in times of need. "You are the sword, shield, and support of the Russian land, the two-edged swords with which we suppress the insolent pagans." It is with this hardly peaceful encomium that one hagiographer ends his story of the death of the two brothers. Later, unfortunately, their help was even invoked in internecine wars, but for the Christians of the eleventh century the two brothers were first and foremost the patron saints of peace.

Feuds Among the Princes

In works written in the eleventh century feuds between princes always meet with disapprobation; sometimes the aggressor and sometimes both parties to the fighting are condemned. After years of fighting, from 1015 to 1019, Prince Sviatopolk, the fratricide, was driven into exile by Yaroslav of Novgorod, but after further warfare Yaroslav was forced to share his power with another brother, Mstislav. This peaceful solution, the partition of the state, was applauded by the chroniclers. After the death of Mstislav I in 1036 Yaroslav became the "sole ruler."

For a long time the power of the princes was considered to "derive from rights of property." Yaroslav, who died in 1054, therefore divided his land among his three sons, but they were not able to live together in peace, and since that time contemporaries again and again condemned the feuds of the princes. Subsequent remarks about the struggles between St. Vladimir and his brothers also originate in the eleventh century, and for a long time the chroniclers agree in their judgments. While the attacks on pagans took place "with God's permission," the feuds were the result of the devil's corruption: "The devil takes pleasure in evil murder and the shedding of blood, instigates quarrels and envy, calumny and the falling out of brothers." God, in return, punishes the land in which feuds break out: "If a country sin [by having feuds], God punishes it with death or famine, with invasions by pagans, with drought, with hordes of caterpillars or other plagues." This quotation from the *Chronicle* for the year 1068 is taken from a sermon attributed to John Chrysostom and serves as the introduction to the report of the feuds in which Yaroslav's sons became embroiled.

From the account of the life of St. Feodosii the Abbot it is known that during the feud Feodosii recognized as the legitimate ruler the exiled prince, who for years stayed in Western Europe seeking aid from the emperor and the pope. In his epistles Feodosii asserted that the exiled prince's successors to the Kievan throne were no different from Cain, and Feodosii refused to visit the victors: "I will not go to Beelzebub's banquet, nor will I take any part in a feast which is full of blood and murder." Rumors that the two brothers intended to drive him from the Kievan Cave Monastery made Feodosii even more obdurate in his attitude toward them. He even expressed the hope that

34

he might "suffer for righteousness," and he "wished with all his heart that they would banish him."

Here, as in other instances, historical fact—the way Feodosii acted—is not as significant as the views of contemporaries, in this case Nestor, who wrote down the legend and who was also one of the compilers of the *Primary Chronicle*. Nestor condemns the feuds of the princes most sharply, and he expects a truly just man, like Feodosii, to be completely independent in his political views.

A century later, when Eastern Europe had broken into a number of appanage principalities, secular writers, such as the author of *The Lay of the Host of Igor* (1185/1187), were of the same opinion. The princes ought to defend their lands against the pagans, at that time the Cumans (Polovtsy), and an ideal prince was now one who in the face of danger urged his brothers to unite. *The Lay of the Host of Igor* depicts Prince Sviatoslav of Kiev as such a man, but in reality such powerless rulers as he is shown to be did not exist.

In the saint's life the concise but utterly clear formulation of the relationship between the princes and the clergy is attributed to Feodosii: "We should instruct you, and you should pay heed to what we say." What is meant, of course, is that the princes should "pay heed" and also follow the "instructions." Reality was a far cry from the ideal.

The Ideal Prince

It was the duty of the prince to defend the country against "pagans" and to preserve peace in the land. This theme recurs in the *Chronicles* as late as the second third of the twelfth century, after peaceful relations between princes had become an idle dream and energetic resistance to "external enemies" was therefore out of the question. Royal power, however, was thought to lie not solely in the fulfillment of certain military duties. The prince was also the chief administrator of his country; he was judge and tax collector.

Around the year 1100 the ideal peaceful prince was Vladimir Monomakh, who was born in 1053 and reigned as prince of Kiev from 1113 to 1125. The *Chronicle* presents in addition to detailed descriptions of his activities his "autobiography," a work which he had written for his children as a supplement to his *Testament*. These sources make it clear that throughout his life the prince, in conjunction with other princes, endeavored to organize the defense of the country against the Cumans. Appended to the *Testament* is a letter from Vladimir which is meant to emphasize his desire to live in peace with other princes. This aspect of his policy is also occasionally confirmed by the *Chronicle,* but in his autobiography Vladimir is unable to conceal the fact that he was involved in numerous feuds. In enumerating his campaigns he mentions not only those against the Cumans but also those which were undertaken against the Poles and the Czechs and which can hardly be classified as "wars against the *pagans.*" He reports, furthermore, the following: "In the same year (1077) my father and Iziaslav and I marched to Chernigov to do battle with Boris (Viacheslavovich), and we defeated Boris and Oleg (Sviatoslavich)." A campaign against Vseslav of Polotsk followed, and when it was completed Vladimir "burnt out" the land. A few years later, during a campaign against Minsk, "we occupied the city and spared the life of neither man nor beast." On this occasion the pagan Cumans were Vladimir's allies. Then, in 1084, Vladimir fought against several Russian princes in order to restore Prince Yaropolk (Iziaslavich) to his throne in Vladimir (Volynia). And Vladimir Monomakh's career continued in much the same fashion. It may be that some of these feuds, like the major one of 1097, were undertaken in a just cause and that many of his campaigns were indeed directed against "external" enemies, but the fact remains that there was no such thing as a lasting peace at that time. Then, as later, fighting for a "just cause" all too often led to destructive civil wars, and in the eleventh and twelfth centuries the chroniclers all too often regard such wars as normal, albeit regrettable phenomena. The chronicle of the twelfth century, the so-called *Hypatius Chronicle,* included for the year 1185 the remorseful observations of a bellicose prince, which are of course the work of the chronicler, and these seem almost to represent the exception to the rule.

Vladimir Monomakh's *Testament* is of interest because in it Vladimir states, although only in a few words, his views on the duties of a prince. First of all, the prince should be a zealous and vigilant administrator: "Do not be lazy in caring for your household, supervise everything, trust neither overseers nor servants." And Vladimir often refers to his own experiences: "What a servant has to do, I did . . . day and night, granting myself no rest; I trusted neither viceroys nor public officials (*birich*) but did everything that needed to be done, even in my own house." Some facts which we know about Vladimir's economic policies, such as his legislation and his attempts to stamp out usury and indentured servitude, bear out this self-appraisal. To be sure, in pursuing such policies he was merely continuing the work of his grandfather, Yaroslav.

One important function of the prince was to dispense justice. Justice was supposed to be the chief attribute of a judge, and justice (*pravda*)[4] was what the people expected of their prince. In his *Testament* Vladimir lists judicial obligations immediately after the religious duties of the prince. He interprets the judicial activity of the prince as the protection of the "weak" and the "poor": "Protect a widow and do not allow the mighty to ruin a man." Here too Vladimir was following in the footsteps of his grandfather, who was the author of an important juridical work, *Russian Justice (Russkaia pravda),* a work which was supplemented by his successors, first by Yaroslav and then by Vladimir himself. Moreover, important original works and compilations concerning Church law also appeared during this century. All the paragraphs of these law books which deal with judicial investigation, assessment of testi-

36

mony, and civil complaints attest to the efforts which were made to see that justice was served. All prove that there was the will to see justice done.

The *Weltanschauung* of the age is documented in the regulations found in these law books. The nature of the punishments which they prescribe is particularly significant. An effort was made to keep pagan blood revenge within certain bounds, and those persons entitled to take such revenge were specified. In the case of the murder of a father the legal avengers were the victim's son, brother, cousin, or paternal nephew; in other cases blood revenge was abolished and replaced by a fine (*vira*). Equality before the law, of course, simply did not exist. Murder of a royal vassal or of a public official was punished with a fine twice as large as that for the murder of a merchant or of a boyar's servant, and the fines for the murder of a tradesman or of a common servant (*kholop*) were even smaller. The right to avenge an insult was completely abolished. The nature of the fines shows that this "barbaric" law was far less barbaric than was Russian law from the fifteenth to the nineteenth century. It might be added that clerical and secular authors alike always severely condemned injustice (*sud kriv*) and punishment "without investigation" (*ne ispytav*).

Cultural Matters

One characteristic of the first centuries of Eastern European intellectual history, the high esteem in which culture was held, is manifest in the frequency with which works of literature remark on the "erudition" of individual churchmen and princes. Among the churchmen Hilarion (eleventh century) and Klim Smoliatich and Kirill of Turov (twelfth century) should be mentioned. Princes singled out for such praise included Vladimir Monomakh's father, Vsevolod, who knew five languages, and Prince Vladimir Vasilkovich (thirteenth century), who was called "the philosopher." Every cultural activity, from literary efforts and sermons to the copying and binding of books, was noted by the writers of the time. For example, it is reported that St. Feodosii helped bind books. Occasionally there are reports of intellectual activity at princely courts—the reading aloud of theological epistles; and fragments of the literary efforts of some princes have come down to us. Even the nobility engaged in copying books—Vladimir Vasilkovich is an example.

Other cultural activities included the founding of schools and the construction of churches and monasteries. The *Chronicle* traces the founding of schools back to St. Vladimir, who required that even the children of the "best families" attend school. Although it was long believed that schooling was not widespread, there can be no doubt that at least reading and writing were. For one thing, in the ruins of old churches there are numerous inscriptions made by tradesmen. Of particular significance, however, are numerous letters and documents found in Novgorod; these were scratched on strips of bark, and some of them were written by people from the middle class.

A note in the *Primary Chronicle* concerning the cultural activity of Prince Yaroslav the Wise reveals how highly education was esteemed: "Yaroslav applied himself to books and read them continually day and night. He assembled many scribes and translated from Greek into Slavic; he wrote and collected many books." The author of this note devotes an entire page to the praise of books, "the rivers that water the whole earth; they are the springs of wisdom. For books have an immeasurable depth; by them we are consoled in sorrow. They are the bridle of self-restraint. If you seek wisdom attentively, you will obtain great profit for your spirit. He who reads books often converses with God or with holy men." Similar praise of books can also be found in a collection of writings dating from 1076. We might note here that in the eleventh century the literature with which the East Slavs were familiar was quite extensive and by no means exclusively religious in character; there were also histories, romances, and books on geography and the sciences. The content of these works was in large measure that of early medieval Latin literature in the West, but because they were available in Slavic they were accessible to every Slav who could read.[5]

Churches, icon painting, church art, and the liturgy were as highly prized as were books. This can be seen from the charming encomium to the city of Kiev which was written during the time of that same Prince Yaroslav by Metropolitan Hilarion, probably about 1051: "Look at the city and how it shines in sublimity. Look at the churches, and how they blossom forth. Look at Christianity and how it grows. Look at the city and how it glistens, illuminated by the icons of the saints, enveloped by incense, filled with the sound of praise and with religious songs."

It cannot be denied that with time portrayals of culture became more and more ostentatious, but also more and more superficial. In the twelfth and thirteenth centuries descriptions of church buildings, works of art, and books shine with all the colors of the rainbow, mostly gold. If we are to judge the actual cultural level, however, we must turn to the literature which has come down to us, and when we do this we can determine that until well into the thirteenth century there were not only beautiful and sublime works of literature but also excellent translations.

Another aspect of culture was improvement of the land, and it too received recognition. There are numerous comments on it in the *Chronicles*. Streets had to be laid, and *"mosti mostiti"* (to lay streets) is a phrase which occurs again and again. Vladimir Monomakh even considered it his royal duty to extirpate wild animals and therefore describes his hunting successes: "I hunted and killed all sorts of animals . . . . I tied wild horses with my own hands. Two wild bison threw me and my horse on their horns, a stag gored me, one elk trampled me, another gored me, a wild boar tore my sword from my swordbelt, a bear bit the saddle cloth of my horse, a wild beast [probably a lynx] leaped onto my hip and threw me and my horse down, but God kept me hale . . . . Thus did I trouble myself whilst hunting." As late as the thirteenth century we find words of praise for the hunting feats of a devout prince.

Relics of the Christian Utopia

It is interesting that vestiges of the utopian concept of the state, which the *Chronicle* attributes to St. Vladimir, can also be observed in Vladimir Monomakh. Monomakh too entertained the idea of welfare contributions by the state and had doubts about his right to impose the death penalty. Nevertheless, he does not go as far in his statements as St. Vladimir had gone (as told in the *Primary Chronicle*). Vladimir Monomakh does, however, reject the death penalty: "Kill neither the just nor the criminal, and do not command that such a person be killed, even if he deserves to die . . . ." At the same time he gives his children the following piece of advice: "Above all, do not forget the poor, provide for them . . ."; to be sure, Vladimir qualifies the statement by adding "if that is possible." These two statements about Monomakh's conception of government must be considered no more than pious wishes, for it can hardly be assumed that Vladimir and his children never pronounced the death sentence, and we know with what modest means Vladimir sought to combat the poverty and indebtedness of his subjects. The means at his disposal could naturally ease the need only in part. However, if the *Chronicles* and other writings are to be believed, the idea of the peaceful welfare state had not completely disappeared.

As early as the twelfth century, another sort of Christian utopia emerged, a much more fateful one, in fact the first signs of the concept of the *theocratic* state became visible. In descriptions of the princes, even those written by secular writers, *external* piety came to occupy a more and more prominent position. The ornate church buildings, the luxurious accoutrements of the churches, and the "love" of the clergy now often received greater emphasis and more praise than the prince's care for specific state duties and for the "poor." As early as 1175 the *Chronicle* contains a statement which was later to play a fateful role in Russian intellectual history: "In his natural person the sovereign is the same as all other men, but by virtue of the power of his position he is, like God, above other men." This is a quotation from a panegyric to Emperor Justinian which was written by a Byzantine author named Agapit (Agapetos); it was merely a rhetorical flourish, but later it came to be taken seriously. The use of this quotation is particularly serious because it is applied to Prince Andrei Bogoliubskii, who was in no way the ideal type of monarch. Prince Andrei was murdered by his boyars in 1174 because, to judge by all that is known about him, he was a ruthless politician and a blackhearted tyrant. In his struggles with other princes in 1171 he also became the first to destroy the old city of Kiev, and in so doing he did not hesitate to rob and burn the churches and monasteries. He did not remain in the conquered city, but took up residence in a city in the northeast, Vladimir, which he beautified with handsome buildings. Even from the encomium, which was dedicated to him by a faithful servant, we can discern in Andrei the "classical" features of the tyrant. The author of the encomium was prepared to declare the prince a saint because of his "martyrdom," and this too was an ominous portent of things to come.

The Beginnings of Christian Life and Literature

For the modern reader Russian piety during the eleventh and twelfth centuries is easier to comprehend than the Russian concept of the state. This piety, it must be conceded, was at first not uniform in character, but in considering it we are confronted not with a multiplicity of different types of devoutness but with a rather sharp contrast between two tendencies. The struggle between them can be traced through the centuries and assumed in the fifteenth century the form of new intellectual movements.

The earliest documents which concern the propagation of the new religion point in two different directions, one toward the churches and monasteries, the other toward those pious souls who remained a part of the "world" but wished to serve God and fulfill his commandments. As early as the middle of the eleventh century there was a Slavic metropolitan, Hilarion, who, to be sure, was soon forced to yield his post to a Greek. Soon Slavic bishops are also found in various cities. The ever increasing number of literary monuments was for the most part written or translated or copied by churchmen, and these writers, translators, and copyists must have been Slavs, although some of them, mostly Bulgarians, may not have been East Slavs. Moreover, the Greek hierarchs had to use Slavs as secretaries to assist in translating their circular letters and their other writings, and by the same token Slavs who worked in Byzantium composed or altered the style of the documents which emanated from the episcopal chancellory. The role of Slavic secretaries assigned to Greek bishops in a foreign land was even more important. Soon there developed a group of professional "literati" which was independent of the episcopal chancellories. In the early years only a few Russian bishops were active in the field of literature; monks and abbots played a more important role.

The Kievan Cave Monastery

Originally old Russian monasteries probably had very few connections with the Greek hierarchy. In the beginning they arose as a result of the private initiative of pious "converts." Such was the case with the famous Kievan

Cave Monastery. The *Primary Chronicle* describes how the monastery came to be founded, probably after 1040. According to the *Chronicle* for the year 1051, the priest Hilarion of Kiev, an ascetic (*postnik*, i.e. "one who fasts") and a devout and erudite man, "was in the habit of going to a hill by the Dnieper to pray. [At that time] a dense forest stood there. He dug a small cave, two fathoms wide . . . and went there to read the *Book of Hours* and to pray secretly to God." In 1051 he became metropolitan; he was the first native of Kiev to hold this position. Hilarion's cave, a sort of hermitage, was the seed from which the Monastery grew. "Some time later," the *Chronicle* continues (this part was written later by a monk of the Monastery), "there lived in the city of Liubech a worldly man. God put into his heart the wish to go to foreign lands. He went to the Holy Mountain [Athos], saw the monasteries there, visited them, and found monastic life pleasing to him. He went to a monastery there and asked the abbot to invest him as a monk. The abbot gave heed to his plea, gave him the tonsure and the [monastic] name Antonii, and taught him and instructed him in the monastic rules." Antonii later came to Kiev, "considering where he should live; he visited the monasteries [of Kiev] and, in accordance with God's will, did not find them pleasing to him. He began to wander through the mountains and forests and came upon the hill where Hilarion had dug his cave, and he came to love this spot, settled there, and with tears in his eyes began to pray to God." This is the rather naive account found in the *Primary Chronicle.*

Antonii "became famous as 'Antonii the Great'." At first "good people" in the vicinity visited him. Later, after 1054, even Grand Prince Iziaslav paid him a visit, "and all learned from Antonii the Great and venerated him, and brothers [monks] began to come to him, and he accepted them and invested them." When the number of new monks reached twelve, they dug other caves and built a church. Antonii "appointed" one of them abbot and again withdrew to solitude. The next abbot, Feodosii, moved the Monastery above ground, and under his guidance it became a center of intellectual and particularly literary activity.

Among the monasteries already in Kiev there were presumably some which were founded at the initiative of the Greek hierarchy, but the monks were native Slavs. Soon there were monasteries in other large cities, and before long Kiev and Novgorod were encircled by them.

In the beginning, life in the monasteries was surely thoroughly ascetic. Antonii himself "ate only dry bread, and that only every other day, and drank a little water." The *Chronicle* (for the year 1051) goes on to report that he "rested neither by day nor by night, making every effort to stay awake and to continue praying." Feodosii, whose views can be ascertained from the *Chronicle,* from a long account of his life, and from those of his sermons which have come down to us, was also an ascetic, but he was an advocate of moderate asceticism. He retired to his cave only for the forty days of the "great fast," and one of his sermons, which is reproduced in part in the

41

Chronicle (for the year 1064), remarks that man, even the monk, should give a tithe to God and that this tithe is a fast of forty days. The saint's life devoted to Feodosii makes it clear that he particularly wished to see moderate asceticism combined with productive labor. This view is in the tradition of Palestinian monasticism and its outstanding proponent, St. Sabbas, whose legend had been disseminated in Slavic translation since the earliest period of East Slavic Christianity. Strict asceticism was unknown at the Kievan Cave Monastery until later, and in the eleventh and in part of the twelfth century the monks of the Monastery were adherents of moderate asceticism and, more importantly, of lay piety.

Lay Piety in the Eleventh Century: The Pious Prince

Two works of significance attest to the presence and character of piety among the laity. The first is Prince Vladimir Monomakh's *Testament,* the central part of which offers advice to Vladimir's children and for "others who will listen to this work when it is read." This part of the *Testament* is organized according to a definite plan. First there are observations about man's religious duties, and since the *Testament* was intended for the use of future reigning princes—some of Monomakh's sons were, in fact, already appanage princes when the *Testament* was written—Vladimir was obliged to speak about the religious obligations of a person who remains active in the world, and he did indeed emphasize that God has imposed on man duties which are sufficient to save his soul and are "not difficult to fulfill." Man can receive God's grace if he performs little acts; "solitude, monastic life, and fasting, which some take upon themselves," are not the only way to earn it. Three "little acts" which God has specified as means to resist the temptation of the devil are in themselves sufficient: "God showed us the way to vanquish the enemy [the devil]. With three good deeds we can free ourselves of him and conquer him: penitence, tears, and almsgiving. For you, my children, that is not a difficult commandment of God. Through these three deeds one can purge oneself of sin and be assured of a place in heaven. I beg you, for the sake of God, not to be lax and forgetful of these three duties, for they are not difficult." Vladimir goes on to implore his children "to meet at least half of these three obligations, if not all of them," most important of all "to weep for your sins" "when God softens your hearts." One must pray every evening, for prayer helps to vanquish the devil, but one should pray at other times too, while on a military campaign, for example; one should pray whenever there is no work to be done, and if one knows no other prayer one should at least "repeat to oneself over and over again 'God have mercy on us!' " Uttering this prayer is better than "thinking of all sorts of trifling things."

Even when Vladimir in the next part of the *Testament* goes on to the specific duties of the prince, he does not fail to emphasize that in making decisions one must not forget God's commandments and that one must keep alive in his heart "the fear of God." The individual duties of the prince, for example the obligation to keep one's word, are also given a religious motivation.

It is clear from a circular letter from Metropolitan Nikifor to Vladimir that the Greek clergy approved of the prince's "lay piety." Even if the last part of the *Chronicle* of the eleventh century, as some historians of literature suspect, was written at Vladimir Monomakh's command, and although it emphasizes the positive side of his political activity and presents an idealized portrait of Vladimir, this portrait nevertheless shows what the chronicler and Vladimir himself, who directed the chronicler's work, conceived to be the characteristics of the ideal "Christian prince." And one of the characteristics of the ideal prince was precisely that lay piety which Vladimir depicts in the *Testament.* Vladimir does not reject monastic asceticism, but he does emphasize that it is not the only possible form of piety and not the only path to spiritual salvation.

An "Instruction to the Wealthy"

A second, somewhat older literary monument, the so-called *Miscellany (Isbornik),* is no less interesting. The manuscript of this work was written down in 1076, but it is a copy of an older original Slavic manuscript. The work itself is a collection of aphorisms consisting of quotations from Holy Scripture, excerpts from Greek works on religion, and proverbs which were in all probability Kievan in origin. Those parts of the text which are translations are treated very freely; they are abridged or modified. The significant thing about them is that they are directed to the laity and in part to persons of means. One series of aphorisms is even entitled "Instructions to the Wealthy." If it were necessary to characterize the contents of this section in modern terms, it would be fair to say that the main topic of the *Miscellany* is "the social question," or, to put it in other terms, "charitable activity."

The *Miscellany* places particular emphasis on almsgiving, one of the three "easy duties" of a worldly man of which Vladimir Monomakh speaks. The authors of the *Miscellany* do not waste a single word on asceticism as a path to heaven. Helping the poor is sufficient. The prayers of almsgivers are heeded by God, their sins are forgiven them, their souls are as purified by almsgiving as the souls of monks are by acts of asceticism. "Fasting purifies the spirit of man," the chronicler wrote in reporting on the establishment of the Kievan Cave Monastery. The *Miscellany* of 1076, on the other hand, asserts: "Water extinguishes fire, and almsgiving purifies one of his sins"; "he who is merciful to the poor will receive the grace of God, and his prayers will be heard in heaven." In such passages, to be sure, there is an echo of the *do ut des* theme, for almsgiving is on the one hand the way to receive God's grace

43

and on the other the gift which man gives in return for the benefits God has bestowed upon him: "Since you have received great gifts from God, you should in return bestow great gifts." This almost businesslike concept is expressed espcially clearly in the story which concludes the *Miscellany*, "The Tale of Merciful Sozomen." This story is surely a translation; it is also found later, as late as the nineteenth century, in religious manuscripts. Sozomen, who gave his cloak to a beggar, saw in a dream what he would receive in return when he got to heaven—several chests full of costly garments—and this dream moved him to continue to be charitable. In later versions of the tale, Sozomen enters a monastery. This change in the plot actually destroys the real meaning of the story, for it was intended to influence the actions of people who continued to live in the world.

This basically "egotistic" motivation, however, is not predominant in the *Miscellany*; quite a different motive prevailed. The authors wanted to arouse the compassion and sympathy of the wealthy, and for that reason they portrayed the suffering of the poor in words which were meant to move the reader and leave an indelible impression on his mind: "When you are lying in a well-appointed room and you hear the rustling of a heavy rain, think of the poor and how they are lying out of doors, with the raindrops striking them like arrows; some of them are sitting up because they could not get to sleep and got up because of the rain. . . . When in the winter you are sitting in a warm room and have taken off your clothes, without a care in the world, think with a sigh of the poor and how they cower over a little fire—their eyes smart from the smoke, they are only able to keep their hands warm, but their backs and their whole bodies are cold from the frost." From this the reader cannot but conclude that the poor must be helped. "O child, give food to the hungry, . . . give drink to the thirsty, give lodgings to the wanderer, visit the sick, visit those who are imprisoned, see their need, and sigh!"

It is most significant that helping the poor is placed above concern for splendor in the churches: "When one makes donations to churches which do not have things they need, then it is right to give them something and to make donations. But one who donates something to a wealthy church cannot know what will happen later to his gift. . . . Later the gift may be neglected or lost or stolen by bandits or looters." Alms given to the needy, by contrast, represent a "gift made to God."

While this point of view may sound somewhat "commercial," somewhat like establishing a bank account in heaven, it is by no means the sole motive for the mercy and charitableness which are here being recommended to the wealthy. With great severity the *Miscellany* characterizes *ill gotten gains* as *plunder*, and failure to be charitable is put in the same category: "There are two kinds of robbery: one is when one takes the clothes off a poor man's back, the other is when one fails to put clothes on a poor man's back." As in Monomakh's *Testament*, one aphorism in the *Miscellany* asserts that God expects from man only "small gifts" (duties).

In the twelfth century there appeared a compilation of two sermons attributed to St. John Chrysostom. This work characterizes charity as a sort of "business," "buying one's way into heaven," but it also cites a new reason for being charitable: the life of the wealthy is described in an exaggerated and in part grotesque way so that it will seem senseless and absurd to the reader. This work too is an "Instruction for the Wealthy" and a recommendation that man be pious while remaining *in the world*.

An Anti-Ascetic Monk's Legend

Especially strong evidence for the existence of anti-ascetic tendencies is provided by a legend which appeared in the *Primary Chronicle* (for the year 1084) and was meant to point out the dangers inherent in exaggerated asceticism. Since this legend was obviously meant to characterize life in the Kievan Cave Monastery, its anti-ascetic bias is particularly significant.

The legend is simple and its bias obvious. After describing the death of the abbot, Feodosii, the legend turns to a discussion of life in the Cave Monastery. The monks who joined Feodosii "shine like stars in Rus'." Their acts of asceticism are briefly described. They kept vigils, prayed, and fasted. Some ate only every other day, some only every third day, some took only bread and water, some ate only vegetables, some ate only uncooked vegetables. They were obedient to their elders, lived in harmony together, consoled the older monks, and instructed the younger ones as if they were their own children. This first part of the legend is still written from the standpoint of the ascetic, but the rest of the tale expresses grave reservations about asceticism.

Among the monks were some who possessed various "gifts of the spirit," gifts like those which the apostles were promised by Christ (Matthew 10:8; Mark 16:18). A few examples are cited. One monk, for instance, possessed the gift of healing, another could read the secret thoughts of men, and yet another had the gift of visions and could see clearly the supersensual world. Examples of the gift of consolation and the gift of prophecy are also given. Almost no mention is made of the ascetic deeds of these specially endowed monks. Then a monk whose monastic name was Isaakii is described, and his story is told for the sole purpose of warning against extreme asceticism and against "ascetic pride," which can lead the ascetic to perdition. The significance of the story about Isaakii is in no way diminished by the fact that the author of the story used as a model a novella from the translated version of the patericon[6] of Palladius, the story about Valens, which is found in Chapter XXV of the so-called *Historia Lausiaca*.

In secular life Isaakii had been a merchant. He decided to become a monk, gave away all his possessions to the poor and to monasteries, and came to Kiev to join St. Antonii. Antonii accepted him and "put on him monastic habit." Isaakii, however, put on a hair shirt and over that a still damp goatskin which dried and pressed the hair shirt to his body, thus irritating his skin. Then Isaakii locked himself in a small cave which was only four ells wide [and thus four times narrower than St. Antonii's cave]. There Isaakii prayed and wept, eating only one communion wafer every other day and drinking only a little water which St. Antonii handed in to him through a small window. He slept for only short periods of time, and this in a sitting position. He spent seven years in this fashion, and despite this most severe ascetic life he still had not progressed far enough to be able to "distinguish between spirits." He succumbed to the temptations of the devil, who appealed to Isaakii's ascetic pride. In short, Isaakii believed that he had already progressed so far that he had been granted the gift of divine visions.

One night when Isaakii was sitting in the dark and praying, "a light, as bright as the sun, suddenly appeared and blinded him. And two beautiful youths approached him and said: 'Isaakii, we are angels. Christ is coming to you, so bow down to the earth before him.' " Isaakii did not understand that the devil was deceiving him, and he forgot to cross himself, as St. Juliana, according to legend, did on a similar occasion. Isaakii bowed down before the figure whom he took to be Christ and thus succumbed to the power of the devil.

His cell was invaded by devils who played on musical instruments and forced Isaakii to dance. In this way they "made fun of him" and "mocked him," and when they departed they left Isaakii more dead than alive. The next morning St. Antonii brought him a piece of bread, and when St. Antonii received no answer from Isaakii he had an entrance dug to the cave and found the ascetic paralyzed. It took two years for Isaakii to recover so that he could walk and talk again.

While the story up to this point is similar to the tale of Valens, for the remainder of the tale the author probably had in mind another story from Palladius' work, the story of Chronius and Paphnutius, which appears in Chapter XLVII of the *Historia Lausiaca.* According to this tale, monks who attribute their deeds "not to God, the bestower of all good, but to their own will power, insight, and strength" are "left by God to their own devices. . . . The proud man, that is, attributes ability and knowledge not to God but to his own natural talent and his industrious use of it; for that reason God takes away from him his guardian angel, and the proud man then falls into the clutches of the devil." This is the psychological interpretation of Isaakii's fate. But for the ascetic whose pride has brought him to a fall there is nevertheless still hope for salvation. Palladius too speaks of this: "bent down and ashamed they gradually lay aside their pride in the virtue they thought they possessed." This is what happened to Isaakii.

46

Salvation from Ascetic Pride

Even after his recovery Isaakii led a "hard life," but now it was a life of a different sort. He no longer locked himself in a cell but instead stayed in the monastery and even went into the city. He worked in the kitchen, for labor was one of the rules handed down by Feodosii. Isaakii attended religious services and "did all sorts of strange things," that is, he was one of the first Slavic *yurodivye,* or "holy fools," a type of ascetic which will be discussed in detail later. Unfortunately, the author of the legend gives few details about Isaakii's "strange" behavior.

Soon Isaakii was indeed granted the "gifts of the spirit." Examples of how these manifested themselves are given. He was able to stamp out with his bare feet a fire which broke out in his cell (in European hagiographic literature this miracle has a special name, *ignis impotens*). He was able to seize wild ravens with his bare hands, and we should bear in mind that in older literature the raven is the "wildest" of birds and is mentioned in the same breath as the eagle. This too is a "reconciliation" with wild nature which is typical of both Eastern and Western saints, and in other legends saints make friends with lions, bears, and stags. Isaakii was soon no longer afraid of devils who appeared to him, sometimes as wild animals, sometimes as snakes and toads. They were forced to confess: "You have vanquished us, Isaakii," and Isaakii replied, "You first vanquished me by assuming the form of Christ and of angels when I was still unworthy of this vision, and now I see you in your true form, as wild animals, beasts, and snakes." And so, Isaakii's life did end with a victory over the devil after all.

The Proud but Impotent World

Political and ideological reality underwent a basic change in the twelfth century. The last prince who was able to maintain, even in part, the unity of the East Slavic lands was Vladimir Monomakh's son, Mstislav, who reigned as Prince of Kiev from 1125 until 1132. After his death begins the age of the appanage princes, rulers who often fought bitterly with each other and who undermined the prosperity and political importance of the country. The feuds of these princes, however, were not the primary reason for the economic and political decline of Eastern Europe. Probably a more important factor was discovery of new routes which connected the Occident and the East and which could serve in lieu of the overland trade routes from Eastern Europe to the Orient. These new routes, which led directly over the Mediterranean, had been opened up by the Crusades.

The East Slavic world became poorer and less powerful, but as is so often the case, this decline evoked a compensatory increase in self-esteem. The "world" to a great extent loosened its ties with religion and proudly began to

47

oppose the Church. While real life became more insipid and insignificant, the literary portrayal of this real world became more colorful and grandiose. Now choice tropes and figures became the favorite stylistic devices in literary works, and many pages of the *Chronicle* and of other works glitter with all the colors of the rainbow, especially with the splendor of gold, pearls, and precious stones. This development in literary style is only one aspect of the ideological trend, but it is a characteristic one. The age produced extremely ostentatious descriptions in the so-called *Hypatius Chronicle* (twelfth to thirteenth century) and in the only old epic work which has been preserved, *The Lay of the Host of Igor* (1185/1187). And it was this age which gave rise to epic lays which still live on—in altered form, of course—and which are devoted for the most part to lavish descriptions of the immeasurable riches of their heroes, such figures as Churilo Plenkovich and Diuk Stepanovich.

The Ornate Literary Style

Hyperbole is characteristic of this age. In works of literature the descriptions of the accoutrements and the chambers of princes who were often politically quite insignificant glitter with gold: their thrones, their stirrups, their saddles, even their arrows are "golden." In *The Lay of the Host of Igor* the palace of the Kievan prince is "roofed with gold." The *Hypatius Chronicle* describes the attire of one prince, Daniil of Galicia, as follows: "The horse on which he rode was a wonder to behold, and its saddle was made of a burnt gold *(aurum coctum)* and his arrows and his sword were adorned with gold, . . . and his cloak was made of Grecian silk interwoven with gold, and it was trimmed with flat golden lace, and his boots were made of Morocco leather and were embroidered with gold."

The boldest possible literary hyperbole serves to disguise the military weakness of the princes. In *The Lay of the Host of Igor* Sviatslav, the Prince of Kiev, is portrayed not as a human being but as a cosmic force, and his victory over the Polovtsy is depicted as an elemental catastrophe: "He stepped on the land of the Polovtsy, trampled the hills and gorges to pieces, muddied the rivers and lakes, dried up the streams and swamps, tore like a whirlwind the pagan Kobiak [one of the Polovtsian chieftains] from the bosom of the sea, out of the great iron armies of the Polovtsy, and Kobiak fell into Sviatoslav's banquet hall in Kiev." Kobiak's flight from the "bosom of the sea" to Kiev was, of course, one of several hundred miles. Prince Yaroslav of Galicia "sits upon his throne adorned with gold, supporting the Hungarian Mountains [the Carpathians] with his iron armies, barring the path of the [Hungarian] king, closing the gates of the Danube, hurling weights over the clouds, and holding court as far as the Danube. His storms inundate the lands: he opens the gates of Kiev; and from the golden throne of his forefathers he shoots at sultans who live many countries removed from him." The Prince of Suzdal "can splash all the water out of the Volga with his oars and empty out the Don with the helmets of his men." These descriptions ignore the fact that the very princes who appear in literary portrayals to be so powerful were restricting and often destroying their own power by constantly feuding with each other, and the authors of these descriptions knew that all too well and even spoke of it—elsewhere.

Besides the "great" princes there were numerous lesser monarchs who thirsted for power. The complicated political system of the time was unstable, and rulers large and small weakened each other not only by constantly fighting with each other, but by merely existing as rulers. They were incapable of uniting to face a common foe. In the twelfth century the enemy was still the relatively harmless Polovtsy, but in the thirteenth it was the destructive force of the Tatars. Even in depicting the feuds of the princes the poets were able to wax enthusiastic and to portray a clash of small armies in a grand manner. One battle reminds the author of "Judgment Day and the end of the world," and we hear how in battle "the warriors in their golden helmets swam in blood," and so on. The *Chronicles* of the twelfth century are devoted in large measure to the feuds of the princes and afford insight into the spiritual and intellectual attitudes of the ruling class.

East Slavic Knighthood

The mentality of the East Slavic princes in the twelfth and thirteenth centuries is "chivalric," with all the strengths and weaknesses which that entails. The princes at that time were primarily warriors, and frequently they simply did not have the time to build up their lands in an orderly fashion, because a prince often remained on the thone for only a few months. Most thrones were contested and objects of armed conflict, and not infrequently, especially in Novgorod, they were "precarious" because the prince could be deposed and driven into exile. Thrones were "sought after" because possession of them meant power and because they were thought to be "golden." The struggle for a throne to which there were pretentions was stubbornly pursued because "honor" and "fame" could be achieved in this way. Reports of victorious campaigns always end with the same formula: the princes "wipe the sweat from their brow" or "wipe the tears from their eyes" and return home or ascend the throne which they have won "with honor and great praise," "with great fame and honor," "with great honor," or "with great honor and great praise." But defeat, or even the "turning away of the army" without "having achieved anything," meant "disgrace."

Honor is always mentioned as at least one of the basic motivating factors of the foreign policy of the era, and since in every war there is a loser as well as a winner the feuds could never end, because the loser, who had "brought on himself the disgrace" of defeat, was obliged to continue the fight in order to restore his honor. Men fought "because of an insult" (*obida,* which also means "injustice"), and an insult "could be avenged only by risking one's own neck": "It is better, brother, to die here than to bring disgrace upon ourselves." Death was preferable to "dishonor" and "disgrace," and a nobleman's honor was sullied not only when he suffered a military defeat but when he was in any way treated "unjustly," or even when another nobleman intended to treat him unjustly. A statement ascribed to various princes who were offered as consolation the rather unattractive throne of Kursk is typical: "It is better for me to die here with my army than to accept the throne of Kursk." Thus there were always reasons which could move a prince to avenge actual or intended damage to his honor.

Of course, this was not the same as the primitive revenge of pagan times. Instead, feelings of hostility were now sublimated and transfigured, raised to a higher power, as it were. Members of the nobility lived in a state of constant turmoil. No knight could ever forget his own disgrace, and he was obliged to seek in every possible way to restore his honor, but on the other hand he could not ignore the fact that he himself had probably caused some other knight to "bring disgrace upon himself" and that this person also wished to "rid himself of his disgrace" and was likewise prepared to go to any lengths to do so.

Honor, in and of itself, was a goal worth striving for, even for the knight who had no need to "rid himself of disgrace," and for this reason fights often started for no good reason at all, simply because the field of battle was the place where it was easiest to achieve honor. The reason for military adventures is frequently found to be nothing more than the desire for honor: "Let us take our honor," "I find my honor and the fulfillment of my dearest wish."

Admittedly, this consciousness of personal honor could rise on occasion to a consciousness of *national* honor. Before a battle one prince is reported to have addressed his army in the following words: "Brothers and fellow warriors, God has not delivered the Russian land and the sons of Russia up to dishonor; everywhere we have won honor through our struggles. Today, brothers, in these lands, confronted by foreign peoples, may God grant that we uphold our honor." This statement, of course, may merely express the views of the chronicler, but even *The Lay of the Host of Igor* speaks of battles "for the Russian land." Feelings of national honor were actually aroused, however, only when the enemy was a neighboring people—the Polovtsy, the Swedes, or the Teutonic Order; and only seldom did the appanage princes succeed in uniting in a common military cause. Even against the Tatars in the thirteenth century they found it impossible to mount a united defense. Only later, after the crushing defeat at the hands of the Tatars, did consciousness of *national* honor become somewhat stronger.

As we have already noted, thrones were coveted because of the wealth which fell to those who occupied them, and in the foreign policy of the appanage princes we often discern purely egotistic motives. If, in the chivalric ethic, honor was one side of the coin, then egotism was the other. Every prince thought he had the right to a "share of the Russian land," and the battle for this "share" was conducted ruthlessly. One prince assured his listeners: "I am going to seek to possess Novgorod by fair means or foul." His appeal to his *hereditary* rights is a euphemistic formulation of this claim to "a share in the Russian land": "I am going to sit upon the throne of my father and my grandfather," or, as he also put it, "I am going to follow in the footsteps of my father and my grandfather." But since the royal families were large and all the princes were related to each other, the princes' claims to their "patrimony" were for the most part mere presumptions. Appeals were made on the basis of primogeniture, but these too were in many cases without sufficient basis in fact. The real reasons for the behavior of the princes are often evident in the reports of the outcome of their military campaigns: the spoils of war, which are often described in rather colorful language; the prisoners-of-war, most of whom were probably released in return for ransom (the sale of slaves is hardly mentioned any more at this time); and, at the same time, the destruction of the material wealth of the enemy.

Every struggle for "a share in the Russian land" was carried on just as ruthlessly as were the battles for personal honor. In both instances the characteristic formula is "either/or": "Either I shall lose my life in battle with the foe or I shall win the throne of my father and my grandfather," or "Either I shall lose my life or I shall stand avenged."

The people stood by their prince and his men. According to the reports in the *Chronicles* the townsmen also wished "to risk their lives" for their princes—the rural population played a purely passive role in political events. In some instances, however, it is reported that the burghers resisted the military enterprises of their princes, especially in Novgorod, and also in Galicia, whose burghers the chronicler terms "those godless Galicians." Sources also give ideological reasons for the burghers' resistance to the military adventures of the princes.

The Ideal Christian Knight

The remarkable thing about the picture of these sad and troubled times is that along with the egocentrism of princely honor and the egoism which spurred princes on to possess a share in the Russian land, the Christian view of the "world" also finds expression. The very princes who were behaving for all the world like "pagans" probably thought of themselves as good Christians, and the Christian concept of history is clearly that to which the chroniclers subscribed.

At this time it was believed that historical events were determined by the will of God. Only infrequently do the chroniclers attribute to their princely heroes phrases which speak of a belief in *blind fate* (such as "we will simply have to wait and see what happens") or of the *personal lot* of the individual ("my time has come"). Almost always the phrase is "We place our hope in God." Men wait to see "what God will give us," "how God will provide for us," or "how God will lead us." In conflicts between mortals it is God who decides: "God shall judge between the two of us." The decision rests with "our Saviour"; "the sacred cross" brings victory. "Behind all men stand God and the power of the cross," and men pray "Grant, O God, that we receive our share." Oaths were sworn "by the holy cross," and even though men often broke their promises and violated their oaths, they still believed that promises made and alliances concluded by "kissing the holy cross" were binding. To be sure, as early as the twelfth century we encounter a prince who mocks his oath and the holy cross. Prince Volodimirko of Galich, when reminded of his oath by the cross of St. Stephen (King of Hungary), said cynically: "What, this little cross?" However, the chronicler who relates the incident is able to report with full satisfaction that this blasphemy did not go unpunished: the prince died the night after he had uttered these impious words.

The outcome of any event was not determined by luck or misfortune; rather it was considered the reward or the punishment which was meted out by God, by Christ, or by the Virgin Mary. Some have emphasized, quite correctly, that in the descriptions in the *Chronicles* the victors are for the most part portrayed as the advocates of a just cause. This is a kind of historical optimism which is ultimately connected with the Christian concept of history.

"Russia" is also frequently referred to as a *Christian land* whenever it is cited as justification for political actions, and by "Russia" the *Chronicles* meant almost exclusively the southern territories, the Ukraine. The idea of a country which is singled out as somehow especially Christian in character did not yet exist at all, and, more importantly, the formula "Holy Russia" did not either. The same princes, however, who on occasion concluded military alliances with the pagan Polovtsy justified their actions roughly as follows: "I shall toil for Russia. . . . Grant, o Lord, that we risk our lives for Christians and for Russia and act as the martyrs have acted." On the other hand, and this is significant, similar reasons were given for preserving the peace. This was done "for Russia, for the Christians," or "we do not wish to ruin Russia and spill Christian blood."

It is even more significant that the progress of the Crusades was followed with warm interest and with satisfaction. In 1188 and 1190 the chronicler of Kiev wrote down short reports about the Crusades, and these notations suffice to show the strength of the ideal of the Christian knight at that time (even though perhaps not among the "knights" themselves): "In this year the German emperor with his entire people went to do battle for the grave of Christ. God revealed this [task] to him through an angel and commanded him to go forth. When they had arrived there they fought valiantly against the godless Hagarians [Saracens] ." The chronicler believes that the crusaders will be greatly rewarded: "Those Germans, together with their emperor, have shed their blood for Christ as the holy martyrs did. Over them our Lord made a sign: when one of them had fallen in combat with the foe, after three days his body was taken from its coffin by an angel of God, and the others, who had seen this, strove to suffer also for the sake of Christ. The will of God was expressed in them, and He led them to His chosen flock, to the martyrs."

The chroniclers present quite well-rounded descriptions of some of the pious Christian princes, for example, of Prince Rostislav of Smolensk (later of Kiev) in the twelfth century and of Prince Vladimir Vasilkovich of Volynia in the thirteenth. The pages devoted to the latter, which are actually a necrology and not a report from a chronicle, are characteristic of the style of the time. Prince Vladimir Vaskilovich saw to it that churches were built and furnished, and he also copied church books with his own hand. The *Chronicle* reports: "He placed in the Church of the Virgin Mary burnt gold vessels for divine services. . . . For his monastery he himself copied the Gospel and the Apostles. To the Bishopric of Peremyshl' he likewise gave a church Gospel which he himself had copied and which was fitted with clasps of silver and pearls, and to the Bishop of Chernigov he sent a church Gospel which was written in gold and bound in silver with inlaid pearls, and in the middle of the silver binding was an icon of our Saviour in enamel. . . . He also built many churches; in Liuboml' he erected the stone church of St. George. . . . He adorned it with wrought-iron icons and had vessels for divine services made; he donated velvet vestments embroidered with gold and pearls and with pictures of cherubim and seraphim, and the gold-embroidered altar cloth, and another vestment made of white silk." At his court there was probably also considerable luxury, but none of it was left in the end because on his deathbed (he died of cancer of the lower lip) the prince "distributed his belongings among the poor: gold and silver and precious stones, and the golden belts of his father, and the silver ones too, and he gave away everything which he himself had acquired after the death of his father; and in his presence he had large silver bowls and golden cups, and silver ones too, broken into pieces and melted down into bars, and the large golden necklaces of his mother and his grandmother, he had them all melted down and sent alms throughout his entire land. . . ." This description of splendor is typical of the style of the time and differs from somewhat earlier descriptions only in that the silver, gold, pearls, and precious stones were either used to adorn churches or distributed as alms to the poor.

One striking aspect of this portrait of the ideal Christian prince is the apparently complete absence of any woman in his life. Women are seldom mentioned in literary monuments written before the thirteenth century, but the characterizations of the few women who are mentioned show that they must have played an important role at this time. One of those mentioned was

53

Princess Olga, a harsh ruler of the tenth century who reigned in her own right and led military campaigns herself. Others are devout princesses: Ianka, who founded a monastery in Kiev in the eleventh century; Princess Predislava-Evfrosiniia of Polotsk in the twelfth century; and at the beginning of the thirteenth century Princess Verkhuslava-Anastasiia, who was the recipient of instructive letters and a patroness of pious monks. Mention is also made of politically active women like Princess Maria of Suzdal, who allegedly saw to it that a chronicle was revised. In *The Lay of the Host of Igor* Yaroslavna, the wife of Prince Igor, appears as a widow in mourning and begins to sing a sort of lament, and another passage portrays a Riazanian prince's wife who dies of sorrow after her husband has been killed by the Tatars. But even though the author of *The Lay of the Host of Igor* does expect one of his heroes to keep in mind "the love and tenderness of his beautiful wife," women do not seem to exist for the men of this age. The question arises as to whether this infrequent appearance of women in older literature might be considered proof that the old Russian knight was not exposed to one of the essential humanizing influences. It is a fact that both of the later Russian male types—the rude and uncouth tyrant, and the ascetic to whom women seemed to be only a necessary evil—remained without any contact at all with the world of women. The numerous invectives against "evil women" which were added later to older works, and the later writings which have an anti-feminist bias, were probably without exception the work of ascetics and were enthusiastically received by the "tyrant type" in particular.

Monastic Asceticism in the Twelfth and Thirteenth Centuries

It is quite understandable that when the world, which had become "conscious of itself," became independent, a counter-movement should develop within the Church. The religious literature of the twelfth and thirteenth centuries exhibits several new characteristics which proclaim that a new age was dawning. On the one hand, there was the increasing popularity of the highly ornate style (the "heavily adorned" style, as it is termed in medieval poetics), which dominated secular literature. On the other hand there was an increase in pessimistic assessments of the world and in praise of asceticism as the sole path for Christian life.

The belief in a "pre-established harmony" between Church and State, a harmony which was disturbed only occasionally and "accidentally" by the intrigues of the "enemy," could not help but give way to a profoundly pessimistic assessment of the world when confronted by the political fragmentation of the country and the inability of its rulers to preserve among themselves even a "bad peace"—and a Russian proverb asserts that a "bad peace" is better than a "good quarrel." Perhaps the world was completely under the control of the devil, and perhaps the only way to escape Satan was to flee to a monastery. True monastic life could only be achieved in complete isolation from the "world," which had nothing to offer but temptation and from which no good was to be expected.

We are fortunate to have a voluminous document concerning the monastic ideology of the twelfth and the beginning of the thirteenth centuries, the so-called *Patericon of the Kievan Cave Monastery*. This important work originated in the thirteenth century and was based on correspondence between two monks of the Monastery, one of whom had become a bishop. One of the two later versions of the work retains the epistolary form as a "frame." The content of the frame is in itself significant, for it consists of a letter in which the bishop urges the ambitious monk not to strive for an ecclesiastical position outside the walls of the monastery. At that time such a post obviously did not afford the peace and quiet needed for spiritual life, and to the bishop such a post had revealed that the world seen at close range was "a den of thieves."

The *Patericon* proper consists of individual stories about twenty-four monks of the Monastery. Some of the stories were written by Bishop Simon of Vladimir-Suzdal, who served as bishop from 1215 to 1226, and some by a monk named Polycarp. Inasmuch as Polycarp directed his letters to the abbot who was in office from 1214 until 1231, it is possible to state with some degree of certainty that the document originated between 1215 and 1226. Only a few of the stories tell about monks whom the authors knew personally. Bishop Simon and Polycarp were familiar with the lives of most of the monks through oral tradition or from written reports which are no longer extant. The tone of the stories no longer has anything in common with the cheerful religious mood of the account of the life of St. Feodosii. This new tone is characteristic of the mood which prevailed in the Kievan Cave Monastery around the year 1200.

The main themes of the *Patericon* are asceticism and demonology, and the attitude toward life in the world is completely negative. Life in the monastery, at least the life which pious monks led, was already confined largely to the caves. Strict hermits are the most important heroes of the *Patericon*. Of course, the men who are described are very different from one another. There were even some who attempted to serve both their brothers in the monastery and those in the world beyond the monastery walls, but the more typical figures are monks who remained in the isolation of their caves and devoted all their efforts to the salvation of their own souls and to their struggles with demons. Some of the stories are simple biographies, while others are fairy tale legends, such as that of Grigorii, who forced the devils to help him carry wood.

It is also quite significant that now the ascetics no longer suffered only at the hands of the pagans. Besides the "martyrs," who paid for their lives of fidelity to the Christian faith while living among foreign peoples, there are those who were persecuted by the princes, like Prokhor, who by distributing ashes as a substitute for salt broke the royal exchequer's salt monopoly. There are even some who were murdered at the command of a prince, such as the aformentioned Grigorii, whom a prince, simply out of youthful high spirits, had ordered drowned; two other monks were executed at the order of another prince who had commanded them to turn over to him a treasure which they had allegedly discovered.

It is even more significant that the two authors no longer paint the congregation of the Monastery in such bright colors as were used by the chronicler to tell the story of Isaakii. Many monks no longer observed the vows, that of poverty in particular, and there were already prosperous monks who greedily guarded their treasures. The devil succeeded in leading two monks astray by playing into their hands an old treasure which was hidden in the Monastery. One deceased brother who had no wealth was not buried for a long time, evidently because at that time the entire congregation of the Monastery neglected even the poor within their own ranks. There are reports of quarrels between monks, and of cases of willfulness and insubordination. To be sure, this is part of the literary tradition of the paterica, which customarily depicted not only models of righteousness but also "fallen ascetics."

The *Patericon of the Kievan Case Monastery,* in any case, does document the spread of the pessimistic-ascetic view of life during the twelfth and thirteenth centuries. Punishment for the world was already near at hand: the destructive incursions of the Tatars occurred in 1223 and 1237.

Ascetic Literature

Several of the original literary works of the time attest to the pessimistic view of the world found in the *Patericon of the Kievan Cave Monastery.* The most famous and really extraordinarily talented preacher of the second half of the twelfth century, Bishop Kirill of Turov, devoted his sermons—at least those which have come down to us—to a portrayal of christology which is of high literary quality and is written in the "richly adorned" style found in works of secular literature. He portrays Christian dogma in symbols and incorporates into his sermons dialogues or monologues (elegies and the like), but his numerous prayers, which have been in use among the faithful until recent times, are more characteristic of his religious philosophy. These prayers are perhaps the strongest expression of the pessimistic view of the world and of man written at the time. Here man is described as a completely powerless plaything of sin and the devil, and only through God's help can he be rescued from his profound degeneracy. Kirill therefore prays for God's help and protection. But, Kirill says, man actually no longer dares hope to receive this help because man no longer deserves it. In one prayer the supplicant describes himself as follows: "Neither do I dare look on heaven, for I have harmed my body through evil, nor dare I lift up my hands on high, for they are stained by usury, nor dare I open my mouth to pray, for it is withered by evil slander; my self-adulation makes it impossible for me to sigh; I have burdened my heart with sumptuous meals, blackened my soul with cruelty, wearied my body with sloth; I opened my ears to listen to transitory flattery; I covered my face with impudence; my nose smells the stench of my deeds; I am like a barren tree; I am like a forsaken temple. . . ." (In the last lines Kirill is alluding to Christ's words about the "barren fig tree."). Kirill is not surprised that man, in such a state of corruption, has fallen prey to the devil: "The enemy of my soul is hidden in my heart and wishes to rob me of the last vestiges of my faith, just by waiting for the propitious moment. . . ."

Kirill was not alone in judging mankind this way. Another witness, Serapion (d. 1275), who was preacher in Kiev and later Bishop of Vladimir-Suzdal, may be cited, even though part of his sermons date from after the Tatar invasions and he was thus in a position to point to the terrible punishment which had been visited upon the East Slavic world. Serapion believes that mankind deserves no better fate: "We paid no heed to the Apostles, we paid no heed to the prophets, we paid no heed to the great saints, . . . they instructed us without surcease, and we have clung to lawlessness." "The robber has not left off robbing; the thief has not given up stealing; the misanthrope has not banished hatred from his heart; the oppressor and exploiter of others is not sated; the usurer has not forsaken usury; . . . the lecher has not abandoned lechery; the reviler and the toper have not mended their ways." Not even God's punishment has had any effect: "We have not turned to God, we have not repented of our lawlessness, . . . we have not cleansed ourselves of the filth of our sins." "Envy has increased, evil rules us, praise has made us haughty, enmity toward friends has come into our heart, insatiable desire for worldly goods has taken possession of us, it prevents us from living a humane life."

The invasion of the Tatars was fresh in everyone's mind, but there were other punishments which God meted out: "We saw how the sun disappeared, how the moon grew dark, how the stars were transformed, and now we have seen with our own eyes an earthquake." That in itself seemed to be a sign that the end was at hand: "The earth, fixed and immovable since the beginning of time, has now moved at God's command, shaken by our sins, it cannot bear our lawlessness." "Today God causes the earth to shake and sway: He wants to shake from the earth numerous lawless sins, like leaves from a tree."

These are the words which Serapion wrote and spoke in Kiev and Suzdal, but in Smolensk, a calmer city, a similar mood prevailed even before the Tatar invasions. Unfortunately, none of the writings of St. Avraamii of Smolensk, a great priest and preacher in that city around the year 1200, have survived, but the legends which sprang up about him reveal that his sermons had a disquieting effect on the city and that his thoughts were dominated by the idea that the second coming of Christ and the Day of Judgment were imminent. His eschatological sermons probably spoke of God's punishments, which then were merely threatening, and it was possible for Smolensk to fall prey to eschatological unrest only because life there afforded a sufficient basis for such spiritual turmoil. The Tatar invasions, which came a few years later, could not fail to give the impression in Smolensk that Avraamii's "prophecies" were being fulfilled, even though the Tatars never reached the city at all. It is useless to try to guess what these prophecies actually were, but they are further evidence of the profound religious pessimism which was spreading at the time, even independently of the "omens that the world was coming to an end," which, of the three preachers mentioned, only Serapion had seen with his own eyes. For Serapion's older contemporaries the state of the world was probably a convincing sign that this world, wallowing in wickedness, could not long continue to exist in its present state. And they were right. This state soon came to an end, and the way it did so caused the ascetic mood to become even more pronounced.

Lay Piety in the Twelfth and Thirteenth Centuries

The turn to "ascetic rigorism" in the twelfth century, however, was by no means complete. In the twelfth and even in the thirteenth century there are various reports which attest to the fact that even at that time and even among churchmen there were those who did not regard monastic asceticism as the only road to spiritual salvation and who believed that a worldly path to God was open to them. The documents, to be sure, are again from the south, but extant manuscripts indicate that these writings were also known in the north and northeast.

First of all, there is the remarkable sermon held by an unidentified priest of Chernigov on the name day of St. Boris and St. Gleb (it should be noted that this sermon obviously dates from as early as around the year 1200). The preacher proceeds from praise of the two royal saints to his general theme, which is given in the title of the sermon: "Concerning Princes." The preacher addresses the princes directly, and since he does not call them "Your Lordships" but rather sometimes "Princes" and sometimes "Children," it seems safe to assume that he was a bishop. He takes as his point of departure an actual event, a planned or already initiated feud during which the preacher's "spiritual children" had either concluded or intended to conclude an alliance with the Polovtsy, among others. Because the royal saints, Boris and Gleb, had preferred death to armed conflict with their older brother, the preacher feels that he may cite the two saints to later members of the dynasty as models to be emulated. Like the saints, the present princes of Chernigov should keep the peace, even if that were to mean "suffering" for it. Another model whom the priest is able to cite is a more recent ancestor of the princes of Chernigov, Prince David Sviatoslavich, who had died in 1123 and whose life story the preacher knew from a literary source or from oral tradition. Prince David had achieved renown because he always kept his word, even when the other party to a contract did not. God rewarded him for this by granting him a happy reign and by giving a wondrous sign after his death. "When his brothers [i.e. the other princes] saw him like this, they paid heed to him as if he were their father and obeyed him as if he were their master. And his reign passed in complete peacefulness." The preacher, however, draws even further conclusions from this: some may think, for instance, "that you cannot fulfill God's commandments and save your soul if you have a wife, children and a house [private property]." Prince David, however, had a wife and children—five sons—and owned not merely a house but a whole kingdom, and he fulfilled God's commandments, for "he was an enemy to no man." And at his funeral, when he lay on the bier in the church, a white dove, the sign of the Holy Ghost, flew into the church and alighted on his chest.

We need not be concerned about whether the preacher had access to a biography of the prince written in preparation for canonization proceedings which were planned but not carried out. What is more important for us is the knowledge that as late as the end of the thirteenth century a preacher could speak with such polemical vigor about spiritual salvation *within the world.*

The *Chronicle* indicates that other clergymen shared the views of the priest of Chernigov. It is common knowledge that there were innumerable feuds among the children and grandchildren of Vladimir Monomakh. One of Monomakh's grandsons, Prince Rostislav of Smolensk, participated in these feuds between 1142 and 1154, though only in a rather passive way—as the companion of his brother, Iziaslav II of Kiev. After Iziaslav had fallen in battle in 1154, Rostislav became for a short time Prince of Kiev, but he was driven into exile by another pretender and did not regain the throne until 1160. Even after Iziaslav's death Rostislav's policies were by no means exclusively peaceful. In 1168, when he was nearly sixty years of age, Rostislav fell ill during a visit to Novgorod. On the journey home he refused to stay with his sister in Smolensk and instead hastened on to Kiev, for if he recovered from his illness he wanted to become a monk in the Kievan Cave Monastery. He is said to have expressed such a desire earlier to Polycarp, the abbot of the Monastery: "I would like to rid myself of this vain and transitory world and of this turbulent and shallow life," he said to Polycarp, who replied: "You [princes] are destined to live this way: you should act justly in this world, hand down just decisions in court, and keep your word when you have given an oath." The abbot did not even want to have the "good cell" built which the prince had requested for his declining years. Only now was the abbot prepared to invest the dying man as a monk, but this did not come to pass, for the prince died on the journey: "He looked upon the icons of the Creator and with tears in his eyes began to speak in a soft voice:

'O Lord, keep Thy word and now release Thy servant in peace'—and the tears on his cheeks looked like pearls, and so, wiping away the tears with a cloth, he died. . . ." The question of the reliability of this report of Rostislav's pious attitude and intentions is another matter, but it is significant that the abbot of a famous monastery related how he constantly resisted the prince's intentions to become a monk, a plan the prince had mentioned "often" since 1164. It is also significant that this same abbot obviously deemed it important that a report of it appear *in the chronicle,* for the report in the chronicle can be based only on information provided by Abbot Polycarp himself. The abbot of the Kievan Cave Monastery may therefore be considered an adherent to the view that monastic asceticism was not the only path to heaven a pious man might follow.

There is other evidence that in the twelfth century monasticism was by no means considered the only path to spiritual salvation. For example, in 1174 the *Chronicle* reports the death of a prince's son who had been ill since birth and whom his family refused to "consecrate" to God, as would later certainly have been the normal thing to do. Moreover, the Chronicle pays little attention to Nikola Sviatosha, a member of the house of the Chernigov princes who became a monk at the Cave Monastery in 1106. For Igor, another member of the house of Chernigov, becoming a monk was simply a way of proclaiming that he was renouncing all political activity (this did not help him at all; in the same year in which he became a monk, 1147, he was murdered by a Kievan mob).

Not until the end of the twelfth century (1194, 1195, and 1198) did several dying princes have themselves invested as monks; toward the end of the thirteenth century this became the rule. The custom is evidence that people were already beginning to believe that purely external attestation of piety was sufficient to save one's soul. In this context the story of the last days of Prince Rostislav assumes special significance. He died without taking the easier "imperial" road to heaven on which, in later times, all the Muscovite grand princes and tsars set out shortly before their deaths.

That one could get to heaven by this easier path and that as a monk one was assured of heavenly bliss was by no means the generally accepted view, however. In fact, more attention was paid to the other path to salvation, that of inner piety—a path accessible to those who remained "in the world."

The Sources of Anti-Ascetic Writings

The ascetic literature of the Eastern Church is sufficiently well known, and even in the tenth and eleventh centuries numerous such works were available in Slavic translation and were also being disseminated among the East Slavs. Ascetic tendencies and ascetic writings among the East Slavs are thus easy to account for. But where did "anti-ascetic" ideas come from? What tradition led to writings like the story about Isaakii? And what were the sources of the compilers of the *Miscellany* of 1076? These questions have perturbed the few scholars who first called attention to the existence of two religious movements in Old Russia.

Formerly attempts were made to answer these questions by tracing the lay piety of the eleventh century and the cheerful optimism of early Kievan religious literature back to the influence of a "Bulgarian tradition." If it is assumed that until 1037 the Russian church was actually subordinate to the Bulgarian hierarchy, then it can also be assumed that the Bulgarian church was influential in Kiev and Novgorod. This answer, of course, is based on two unproven hypotheses: the existence of a Bulgarian hierarchy in old Russia, and a special variant of "Bulgarian Christianity." The second hypothesis in particular is a very bold one, for precious little is known about the "Bulgarian" church of the tenth and eleventh centuries and nothing at all about its "anti-ascetic, optimistic Christianity." Indeed, religious life in Bulgaria was characterized by the growth of a heretical movement called Bogomilism which was, in fact, opposed to the anti-ascetic movements found among the East Slavs. Moreover, at that time Bulgaria was merely a province of the Byzantine Empire, and even the Bulgarian Church's relative independence, which was soon to come to an end, was hardly suitable soil for an optimistic view of the world. Finally, the Bulgarian hierarchy could have reigned over the East Slavs only until 1037, but all the writings under discussion here are from a later time, when a Greek metropolitan was residing in Kiev and Greek bishops in other cities.

It seems probable that *both* religious movements in old Russia go back to Greek origins. That Byzantine religious literature was not exclusively ascetic was pointed out when it was noted above that the patericon of Palladius served as a model for the story of St. Isaakii. Moreover, it was in the tenth century that Simeon the New Theologian (949-1022), an influential churchman and preacher who publicly advocated a purely anti-ascetic lay piety, was active in Byzantium. In his writings Simeon placed perhaps even more emphasis on the possibility of achieving spiritual salvation within the world than the East Slavs did in their works. Slavic translations of Simeon's works are extant in copies made in the fifteenth century, but it is quite possible that the original translations were made much earlier. Not nearly enough research has been done on old Russian translations to permit us to draw any definite conclusions about the ideological influences of this literature. Even the most thorough descriptions of manuscripts often designate works only by title or by the first words of the text. Furthermore, between the eleventh and the thirteenth centuries, an era when numerous and in part excellent translations from the Greek were being made in Kiev and elsewhere, there were certainly no small number of East Slavs who knew Greek and were able to read Simeon's works in the original. Among these, to mention only well-known East Slav authors, were Bishop Kirill of Turov and Vladimir Monomakh, who was the son of a Byzantine princess. Finally, it should not be forgotten that there were East Slavs who served as secretaries to the Greek hierarchs.

In short, the sources of ascetic and "anti-ascetic" trends in the religious life of old Russia are not known, and it is quite possible that the one or the other of the views presented in religious literature is even indigenous.

CHAPTER III. THE TATAR INVASION AND THE INTELLECTUAL AND SPIRITUAL CRISIS OF THE FOURTEENTH AND FIFTEENTH CENTURIES

The Tatar Invasion

In the year 1223 the Tatars appeared on the political horizon of Eastern Europe when they swept down from the Caucasus and overran and subjugated the Cumans (Polovtsy). This time the Russian princes heeded the plea for help which the Cumans directed to them, but the united Russian armies were soundly defeated at the Kalka River, not far from the Sea of Azov, and several Russian princes fell in the battle or were taken into captivity and never repatriated. The Tatars, however, did not exploit their victory, but withdrew instead to the steppes of Asia. They did not appear again until 1237, this time under the leadership of Batu (or Batyi, as he is called in Russian), the grandson of Ghengis Khan. They came from the northeast, and after subjugating the Volga Bulgars they directed their attacks against the principalities of Riazan and Vladimir-Suzdal. Many cities were destroyed and those inhabitants who attempted to resist were slaughtered. The Tatar hordes did not penetrate to the northwest as far as Novgorod or to the west as far as Smolensk, either at this time or later. The following year the Tatars continued their march, conquering and destroying Chernigov and Kiev and pushing westward through the lands of Volynia and Galich. Now various parts of the land capitulated to the invaders without a struggle.

In spite of their victories in Hungary, Silesia, and Moravia, the Tatars did not continue to move westward. Perhaps they simply planned to halt for a while before pressing on. Whatever the reason, after the Great Khan died in central Asia in 1241 they set out for the East. Russian territories, however, remained under Tatar dominion.

For our purposes only a few of the political events of the thirteenth, fourteenth, and fifteenth centuries are of interest. The Mongol Empire,[7] the "Golden Horde," whose shock troops Batu commanded, did not survive its greatest victories. In the west in particular it began to weaken and then to disintegrate as a political entity. One part of this empire, which had its capital on the Volga, achieved first relative and then complete independence. As a result of internal dissension and quarreling, by the sixteenth century there were several Tatar Khanates—Kazan, Crimea, Astrakhan. The Russian appanage princes soon reestablished themselves as rulers, but they did have to be confirmed in office by the Khan. At first they were required to appear in person to receive the document of confirmation, the *Yarlyg*, but later their presence in the capitol of the Golden Horde was no longer necessary. Of yet greater significance was the fact that at the beginning of the fourteenth century the right to collect and transmit taxes was delegated to the princes. The influence of the Tatar tax officials *(Baskak)* and especially of the Tatar supervisors *(Darugas)* steadily diminished. In assigning *Yarlygs* to the kingdoms, the Tatars at first took care that no one branch of a royal Russian family was strengthened as a result of receiving the *Yarlygs,* but from the fourteenth century on, the Muscovite princes, with few exceptions, were able to have the office of grand prince made hereditary in their families.

It is important that the religious policy of the Tatars was from the beginning one of tolerance and that the Church was relieved of all taxes and tributes.[8] With one lone exception there is no evidence of punishment imposed for religious reasons, and this exception, the murder of Prince Mikhail of Chernigov, can be explained as the result of his refusal to pay homage to the Khan. Of course, the churches and monasteries did suffer from occasional Tatar punitive expeditions against individual cities and lands, but such incidents were hardly more frequent and more violent than during the feuds among the princes.

In the early years *direct* cultural influence by the Tatars can scarcely be discerned. The Russians only later adopted for their state organization some of the features of Tatar government. This is evident in Tatar loan words, especially those concerning finance, such as *den'ga* (money), *altyn* (custom house), *tamozhnia* (tax office), and *kaznachei* (cashier)—and those concerning the postal service—*yamshchik,* the Tatar word for a post coachman (these words were in use in Russian until recent times). The cultural influence of the Tatars did not increase considerably until the Russians conquered the Tatar Khanates of Kazan and Astrakhan in the sixteenth century.

One should certainly not imagine that the Tatars were settled throughout the land or were roving about and in this way able to spread their culture (or lack of it) to all parts of the country. The Tatar finance officials and supervisors in the capitol cities of the principalities could not exert such influence, especially since Christianity placed a barrier between the Russian people and the Tatar world.

It is worth noting that the Golden Horde without any particular difficulties relinquished to Poland-Lithuania the western and southwestern territories of White Russia and the Ukraine. From that time on, the intellectual and spiritual development of these territories proceeded along independent lines, and neither became of significance for the Great Russians again until the seventeenth century.

It may be pointed out here that the severity of "the Tatar yoke" is a debatable point. The view that the land was completely devastated and even depopulated can no longer be defended today, but there is just as little reason to overestimate and evaluate positively the cultural influence of the Tatars, as various scholars (such as G. Vernadsky) have done. Opinions vary concerning the motives and the significance of the deeds of Alexander Nevskii

(d. 1263), the prince of Novgorod and then of Suzdal who was later canonized. On the one hand he defended his kingdom against attacks from the west by the Swedes and the Teutonic Order, and on the other he sought and found a *modus vivendi* with the Tatars. This policy can be regarded as an expression of Russian anti-Westernism, but it can just as well be explained as the result of a thoroughly realistic assessment of the powers in both the East and the West. Somewhat earlier Prince Daniil of Galich had turned to the West and had even received his crown from the hands of the pope, but he profited from this less than Alexander Nevskii did from his "Eastern" orientation. Alexander at least did assure his country a lasting peace, but that Alexander was attuned to the Tatar world spiritually and intellectually is simply out of the question. In any event, there developed under Tatar rule several new intellectual movements in which no traces of Tatar influence can be detected.

The Intellectual Situation

Whereas the political structure of the East Slavic world began to consolidate soon after the violent upheavals of the thirteenth century, the Tatar invasion did bring on a severe intellectual crisis. The East Slavic intellectual organism was seized by a debilitating illness which required a doctor's attention. The Tartar invasion had severely shaken the optimistic intellectual attitude which can be observed in the eleventh century and the faith in a better future which was still present in the twelfth. A Christian land had been conquered by a pagan people and was obliged to find some way to get along under their rule. The new masters were unable to exert any intellectual influence on the East Slavs—indeed, they made no attempt to do so; one of the virtues of the Tatars, as has been mentioned, was religious tolerance. But Tatar rule severed the spiritual and intellectual ties which bound the East Slavs to Byzantium and, though to no great degree, to the West. The political and economic decline of the twelfth century reached its logical conclusion. The feuds between petty princes which devastated the land were merely the symptoms, not the cause of this decline. The flourishing literature of the late twelfth and early thirteenth centuries was only a twilight, and the fact that night now fell was the consequence of internal causes, not solely of Tatar rule. The devastation during the Tatar invasion should not be overestimated. The Tatars never set foot in large areas of Russia and in some wealthy cities, such as Novgorod and Smolensk. Even though there was no hope that the lands which were spared during the Tatar invasion could carry on independent and vigorous policies, the situation of the Russian princes was by no means hopeless. They soon found a *modus vivendi* with the Tatar Khan.[9] It is significant that Prince Mikhail of Chernigov, who had fled to Hungary when the Tatars invaded, returned home within a few years. Alexander Nevskii's policy, discussed above, is equally revealing. Temporal rule remained in the hands of the old royal dynasty, but spiritual and intellectual vigor seemed to have departed the land.

Although the Church had suffered far less than the "world," the shock to the spiritual and intellectual life of churchmen seems to have been quite severe. This can hardly be explained by external conditions. The impoverished princes, of course, could no longer serve as patrons, as some of them had done in the past. The feuds among the princes, which were often conducted with the aid of the Tatars, did not stop, of course, but they were not as devastating to the country as before. And despite this, in cultural life a process of decline continued which in intensity exceeded by far the decline in the economy.

The main reason for the spiritual and intellectual decline was perhaps the conviction, apparent as early as the twelfth century, that "the world was wicked" and that the only way to remain religiously and morally pure was to flee from the world. The Russian of the time witnessed not only the victory of the pagans over the Christian Russian people; he also saw beleaguered Byzantium become less and less able to repel the attacks of the Turks and finally, in 1453, fall into their hands. Even before this occurred, the Russians had doubted the "orthodoxy" of the Byzantines, who, after all, had entered into a union with the Church of Rome.

But political and ecclesiastical events were only secondary causes of the crisis. The real cause lay deeper: the failure of the East Slavs, before the catastrophe of the thirteenth and the following centuries, to develop a spiritual and intellectual culture which could stand on its own feet. G. Florovsky, a penetrating investigator of Russian intellectual history, has termed this era in which there was a lack of independent cultural creativity "centuries of silence" which he is unable to explain and terms a "riddle." Even Soviet Russian scholars, who have at their disposal the magic wand of dialectical materialism, an instrument which allegedly solves all riddles, are unable to give any convincing explanation. Whatever the reason, the East Slavs, with no spiritual and intellectual weapons of their own, had to find a way out of the crisis, and this is what determined the course which events took. They made no attempt to overcome through their *own* strength their spiritual ills; instead they searched for a physician from *outside* their own cultural sphere. The search lasted for two centuries, from 1300 to 1500, and only then did the idea of "Holy Russia" originate, an idea which did *not* exist before the end of the fifteenth century.

This image of "Holy Russia" was not an ideal; rather it corresponded to the Russian present as it then was. "Holy Russia" was thus not an image which pointed to the future and called for and gave direction to creative activity; it was a reassuring fairy tale which induced spiritual stagnation, a sort of pillow on which the mind could drop off to sleep. The inexorable dynamics of history saw to it, however, that the Russian mind did not go to sleep completely. In the sixteenth century Russians believed that their country was above and beyond history or that "Holy Russia" represented the end of history. This idea, which has never since completely disappeared from Russian spiritual life, is the reason for many aberrations in Russian intellectual history and possibly dominates thought in present-day Russia more strongly than ever before.

The Turn to the East. The "Judaizers"

The writings of a "heretical" movement which played an important role in the fifteenth century and is still on the whole not clearly understood are typical of the efforts at that time to find help outside of Russia. These heretics were the "converts to Judaism" or "Judaizers" *(zhidovstvuiushchie)*, a name given them by their enemies, obviously not until after the movement had been suppressed. This "heresy" appears to have first begun to spread in the Ukraine and in White Russia. Both countries at that time belonged to Poland-Lithuania and did not participate in the intellectual life of Russia proper—Great Russia.

The movement then sprang up in Novgorod and Moscow, and, remarkably, there were among its adherents courtiers, diplomats, and even a large number of churchmen. Enemies of the movement spread rumors to the effect that the "heretics" had converted to the Mosaic faith, but the fact that some of the clergy participated in the movement is the best proof that these allegations are false. At that time it would hardly have been possible to practice in secret the ritual prescribed by the Jewish faith.

The doctrines of the Judaizers are known from the polemics directed against them. In these they are accused of holding views that could be termed "Protestant": they neglected, or ignored, external ritual forms; they put "inner prayer" above the liturgy; they rejected the worship of icons and saints and allegedly even doubted the divinity of Christ. Taken together, these accusations form a picture which strongly resembles radical Hussitism, the fifteenth-century Czech precursor of Protestantism. When one considers that the heresy was introduced to Novgorod by a Kievan prince and that in Moscow one of the most zealous adherents to the doctrine was F. Kuritsyn, a diplomat who had formerly served in Hungary, it seems quite probable that there was a connection between the Judaizers and the Hussites. At the time Kiev was a part of Poland-Lithuania, where for a time the Hussites threatened orthodox Catholicism; many adherents of radical Hussitism fled from Bohemia to Hungary; and Novgorod maintained close ties with the West, including the Slavic West—in fact, some of the Novgorod saints appear to have been Slavs from the West.

Several works have survived from these heretical circles, all of them translations of Arabic scientific works, translations made from the Hebrew.

This may well explain the origin of the pejorative name given to the heretics. These works were: the so-called *Secreta Secretorum,* a pseudo-Aristotelian treatise on character and physiognomy which was supplemented by excerpts from Galen's writings on medicine and by other additions; the logic of Moses Maimonides; two works of the Arab philosopher Algazali; and astronomical tables of lunar movements. In the West some of these works—the *Secreta Secretorum,* for instance—were already known earlier in Latin versions, and some, such as the works of Maimonides and Algazali, appeared in print, also in Latin, after the invention of the printing press. The religious works of the Judaizers, if indeed there were any such original works at all, have not survived. It is known that the Judaizers were primarily interested in those books of the Old Testament which at that time were not yet available in Slavic translation,[10] and interest in the Old Testament is likewise characteristic of the pre-Reformation Protestantism of the Hussites. A new translation of the psalms which was made at that time from the Hebrew has been preserved, and like the Hebrew psalm-prayer book, it is divided into *"parasha's."* This translation, however, is not necessarily the work of the Judaizers; G. Florovsky believes it possible that it was intended for the use of Jews who no longer knew any Hebrew. In any case, the interest of the heretics was focused on religious and profane-scientific literature. They sought to find new intellectual and spiritual sources which might supplement or even replace the old Byzantine ones.

Translations of the Orthodox

The translating activity of the Judaizers had strange after-effects. While the heresy itself, as will be seen, was extirpated by fire and the sword, members of the victorious Orthodoxy discovered to their chagrin that the heretics had in Slavic translation books not available to the Orthodox Church. After a fruitless search in monastery libraries for the missing books, the churchmen had to do the translations themselves, and the result was the first complete Slavic Bible, the Gennadii Bible, so called after the archbishop of Novgorod who organized the new translation. Typically, however, the Orthodox Church turned not to Byzantium but to the West for the texts on which the translations were based, and the Orthodox translators worked partly with Latin texts and consulted German translations. Whereas the "heretics" presumably in all seriousness wanted to be able to read the Bible in its entirety, the Orthodox churchmen were more interested that the new Bible be complete than that it be intelligible to the reader.

This same tendency is even more evident in the "scientific" translations which Orthodox churchmen made at the time. The heretics' example possibly also provided the stimulus for these translations, but the churchmen selected works which were already outmoded. They elected to translate the *Lucidarius* (a primitive medieval encylopedia of natural science), the *Donation of Constantine,* and other similar works. They left untranslated words which they did not understand. For example, in the middle of a translation into Church Slavic the German word "Schlange" (snake) is rendered as "slangi," a word which does not exist in Slavic. This helpless turning to the West for aid is characteristic. It is significant that even the methods for persecuting heretics were influenced by the inquisition in the West: specific reference was made to the example of "the pious kings of Spain."

Byzantine Mysticism

Byzantium did provide one stimulus to Russian spiritual life: *Hesychasm.* This movement, which flourished in the thirteenth century, taught a specific "technique" for inducing mystical visions: one remained standing, motionless, head bowed, holding one's breath, and prayed. In the West and even in Byzantium this practice of "contemplating one's navel," of forcing mystical experiences by "soul techniques," met in part with serious objections, in part with ridicule. The Hesychasts, who desired to achieve inner peace (Greek *hesychia*) in this way, also developed theological and speculative doctrines on which their *praxis pietatis* was based. It is not clear whether these doctrines (and for that matter the instructions for mystical contemplation) were widespread and had any great influence in Russia, although translations of several Hesychastic works did exist. But no matter how insignificant the spread of early Hesychasm in Russia may have been, it did influence, though not until the fifteenth century, the spiritual movement which is one of the most significant and original phenomena in the intellectual history of Russia: eremitism.

Eremitism

Eremitism—the "hermit movement"—was a mass movement in Russia in the fourteenth and fifteenth centuries. It was peculiarly in keeping with the character of the times, for it too was based on foreign models, this time very ancient ones, and at first it had all the symptoms of a "spiritual epidemic."

Neglect of this movement is one of the major shortcomings of scholarship in the field of Russian intellectual history, and it is particularly regrettable that the literature of the movement, mainly short saints' lives, has still been edited only in part. Most of these lives, known from excerpts or descriptions of their content, have been published in conjunction with work which has little or nothing to do with intellectual history—in treatments of Russian colonization, for instance.

To struggle against a world engulfed in wickedness makes sense only if the world in question is powerful and self-confident, and for many a thinking man of the time the fall of this world, the fact that pagans had been able to vanquish it, was ample proof that it was not strong and self-confident. There was no need to struggle against this world. If a man wished to save his soul, the best thing he could do was to turn his back on this impotent world to which God had already meted out His punishment. A movement arose which is reminiscent of the earliest days of monasticism in Egypt and Sinai, although, of course, this new movement had special problems which were unknown to the ascetics of old.

Asceticism was now no longer conceived to be merely castigation of the flesh; instead, its object was to purify the soul. This change of direction represents a break with the venerable tradition of the last decades of the Kievan Cave Monastery. Eremitism, of course, had its leaders, and at first they probably influenced others only through oral instruction and their own good example. Their ideology did not crystallize in literary form until later, and not until the end of the age did some written works appear which provided, after the fact, a justification and a sharp profile of the entire movement. Eremitism began in the fourteenth century under the sign of the old Christian paterica and the old Christian saints' lives (indigenous Russian literature of the eleventh, twelfth and thirteenth centuries could scarcely give the new hermits any guidance).

The hermits of this time were not satisfed to live in a monastery. There are many stories of people who left inhabited areas and withdrew into the depths of the forests where "no man could find them"—even if that were only a few miles from a city. Even more often they fled into the extensive forested area north of the upper course of the Volga. Pushing on northward from there, they reached the White Sea before the beginning of the sixteenth century. We must keep in mind that in these impenetrable forests things far worse than complete solitude awaited the hermit. He had to spend several months a year in ice and snow, and his life was threatened by wolves and bears, by half-civilized Finnish hunters, and by people who had fled to the North for quite different reaons. To be sure, the northern Finnish tribes were more peaceful and less dangerous than the Russians. Legends tell of the peaceful Finns, perhaps the Syrianes, who did not attack a missionary even when he set fire to their pagan temple because, "after all, he didn't start a fight; if he'd started a fight we would have torn him limb from limb." By contrast, the legends repeatedly mention Russian robbers and even Russian serfs who had fled to the North to escape the heavy burdens placed on them and who tried to rid themselves of a hermit, to them an unpleasant neighbor, either by setting fire to his hermitage or by murdering him. There were certainly many men who were driven into the wilderness by the spirit of the times but who "were not able to bear the hardships of that life" and returned to the world to become "normal" churchmen and even to achieve high positions in religious and secular society. But how many perished in the wilderness as a result of these "hardships?" One could freeze to death too, or die of an illness. Some were discovered in the wilderness years, even decades later. There is one report of a hermit named Pavel of Obnora whom a younger hermit found in the depths of a forest feeding wild animals, with birds perched on his head and shoulders. During a campaign in the north a prince found two hermits in a completely uninhabited region on an island in a small lake.

In L. Tolstoy's story, "The Three Old Men," a bishop finds three very old hermits on a lonely island in the White Sea. This motif clearly comes from oral or written stories handed down about the hermit movement. Tolstoy goes on to tell that the hermits "did not know how to pray," (that is, they did not know any of the traditional prayers) but were nevertheless more pleasing to God than well-educated monks; this detail corresponds to the hermits' views on "inner prayer." Admittedly the uneducated but pious person who is pleasing to God is a universal motif, one also known in the West.

Descriptions of the Wilderness

Accounts of saints' lives occasionally also describe life in the wilderness, usually, it should be noted, in only a few words. These descriptions are a far cry from the beautiful nature descriptions found occasionally in older literature and composed in accordance with a tradition which is termed in classical poetics the *locus amoenus,* "the charming spot." The saints' lives of this time seem intent instead on sketching a picture of what could be called a *locus horridus.*

One such *locus horridus* was the wilderness where St. Sergii of Radonezh lived with his brother Stefan at the end of the fourteenth century. Stefan could not endure this life, for it was "a life full of sorrow, a life full of hardships, everywhere limitations, everywhere need, without food, without drink, without any of the necessities of life; no one came and brought anything, for at this time there were in the vicinity of this wilderness neither villages nor farms nor people who live in them; no path led to this place from any direction; no one came past and came to see this spot; instead on all sides in this area there was nothing but forests, nothing but wilderness. He [Stefan] saw this and was filled with sorrow. . . ."

We find much the same description of the wilderness where a century later St. Nil Sorskii, one of the last representatives of the hermit movement and the formulator of its ideology, wrote his works: "In this wilderness there were all sorts of trees: fir trees, aspen trees, and in some places birches and pines, and much moss in the forest; there were also berries there, swamp berries and red bilberries and blackberries and whortleberries; no other fruits

71

and trees could be found in this wilderness. There was not the slightest
thing in this wilderness which could have tempted man into the desires,
struggles, and toils of this world; and because in this wilderness there were
neither cattle nor asses, neither servants nor masters nor domestics nor anyone else who was a part of human society, our blessed father Nil chose this
place. . . and blessed his likeminded disciples to live there." A description of
this region written in the nineteenth century reads as follows: "The place
where Nil established his hermitage is wild, desolate, and forbidding. The
ground is level and swampy; round about there is a forest consisting mostly
of conifers. . . . It would be difficult to find a place more solitary than this
wilderness."

St. Sergii and the Bear

Many dangers threatened the lonely hermit in the depths of the northern Russian forests. Besides the devil and human beings (who were sometimes
as wicked as the devil), there was nature, particularly the wild animals and the
winter cold. Sometimes, however, the wild animals proved to be friendly
neighbors. Just as St. Gerasion made a friend and servant of a lion in the
wilderness along the River Jordan, St. Sergii of Radonezh, according to
legend, lived together peacefully with a bear. This passage in the saint's life is
also a good example of the descriptive art and the style of Epifanii the Wise,
the most important Russian hagiographer of the late fourteenth and early
fifteenth century. The modern reader may find his long-windedness, his repe-
titions, and his partiality to detailed descriptions tiring, but they are surely
in accord with the taste of his time and succeed in presenting vivid pictures
which exude gentle humor. Moreover, such unforgettable passages occur
frequently in Epifanii's writings.

"Sometimes it was the devil's wiles and terrors, but sometimes also
attacks by animals; it is said that there were many of them in the wilderness.
Some went past in herds, howling and roaring, but others went by in small
groups of two or three or even singly, some far off, some close by, some approached the blessed man, surrounded him, and even sniffed him. There was
among them one animal, . . . a bear, which got in the habit of going to him,
but he saw that the animal came to him not with evil intent but to receive
food and nourishment, and he brought it a small slice of bread from his hut
and put the piece of bread on a tree stump or on the trunk of a fallen tree so
that the animal would find its meal prepared for it, as it were. It took the
bread in its mouth and went away. When the bread was not there one time,
however, and the animal, which came as it was accustomed to, did not find
its usual slice of bread, then it did not depart for a long time but instead
stood there, looking here and there, full of expectations, like a mean credi-
tor who wants to take possession of what is his. When there was only one

slice of bread available, Sergii had to divide it into two pieces so that he had once piece for himself and served the animal the other piece. For at that time Sergii did not have a variety of foods in the wilderness but only bread, and water from a spring that was there, and precious little of these; often, however, he did not even have his daily bread, and when that happened they both went hungry, he and the animal. Sometimes, the blessed man did not satisfy himself but went hungry; when he had only one piece of bread he threw it to the animal and decided to fast and not to eat anything that day rather than hurt the animal's feelings and let it go away without food. And the animal came not once, and not twice, but rather it came every day for a long time, longer than a year."

The Lives and Deeds of the Hermits

Often the life of a hermit passed according to a "cycle." The hermit, usually a young man, flees to the wilderness of the North, this "northern Thebais." Years later a second man joins him, and then a third. Soon a small hermitage develops, but the hermits do not wear monk's garb. The hermits can pray, but they have no priest. With great difficulty, sometimes after a long journey, one of them reaches a bishop who ordains him as a priest. Thus the hermitage becomes a monastery. Word of the existence of the monastery spreads and a small congregation, usually only ten or twelve monks, joins the original hermit. Frequently serfs come to settle in the region, and the monastery has to provide them with ministers, with advisors, and often with men to organize the secular life of the region. In this way the hermits return to the world, or rather the world intrudes on the solitude of the wilderness. But "organizing the secular life" of a village community of necessity meant establishing relations with the secular authorities from whose jurisdiction the peasant settlers had fled, and that is the reason why the serfs treated the hermits with such caution and often with such hostility. In this way the network of monasteries spread as far as the White Sea—the famous monastery on the island of Soloviki—and Petsamo on the Kola peninsula.

The best known example of lives following this cyclic pattern is found in the accounts of the lives of St. Kirill of Beloozero (White Sea) and St. Sergii of Radonezh. The life of Nil Sorskii (from Sorka), which will be treated below, followed a similar pattern. Excellent saints' lives, somewhat discursive and ornate, as the style of the time demanded, treat St. Kirill of Beloozero and St. Sergii of Radonezh, who bring the hermit movement to an impressive conclusion. Their works were usually depicted in the wrong light and have been completely misinterpreted by later generations and even by present-day scholars. The life of the missionary hermit St. Stefan of Perm might also be mentioned, but from the point of view of intellectual history the short saints' lives are much more interesting because they contain unmistakable traces of mystical Neoplatonism, which is characteristic of Hesychasm.

In these stories the life of the hermit is portrayed as an "intellectual-spiritual struggle." Even though the authors do not always find words to describe the inner life of their heroes, they do sketch "inner activity" as *the* way to progress spiritually, employing short formulae which reproduce the traditional view of the mystic life. The hermits are praised because "they were never free of inner activity." Inner activity is first and foremost "purification of the spirit," "purification of the heart" (Greek *katharsis*); and "purifying the heart of all passions" is emphasized. Pavel of Obnora, who according to legend spent his life with bears and birds of the forest, "worked tirelessly to purify his strength of spiritual vision." Strength of spiritual vision is precisely that spiritual quality which makes mystical visions possible. "Purification," however, is but the first stage of mystic ascent. Such expressions as "directing his spirit to the heights" are used to characterize this ascent. One legend contains the following instructions: "Direct your spirit to seek only God." It is reported that Pavel of Obnora "saw the magnificence of God; thereby he became the chosen vessel of the Holy Ghost." All these expressions occur again and again in mystic literature. "Pavel collected in his heart the light of the Holy Ghost." The idea of "divine light" (Greek *photismos*) as an object of mystical vision is also typical of Hesychasm. Even the long saints' lives, which for all their beauty pay relatively little attention to the inner life of their subjects, speak often of the saints' visions of light. Images and symbols of "divine light" and of mystical "illumination" are perhaps employed most frequently in the life of St. Gregory of Sinai, which was translated from the Greek in the fifteenth century.

Visions of Light

Visions of light are not "anthropomorphic"; they are not visions of angels, of saints, or even of the Virgin Mary (there are, occasionally, reports of such visions). Furthermore, these visions made no acoustical impression; the hermit heard no words spoken to him. What appeared to him as light was "the magnificence of God" (Greek *doxa*). According to the Hesychastic view, divine light was a substance, a phenomenal form of divine existence which was still perceptible to man.

St. Kirill of Beloozero left Moscow after he saw one night a light in the North which he took to be a sign to travel to the north (to be sure, the Virgin Mary had already commanded him to go to Beloozero). Ferapont of Menzen (d. 1591) also considered a vision of light to be a command to leave his monastery. The life of Ferapont says: "Once he came out of his cell, looked to the East, and saw on the eastern side a thin column of light rising up to heaven. The old man stopped and bowed his head. Then he

74

looked up again and to the left of that thin column he saw another column, a large and brightly shining one. . . . He was filled with wonderment. . . and decided to wander to the East."

The most vivid description of a vision of light is found in the life of St. Sergii of Radonezh. Simon, a disciple of St. Sergii, saw the "divine light" (the exact words used) during a mass at Sergii's monastery: "When the saint was celebrating mass Simon saw a light move across the top of the altar and hover over it and surround the Holy Eucharist. And when the saint was about to celebrate communion the divine light rolled together like a veil and went into the consecrated chalice, and this is how St. Sergii celebrated communion. When Simon saw this he was filled with fear and trembling and wonderment. When the saint left the altar he knew that Simon had been vouchsafed a wondrous vision, and the saint said unto him: 'My child, wherefore do you take fright?' And Simon replied: 'Lord, I saw a wondrous sight, the grace of the Holy Ghost working together with you.' The saint forbade Simon to make report of this, saying: 'Tell no one what you have seen until the Lord commands me to depart this life.' And together they sang the praises of the Lord."

Nil Sorskii and his Doctrine of the Inner Life

The canonized hermit who expressed in his works the ideology of the hermit movement was Nil Sorskii. His real name was Nikolai Maikov. Born in 1433, he was as a young man a court clerk for a short time. He referred to himself occasionally as a farmer *(poselianin),* but this was probably no more than a sort of customary self-deprecation, for at that time a peasant could hardly have become a public official (after all, Horace too called himself *rusticus*). At a rather early age Nil had himself invested as a monk in the monastery of Kirill of Beloozero, but he did not stay there long before going to sacred Mount Athos where he had the opportunity to become familiar with the teachings and practices of the Hesychasts. When he returned a few years later—his biography unfortunately includes no chronology—he settled near Kirill's monastery in a forest on the Sorka River (*not* on the Sora, another river, which is frequently cited erroneously as the location of Nil's hermitage). He soon became so well known as the ideologist of the hermit movement that he had to answer numerous letters and was often consulted on various occasions by the higher clergy.

Nil participated in various synods, but he first appears as a leading personality in reports of the Synod of 1503, where he "began to speak," apparently on a subject unrelated to the business of the council, stating that the monasteries ought not to own any lands or serfs and that "monks ought to live in hermitages and support themselves by the labor of their own hands." These proposals were very nearly adopted as resolutions, but Josif

Volotskii, who was the most influential spokesman for the opposite view and who had already left the Synod, was brought back and was able to prevail on the council to support his point of view.

This brief note is the only contemporary report of Nil. It is significant that there is no saint's life devoted to him and that he came to be generally venerated as a saint without ever being canonized. His sixteenth-century followers, however, have passed on some reports about him, and his works, available in numerous copies, tell more about the ideology of the hermit movement than does any other literary source. Nil's works are the *Predanie* (which could be translated "Instruction"), several epistles, an extensive set of monastic rules, a prayer, and some translations, the exact number of which has not been determined. In addition, he revised several older saints' lives, but unfortunately these have not yet been identified from among the numerous extant manuscripts of saints' lives. The works of Nil, as far as is known at present, are the first relatively independent Russian theological writings, and they played a role of considerable importance in the history of Russian religiosity during the sixteenth and seventeenth centuries, even though they have by no means enjoyed universal recognition, especially among Church authories.

The main concern of Nil's writing is the "spiritual perfection" of a man who has already chosen the "narrow path" of asceticism or is about to set forth on it; that is, his works were meant primarily for monks. Nil certainly did not believe, of course, that an ascetic absolutely had to live as a monk in a monastery. In fact, living in the wilderness was to his mind more conducive to the spiritual struggle, to inner activity. In Nil's philsophy traditions of the hermit movement and of sacred Mount Athos are combined. He moderated the demands of the hermit movement to the extent that he considers a hermitage a place where ascetics live in groups of two or three, supporting each other in their spiritual activity and providing for themselves by the labor of their own hands. It was not absolutely necessary that an ascetic engage in physical labor; he needed no riches "to be able to give alms," a remark directed against the wealthy and benevolent monasteries of the time. Nil believed that the assistance an ascetic could give his fellow man was his "word," that is, counsel, instruction, consolation, and spiritual guidance.

Nil's statements concerning "inner activity" are perhaps not very original; he himself always preferred to support his basic theses by citing either the Hesychasts or older thinkers, perhaps with the intention of demonstrating that what he was saying was nothing new. And yet his demands met with opposition and provoked attacks. Man, Nil asserted, must be guided in his spiritual struggle by the Holy Scriptures. Unlike other Russians of his time, he did not consider all instructive and religious works equally authoritative. For him Holy Scriptures, in the narrowest sense of the word, occupied a primary and unique position. He believed that one ought to learn to understand them and that man has been endowed with reason *(razum)* so that he may have the means to make judgments. Moreover, he thought, Holy Scriptures certainly do not provide answers to all questions concerning spiritual struggle; one ought to entrust oneself to the guidance of an experienced ascetic, but Nil doubts that it will be easy to find one. He warns expressly against believing and acting in accordance with everything found in religious literature. Some have viewed these ideas as "rationalism," but nothing could be further from the truth. They represent merely a sound critical assessment of the enormously varied religious literature extant in Russia at the time, including numerous apocryphal works, even some explicitly rejected by the Church. Moreover, Nil's "critical attitude" could hardly go much beyond views he was able to find in Byzantine religious works, among them those of the Hesychasts. Nil was later accused of having "spoiled" the saints' lives which he revised, primarily, it turns out, because he omitted from them stories of miracles. Even in this he was justified, for the Church itself rejected legends which contained improbable and offensive reports of miracles. Nil may have been attempting to restore the saints' lives to their original form, which could frequently be done by omitting anachronistic details.

The advice which Nil gave his readers was not based solely on the Bible. He relied on patristic and Hesychastic literature and on works which the Greek ascetics had already accepted as authoritative. He first appropriated psychological insights which could serve as a basis for his own counsel. Most people, including ascetics, are governed by their "passionate will," and the passions do not seize and overwhelm man all at once but rather conquer his soul step by step. Nil differentiates five stages in the development of a passion (John Climakos, whom Nil looked upon as an authority, mentions six). The five stages are: 1) the *image* of the object, 2) *retention*, i.e., keeping this image in mind; 3) *union*, i.e., constant and more intrinsic connection of this image with one's whole spiritual life; 4) *captivation* of the will by the image of the object, i.e., the inability to rid oneself of the thought of the desired object; and only then does there follow what we call 5) *passion*, i.e., constant attraction to the image of the object. The problem was to find ways and means of counteracting each of these stages in the growth of passion, and Nil describes in detail these ways and means.

Nil analyzes the passions in a similar way according to the nature of the desired object. There are, he states, eight vices which arise as a result of passion: *gluttony, fornication, covetousness, wrath, sadness, pusillanimity (accidie), arrogance* (vain glory), and *pride*. He also recommends ways to combat these vices. Characteristically Nil considers the last two vices mentioned, arrogance and pride, to be the most dangerous and deduces from them psychic effects which would be characterized today as a "Caesar complex."

It is worth noting that Nil does not simply cite God's commandments. Man should fight against passions and vices because they divert him from his duty, which is to become spiritually perfect, and in this way they hinder him in his spiritual struggle. When Nil then gives special emphasis to two ways to combat vice which seem to be within the ascetic tradition, prayer and fasting, his concrete advice does exude a new spirit. By prayer Nil means essentially "spiritual prayer" *(umnaia molitva)* or "inner prayer." He does not mean the mere recitation of a prescribed number of prayers. One's inner mood, not the enunciation (or singing) of some required words, is the essence of prayer. In fact, "external praying" or singing can distract man from his "inner activity." "He who prays with his mouth and neglects his spirit is praying to empty air." Moreover, prayers should be addressed only to God, not to either angels or men (a reference to prayers addressed to saints).

Nil has the same "spiritual" conception of fasting and of other ascetic practices. Here too all things "corporeal" are merely a means to achieve spiritual perfection: "an act of the body is only foliage—but an act of the spirit is fruit." For this reason Nil developed views on fasting which were contrary to those on which the monastic rules of the time were based. All one had to do, Nil believed, was to avoid gluttony and gormandizing; otherwise one could eat "whatever one needed to." Furthermore, he said, there were no forbidden foods. Anyone who rejected good-tasting foods "was scorning the good which God had created." Fasting, like "external prayer," could be dangerous if one deemed fasting a virtue. In this way one could fall prey to the devil, who plants in the faster's soul seeds of self-satisfaction which grow into the "the inner pharisee," as one of Nil's followers expresses it. In fasting it is necessary to consider the physical constitution of the individual, for "wax must be treated differently from copper and iron." Instead of strict asceticism Nil recommends ascetic exercises consonant with the capabilities of the individual, but along with them manual labor, conversations with one's brothers (about spiritual questions, of course), reading, contemplation of death, and, most important of all, spiritual prayer. Although Nil also described the ideal daily schedule of a hermit, he granted every hermit a measure of freedom in his actions: a monk is not forbidden to engage in any sinless pastimes, and he may pursue them "as the occasion demands." Nil concludes his rules for monastic life with the following statement: "But if anyone know something better and more useful about his matter let him act accordingly, and I shall be happy. . . ."

On the whole, Nil's thought has about it the spirit of freedom, but he harbors the unshakeable conviction that one means of carrying on the spiritual struggle—genuinely inner, spiritual prayer— is the highest stage of human perfection. This is an area where Nil follows closely the practice of the Hesychasts. According to Nil, the Hesychastic praying technique, which has been described above, leads to a state of ecstasy *(izstuplenie)* in which man "considers everything mortal to be dust and ashes and rubbish" and sees "the light which the world does not possess." When Nil writes

"Within me I see the Creator of the world" he is paraphrasing the words of Isaac the Syrian: "To become as united with God as the powers of the inner man permit." Thus Nil attains the ultimate level of mysticism, "union" (Greek *henosis*), at which other writings from eremitical circles only dare to hint.

Nil's theological and mystical philosophy, as already noted, is not original. It can be found in the works of such Byzantine writers as John Climakos (sixth century), Maximus the Confessor (sixth century), Isaac the Syrian (seventh century), Gregory the Sinaiite (fourteenth century), and others. Nil, however, was not a compiler but a writer capable of reproducing the thoughts of others in his own words and in his own style.

Ecclesiastical Questions

Bold as this breakthrough of "anti-traditionalism" was in Russia at that time, the views of Nil were meant *only for monks and ascetics.* As will be seen, they did have a lasting effect, far beyond the boundaries of the Church, in fact. Nil himself, however, spoke only occasionally about "improving things in the secular realm," and for the most part his thoughts have been handed down only indirectly. In the sixteenth century his name became a catchword, first of all for those who shared his view that "monks ought to engage in honest toil with their own hands to earn their daily bread and everything else they require," as Nil had put it at the Synod of 1503. For this reason Nil and his followers were against the practice of the monasteries, which was to own villages and the peasants who lived in them. Such worldly possessions, they thought, were superfluous: "We should neither possess nor wish for nor acquire anything superfluous." In fact, they contended, owning villages and land was actually harmful to the monasteries, for all worldly possessions are ill-gotten, they are "the work of another taken by force," and when such ill-gotten gains are donated to a monastery, they are naturally "of no use" to the monks. Concern about worldy goods, that is about taking care of them, diverts monks from their real task, and possession of them involves monasteries "in worldly affairs." The philanthropy of wealthy monasteries cannot make up for the harm done by owning worldly goods, especially since monks are supposed to help and serve the world in a different way, "through the word," that is, by instructing and counseling. We shall see later what ideological conflicts arose in the sixteenth century when this Christian thought was taken (or so it seems to us) to its logical extreme.

Another issue which concerned eccelsiastical and temporal authorities alike and on which Nil took a position was the condemnation and persecution of the "heretics," the "Judaizers." Nil was of the opinion that one should try to "exert a positive influence on them by word and deed," and if they could be convinced to mend their ways they ought to be taken back into the Church. Of course, one ought to "be careful" not to have anything to do with "stubborn heretics." Unlike Nil and his followers, other Church circles took the position that one ought to follow the example of the Inquisition in the West and turn heretics over to the secular authorities, who would, of course, punish them severely (it was only after considerable hesitation that the secular authorities accepted the task of meting out punishment to heretics). Because Nil believed in the spiritual powers of man he wanted to convince the heretics that they were in error, and his "conciliatory" attitude toward heresy, as it seemed to some at the time, was later to expose his followers to severe trials. In an atmosphere of increasing absolutism and in a time when the belief was widespread that the state had ecclesiastical duties, the followers of Nil were accused of having given aid and comfort to convicted and fugitive heretics and of having sought to protect them from punishment. This amounted to an accusation of high treason. Nil did not live to see these troubled times. He died in 1508.

The Christianity of Josif Volotskii

Nil's audience was not made up solely of people who had no opinions of their own. In fact, monastic life produced one man who held the opposite opinion on most debatable points and who had the determination to combat the views of Nil and to gather about him numerous followers. This was Josif Volotskii, or Volokolamskii (1439-1515), so named after the region where his monastery was located. He was a nobleman of the Sanin family and in his youth entered the monastery of a "tried and true ascetic," Pafnutii Borovskii. After the death of Pafnutii in 1477 Josif became abbot of the monastery. In this capacity he took a trip through Russia in search of a monastery which corresponded to his ideas of the ideal monastic life. He did not find one. He therefore had no alternative but to found a monastery with new statutes, and this he did in Volok Lamskii (Volokolamsk). Many bequests were made to his newly established monastery, and it was outfitted rather opulently. Later many men from "the best families" entered this monastery. The wealth of the monastery was used to a great extent for philanthropic purposes—during a famine in the area, for example—and the rules of the monastery were rather strict. Every monk, of course, was permitted to choose that level of ascetic rigor which seemed best suited to him, but once he had made his choice, no alleviation and no reduction was possible.

Josif wrote numerous instructive circular letters to secular personalities, and, among other things, he attempted to convince the landed gentry to treat their serfs kindly and gently. He believed that philanthropic activity was equally useful to the souls of philanthropists and of those who reaped the benefits of philanthropy.

Josif wrote numerous works which have survived. Besides the circular letters already mentioned, he wrote a set of monastic rules and a collection of polemical treatises which was entitled *Prosvetitel' (The Enlightener)* and was directed against the Judaizers, but Josif's works can be more accurately described as compilations than can those of Nil. They frequently consist in their entirety of quotations from religious works which support, or even only apparently support, the views held by Josif. Josif's writings are a good example of why Nil was right in demanding that distinctions be made as to the degree of authority to be ascribed to religious didactic works. Josif not only cites as "divinely inspired writings" on a par with the Gospels such didactic works by Byzantine monks as the *Pandecta* (instructions for ascetics written by Nikon, an eleventh-century monk who has not even been canonized), he even wants to "place civil laws on a par with prophetic and apostolic writings and the works of the Holy fathers."

Moreover, Josif was not at all selective in his choice of quotations. He was an ecclesiastical politician who had definite views and wished to promulgate them, even if he found little support for them in religious literature. In his monastic rules his religious ideal is expressed with great clarity. His main consideration is not spiritual perfection but "decorum" *(blagochinie)*. Fear is the chief motivation to which Josif appeals; "fear of God," fear of death, fear of punishment. His monastic rules are not strict, they are casuistic; and they require that all regulations be obeyed to the letter. Punishments are not severe either, although Josif once mentions "iron fetters" for disobedient monks. He compares the monastery with a royal palace and God with an emperor who resides there. Josif himself, as he notes, had seen what decorum prevails in royal palaces. Even the spiritual advice which he gives is in the form of rules of decorum. It is easy to believe that Josif was thinking of the soul as well when he wrote such advice as "Press your hands together, put your heels together, close your eyes and concentrate your spirit," but sometimes he explicitly places external decorum above spiritual stance. His rules therefore became, as Feodotov has observed, a sort of "Muscovite *kallokagathia,*" as for example when he writes: "Put your feet down gently; let your voice be moderate and your words decorous; eat and drink quietly; . . . be sweet in giving answers and not excessive in conversation; when you speak your face should be bright so that those who speak with you will be of good cheer." In his rules for monastic life, in fact, the instructions are explicit: "First of all we should care for physical beauty and for decorum, but then also for inner prudence" *(khranenie)*. This last word is characteristic. Josif was primarily interested not in seeking good but in avoiding evil. For that reason he piled prohibition upon prohibition and gave little positive advice. His rules for monastic life are likewise in this tone, and most of his rules for monks and for people in secular life are rules governing external conduct. For example, Josif writes a secular correspondent the following concerning fasting: "Three days a week—Monday, Wednesday, and Friday—one should eat dry bread or dry white bread with water or kvas, but when this is impossible a cooked dish or two without lard; but when Monday, Wednesday, or Friday happen to be a festival of the Lord or of the Gospel or some other Church festival all foods may be eaten. And during the twelve days from Christmas until Epiphany (January 6) and a week after the Sunday of the Pharisees and during Butter Week and after Easter Sunday and in the week after Pentecost anything may be eaten, even on Monday, Wednesday, and Friday; it is also permissible to eat meat, and curds and to drink wine and, as is our custom, mead. . . . And if it is impossible to do as prescribed here on a fast day, then one should if possible give alms on this day. . . . For you it would suffice to give one *grivna* on such a day, and otherwise you should give as much alms as possible." This letter is not the only one of this sort. The following statement by Josif shows how much significance he placed on conformity to regulations: "Anyone, however, who does not fast on Wednesday and Friday is like the Jews who crucified Christ."

Josif regulated prayer and praying aloud in a similar way, determining exactly how many and which prayers one should say each day. All this shows that Josif was one of the founders of the ritualistic Christianity which astonished foreign visitors to Moscow during the sixteenth and seventeenth centuries, even those who were Greek Orthodox, and gave rise to the following question, which was even treated in doctoral examinations: "Whether or not the Muscovites are Christians?"

Ecclesiastic Policy and State Policy

Frequently Josif took a position on political and ecclesiastic problems, as for example in his *Prosvetitel'*. This work certainly contains much that is untrue about the Judaizers, but the basic questions it treats are of interest. Unlike Nil and his followers, Josif demanded that "heresy" be extirpated, i.e., that Judaizers be condemned to death. And he did not look for the way out which the Western European Inquisition had found, namely turning the heretics over to the secular authorities with the request that the heretics be judged "without bloodshed." Josif himself was prepared to kill those who had strayed from the Church, for "killing a sinner and heretic through prayer or with one's own hands is one and the same thing." He does not try, of course, to kill them "through prayer"; instead, to be on the safe side, he would have them executed "by the hands" of the hangman, probably in the interests of the salvation of the latter, for Josif thought that the destruction of heresy was a work commanded by God, and killing a heretic "hallowed one's hands." Josif even wanted to impose the same punishment on heretics who had repented of their sins because he did not believe it possible for them to improve and because he also thought it impossible to judge whether or not their repentance was genuine. The possibility that in the process innocent people might be executed by mistake did not seem so serious to Josif, because the innocent person thus afflicted could only profit from it since he "was right certain of his reward in heaven" because he qualified as "a just person who had innocently suffered." Stubborn heretics, Josif insisted, ought to be treated with "divinely wise cunning," and he believed that any means might be employed to find out their views. To gain their confidence one might pretend to be of their persuasion (Josif seems to have been an early proponent of later Russian police methods). The opinions which Josif held are connected with his high esteem of secular authority. If one is willing to defend Orthodoxy with force, one needs the aid of the *secular* authorities. They ought to be allies and defenders of the Church. It is along this line that Josif developed his political theory.

Josif believed that the power of the Christian ruler, and for him that meant the Muscovite grand prince, was unlimited, for "in essence the tsar is like all men, but in power he is like God," a statement Josif copied from the works of the Byzantine panegyrist Agapit (Agapetos). "You, Lord, have been placed by the right hand of God as sole ruler and master over all Russia, for God has chosen you (the princes) to be God in his stead here on earth and has raised you up and placed you on His throne." In theory the Church was above the state, but the temporal ruler was protector and defender of the faith and of the Church. For that reason, Josif thought that criminals, thieves, and robbers were "like the heretics," and since the cause of the decline of secular kingdoms had always been heresy, or so Josif believed, self-interest should dictate that the secular authorities be concerned with "the purity of the faith." For Josif, church and state became identified with each other to such a great extent that the tsar, the grand prince of Moscow, was also the ultimate authority in Church affairs, for "the court of the tsar is judged by no one," i.e., not by God either! To a certain extent the tsar possessed a mandate from God to regulate *absolutely* all things on earth, including the Church.

For Josif the sole criterion in Church matters was *utility*. Utilitarianism is a most dangerous force which destroys all moral and religious basic principles, and in Josif's doctrine it was all the more dangerous because he did not state clearly whether utilitarianism should apply to the Church or to the state and, more importantly, because he was unable to distinguish between eternal and "transitory" values. It may well be, as some scholars claim, that originally Josif had in mind primarily the eternal interests of the *Church*, but in his own ecclesiastical activity such interests were not much in evidence, and his followers went even further in their willingness to adapt to all demands of the secular politics of the time. For them, and also for Josif, the picture of the ideal Christian state merges completely with the forbidding picture which Muscovy presented at that time. Therefore, Josif

approved of every move which the Muscovite grand prince made to inter-
fere with Church life, and indeed Josif occasionally even provoked such actions himself. Bishops were deposed for political reasons, theological quarrels
were settled by decisions made by the secular authorities, and all these acts
seemed to Josif a part of the normal life of the Church.

Josif even introduced utilitarianism into the argument about whether a
monastery has a right to hold property. His own wealthy monastery was
able to distribute considerable alms and was therefore "useful" to the world,
and his followers pursued the same line of argumentation: "If the monasteries were not granted the right to have property, then why should any
respectable member of the nobility wish to become a monk?" And "if no
respectable *startsy* (members of the upper social classes are meant) were in
the Church, then where would candidates for metropolitan come from, or
for the office of archbishop or bishop or for other honorable posts?" And
that would be politically harmful from the point of view of the state: "If
there were no respectable *startsy,* then the faith would be shaken," which
would mean that the state would also be shaken. The authenticity of these
statements is scarcely open to doubt, even though Josif himself did not make
them. Various Soviet Russian scholars see in Josif's attitude toward the Muscovite state (that is, in the fact that he supported the idea of the omnipotence
of the state and thus Muscovite absolutism), his "positive historical contri-
bution" and call him a "progressive man" and a "progressive thinker." In
point of fact, Josif was anything but a thinker. It will be shown that the
very tradition which began with Josif turned out to be the cause of the
severest political upheavals experienced by the Muscovite state and, even
more important, the source of disastrous ideological confusion.

Josif, of course, cannot be held responsible for all the grievous wrongs
committed by his followers. He by no means viewed political power as op-
timistically as they did. For example, he spoke occasionally of the possibility that a ruler might "turn his back on the faith." Such a "refractory
tsar," Josif thought, would then be "not a tsar but a tyrant" (*muchitel'*,
a word used in translations to render the Greek *tyrannos*); he would be "not
a servant of God, but a devil," and people should refuse to obey such a
ruler. Naturally Josif had no way of knowing that in the not-too-distant
future a "devil" would ascend the throne of Muscovy. But because Josif
left open the question of who was responsible for determining that the ruler
had "turned his back on the faith"—given Josif's theory, the secular authorities would have had to decide this question—there was basically no solution
of a possible conflict between the Church and a "faithless" and "refractory"
tsar. Such, then, were the conflicts which confronted Russia in the sixteenth and particularly in the seventeenth centuries.

On the question of how to resist a "tyrant" Josif vacillated. Sometimes
he suggested that one "should not obey a tsar and prince who leads his people
astray and into faithlessness and vice *(lukavstvo),* even if he threatens death."

84

Sometimes his advice was more moderate: one should "make supplications" *(umoliat')* to the "refractory" ruler. Josif's followers, however, could not make up their minds to pursue the second, more moderate path either: their spiritual eyes were completely blinded by the bright light of magnificence in which Joseph's political doctrine had suffused the Muscovite sovereign.

Was Josif Volotskii a Reactionary?

It is very difficult to judge the spiritual and intellectual struggles of the fifteenth century. There can be little doubt that more than anything else the victory of Josif Volotskii's faction, which will be examined presently, led to catastrophe in the following centuries. It seems quite wrong, however, to call Josif a "reactionary" or a "conservative." A person who thinks he is a conservative can often be in reality a bold innovator, and Josif Volotskii was just such a person. He created the ideological foundation for the theory of the "service state" *(sluzhiloe gosudarstvo),* which down to this very day, under various names (including "Communism"), has remained the specifically Russian form of government and which grants to the individual hardly any personal freedom, even of the most restricted sort. Whenever the advantage of the state was mentioned, the principles of Christian philosophy were forgotten. From this point of view everyone, insofar as he laid claim to personal freedom, or was able to do so, could be or was harmful to the state. And so, to use the opposite of Hegel's formulation, Russian history became "progress in the spirit of non-freedom." With brief interruptions this development has continued down to our times.

All citizens have obligations but they do not have any rights, at least no rights that the state would have to guarantee. This basic tenet of Ivan the Terrible's conception of the state is implicit in Josif's philosophy. In the name of the Church Josif extended a helping hand to the absolutistic service-state which was then beginning to emerge.

An essential characteristic of Josif's philosophy is his complete disregard for cultural creativity. *Objectively* an *innovator,* he was *subjectively* a *traditionalist,* for he believed that all cultural values already existed in Russia and needed only to be preserved. This conviction is the standpoint, pushed to its extreme, which some, though not a great many, adopted in the West during the Middle Ages: "Our only task is to preserve and pass on to posterity what is old, tried and true; every new thought is either superfluous or wrong." Strangely enough, this attitude recurs in somewhat altered form in nineteenth-century Russia. Josif Volotskii believed that the task of culture (although he did not use this word) was to preserve old values; in his ideal world there was no place for any new values whatsoever. But he had no criterion by which he could distinguish old values which were genuine from those which merely seemed to be genuine, or tell those which were

85

worthwhile from those which were worthless. He considered all written works equally authoritative, and because he lacked critical acuity he thought his innovations were "old." His followers revealed a true understanding of his views when in the sixteenth century they considered the collection of old works (by Metropolitan Makarii) their most important task, a fact which one nineteenth-century scholar, I. Krushchev, has correctly pointed out. Little effort was made even to propagate supposedly old ideas, either by popularizing them or by preaching them and the like.

In misinterpreting the old values and ideas—and simply repeating them in a new context really amounts to misinterpreting them—Josif Volotskii founded a new tradition, an essentially new ideology. In the course of the sixteenth century the negative aspects of Josif's ideology were intensified by his followers, and that is how it came about that after a hundred years even Greeks travelling in Russia were confronted with a variant of Christianity, the nature and origin of which they could not comprehend.

Under the surface of this Christianity, frozen in ritual, there slumbered of course a spiritual and intellectual life of quite a different sort, and Nil and his followers are largely to thank for the fact that it was kept alive. With the end of the fifteenth century, in any case, a new chapter in Russian intellectual history began. The crisis of the fourteenth and fifteenth centuries led to a chronic disease which infected the entire spiritual and intellectual organism of Russia. For a long time no cure for the disease could be found.

The Consequences of the Spiritual and Intellectual Struggles

One question still remains to be answered: Could one have expected—as some historians, particularly historians of the Church, seem to believe—that "Russia would have been spared" the crises and catastrophes of the following centuries if the views of Nil Sorskii had prevailed? This question, like all others which concern "what might have been," cannot be answered with certainty, but one could argue against an all-too-optimistic assessment of the historical potential of Nil's philosophy.

Nil's ideology was that of an *ascetic* who was prepared to improve "the world" with his counsel, but the religious sphere was the only area which Nil, whose environment was the tranquility of the hermitage, deemed worthy of consideration, and by and large his "school" fought to make the religious sphere even more isolated from the world than it already was. One has the distinct impression that Nil's school was originally rather indifferent even to ecclesiastical questions and that Nil and his followers came forth with their ecclesiastical proposals and demands only when the "world" grew dubious about the value of their tranquil hermitages, especially when rich bequests and presumed "benevolent acts" threatened to draw monks into "the toils of the world."

86

Later followers of Nil and his philosophy, to be sure, were almost the only people who made a serious attempt to resist the Moloch of the Muscovite state, which was gaining more and more power, but their efforts were in vain because their ideology was not a universal philosophy but merely a theory about monastic "inner activity," about "the spiritual struggle" of the anchorite.

This is by no means an underestimation of Nil's philosophy. Indirectly, if conditions had been favorable, it could have had a salutary effect on the general mentality of the time. People could have learned in particular to revere the inner life and not to confuse it with the external trappings of piety, and that would have been of decisive significance for the political and cultural life of Russia in the sixteenth and seventeenth centuries. It is significant that the men who resisted—morally, if not politically—the immorality of Muscovite absolutism as manifested by Ivan the Terrible were, directly or indirectly, pupils of Nil. Furthermore, the Russian schism of the seventeenth century would probably have been out of the question, or at least it would have taken a different form. The fanatical character of this schism can be explained as the result of overestimating "ritualistic" Christianity, which derived from Josif Volotskii and his disciples. Moreover, the pseudo-pious human type, whom A. Blok, a twentieth-century Russian poet, portrays in one of his most beautiful poems, could not have developed. The primary characteristic of this type is a piousness which colors "the surface of the soul" but does not penetrate to the deeper levels of spiritual life and is incapable of shaping man's life from within. Pseudomorphic piety, so dangerous to the fate of the individual, could not have played as great a role in the later spiritual and intellectual life of Russia as it has, from the pseudomorphism of "Holy Russia" of the sixteenth and seventeenth centuries down to the pseudo-socialism and pseudo-pacifism of the twentieth century. In all probability, the resistance of inwardly-pious people to the political and moral decay of Russia would not have met with any success, but at least there would have been an indelible memory of this struggle in the consciousness of the people, and not only the "sufferer," a type so highly esteemed by the people, but also the "activist," the person who fights against injustice, could have developed as an ideal for future generations.

This did not happen. Josif Volotskii's philosophy was victorious, and it bears part of the responsibility for the darkest aspects of Russian life in the sixteenth, seventeenth, and the following centuries, right down to the present. We can only conjecture about the significance Nil's school could have had for Russia, but we can see clearly the actual importance of the ideology established by Josif Volotskii and propagated and perpetuated by his followers. This ideology infected Russian life with the poison of arrogance. It injected into the life of Russia that most dangerous of all viruses, the illusion that the ideal has already become a reality, and this illusion was all the more dangerous because here ultimate values, all that is holy, were at stake. The

87

idea of "Holy Russia," which was connected with this ideology, became a pernicious disease which gnawed away at Russian consciousness. While some were misled and held blindly fast to real or supposed "old ideals and values," others, who perceived the true condition of Russia, were forced to flee from this reality, either in the traditional way, by becoming hermits, or else by espousing various types of utopianism. Both traditionalism and utopianism, the two tendencies which were especially powerful in Russian life during the nineteenth and twentieth centuries, are rooted in the spiritual and intellectual situation brought about by the crisis of the fourteenth and fifteenth centuries. For that reason the historical importance of this crisis can hardly be stressed enough.

"Ruler by the Grace of God"

It is important to know how the princes themselves conceived of their calling and their position, because their views quite soon penetrated the consciousness of Russian society. In the fourteenth and fifteenth centuries royal power was conceived to be based on *heredity* and *genealogy*. In the *Tver Chronicle* of the fifteenth century we find for the first time a carefully constructed genealogy of a royal dynasty. This was probably the model for the Muscovites' genealogical scheme. When Emperor Frederick III suggested, at the end of the fifteenth century, to Grand Prince Ivan III of Muscovy that he acquire the title of king, Ivan replied: "By the grace of God we have been since the beginning of time rulers of our country. . . . We, like our ancestors, were installed on the throne by God." This idea—installation on the throne by God—soon supplanted completely the notion that royal power was hereditary, that the country belonged to the prince by inheritance *(votchina);* and soon the thought of genealogy was taken far beyond the confines of the Riurik dynasty.

In 1472 Ivan III married a Byzantine princess who was then residing in Italy. This marriage contributed a great deal to the pomp of the grand prince's court in Moscow, but the view that the Muscovite grand prince, by virtue of marriage, had become to some extent the successor to the Byzantine emperors was of only slight importance, probably because the fall of Byzantium was considered a punishment meted out by God, and, as will be seen, in Moscow it was believed that the Muscovite state was destined not so much to fall heir to Byzantium as to supplant it completely.

Gradually the view that royal power was exercised at God's command became firmly established, and by the beginning of the sixteenth century, according to reports of foreign visitors to Russia, the Muscovites considered the grand prince to be the deputy of God and the will of the grand prince to be the will of God. This view was probably not generally accepted in Russia. After 1480, when Ivan III during a crucial campaign against the

Tatars left his army at the River Ugra and returned to Moscow, Archbishop Vassian Rylo wrote him a letter which clearly indicates that the old prerogative of the clergy "to instruct" the princes had not yet been forgotten: "When, O Master, you rule us in times of peace you impose heavy taxes upon us, but now you have angered the Khan and delivered us into the hands of the Tatars." Vassian calls the prince a "coward" and threatens that God will call him to account for the Christian blood which has been shed. And at the beginning of the sixteenth century Josif Volotskii took the liberty of giving Grand Prince Vasilii some unsolicited advice. These were the last steps taken by the still relatively independent Church. "Rulers by the Grace of God" had no need of advice from prelates.

CHAPTER IV. MUSCOVITE ABSOLUTISM

The Origin and Establishment of the Muscovite Empire

Under the rule of the Tatars the Muscovite princes "collected together the Russian lands," by peaceful means, by taking individual small kingdoms under their protection and even by purchasing land, and by military campaigns, which ended with the destruction of the cities they conquered and with all manner of atrocities. After the fall of Tver the only territories left were Muscovy and a few small lands which were completely dependent upon it. In the campaign of 1480 against the Tatars Ivan III (1462-1505) did indeed "shake off the Tatar yoke," that is, he achieved complete independence from the Tatars.

Autocracy became more firmly established during the long reign of Ivan's successor , Vasilii III (1505-1533). This was done in part by breaking promises made to the kingdoms of Novgorod and Pskov and depriving them of most of their rights. Vasilii ruled with a strong hand, and there are many tales about his despotism and injustice, but Muscovite absolutism in the full measure of its menacing and loathsome power did not become evident until the reign of Vasilii's son, Ivan the Terrible (1533-1584).

Ivan ascended the throne as an orphan of three years of age, and a clique of boyars ruled for him until, as a young man, he followed in the footsteps of his forefathers. His fame is based upon his conquest of the two remaining Tatar khanates on the Volga: Kazan and Astrakhan. In an attempt to regulate religious life he convened a Church council, and for a long time the decrees of this council, consisting of 100 chapters, remained the basis for religious life in Russia. He was less successful in later wars with Poland, and the last years of his reign proved to be the most terrible pages in Russian history.

Descriptions of this reign of terror can be found in most histories of Russia. He had countless people executed, some of whom were certainly innocent. He destroyed whole families, together with their children and servants. He was guilty of numerous homicides—in fact, he murdered his own son and heir to the throne. He treated women with contempt. He destroyed Novgorod because of an unfounded suspicion—as Kliuchevskii puts it, "without investigating, merely on grounds of suspicion, and without reason Ivan inhumanly and godlessly laid waste to a great old city and a whole territory in a way the Tatars had never done." Finally, he divided the state into two parts *(oprichnina)* and removed one part, which was deemed the tsar's private property, from the normal administrative system (a move which baffled contemporaries and historians alike). All these deeds undermined the foundations of normal political life.

The psychological shock, however, was even more severe, as the following decades showed. In the bloody atmosphere of that time of terror it could not be discerned that Ivan was pursuing certain goals which he, having absolute power anyway, could have achieved by other means. The most important of these goals were the centralization of the state and the replacement of the hereditary nobility by appointed government officials *(sluzhiloe dvorianstvo)* who at the time were also noblemen. The Tsar's actions toward those about him, deeds which ignored all laws of God and man and which he perpetrated in Moscow and in his residence, would not have become common knowledge if the Tsar himself had not taken pains to see that they became as widely known as possible. Reports of his reign made at the time and later show what a strong—and overwhelmingly negative—impression the Tsar made.[11]

The age required the solution of important political, social, and cultural problems. Numerous works written at the time indicate that members of various social classes were conscious of these complex problems. Their answers to the questions facing them were varied and are the best information we have about the spiritual and intellectual life of Russia in the sixteenth century.

"Political Journalism" in the Sixteenth Century

One characteristic of Russian literature in the sixteenth century is the important part played by polemical writings. With some justification the modern term "political journalism" has been used to describe these works. They are devoted primarily to political and social questions, making suggestions for reforms, attacking existing conditions by various means, and sometimes functioning as a defense of the status quo (Ivan the Terrible himself engaged in polemics).

Most of these works of political journalism were distributed in handwritten copies, but some did later become accessible to a more or less large circle of readers; even those writings which no one was able to read at the time can be utilized in our intellectual history because they represent the views of men who could, and indeed actually did propagate their ideas orally.

Part of this political journalism goes back to the religious polemics of the fifteenth century, but by and large religious questions now fade into the background. Only a few authors added anything to the stock of quotations from religious writings. In the literature of the time, however, two themes emerge which are highly characteristic of Muscovite absolutism and are summed up in the two pithy formulae, "Moscow—the Third Rome" and "Holy Russia." These two phrases express a view of the historical position and calling of Russia—that is, of Muscovy—which form the basis for many of the discussions in works of political journalism, even though no

91

explicit reference to the two phrases is made. For many people of the time the two formulae seemed to be axioms of Muscovite political philosophy. Strangely enough, the two formulae appear in rather off-hand contexts and are neither substantiated in any way nor elucidated in any detail.

Moscow—the Third Rome

The idea of "Moscow the Third Rome" first occurs in the works of Filofei (Greek Philotheos), a monk of Pskov, and it must be emphasized that the significance which this idea later acquired and the ideological importance which historical scholarship has ascribed to it are quite incommensurate with Filofei's writings, which are primitive in both form and content. To call this monk "a progressive man" or to term his views "a harmonious, pithily formulated theory" as Soviet scholars have done is certainly unwarranted. Malinin, the Russian scholar who edited Filofei's writings in 1901 and wrote an exhaustive monograph about him, was rather sceptical in his assessment of the value of Filofei's "works" and expressed the suspicion that Filofei's writings were nothing more than compilations.

Filofei's works consist of a few letters written to various persons on various occasions. Two of them are "letters of consolation," both composed in the same format and containing no more than the recommendation that all suffering be borne with equanimity. In addition, he wrote three letters attacking astrology; in so doing he cited only some (in part fictitious) statements from the Apocrypha and from the "councils" which forbade Christians to devote their energies to an investigation of nature. Another of Filofei's letters is the answer to a question about "good and bad days." Filofei rejects such concepts, and at the conclusion of the letter, in a passage completely unrelated to the rest of the letter, he begins to speak about the fact that "our Lord [the Muscovite grand prince] is the only Christian tsar in the whole world," an assertion which is correct if "Christian" is construed solely as Greek Orthodox. Filofei continues: "All Christian kingdoms have been united in this one single kingdom *(snidoshasia):* two Romes have fallen, the third one stands, and a fourth one there shall not be." These words are followed by quotations from the Apocalypse.

Filofei's fame is based on two other letters, the first, written about 1511, to Grand Prince Vasilii III, and the second, probably written shortly after 1533, to Ivan the Terrible, who was still a child. Both letters were written in response to specific conditions. Filofei urged Vasilii to combat "immorality," by which he presumably meant homosexuality, which seems to have been widespread at that time among the Muscovite upper classes, and to introduce the "true sign of the cross" to replace the "Greek sign of the cross" used by many people. Filofei goes on to assert that the Grand Prince, whom he already addresses as "tsar," rules in "the Third Rome" and is the sole Christian ruler. Filofei gives him the title "The Ruler of the Holy and Divine Throne of the Ecumenical Apostolic Church" *(sic!)* and considers him to be the lawful successor of St. Vladimir and Yaroslav the Wise. It is quite clear from the grotesque title he gives the "tsar" that Filofei regards him not only as chief of state but also as head of the Church. Filofei, of course, does not forget to remind the Grand Prince in passing of the inviolability of Church property, citing as authority the "decrees of the Fifth Ecumenical Council." These decrees are almost certainly Filofei's invention, for no such decrees have come down to us. In his letter to Ivan the Terrible Filofei asks Ivan to take action against simony. This request is introduced by a long quotation from *Climax* (a didactic work by John Climakos which is in no way related to the topic of the letter), by excerpts from the Apocalypse, and by a reiteration of the now familiar statement that "Moscow is the Third Rome" because Byzantium "turned away from the true faith." The allusion to the union with Rome was an anachronism, for in the sixteenth century this union no longer existed.

The formula "Moscow—the Third Rome" actually seems to have been Filofei's invention, but it was suggested to him by a similar phrase in the Bulgarian translation of the *Chronicle of Manasse,* and there is some question as to how Filofei interpreted the phrase. The quotations from the Apocalypse which accompany the phrase in two instances and the conclusion of the phrase in the letter about "good and bad days,"—"a fourth Rome there shall not be"—lead one to suspect that Filofei thought the *end of the world* was imminent and that "the Third Rome," the concluding chapter in the history of the world, was destined to be short-lived. This is how G. Florovsky, a historian of Russian theology, interprets the statement. Ivan the Terrible and his contemporaries interpreted the term "the Third Rome" differently. For them, being "the Third Rome" meant being the central point and fulfillment of world history, and Ivan did not hesitate to exploit Filofei's phrase politically.

Fake Genealogies

The Muscovite rulers were no longer satisfied to trace their dynasty back to the old Kievan princes, and as the power of the Muscovite kingdom began to increase several legends arose concerning the Muscovite dynasty and the origins of its power. These legends were thoroughly fantastic and were presented in works marked by extreme literary awkwardness, but for a long time they were able to achieve the desired effect. They need not be treated in detail here.

One legend reports that the dynasty of Riurik goes back to none other than Emperor Augustus of Rome. Augustus, it seems, had a brother named Prus who ruled in ancient Prussia and who was the ancestor of Riurik. In

1498 the "coronation" of the youthful prince Dmitrii Ivanovich as heir to the throne took place in Moscow (later he was deposed by his grandfather, who had devised the solemn coronation ceremony, and he died in prison). In this public ceremony an ornate cap was used as a crown, and a broad fur stole *(barmy)* was placed on the shoulders of the heir apparent; he was also handed a little box made of carnelian. There was a legend connected with these objects, which were later used at the coronations of the Muscovite tsars. A Byzantine emperor was supposed to have given these objects to Prince Vladimir Monomakh at the beginning of the twelfth century in recognition of his royal dignity, and the carnelian box was said to have once been the property of the Emperor Augustus. By means of these regalia, then, a link was established between the "First Rome" and the "Second Rome." They were, in fact, unknown before 1498. Where they came from is not certain; the "crown" was presumably Byzantine, but possibly it too was put together in Russia from various individual pieces. The legend about the crown, however, is certainly not true.

The legend spun its web further. The final stage in its development traced the coronation regalia of "the Third Rome" back to Babylon. The fantastic tale of "the Babylonian Empire" told the early history of these objects. They had belonged to King Nebuchadnezzar. After the fall of the Babylonian empire, Babylon had become infested with snakes. Three emissaries of the Byzantine emperor—a Greek, a "Russian," and a Georgian—went into the city and took Nebuchadnezzar's regalia. From Byzantium the objects then were brought to Russia. In this way the "sole Christian realm" became successor to Babylon and the "sole Christian ruler" successor to King Nebuchadnezzar. This shows how fatuous the historical and genealogical fabrications of Muscovite patriotism were. This legend sounds almost like an unintentional mockery of Muscovite claims. The new Rome—a second Babylon. This thesis, which was not advanced at the time, well fitted the true nature and the ideology of Muscovite absolutism.

The "Most Christian Ruler"

The letters which Feodosii, bishop of Novgorod after 1547, wrote to Ivan the Terrible are significant. Here a prelate spoke and admitted that the Church was in the hands of the secular ruler, and rightly so. The Tsar himself ought to attend to the spiritual welfare of his subjects, for, "following the model of heavenly power," the scepter of the temporal world has been entrusted to the Tsar: "Just as the severe and all-seeing eye of the heavenly tsar sees into the hearts of all men, your royal wisdom likewise has the greatest capacity for arranging harmoniously your good government." "You should support devoutness in every way and spare your subjects physical and spiritual unrest." The following statement is the most important of all: "I am writing to you, divinely appointed master, not to teach you wisdom nor to instruct your noble mind, because it is unseemly of us to forget our place and dare to do such a thing; rather I am writing as a pupil writes to his teacher or a servant to his master." How vastly different the views of this Archbishop Feodosii are from those of St. Feodosii, the modest abbot who considered it his duty to instruct sovereigns and admonish them with harsh words in the name of Christian morality! And in 1480, less than a hundred years earlier, Vassian Rylo had not hesitated to direct blunt words of admonition to the Muscovite grand prince.

The Ideal State

The successes of Muscovite foreign policy and Tsar Ivan's attempts to bring about reforms moved some people to express in writing their advice, warnings, and admonitions. It is impossible to cite all these works here, but some of them do deserve attention.

Ermolai-Erzam, a member of the literary coterie of Metropolitan Makarii, composed saints' lives and a few writings which contained concrete advice on state policy. Ermolai developed, along with suggestions on how to improve the conditions of the peasantry, his own views on the ideal state. He believed that through "good will" the ruler could overcome all difficulties. The sovereign ought "to rule not with severity *(yarost')* but with clemency and justice." He should devote himself not to the interests of "the strong" alone but to "the welfare of all who are his subjects, down to the lowliest" *(do poslednikh)*. Furthermore, all subjects have the obligation to help improve conditions. No one, Ermolai-Erzam thought, should envy his betters or look down on his inferiors: "Most important of all, despise pride, not only in its outward appearance, but also in your heart." Pride—and it will be recalled that Nil Sorskii designated pride, the Caesar complex, a particularly grievous sin—has the tendency, Ermolai-Erzam thought, to keep on growing larger: "The proud man who has achieved a high position will rise still higher and thinks of rising higher and higher." Erzam's views on social policy were derived from this concept of the moral state. He considered Russia a purely agricultural country, and therefore the peasants ought to form the foundation of this state. The upper classes ought to serve the state because otherwise there would be no justification for their wealth: "All riches are gathered by force or by intrigue alone." Members of the upper classes, he believed, were responsible for the sins of their subjects. This picture of a Christian peasant state was, of course, utopian.

Ivan Peresvetov thought more realistically. Ivan was a secular writer whose personality remains obscure even though he relates in his works many details of his life. Even his name presents problems; it may be a pseudonym. It does appear that he spent some time in Central Europe—in Hungary,

95

Poland, Wallachia, and Bohemia or in the one or the other of these lands. His concrete proposals for reform were brought to the attention of the Tsar, but it is difficult to judge them because it is not known whether he made them before or after the beginning of the reign of terror. The general tendencies of his thought, however, are clear enough.

Peresvetov's works are directed against "strong men" but give no specific details. Even one of his works written as a petition contains no indications of any wrongs which Peresvetov may have suffered at the hands of "strong men." Peresvetov believes that the willfulness of the "strong men" was able to take root in Russia because there was no "justice" *(pravda)* there. A Muscovite is said to have told Prince Peter of Wallachia: "In Russia the Christian faith is good, . . . and the beauty of the churches is great, but there is no justice." When Prince Peter heard that, he wept and said: "If there is no justice there, then there is nothing at all there." Peresvetov considered justice a purely political and social virtue which, to be sure, has a religious basis: "God helps not the lazy but those who labor and call on God for help, those who love justice and make just decisions in courts of law: Justice is pleasing to the heart of God and is the great wisdom of the tsar." He stated this repeatedly: "God prefers justice to all other things"; "true justice is brighter than the sun"; and even "God loves not faith but justice." Peresvetov calls Mohammed the Great, the Turkish sultan who conquered Constantinople, the model of the just sovereign. The reasons for the fall of Constantinople, in Peresvetov's opinion, were the weakness of the last emperor, Constantine, and the perfidy of his servants.

Peresvetov believed that justice could be established only by disciplinary measures. He demanded the harshest punishments for perfidious officials and office-holders, whom he termed "magicians and heretics": "Such people should be burnt with fire and executed in other cruel ways." Peresvetov cites in support of his own proposals examples of the supposedly cruel acts by which Mohammed established justice in his empire: "When an emperor rules with gentleness and clemency, his empire grows poor *(oskudeet)* and his empire and fame is diminished."

"A Realm Without Strict Discipline is Like a Horse Without Reins"

Strict discipline, but without justice, certainly did prevail in "the Third Rome" of Ivan the Terrible. It should be kept in mind, however, that Peresvetov did not develop his views solely in general terms. He made a series of very concrete proposals. He was against the rule of the magnates *(velmozhi)*, who received administrative posts because of their family connections and as virtually independent viceroys acted in their own best interests and not in those of the tsar. Peresvetov advised the ruler to establish a professional civil service and to pay government officials fixed salaries.

Officials should be chosen without regard for family background, as had been the practice of the Sultan. Peresvetov recommended that the army be given particular attention, and, because for him the strength of the state was the true mark of a successful policy, he advocated the abolition of those forms of personal dependency *(kholopstvo)* which he termed slavery *(rabstvo, poraboshchenie):* "If the people of a state are enslaved they are not brave and valiant in battle with the enemy; for an enslaved man has no fear of shame and does not strive for honor, . . . for he says to himself: 'I am a slave *(kholop)* anyway and will never be called anything else.' "

Peresvetov himself characterized his ideal state as a unique synthesis of nearly irreconcilable opposites. In Muscovy he found true faith, in Turkey true justice, and "if one could add to the true Christian faith [of Muscovy] Turkish justice, then the angels would consort with us." In other words, Muscovy could become heaven on earth.

Opponents of Absolutism

Of course, those who may be designated opponents of Muscovite absolutism thought differently about life in Russia at the time. Most of them put the interests of the Church above "reason of state" and piety above politics. They saw in the victory of Josif Volotskii's philosophy and in the ever-increasing dependency of the Church on the state, in the rule of such prelates as Metropolitan Daniil, not only easily corrected flaws but also portents of impending decline. Their efforts to put into effect Nil Sorskii's program were from the outset doomed to failure. If their demands had been met, Church property would have been expropriated and the Church would have become to a great extent independent of state authority and control. That would have meant revolution. The Russian autocrats were in fact often "revolutionaries" and did not hesitate to destroy by force old values and traditions. This was especially true of Ivan the Terrible, but he could never have made the program of the pious anchorites his own.

Vassian Patrikeev

Members of the opposition were usually able to formulate their views more pregnantly and more impressively than were the defenders of the status quo. This was not merely a matter of the personal talent of the members of the opposition but rather of the more advantageous position which they enjoyed as attackers of the established system.

The opponents of the Muscovite political system include some outstanding figures. The first who might be mentioned was the royal monk Vassian Patrikeev. Born around 1460, the son of a general and high government official who was related to the Grand Prince, Vassian, together with his father, became involved at the turn of the century in conflicts at the court concerning the succession to the throne and was forced to take monastic vows—then and later a favorite method of eliminating a political opponent. He was held prisoner in the Monastery on the White Sea, and there he met Nil Sorskii and became his enthusiastic disciple. It was not until after the death of Nil and of Ivan III that Vassian returned to Moscow to play an important role at the court of Grand Prince Vasilii III. At about this time he was also in contact with Maksim Grek, who was essentially in agreement with Nil Sorskii's philosophy and strengthened Vassian in his views. At this time, however, the higher clergy were followers of Josif Volotskii. Metropolitan Daniil, an unscrupulous man, brought charges of heresy against Vassian, and after a trial conducted by the most ignoble means Vassian was found guilty and banished to a monastery controlled by his enemies where he died. Some of his works and the records of his trial have been preserved, and they afford a rather clear picture of his views. His ideas were not new; they were penetrating and vibrant re-statements of Nil Sorskii's thought: monasteries should own neither serfs nor property; "heretics" should not be punished with death; instead intellectual and spiritual weapons should be used to discredit their views.

Vassian was particularly opposed to the state of the Church in his time, the excessive attention given to the external splendor of its buildings and the ostentatious services which turned the church into a theatre *(sen' pozorishchnaia)*. "The loud sound of singing and shouting" was incompatible with heartfelt prayer and genuine piety. The clergy, Vassian insisted, should engage in "spiritual therapeutics," i.e. care for the soul, and in the study of Holy Scriptures. Like his master, Nil, Vassian addresses his writings primarily to monks.

In the question of monastic ownership of property and serfs and in that of the position of the Church in the state, Vassian was more radical than Nil. First of all, he emphasized that all ownership rests on "theft" and that monasteries must not go the way of the world. Vassian made no suggestions about how the world should be improved, but his description of monks "caught in the toils of the world" shows how profoundly pessimistic his judgment of the world was. Monks who own property, like property-owners in the *world*, are "ruled by greed for money and insatiability; the poor brothers who live in the villages are harassed in various ways; more and more burdens are imposed on them, more and more deceits, more and more usurious interest; their possessions, their little horses and cows, are taken away from them without compassion, and they and their wives and children are driven into exile." "We," Vassian says, speaking for monks who own property, "harass, rob, and sell Christians, our brothers, tormenting them mercilessly with the whip and throwing ourselves on their bodies like wild animals."

98

Vassian also spoke of a political problem, the problem of absolute monarchy. He expressed doubts that autocracy was a suitable means to an end: "Often the ruler's weakness of mind brings misfortune to his land and to his people." It would therefore be better if the ruler consulted his boyars on all questions. In this view vestiges of the old "feudal" psychology can perhaps be discerned, views of times gone by when the power of the grand prince was limited by the appanage princes. In his political program Vassian also demanded the complete separation of Church and state. He believed that whereas the Church should be completely independent of the state, the clergy for its part ought not to become involved in the business of the world, and churchmen who strive for secular power "do not love God but rather give offense." Vassian recognized that God had given the tsars their power, but he was, it seems, the last Muscovite writer who makes *no* mention of the "divine" or "God-like" *nature* of this power.

For Vassian it was important that every Christian has the obligation and right to give instruction in religious matters; the followers of Josif Volotskii were at this time of the opinion that only bishops might "preach about the paths to salvation."

Vassian was found guilty and banished. At his trial he preserved his independence and defended himself and his views, which has led some Soviet scholars to charge that Vassian was a "reactionary." Vassian disappeared from the political and ecclesiastical scene, but copies of his works continued to be made and disseminated. He represented, even more consistently than Nil, the purely monastic point of view, and he found for the "world" only words of condemnation and contempt. He was certainly not the man to reform the conditions which existed at the time.

Maxim the Greek—Maksim Grek

Maksim (1480-1556), the monk of Athos, may be included among the opponents of Muscovite absolutism, and at least one of his works must be mentioned. Maksim, a member of the Greek Trivolis family, studied in Italy, where he travelled in humanistic circles and heard the sermons of Savonarola, but after his return to Greece he became a monk at Mount Athos. In 1518 he came to Moscow to assist in making translations of theological works. He was destined never to leave Russia again, and later in two trials he was found guilty of "heresy" because he had made changes in the old translations, had taken an independent stand on some delicate questions (such as the divorce of the Grand Prince), and had supported Nil Sorskii's school. Despite his own pleas and entreaties and despite the attempts of the Eastern patriarch to free him, he was held prisoner in a monastery until his death in 1556 and at times was even denied communion. He wrote many works (in Church Slavic), most of them theological in nature, but they contain scarcely any traces of his humanistic studies.

One of Maksim's small works show what impression life in Moscow made on an Orthodox non-Russian. This work is a lament of "tsardom" *(Basileia)*. "I trod," Maksim writes, "a difficult and sorrowful road and met a women who was sitting by the road groaning and weeping inconsolably, her knees bent, her head resting on her hand, and dressed in black, like a widow. Around her swarmed wild animals, lions and bears, wolves and foxes." When asked who she was, she replied: "Wanderer, I am one of the noble and glorious daughters of the Emperor of all that is, of the Creator and Lord. . . . I have not one name but many, for I am called Authority and Power, Government and Rule. My real name, which comprises all those I have mentioned, is *Basileia*. I was given this beautiful name by the Almighty, and those who rule me must be the supports and strongholds for the people who are subject to them. . . ." In reality, however, these rulers are the cause of "decline and constant confusion." "Many who do not understand my name conduct the affairs of their subjects in a way unworthy of the title of emperor and become tyrants instead of emperors, dishonoring me and plunging themselves finally into terror and impotence, and thus the Almighty visits upon them retribution in accordance with their fury and their folly." These words sound a prophecy of God's punishments to come. *Basileia* gives no thought to a way to avoid these punishments: "And so I, a poor widow woman, sit by the wilderness road, deprived of those who might defend me and be zealous on my behalf. That, wanderer, is my misfortune, one worthy of many tears."

Metropolitan Filipp

The "political journalists" of religion in the sixteenth century really saw no way out of the hopeless situation, or, like Maksim, they prophesied that severe punishment by God was forthcoming. The conflict between Metropolitan Filipp and Tsar Ivan the Terrible ended with the deposition of the metropolitan and his subsequent murder in the monastery where he was imprisoned. During the reign of Ivan's son and successor Feodor, who was a gentle tsar (and probably also a man of limited mental capacity), Filipp was canonized, and at that time the saints' life of Filipp originated. In it the author put his own opinion of the reign of Ivan the Terrible into the mouth of the saint. The opinion was a highly characteristic one, and the author of the life was probably not the only person who held it.

Filipp was chosen metropolitan at a council, and, in accordance with the conditions which he had put forth at the election and to which the Tsar had agreed, he wanted to make use of the traditional right of the clergy to intercede on behalf of the condemned and persecuted. When the Tsar, during the reign of terror, entered the cathedral where Filipp was celebrating mass and asked Filipp to bless him, Filipp refused and attempted to move the Tsar to clemency. Ivan had no desire to listen to any advice, however, and said: "Be silent, I tell you, holy father, be silent and bless me!" Filipp is said to have answered: "Our remaining silent exposes your soul to sin and will bring death." The general tendency to keep silent in the face of events which were bringing the state to the brink of moral and political ruin was probably the most grievous political sin committed by the Russians of Ivan's time. People did not become conscious of this until a generation later, and the author of Filipp's life expressed this consciousness in the words he put into the saint's mouth.

Fedor Karpov

Among the opponents of Muscovite domestic policy in the sixteenth century there was one who posed the question of the nature of the state *in terms of principles*. This was the diplomat Fedor Karpov, a few of whose works have come down to us. Karpov's views are expressed in a letter in reply to a work which was written by Metropolitan Daniil between 1536 and 1539 but which unfortunately has not been preserved. Karpov surely shared those views with his circle of acquaintances, which included Maksim Grek and Prince Kurbskii. The quotations from Aristotle and Ovid which Karpov includes in the letter lead one to assume that his thought was influenced by Western literature, but the exact sources of his views remain unknown and are of no consequence for our purposes. Karpov attempted to draw a sharp line between the demands of religious and those of secular morality. He wanted to demonstrate the principles on which a sound civil political life could be built. Karpov did not live to see Tsar Ivan the independent ruler of Russia, for Karpov was already well on in years in 1536-39. His letter to some extent condemned Ivan's domestic policy in advance.

In the letter known only from Karpov's answer to it, Metropolitan Daniil had praised patience *(terpenie)* as a virtue which helps subjects bear the burdens—even personal persecution—imposed on them in civil life. Karpov emphasized, by contrast, that while patience, and particularly the willingness to bear suffering patiently and for a long time *(dolgoterpenie)*, was a monastic virtue, it could by no means constitute the basis of civil life. If a person bears everything that happens to him with patience, then "the strong will be able to oppress the weak" without encountering any resistance. In that case "princes and laws would be unnecessary," nor would judges be needed, for "patience would satisfy everyone," i.e., it would silence any protests which could arise and it would suppress the will of the individual to defend himself. Then one would live not in a state but "without any order." But organized society requires justice and rights *(pravda)*, and where these prevail, patience loses its value. Only those who have nothing, Karpov states, can be patient, because they have nothing to lose, but even they can be subjected to force. Patience "without justice and law destroys all society's goods," for patience "abets evil ways and creates people who because of their poverty are disobedient to their ruler." They do not fear punishment because they have nothing to lose. Karpov could not have suspected, of course, how widespread the most cruel tortures would become under the rule of Ivan the Terrible, tortures which were able to intimidate even those "who had nothing to lose."

The state, Karpov contended, ought to be "governed by rulers according to justice and law," and rulers ought to "defend those who are innocent, free those who have been wronged, punish those who have wronged others and caused annoyance, and remove from decent society those who are completely incorrigible." Harmony ought to prevail in the state, and it is the task of the princes, whom Karpov compares to musicians, to establish this harmony.

In a word, Karpov insists that subjects must not live "under the slavery of patience." He even drew up a scheme of the way mankind has developed from its natural state to the strict laws of Moses and down to the "Age of Grace." Unlike Peresvetov, Karpov believed that if the letter of the law were followed the state would degenerate into tyranny. Justice must be tempered with mercy: "Mercy guided by justice and justice tempered with mercy will preserve the state for a long time."

Although these ideas are rather primitive, their importance should not be underestimated for the simple reason that they were directed against the utopian identification of the Church with the state. Karpov even hinted that a state based on patience, the monastic virtue, could not "long be preserved," yet another pessimistic prophecy which was to be fulfilled in less than a century. Patience *(terpenie* and *dolgoterpenie),* however, has remained down to our times the most frequently praised virtue of the Russian people, and almost all Russian rulers have counted on this Russian virtue to help them through difficult times. Karpov realized that a state based on the patience of its subjects was actually like a monastery. This identification of the sacred with the profane was at that time already present in the concept "Holy Russia."

Prince Andrei Kurbskii

The term "Holy Russia" or "the holy Russian Land" or "the holy Russian empire" *(sviatorusskaia zemlia* or *tsarstvo)* first appears *expressis verbis* in the biography of Ivan the Terrible written by Ivan's opponent, Prince Andrei Kurbskii (1528-1583). Kurbskii had formerly been one of Ivan's important generals and his personal friend. In 1564 he fled to Lithuania and wrote a letter to the Tsar; two other letters followed in 1577. The

102

Tsar wrote a letter of reply to the "traitor," and Kurbskii thus deserves credit for having prompted the Tsar to describe in his own words his political ideology. Kurbskii also wrote the "biography" mentioned above, and it is an important historical source in spite of its polemical character.

Kurbskii's letters have been cited and reprinted frequently, and they have been regarded, not completely justifiably, as the most important works written in opposition to Ivan's political system. These letters, particularly the first one, are in reality outstanding pieces of rhetoric, but Prince Andrei barely comes to grips with basic issues. His letters are passionate excoriations of the amorality of the tsar's policies. Kurbskii seems to have been not totally unfamiliar with the view which equated state and Church. Tsar Ivan, however, was not fulfilling the duties of a Christian monarch, and Kurbskii, who knew the Tsar personally, gives a psychological interpretation of Ivan's character which was long accepted by historians as accurate. For our purposes, the Tsar's replies to Kurbskii's letters are of much greater interest.

Ivan the Terrible

Once again, as Vladimir Monomakh had done earlier, a ruler set forth his views on his duties and rights. Whereas Vladimir had spoken primarily about the *duties* of a prince, Tsar Ivan in his broad description gave priority to the *rights* of the ruler. Ivan's style is rather awkward, and his letters bristle with quotations which are too long and too numerous. His letters are rambling, even loquacious, and are not organized along a uniform line of development. Despite this, the Tsar can be termed "one of the best Muscovite writers of the sixteenth century," as Kliuchevskii has called him, even though Kliuchevskii's explanation for Ivan's literary ability— "because he was the most inspired Muscovite of that age"—does not lead one to expect much from the content of the works.

Ivan's main ideas are clear, even though his concept of the state has, as it were, an "autobiographical" basis. He considered himself a monarch "by virtue of God's decree, not man's discretion" *(mnogomiatezhnoe khotenie)*, but he did not forget to emphasize his genealogical rights, which went back to the Riurik dynasty and beyond that to the Emperor Augustus. He expressed his attitude toward his subjects in the lapidary statement: "I have the right to reward and to punish my slaves *(kholopy)*." Although Kurbskii had asked the Tsar whether his punishments were always just, Ivan was not interested in justice when he was rewarding and punishing his slaves. He believed that suffering was the lot of man and was ordained by God: "It is God's will that man be good and suffer." On the other hand, this suffering seemed to him actually to profit the sufferer. He wrote to Kurbskii: "If you are good and just, why are you unwilling to bear suffering caused by me, your refractory monarch, whereby you could obtain the crown of life [presumably he meant the martyr's crown]." Moreover, Tsar Ivan was still firmly convinced that his state was most intimately linked to the kingdom of heaven. Naturally, he shared Kurbskii's idea of "Holy Russia," but unlike Kurbskii, Ivan would certainly have spoken of the holiness of *every* tsar. The way he judged Kurbskii's defection is typical. According to the "feudalistic" ideas of the time, Kurbskii's departure from Russia was a permissible change to the service of another monarch; after all, Ivan himself had taken servants of other states into his own service—Ivan Peresvetov, for example, not to mention non-Russians. And yet Ivan considered Kurbskii's flight not only "treason" but "heresy," and he even believed that through his "treason" Kurbskii had destroyed "the souls of his ancestors," among whom was a prince who had been canonized. Such an estimation of his power and dignity logically led Ivan to give free rein to his personal whims. His political reforms may have been meaningful historically—they did establish a centralized government, and they did curtail, once and for all, the power of the appanage princes and their descendants, who served the state as boyars; but his reforms assumed such grotesque forms and were carried out in such cruel fashion that now we must share the view of earlier scholars that Ivan "sacrificed himself, his dynasty [by murdering his successor to the throne], and the interests of the state to hatred and caprice."

The Church in "Holy Russia"

The position of the Church in "the Third Rome," in "Holy Russia," by no means lived up to these high sounding names, and the ostentatious church services in no way reflected the real situation of the Church in Russia at the time. In 1547, 1549, and 1551 important church councils were held which regulated the external organization of religious life and canonized a number of pious men who were already being worshipped as saints (Nil Sorskii, who was venerated far and wide, was not one of them). Metropolitan Makarii (1542-1563), the former archbishop of Novgorod, also succeeded in initiating works which were meant to be worthy of the greatness and universal historical significance of "the Third Rome." On his initiative historical compilations were made: *Tsarstvennaia Kniga,* a world history in several volumes adorned with thousands of miniatures; *Stepennaia Kniga,* a history of Russia by dynasties, i.e. the history of Russia in the form of genealogies of the royal family; and, finally, the greatest of all literary works, the *Reading Menaea,* which included not only the lives of the saints but also all other extant Russian literary works (it was arranged according to the calendar and was meant to be read aloud in family circles or in monasteries). In choosing works for inclusion the compilers of course applied religious standards, with the result that older secular literature, such as the magnificently translated romances and some apocryphal works, were excluded.

In the *Reading Menaea* there are, among many other things, parts of books of the Bible, extensive works like the *Areopagitica*[12] with exhaustive commentaries by Maximus the Confessor, and the *Climax (Ladder)*, a religious moral tract which treats the step-by-step ascent of man to perfection.

The plan for this undertaking is consonant with Josif Volotskii's cultural ideal. It was to be a collection of all older works of value. The men who compiled it gave hardly any thought to creating new cultural values. Some older lives of saints were revised, of course, and some new ones were composed, for the most part about saints of whom nothing but their names was known; but these new works were for the most part crude falsifications. A Greek legend about a saint of the same name or of a similar type (martyr, confessor, bishop, ascetic, etc.) was chosen, and to this framework was affixed a "wreath of words" with short fictitious intimations about the life of the saint and unctuous and effusive encomia. This literature reflects the state of the Church at the time: its outward splendor, its inner helplessness against the unlimited power of secular authority, and the paralysis of its creative powers.

As has been noted, the position of the Church in "Holy Russia" was anything but easy and serene. Metropolitan Filipp, who took his duties seriously, was deposed and murdered. The other metropolitan, German, who was also later canonized, was prevented from assuming the office of metropolitan and died a prisoner in a monastery—it was believed at the time that he had been poisoned. Even so faithful a servant to the Grand Prince as Metropolitan Daniil was forcibly removed from office. It appears that seven of the nine metropolitans who served in the sixteenth century were deposed at the command of the civil authorities. The canonization of Filipp and German certainly shows that Church circles were by no means optimistic in their assessment of the Church's position, but in spite of everything the Church remained completely dependent on the state and thus on the sovereign reigning at the time, who with great accuracy could assert: "I am the state."

The Saints

One modern scholar, G. P. Fedotov, is surely right when he speaks of the "crisis of Russian hagiolatry" in allegedly "holy" Russia, of all places. This is indicated not only by the small number of newly canonized saints, but by the names of these saints, most of which were "mute," "nondescript," i.e., neither written nor oral tradition reports anything about these men.

More characteristic of the age is the type of saint widespread at that time, the *yurodivyi*, the "holy fool," as it should but actually cannot be translated. Every age has a sort of charisma which it needs, which it deserves, and which it can comprehend. The series of "holy fools," which begins in the fifteenth century, did not produce its most important representatives until the sixteenth century.

The "holy fool," as a type, is by no means specifically Russian. Such remarkable saints were known to Byzantium, where they were called *saloi*, which roughly translated means "monsters." The two most famous Greek *saloi*, Andreas and Symean, were well known in Russia, for the voluminous legends about them were translated quite early. This type of devout person, the pious eccentric, was also not unknown in the West; he is even found in the Protestant world. But this type appears to have been most widespread in Russia, exclusively in the Great Russian lands. More than thirty *yurodivye* were venerated as saints. It should be noted, of course, that often official circles only reluctantly recognized the worship of *yurodivye* after the people had long been worshipping them without Church sanction. Reports about the lives of some of them were passed on orally and not written down until modern times. There is evidence that they were frequently held in higher esteem than the other saints. For example, the famous Muscovite church *Vasilii Blazhennyi* (St. Basil's) is generally known by the name of this particular "holy fool," but the church is actually dedicated to the Ascension of the Virgin Mary and was built before the birth of Vasilii, who lies buried there!

The "holy fools" were not real fools, like the mentally deranged who were worshipped in the East. *Yurodivye* merely pretended to be fools, playing a role which for various reasons it seemed advisable to the devout of that time to play. First of all, they avoided the general veneration which genuinely or supposedly devout persons enjoyed: they "did not wish personal fame," "they fled from praise," as the accounts of their lives put it. Moreover, at a time when it was impossible to speak one's mind openly—as the fate suffered by Vassian Patrikeev, Maksim Grek, or Metropolitan Filipp shows—they expressed their views through silence and through symbolic acts which were intended to expose the vanity of the world. As the power of the state and the wealth and self-awareness of the world increased and became established, the *yurodivye* flourished. Fifteen canonized *yurodivye* lived in the fifteenth century (they were canonized in the sixteenth), fourteen in the sixteenth, and seven in the seventeenth.

Almost without exception the *yurodivye* struggled against a world which had grown too powerful, and they contrasted the folly of Christian faith with the "wisdom of the world," the wisdom of a *Christian* world which was threatened not by forces alien to it, such as the pagans and Tatars, but by its own internal weaknesses. It is no accident that the *yurodivye* appeared in Moscow, a flourishing city, and in the large and wealthy mercantile cities of North Russia—Novgorod, Pskov, and others.

The *yurodivye* used folly as a mask to flee the fame of this world, but if such a mask rendered its wearer ineffective in the world, he would be guilty of "the sin of keeping silent." Some *yurodivye* were indeed condemned to keep silent because they were not Russians. Reliable reports indicate that this was the case with Prokopii of Ustiug, an early representative of this type who died in the kingdom of Novgorod in 1302, and with Isidor (d. 1474) and Ioann (d. 1581), two saints from old Rostov, a city northeast of Moscow (for a long time a Latin psalter which had belonged to Ioann was preserved in a church in Rostov). Even *yurodivye* of Russian birth, however, preferred either to cloak their thoughts in obscure words which required interpretation or to express their views of the world through deeds and symbolic acts. They usually demonstrated their piety by attending church frequently or by spending their lives on the church steps or out in the open near a church. They dressed in pitiful rags—some went completely naked—and their sole means of livelihood were the alms they received. They were different from the monastic ascetics, however, for they neglected the ritualistic aspects of religious life. Frequently they did not fast, and they showed little reverence for the clergy and even for churches and icons. Through all these actions they proclaimed "the inner church," which attached no importance to external forms.

The legends present the *yurodivye* as "charismatic men" whose most important attribute was the gift of "distinguishing between spirits." Behind the phenomenal world they perceived spiritual reality. One story tells of a *yurodivyi* who threw stones at a church when evil spirits had assembled in front of it because they could not enter it along with the people whom they wanted to lead astray. There is a story of how another "holy fool" hurled a stone at a famous icon which possessed miraculous powers. They saw behind the profane world the spiritual essence of that world. Legendary deeds and feats which were heretofore attributed to saints and angels wandering on earth and even to Christ were now attributed to *yurodivye*. The angel in L. Tolstoy's story *What Men Live By* is modeled on the *yurodivye*. When a man orders boots which will last a long time the angel laughs because the man will soon die, and instead of the boots the man ordered the angel makes slippers for the burial of the customer, who does not suspect his fate. One story tells how a *yurodivyi* gave gold not to the poor but to an apparently wealthy merchant who in reality had lost his fortune and was already going hungry. In the marketplace *yurodivye* destroyed wares with which tradesmen intended to cheat their customers. One *yurodivyi* drove away a beggar because he recognized him to be a devil who "rewarded" those who gave him alms with happiness on earth and in this way led them astray and ruined them morally. Even though some of these tales may derive from non-Russian legends, they all do show how people of that time were taught to see, beneath the deceptive forms of the transitory world, eternal spiritual truth.

Several reports also describe the *yurodivye* as political opponents of precisely those sovereigns with whom the "politicians" of the time, both clerical and secular, had struggled without success. One *yurodivyi* is said to have reproached Ivan the Terrible for thinking in church only of the palace which he was in the process of building. Vasilii Blazhennyi (the Blessed) is described, anachronistically, as opposing Ivan's reign of terror. The Pskov chronicle, on the other hand, reports that a "holy fool" named Nikola prevented Ivan the Terrible from destroying Pskov in 1570 as he had Novgorod. When the Tsar asked the *yurodivyi* for his blessing, Nikola told him "with terrible words to stop the bloodletting." As the saint had prophesied, Ivan's best horse died, and the Tsar withdrew from Pskov. The legend gives a well-rounded portrayal of the meeting between the two men: Nikola served the Tsar raw meat, and when Ivan objected that as a Christian he ate no meat on fast days, Nikola is said to have replied: "But you drink Christian blood." There are other reports in a similar vein. St. Mikhail of Klopovo (d. 1453) allegedly prophesied the end of the independence of Novgorod. He saw the authorities of Novgorod sitting at a table without their heads. In Novgorod two *saloi* performed on the bridge a parody of the struggles between the political parties of that city. According to the English traveler Fletcher, a *yurodivyi* in Moscow "walketh naked about the streets and inveigheth commonly against the state and government, especially against the Godunovs, that are thought at this time to be great oppressors of that commonwealth." Fletcher describes the role of the *yurodivyi* from the political point of view of the English: "besides these [friars and nuns], they have certain hermits, whom they call holy men. . . . These they take as prophets and men of great holiness, giving them a liberty to speak what they list without any controlment, though it be of the very highest himself." Fletcher also reports, to be sure: "for this rude liberty . . . they are made away with in secret, as was one or two of them in the last Emperor's time [that of Ivan the Terrible] for being over bold in speaking against his government."[13] In any event, the *yurodivye* were permitted to act and speak more boldly than were the prelates—at least the people imagined this to be the case. A metropolitan could be removed from office and imprisoned, but the only thing that could be done to a *yurodivyi*, who occupied no specific position in the church hierarchy, was to murder him, but in Russian reports there is absolutely no mention of such action. The *yurodivyi* attained his "rank" through his personal effectiveness and his charisma alone. At certain times these "fools" were perhaps the only intellectually free men in Russia.

In the seventeenth century and later there are reports of such persons (cf. Dostoevsky's portrayal of such a type in *The Possessed*). The official and enlightened Church of the eighteenth and nineteenth centuries, however, attempted to restrict or do away completely with the worship of canonized Russian *saloi*. There are reports that the prelates of these times even went so far as to destroy old saints' lives which treated *yurodivye*.

Documents about private life in Russia at the time are supplemented by the *Domostroi (Oikonomikos)*, a work of obscure origin which depicts the ideal life of a well-to-do man around the middle of the sixteenth century. Whether this book reflects the real life of any Russian social class cannot be determined, but the description which it gives of "ideally" arranged family life is not heart-warming. Unlike almost all other works of this sort in world literature, the *Domostroi* almost completely ignores spiritual life and moral problems. The portrayal of the life of the family is limited to day-to-day living and strict observance of the formal regulations of the Church. Within the family the *pater familias* is an absolute ruler who may even use physical force, if need be, to see that his orders are obeyed. Neither love and harmony nor genuine devoutness is depicted. Unfortunately, it must be conceded that this same life style still obtained in the nineteenth century, particularly in the merchant class, but also in families of the lesser nobility and in wealthy peasant families (nineteenth-century literary works indicate such to be the case).[14] Moreover, the *Domostroi* family is depicted as totally isolated from its immediate surroundings. The absence of all social and political connections is quite characteristic of the times, and the very life-style of the family is inwardly connected with the unlimited autocracy of the monarch, whom no one dared to oppose or even thought of opposing. The same isolation of the individual from society can also be discerned in the following age of confusion when the disintegration of the state was brought about by precisely this complete indifference and lack of principle on the part of the moneyed classes and their representatives.

CHAPTER V. THE CRISES OF THE SEVENTEENTH CENTURY

Muscovite Absolutism

Foreigners traveling in Russia characterized sixteenth- and seventeenth-century Muscovite absolutism in the same way. Herberstein,[15] for example, wrote of Vasilii III, father of Ivan the Terrible, as follows: "In the power which he holds over his subjects he surpasses all monarchs of this world. . . . He oppresses all equally with cruel slavery. . . . He holds sway over clergy and laymen alike and without resistance disposes over the life and property of all in any way he wishes." Herberstein believed that the Muscovites were firmly convinced of the omnipotence and omniscience of the grand prince and that they believed the sovereign was fulfilling God's will. A century later Olearius[16] made the same assertion: "Their ruler, who inherited the crown, is the sole ruler of the entire country; all his subjects, princes and noblemen and the simple folk alike, are his servants and slaves, and he treats them the way a master treats his servants."

Similar statements are found in several sources written in these two centuries. The Pole Maskiewicz, who wrote down his conversations with Russians, reports that a Muscovite said to him: "Your freedom is dear to you, but our lack of freedom is to us. . . . If the master acts unjustly, then he has the power to do so: he bestows punishment and pardon like God." The tsars shared this opinion. The views of Ivan the Terrible have already been noted. But even Aleksei (1629-1676), the "quietest" *(tishaishii)* tsar, believed that "the heart of the tsar is in God's hand" and that "God instructs *(izvestit)* the tsar" when the tsar must make decisions. He demanded of his subjects "cheerful obedience," because people "must belong to the tsar with all their heart." In their dealings, Aleksei thought, men should be led "by the fear of God and of the tsar." This "mild" tsar did not hesitate to reproach as follows a subject who had not carried out orders: "Whom are you not obeying? Christ Himself!" This will suffice to demonstrate that even after the Interregnum and after several uprisings the intellectual and spiritual situation remained the same and that even in the seventeenth century Muscovite absolutism remained unchanged.

The Interregnum and the New Dynasty

Nevertheless, at the time of Ivan the Terrible some people did believe in the possibility of political catastrophe. Maksim Grek, who reminded his readers of the fall of the Byzantine empire, and Fedor Karpov, who alluded to the same event in a letter, certainly had this possibility in mind; and perhaps even Metropolitan Filipp, if every detail of the legend devoted to him is to be believed, possessed such far-sightedness. We even find the following prophetic lines in a sixteenth-century pamphlet entitled *A Conversation of the Miracle-Workers of Valaam Monastery*, a work which is puzzling in many respects and which combines the philosophy of Nil Sorskii with the firm belief in the divine right of the tsar: "There will come times of famine and frequent plagues, there will be earthquakes and floods of all kinds, there will be wars, civil wars *(mezhduosobnye brani)*, great unrest, and times of terror, and districts, villages, and Christian homes will be empty." When Fletcher in 1588 considered the possibility of great unrest in the Muscovite empire, this thought was perhaps suggested to him by the Muscovite authorities with whom he conversed. Some opponents of Muscovite absolutism knew why this tyranny was unbearable even for native Muscovites. Fedor Karpov saw in Moscow a transgression of "natural law" *(pravo estestvennoe)*. Kurbskii, who accused Tsar Ivan of having "locked up free humanity as in an infernal fortress," felt much the same way. It is obvious that many people were aware of the absence of justice to which Ivan Peresvetov had referred. The reason why people came to recognize this was that *everyone was dissatisfied with everything.*

This dissatisfaction might not have arisen, however, if the dynasty had not come to an end. Tsar Ivan's successor was Tsar Feodor, a man weak in body and mind. During his reign the Muscovite empire achieved new glory by establishing the patriarchate. The patriarch of Moscow, as the dignity of "the Third Rome" required, was now on almost equal footing with the four patriarchs of the Eastern Church. Feodor died without heir in 1598. His brother Dimitrii had already died a tragic death in 1591;[17] Dimitrii, to be sure, could scarcely have been considered a successor to the crown, because as the son of Ivan's seventh wife he was illegitimate in the eyes of the Church. It was all the more natural to choose as tsar Boris Godunov, the brother of Tsarina Irene, Feodor's widow, because during Feodor's lifetime Boris had conducted the affairs of state. During Boris' reign Russia was visited by natural catastrophes, particularly by drought followed by famine. In 1604 a civil war broke out. The dynastic interpretation of tsarist power was exploited by a usurper called the False Demetrius (Dimitrii) who appeared in Poland claiming to be the son of Ivan the Terrible and whose true identity is still a mystery. When Boris died unexpectedly the usurper was able to eliminate Boris' young successor, his son Feodor, and quietly seize power, but Dimitrii, who had entered Moscow escorted by Polish troops, was in turn murdered during an uprising instigated by the boyars, and then Prince Vasilii Shuiskii was chosen tsar in 1606. Vasilii's power soon proved to be illusory when a second usurper appeared and gained the support not only of all who were dissatisfied with the regime but also of the Polish troops and the Ukrainian Cossacks who came from Poland. Muscovy was now in a state of complete disorder, and the inconclusive battles for power degenerated into murder, rape, and pillage. In descriptions written later all this left behind the impression that an entire society had plunged into most extreme moral degeneracy.

Political disintegration seems to have been even more severe, since in many instances members of the most notable and influential families were parties to foul deeds. An attempt was made to procure a legitimate sovereign in 1610 when the Polish prince, Vladislav, who later became King Vladislav IV of Poland, was chosen tsar, but for religious reasons negotiations with him remained fruitless: he could not be convinced to convert to the Greek Orthodox Church. The intervention of the Poles in the West and the Swedes in the North, in Novgorod, was frustrated, however, by resistance mounted by forces which gradually became organized in northern Russia, in Nizhnii Novgorod. The *zemskii sobor,* an Assembly of the Land made up of representatives of various territories and social classes, did not succeed in choosing a tsar until 1613. Their choice fell on young Mikhail Romanov, whose family was related to Ivan the Terrible through Ivan's first wife. Mikhail ruled in conjunction with his father, Patriarch Filaret, and when Mikhail died in 1645, he was succeeded by his son Aleksei, who reigned until 1676. After the early death of Aleksei's son and successor Feodor in 1682, the crown passed to two powerless tsars—Ivan, who was sickly and incompetent, and Peter (Piotr), who was still a child. For a number of years their older sister Sofia ruled in their stead. During this time the gradual Europeanization of Russia, which will be treated below, was already beginning.

The restoration of the monarchy, however, did not bring with it complete domestic political tranquility. The seventeenth century was filled with popular movements and uprisings during which the insurgents sometimes took control of large areas of the country and to a great extent replaced the authorities in office, as, for example, in the rebellion led by the Don Cossack Stepan Razin between 1667 and 1672. Even the Muscovite masses rose up on occasion and were able to force their way into the presence of the tsar and present their demands to him. But despite all the threats and disturbances, the power of the tsar was undiminished and remained as unshakeably firm in the consciousness of the population as it had been when Herberstein and Olearius had observed it.

Even more important was the upheaval in religious life, for it led to a division in the Russian Church which was never overcome, the Russian schism *(raskol)* of 1666. Attempts to "improve" religious life undertaken by Tsar Aleksei in conjunction with Patriarch Nikon aroused in wide circles such resistance that these circles, themselves without adequate leadership, remained separated from the "official" Church for centuries. The Interregnum and the subsequent unrest are ideologically just as characteristic as the schism. We must attempt to understand the intellectual-historical side of these events.

112

During the relatively calm reigns of Tsar Feodor and Boris Godunov which followed the death of Tsar Ivan a strange pause occurred in the development of Russian literature. Not until around 1605-06 was a work written—the so-called *Inoe skazanie,* or *Other Story*—which was concerned with the historical events of the time,[18] and not until after the Interregnum did works appear which attempted to depict the period after 1584. Unfortunately, most of them are extremely subjective, and most were written by people who today would be termed "collaborators." One of these authors was a member of the inner circle of the first usurper, the False Demetrius; another was one of the supporters of the Polish candidate for the Muscovite throne; yet another collaborated with the Swedes. During the Interregnum Russian magnates, politicians, and writers, vacillating among the various hostile camps, exhibited an unparalleled opportunism and revealed the frightening inconsistency of their political views. Patriarch Filaret, who had great influence during the reign of his son, Mikhail Romanov, had become metropolitan under the first usurper. In the "robber's camp" of the second usurper, whose political dishonesty no one doubted, Filaret had risen to patriarch. And in the years following 1610 he came out strongly in favor of Vladislav as tsar.

Not all the writings of the time, it should be noted, were content to interpret the years of misfortune and disturbances—which are known in Russian history as the "Time of Troubles"—as "permitted by God." The events of those years were also considered to be "God's punishment," and punishment presumes guilt. But since people had long since ceased to expect justice from civil courts, they actually expected justice only from God. There are indeed interpretations which are characteristic of this view. One was that the country had incurred guilt when the dynastic principle was renounced and Boris Godunov was chosen tsar. The importance of the dynastic principle in the eyes of the Russian people is evident in the success enjoyed by "false tsareviches" and "false tsars"—besides the two Dimitriis there were several other false tsars, the last one toward the end of the eighteenth century. Pseudodynastic motives played no small role in the choice of the new dynasty, the Romanovs, even though that family, like Boris Godunov, was related only by marriage to the old tsarist family. On the other hand, people believed that Russia was "guilty" of exercising too much restraint in dealing with "the Latin and Armenian heresy" during the reign of Boris. To Russians of the time, Greek Orthodox members of the Polish state were just as much heretics as the Poles, whom the Russians often considered Lutherans! We even encounter the wonderful term "the Papist-Calvinist-Lutheran faith."

People thought it a particularly grievous wrongdoing that during the famine, bread for communion had been made of rye instead of wheat. In any case, a serious note was sounded which had been heard before in the saint's life devoted to Metropolitan Filipp: Russia was being punished for the "mad silence *(bezumnoe molchanie)* of the whole world." In the passage in question, only the silence during the reign of Boris Godunov is meant; that the people might say something to a "legitimate tsar" like Ivan the Terrible was beyond the powers of imagination of the author, a monk named Avraamii Palitsyn.

Attempts to Limit Absolutism

There were attempts to limit the power of the tsar. Whether these were serious is still not clear today. Even earlier certain institutions and norms did stand in the way of the power of the tsar, but it was never possible to organize them into a constitution. These institutions were the church councils and the *zemskii sobor,* an Assembly of the Land, which was a sort of parliament. It would not be far from the truth to term both bodies, which were convened at the wish of the tsar, no more than organs of tsarist power. Ivan the Terrible destroyed the influence of the princes, who were formerly hereditary rulers, and completely wiped out those families which seemed to him to be especially dangerous.

The ranking of the nobility according to service *(mestnichestvo)* was, in fact, more important, for it restricted the power of the tsar to dispose over his noble "servants" as he wished. The rank of the nobility was determined by services performed by members of the various noble families. If a member of Family A had formerly been the superior of a member of Family B, then no later member of Family A could be made the subordinate of (i.e. ranked below) any member of Family B. This ranking played a role of considerable importance in social life and led to interminable squabbling until the principle of *mestnichestvo* was abolished at the end of the seventeenth century. The ranking of the noble families, of course, prevented neither Ivan the Terrible nor Boris Godunov from persecuting members of high-ranking families and excluding them from political life by banishing them, executing them, or forcibly investing them as monks.

The events of these times indicate that the idea gradually began to dawn on both the hereditary and the service nobility that it was possible to limit the despotism of the tsar through constitutional means, but it never proved possible to organize the proposals into a regular constitution. The nobility merely attempted to obtain certain guarantees from the elective tsars. Tsar Vasilii, for example, was prevailed upon to promise not to persecute members of the nobility without investigation and court judgment, a promise which was in fact not binding on him. The nobility hoped to get more concessions from the Polish princes and proposed two contracts which were intended primarily to safeguard the Orthodox faith, but they also

114

demanded "judgment according to the law," specifically demanding that in judicial matters the tsar act "in conjunction with the boyars" and that innocent relatives of persons found guilty not be persecuted (the arrest of all members of a family was common practice during the reign of Tsar Ivan). They wished to retain the council of boyars *(boiarskaia duma)* and the Assembly of the Land *(zemskii sobor)* as permanent institutions, and they also wanted to be permitted to travel "in Christian states for purposes of study." They even emphasized the possibility of rising in rank "according to merit." The second contract proposal, which was formulated in 1610 after six months of deliberation, actually stressed only the guarantees for justice and was mainly intended to restrict the appointment of foreigners—primarily Poles—to government posts. The second contract made no mention at all of "merit" promotions or of authorization for travel in foreign countries.

Obviously certain demands were made of young Tsar Mikhail and were met by him. These demands are not documented, but to all appearances they did *not* go beyond demands for guarantees of justice.During Mikhail's reign the *zemskii sobor* was indeed active almost without interruption, but it was an old institution, and it had not had in the past, nor did it now receive any guaranteed rights. During the reign of Mikhail's son Aleksei, the *zemskii sobor* was convened only occasionally. It does appear, according to reports which are not completely reliable, that the *zemskii sobor* finally did confirm Aleksei's ascension to the throne, but this did not mean that a *new concept* of the powers of the tsar had arisen; that concept remained exactly as it had been in the days of Tsar Ivan.

Thus no new view of the power of the tsar is to be found, and the many disturbances and insurrections which occurred were directed not against the tsar but against the lords who were subordinate to the tsar. In the minds of the rebels the fault lay with the lords, not in the ill will of the tsar, and even the cruel punishments meted out to the rebels in no way affected the esteem in which the power of the tsar was held. These punishments were harsh enough. Reports of the time tell that after a revolt caused by inflation, which had resulted from the "devaluation" of the currency and the unlimited minting of copper coins, 7,000 people were executed and 15,000 had one hand chopped off and were sent into exile. But "the Tsar is merciful, his officials are the cause of it all" remained the view generally held by the Russian people down to the twentieth century.

Even though no new political *concept* arose at this time, political reality in Church and state did change appreciably, and it is these changes, insofar as they are important for the intellectual history of Russia, which must now be examined, even though the Russian of that time was not always aware of them.

The Individual and the State

In the seventeenth century the position of the individual in the Muscovite state underwent a change. At first this change found no adequate means of expression in the ideology of the time. Perhaps the new ideology was destined to develop only gradually, but the first signs of it in literary monuments are rather insignificant. In the second half of the seventeenth century several new ideological processes begin. By and large, as has been seen, the attitude toward the state remained the same: the state, represented by the person of the tsar, was everything–the individual nothing. The participation of Patriarch Filaret in the government of his son, Tsar Mikhail, and the special role which Patriarch Nikon played as a personal friend and confidant of Tsar Aleksei appeared to give rise to a new idea, namely that the power of the state,was dual in character, civil and ecclesiastical, but the fall of Nikon and the inactivity of his successor revealed that this synthesis of Church and state was illusory.

Social processes which reached their logical conclusion in the seventeenth century led Russia in another direction. Despotism, despite all the revolts and upheavals, became more firmly established. Various factors contributed to this. First of all, the old royal families and the upper nobility were still further weakened by the disturbances, and some even disappeared completely. Ivan the Terrible had systematically eliminated them, and during the Time of Troubles they destroyed each other. Some families became impoverished and withdrew from political life. The offspring of ruling royal families gradually lost contact with their ancestral lands, from which they were now physically separated, and they became completely dependent upon the favor of the tsar. This was particularly true of new families which were now close to the throne. During the reign of Peter the Great and his successors the hereditary upper nobility was dealt yet further blows.

The lower classes of the population, the serfs, underwent the most important change. The process of reducing free men to serfdom continued without surcease, and at the end of the seventeenth century all peasants were either serfs or in some other way dependents with no rights of their own. Although our idea of "the terrors of serfdom" may be exaggerated, the fears of Fedor Karpov proved to be true: the serfs became not only objectively mere "things subject to the law," they also subjectively ceased to realize that they could and must make decisions in political life. There were only two things the serfs could do to improve their position. They could flee, or they could rebel, mostly against the boyars and government officials and "in the interests of the tsar." They could flee to the "free territory" outside the borders of the state and there swell the ranks of the so-called "Cossack armies"; or, keeping their identity and class a secret, they could lead a vagabond life inside the borders of Russia. For now they considered their status as serfs to be "perpetual" and immutable. On the other hand,

116

owners of lands and serfs became convinced and inflexible supporters of the status quo, for their right to dispose over their serfs, the labor of their serfs, and even the private possessions of their serfs was not clearly delimited by law, and the status quo assured that the forced labor of the "subjects," who not infrequently were also called "slaves," would continue to form the basis of the existence of the masters. Therefore, the landowners could not be expected to generate a new political philosophy.

There was, of course, one thing which kept alive a sense of nationality, stunted as it was, and even intensified it out of proportion: adherence to the Greek Orthodox faith. The Church, which represented ultimate and "eternal" values and was closely linked to the state, thus became the foundation on which a primitive feeling of nationality developed. In this way the idea of "Holy Russia" re-emerged in somewhat altered form. This idea, to be sure, was somewhat shaken by the trials to which religious life was subjected at the end of the century.

The Schism

In the second half of the seventeenth century something happened which no one could have foreseen. "Holy Russia" was split, and from that point on there were two Russias, each of which claimed to be the real "Holy Russia." It was not easy to determine which side had more right to the title. This first division, which rent asunder the heart of Russia, was followed by others in the next decades and centuries. From that time on, the two parts of the Russian people were separated from each other by a chasm which was more unbridgeable than it might appear to the casual observer. From then on, schisms became a basic characteristic of Russian intellectual and spiritual life. A few decades after the first schism, another one occurred. Such schisms *per se* can enrich and revitalize the life of a people, but in Russia the differences of opinion remained irreconcilable because each party judged its point of view to be an absolute and was not prepared to engage in any conciliatory discussions with other parties. And besides, how could there have been discussion in a country where keeping silent had become the law and where people were forced to express their opinions in whispers and with certain reservations because they knew the tsar had absolute power of decision?

The sequence of events which led to the schism of the Church was simple, "linear," and so rapid as to be precipitous. The tragedy of the Russian Church resulted, paradoxically, from measures taken to cure the ills with which it was afflicted and from attempts at reform which by rights should have had no ill effects. The matters involved were the beauty or "decorum" *(blagochinie)* of the church service on the one hand and the revival of the ministry, i.e. the sermon, on the other. Tsar Aleksei, a man of religious and

117

aesthetic inclinations, had striven from the beginning to bring about this reform, and a small circle of clergymen who were sympathetic toward his efforts soon gathered around him. The first success was not long in coming. Sermons held in Moscow and in a number of smaller cities enjoyed extraordinary success among the faithful, even though some of the older clergy did consider the sermon an infernal innovation or an expression of "hypocrisy." Among those delivering sermons were several men who later became leaders of the opposition to the reforms, and of these, one man whose activities were most intimately connected with the schism of the church should be singled out: Archpriest Avvakum.

The Russian preachers were well-read dilettantes, for in Moscow there was no instruction in theology. It was therefore necessary to import theologians. The nearest source of theological knowledge was in the Ukraine, where, in conjunction with Poland-Lithuania, schools of theology already existed and strong ties with Greece were maintained. The Ukrainian clergy was also far more cosmopolitan than the Muscovite, and this led to the initial conflicts. Clergymen were brought from the Ukraine and were first of all supposed to devote themselves to translating. They soon noticed, however, basic differences between the ritual of the Great Russian and the Ukrainian Church and deviations in the texts of the Church books. They believed the Muscovite traditions to be "errors," and in most instances they were right, but they attributed too much importance to these "errors." The "improvements" which the Ukrainians wanted to make met with immediate resistance, and, as often happens, the resistance became stronger and more obdurate when the improvements were implemented energetically and radically.

Nikon (1605-1681), who was a friend of Tsar Aleksei and a northern Great Russian clergyman, soon became the moving spirit of the reform. He was close to the circle of reformers who had gathered about the Tsar, and in 1652 he became patriarch. Nikon was energetic but by no means better educated than those around him (for an understanding of what happened it is necessary to know that he knew no Greek); and he probably attacked the matter of reform with such energy simply because he had no idea of the problems involved and the effects the solutions would have. He became convinced that the ritual of the Russian Church must agree completely with that of the Greek Church. When the Tsar and Nikon first broached the matter, Paisos, the Patriarch of Constantinople, pointed out to them that only dogmatic differences are of real importance, that church ritual is the product of history, and that differences in ritual do not constitute heresy and should not be a reason for schisms in the Church. Other Greek prelates and Ukrainian scholars did not share this opinion, however, and Nikon was incapable of acting with moderation.

The struggle for Church reform began in 1653 when Nikon forbade worshippers in church to bow all the way down to the ground and prescribed the "new" sign of the cross, which was made with three fingers extended instead of two, as was the custom in Moscow. Those who clung to the old tradition, according to Avvakum, "felt their hearts grow cold and their legs tremble."

The problem of improving religious books proved to be a thornier one. Some Muscovite religious traditions, such as the way of making the sign of the cross, had been sanctioned by the Muscovite church councils of the sixteenth century, and those who refused to observe those traditions were threatened with severe punishment by the Church. As late as the seventeenth century books printed in the Ukraine and in White Russia were forbidden on the grounds that they were suspect or even "heretical." And now the improvements made by the Ukrainians were declared valid and admissible. Moreover, Greeks were involved in making the improvements, and the Greeks had been declared "defectors from the true faith" in the fourteenth century after the Florentine-Ferrara union with Rome, a union which, of course, had long since ceased to exist. In Russia, however, this had not yet been forgotten. Besides, the improvements were carried out harshly and without proper preparations. Instead of turning to the really old Greek texts of books used in church services, the reformers used mostly recent editions, some of which had even been published in "heretical countries," such as Venice. The Council of 1654 rashly decreed the reform of church ritual, and those who opposed the reform—and the extent of this opposition was not known—were punished severely, for example by banishment to Siberia. In his moving autobiography Avvakum later described his own Siberian exile.

Today adherents of both movements recognize that the changes were in themselves slight and in respect to dogma quite insignificant. The struggle over the changes lasted until the Church Council of 1666. From our vantage point it is easy to say that the schism occurred because those who clung to the old rites were uneducated, but it must be conceded that Nikon, Tsar Aleksei, and the relentless Greek and Ukrainian proponents of reform showed absolutely no understanding of the psychological importance of differences in ritual *(obriad)*, and the party from which flexibility was actually by rights to be expected was the party which was supported by the power of the state, the "stronger" party—in short, the reform party.

The reason for the inflexibility of both parties was the same: *the tradition of "ritualistic piety,"* which began in Moscow in the fifteenth century and became almost universal in the sixteenth. Each party considered members of the other not only "schismatics" *(raskol'niki)* but "heretics," "infidels," servants of the devil and the Antichrist. The opposition, which was devoid of power, struggled against the Church, which was supported by the all-powerful state; and the opposition struggled with enormous tenacity, with fanaticism, and with a degree of self-sacrifice which is almost unparalleled in the history of Russia. The state persecuted and punished the schismatics with merciless severity. The leaders had their tongues cut out, their hands chopped off, and were burned at the stake. Their "less dangerous" followers in the old faith were sent into exile or imprisoned. And in spite of this the "Old Church" retained millions of members down to the twentieth century. The number of "Old Believers" and members of other related sects has been put at twenty million. What is of major interest here, however, is the intellectual and spiritual basis of the Great Schism.

The Ideology of the Old Believers

The official explanation of the schism given in Church circles is that it was the result of "lack of education." Occasionally attempts have also been made to explain it psychologically, and although these explanations—such as that given by Kliuchevskii—are somewhat more accurate, basically they all lead to the same conclusion: the schism was a sort of "comedy of errors"—people fought about things which were of no real importance but which they considered important for certain psychological and historical reasons. Church historians only gradually began to realize that the reasons for the schism were inherent in the nature of piety as it was practiced at the time and that although people say that the schism was the result of ignorance and misunderstanding, both parties were in fact equally responsible.

Ritualistic piety, which has already been characterized, was the common ground shared by both the proponents of reform and the defenders of the "old faith"—the term "faith" is used, but actually "church ritual" would be more accurate. In their struggle both parties were seized by a certain "pathos of antiquarianism." An honest effort was made by the reformers to renew "primitive Christianity" and by the "Old Believers" to preserve it. "Thus it was established, and thus shall it remain for all eternity," was the way Avvakum put it. It should not be forgotten that restoration of the primitive Christian faith and primitive Christian life was also the desire of the Reformation and, in fact, of the Hussite "pre-Reformation" too.

The fate of the Russian reform and the opposition to it was determined by two things. First, both parties had in mind not genuine devoutness but solely church ritual, and for that reason they were in no case able to push forward to true primitive Christianity; they could not have done so even if they had actually determined where the old values were to be found. And second, the methodology and mode of thinking at the time were such that neither party could have caught a glimpse of genuine old values. In point of fact, the reformers were fighting for the *new* Greek tradition, or at least the late Byzantine one, while the Old Believers were fighting for the Muscovite ideology and the decrees of the sixteenth-century Muscovite Church councils. At that time it was no easy task to free oneself from the suggestive power of those decrees, and among them was one which forbade the use of three fingers in making the sign of the cross and the singing of "Halleluyah" three times. Both of these practices were now prescribed by the reformers, whereas in the sixteenth century they were considered a "breach of faith" and were condemned. Similarly, a sixteenth-century Russian council forbade men to shave, for that would be "an insult to the image of God in man," and barbers were denied a Christian burial.

Furthermore, there was a symbolic basis for almost every Muscovite custom and rite. To cite just one example, making the sign of the cross with two fingers was supposed to symbolize the twofold nature of Christ. The three fingers required by the reformers, on the other hand, were meant to symbolize the Trinity. In a word: while the efforts of both parties to renew or preserve "primitive Christian values" were doomed to failure from the start, they were nevertheless attempts to solve a problem of the first magnitude by insufficient means.

In the course of the struggle other motives moved into the foreground. In 1656 anathema was pronounced against the Russian way of making the sign of the cross, and the Council of 1667 handed down a decision on the whole complex of questions under discussion between the reformers and the Old Believers. All the decisions were in favor of the reformers and in favor of making the Russian Church conform completely to Greek Orthodoxy. Russian rite and Russian church ritual were declared wrong, erroneous, even heretical. The severe police measures taken against members of the "old faith" probably sufficed to make the weak members waver in their beliefs or to force them to conform to officially approved practices, but they did not convince anyone that he was wrong. And even at this time the Old Believers exhibited not only simple obdurateness but also healthy resistance against the "rape" of the congregation from above. It was recognized, and rightly so, that the entire reform had originated with the Tsar and the Patriarch and was being carried out by them. The resistance had about it something of the spirit which imbued the reform movement against the Papacy in the West. Paradoxically, in Russia the Old Believers were actual "reformers," for they did establish something new—against their own will, to be sure: the liberation of the Church from the tutelage and control of the state. They also brought about a situation in which only those people were members of the "true Church" (for them the old Church) who joined it because they decided of their own free will to do so. In the sort of piety it espoused, the "old Church," which had been declared illegal and had been deprived of the protection of the state, was in the tradition of Josif Volotskii, but it was, in its early days at least, as free as Nil Sorskii and his followers could have wished. It is quite significant that the works of the first generations of Old Believers, among others Avvakum, were, for all their narrow-minded fanaticism, by nature personal confessions; this was a refreshing novelty in Muscovite religious writing and again reminds one of the literature of the Reformation in the West.

There is one motif in the polemics of the Old Believers which can scarcely be considered a step in the right direction: the justification of the national uniqueness of Russian religious tradition. This was the tradition which was now judged, condemned, and damned by the reform. Without hesitation the "Nikonian church" appropriated the old saints of the Russian Church. The Old Believers were of the opinion that the old saints, whom they considered their religious ancestors, were more rightfully theirs. The Old Believers also considered the "Nikonian councils" to be councils made up of foreigners and as such not entitled to hand down decisions concerning the Russian Church. Of the thirty bishops present at the Council of 1667, fourteen were "foreigners." The Greeks were against the Russian tradition, and the Kievan scholars naturally shared their views. Even earlier Nikon had unnecessarily adopted Greek Church rites down to the last detail, including the mitre and robes of the bishops. He asserted that his "faith" was "Greek." All this caused bad blood, and the defense of the "old faith" became in many instances a *nationalistic* defense of old Russian traditions against modern Greek ones. Echoes of nationalism are not infrequently heard. Avvakum, who generally attempted to give theological reasons for his resistance to the innovations, did not hesitate to write the Tsar the following: "Sigh the way you used to . . . and say in Russian: 'God have mercy on me, a sinful mortal.' Leave off saying *Kyrie eleison*—that is what Greeks says. Spit on them. After all, you, Aleksei Mikhailovich, are a Russian, not a Greek. Speak your mother tongue *(prirodnyi yazyk)*, do not debase it, either in church or at home or in daily conversation. . . . God does not love us less than the Greeks. He gave us through Kirill and Methodius a language for our religious writings [Avvakum considered Church Slavic genuine Russian!]. What more do we want? The language of the angels perhaps?"

The decrees of the councils were indeed based on preliminary work done by a Greek, Dionysios, who had spent some time in Russia before the Council was convened. In his opinion, "the differences in ritual and the misleading new practices *(prelesti)*" which he had found in Russia had been effected "by some heretics who had left the Greeks and had not taken counsel with them." The Old Believers maintained that Dionysios had employed threats to make the foreign bishops accept the "Nikonian innovations": "The patriarchs only now came [to Russia] and knew nothing; they knew only what he [Dionysios] told them, and they believed him." He had "poisoned the minds of the patriarchs when he told them: 'Holy fathers, you are strangers here and if you judge on the basis of your own opinions you will receive no honors and presents from the Tsar and the government; you will be banished to a monastery the way Maxim of Athos [Maksim Grek] was, and they will not let you go home if you offer resistance. . . .' The patriarchs paid heed to his words and acted accordingly: they contested nothing, instead they approved everything." Thus the reform was not only considered the work of foreigners, it was even held to be fraudulent. Furthermore, this fraud had been perpetrated by the highest dignitaries of the Russian Church and the Russian state. For that reason it was necessary for the people to revise their attitude toward this state.

The Unchristian Realm

To understand why the crisis of the Church was at the same time a crisis of the state, it is necessary to bear in mind what role the Muscovite state played in the *Weltanschauung* of the Russian of that time. The Old Believers were forced to construct their *Weltanschauung* from the ground up, and the Apocalypse afforded the basis for the new concept of the state. If the one true Christian Church can exist only as a persecuted Church, then obviously the end of the world is near, and if the only Christian state, "the Third Rome," not only does not support the Church but instead persecutes and banishes it, then that state is un-Christian, indeed anti-Christian. Perhaps the Antichrist is about to appear; perhaps he already has appeared. Nikon was often held to be the Antichrist. At the Council of 1666 he was tried, found guilty, and deposed; he had gone too far in his claims to temporal power, had fallen out with Tsar Aleksei, and could not but fall from power. He was sent away to a monastery where he died a simple monk in 1681.

Even if Nikon was not the Antichrist, signs that the end of the world was at hand increased. The Old Believers interpreted the *Book of Faith (Kniga o vere)*, a compilation of Ukrainian works which was made in another age and which linked eschatological thoughts to the successes of the Union in the Ukraine around 1600, to mean that the world would come to an end in 1666. Eschatological expectations spread like a spiritual epidemic, especially in northern and northeastern Russia. Every night people expected to hear the horn of Gabriel call them to the Last Judgment. To be sure, people soon decided that the end of the world had been postponed, or else that the Antichrist was not going to appear in "body" but in "spirit." The fact that the Old Believers were persecuted and that in 1682 Avvakum and two of his followers were burned at the stake showed that there was no longer any hope that the old conditions, now felt to have been ideal, could be restored, nor any hope that the true Church and the true state could be reunited. And so the thoughts of the persecuted "schismatics" turned to the past, and a "utopia of the past" arose.

The Old Believers saw that "the sun of Orthodoxy had been extinguished." According to Avvakum, Christ in Russia was out of the question; instead of Him one saw "armies of devils" in control of the "Nikonian

Church" and the Muscovite state, the very Church and the very state in which heaven on earth had already become a reality. In the decades immediately following 1666, and indeed before that date, various types and groups of Old Believers developed. There were fanatics and ecstatics who were so firmly convinced that the kingdom of the Antichrist had already come that they no longer waited for the fire which would destroy the world but rushed to fiery deaths in advance of the end of the world. There were those who fled beyond the borders of the state or into the northern forests where it was difficult for the authorities to reach them. Finally there were those who chose passive resistance against the reforms and conducted their private lives in keeping with the old ways; to satisfy their religious needs they sought spiritual assistance from priests who had been ordained "before Nikon" and who had not accepted the reforms, and they read the old literature, sometimes in falsified recent copies or even in Ukrainian printings (which by rights Old Believers should have considered especially suspect). The self-immolations of some Old Believers is most significant of all. Avvakum had written the following to his flock: "God will bless you"; "one should be prepared to suffer martyrdom for the true way of making the sign of the cross"; "death suffered for one's faith is blessed; what is better than to stand together with the martyrs, the apostles and the saints in one rank?" And since man is "weak" and the temptation to follow the laws of the world of the Antichrist is so great, it is perhaps best to depart this life. The idea of burning oneself alive probably arose in connection with the idea of the conflagration which was supposed to destroy the world at the end of time. And "one suffers in fire for only a little while." "Are you afraid of the furnace? Do not be afraid. Fear occurs before one enters the furnace, but once one has entered all is forgotten." "When a person has burnt himself up then he has escaped everything." And so the flames in the "furnaces" of confession burned more and more brightly. Even among the Old Believers some soon appeared who opposed this practice, but to many self-destruction seemed easier than the eternal struggle against the powerful forces of the Antichristian world. Only later did there arise in the North the movement which resulted in an illegal, carefully planned organization, but this movement did not really begin to flourish until the eighteenth century. In the seventeenth century Old Believers engaged in passive resistance, mostly unorganized. They hid or fled from this world in the most literal sense of the word.

Soon, however, all these groups and types were faced with a difficult and insoluble problem, that of clerical succession. No bishop had joined the Old Believers, and therefore there was no one to ordain new priests. Thus the grace of the old belief could not fail to disappear from the circles of the Old Believers. The search for a new priesthood—or even the denial that the persecuted Church needed one—and the search for genuine Christian education remained the two tasks of the next century. Nor could a utopia which looked backward long prevail. The governments in power after the death of Tsar

Aleksei showed that there could be no "restoration" of the old theocratic state. The Old Believers suffered the fate which befell so many eschatological sects in Western Europe and in America. They did find a way to survive in this world, but they withdrew from society and lived as much as possible outside history, which was now "Antichristian," taking part in it only under duress. For Russian society and history were now deprived of divine grace, of the priesthood and therefore of the sacraments, and even of genuine tsarist rule!

One question remains to be considered: how did the rejection of millions of Old Believers affect Russian life? It was without doubt a damaging blow to the state organism. The Old Believers were those members of church congregations who took religious problems seriously, who were ardent believers in the Church, and who were not indifferent to the revolution which had taken place in the Church. People who were indifferent, "lukewarm," or even lacking in faith, if such there were at that time, stayed in the officially recognized Russian Church. From a sociological point of view, the Old Believers belonged to those segments of society from which public service and private contributions toward building up the nation could otherwise have been exptected: wealthy townsmen and merchants, but also well-to-do peasants of the North, i.e. approximately the same classes which joined in the Reformation in the West. As a result of the schism, however, precisely these classes were forced to withdraw from Russian public life, and upon their withdrawal the influence of conservative forces on the development of Russia was substantially weakened. Even more important, the Old Believers played no small role in the uprisings and insurrections of the following centuries. Old Believer circles also produced the fanatical sects which rejected the state and were even hostile to reality, and the absolutist government found it more difficult to keep peace with such sects than it did with the Old Believers. The Old Believers were the first Russian utopians, representatives of Russian "rootlessness," even though later specimens of this ideological type were in no way connected genetically with the proponents of the "old faith." From the very beginning, the Old Believer movement regarded as dangerous enemies not only members of the officially recognized Church but also proponents of Western culture.

The Beginnings of "Westernism" in the Seventeenth Century

In discussing the beginnings of Westernism one can speak of Western culture only in a limited sense, for if "culture" is defined as the creative development of values handed down from the past, then seventeenth-century Russia had no idea of Western culture.

From the fifteenth century on, foreign technicians—especially doctors, pharmacists, architects, and soldiers—are found in Russia. They had almost no contact with the population at large, but members of the upper classes do mention occasionally Western cultural advances and thus were probably familiar with them. Fedor Karpov knew Latin poetry and the works of Aristotle, presumably in Latin translation, and he had also heard of astrology.[19] Latin grammars were translated into Russian and served as ill-suited models for descriptions of the Slavic language. Maksim Grek reported on some aspects of the European renaissance, even though he rejected its "pagan" culture. Foreign architects built churches in Moscow, and Russian overseers assisted them and even took over some elements of their art. Most important of all, Russians learned from Europeans how to use firearms and even mined fortresses, as in Kazan in 1552, for example. However, all this amounted to no more than the adoption of the products of Western culture without any attempt to develop something new on the basis of those products. Perhaps it was even believed that creative work was impossible in Russia, but probably the Russians did not understand that without such creative work genuine assimilation of foreign advances is not possible. Even the adoption of foreign innovations did not always succeed. In the middle of the sixteenth century Ivan Fedorov founded the first printing shop in Moscow, but he succeeded in printing only one book, *Apostle,* before his workshop fell victim to the rage of the Muscovites, who considered him a "magician." He was forced to seek a more congenial climate in White Russia and later in the Ukraine.

The Time of Troubles brought Russia closer to Europe, albeit unwillingly. The presence of Polish troops or Ukrainian Cossacks outside the city gates of Moscow and of their Swedish allies in the North did at least permit Russians to see the peculiarities of Western life with their own eyes. Several Muscovite emissaries spent a long time in Poland, first as ambassadors and then as prisoners. No matter how little the Russians may have learned in the process or how little Polish or Swedish life may have appealed to them, these encounters assuredly contributed to the introduction into Moscow of new elements of Western culture after the Time of Troubles had passed, and some of these did have an effect. The first result was perhaps the use of verse in Russian poetry, due to the influence of Polish and Ukrainian lyric poetry. The earliest Russian verse was written immediately after the Time of Troubles.

Then a series of translations, mostly from Latin and Polish, began to appear, for the most part at the order of the crown, especially during the reign of Tsar Aleksei and his son, Tsar Feodor. The works to be translated were chosen at random and often ineptly, the translations were in many instances miserable, the good intention to have them printed was hardly ever carried out, and as in earlier times the translated works were "disseminated" in handwritten copies, often in only two, three, or four copies. This was, therefore, an attempt to appropriate only the finished products of Western culture. The translations remained accessible only to the family of

126

the tsar and to a few high-ranking dignitaries.

Only in the arts, particularly poetry, is some Western influence discernible. In the second half of the seventeenth century Muscovite Baroque poetry originated, primarily as a result of the influence of Simeon Polotskii, a White Russian clergyman who was educated in Kiev. Painters and sculptors likewise began to imitate Western models. The court theater built during the reign of Tsar Aleksei was the creation of a German (Pastor Gregory), a White Russian (S. Polotskii), and a Ukrainian (Chyzhynski).

Characteristically, the Old Believers paid almost no attention to Western influences, except in icon painting. They probably saw in these influences no great danger to the old Russian forms of life and even less danger to the old beliefs. On the other hand, from the beginning of the century on, isolated works appeared which reveal a profound dissatisfaction with Russian life. They usually do not touch on religious questions and contain only allusions to the superiority of the West. One of the authors of such works was Prince L. Khvorostinin, who immediately after the Time of Troubles wrote a scathing attack on the "falseness" of Russian life. In the second half of the century G. Kotoshikhin, a public official who had escaped to Sweden, wrote at the behest of the Swedish government a work in which he painted a depressing picture of Russian life, a work which is an important source for modern scholars. The most interesting observations of all, however, were made by Jurii Križanić, a Croatian Catholic priest who became acquainted not only with Muscovite life, but also with Siberian exile. Although from the point of view of a Westerner he engages in most pointed criticism of life in Russia, he does harbor Slavophile hopes for the further development of the nation.

Tsar Boris Godunov had tried sending young Russians to Europe to study, but of the twelve who went to the West for this purpose not a single one returned to Russia. In the second half of the century Ordyn-Nashchokin, the son of a high-ranking Muscovite dignitary, became infected with Westernism and fled to Europe; to be sure, he later returned home repentant. Even such people as these, however, can hardly be termed disciples of Western culture. Nevertheless, the fact that none of those whom Boris Godunov sent to the West returned can be interpreted as an acknowledgment of the superiority of Western culture. In the eighteenth and nineteenth centuries, as we shall see in Volume II, Russia's relationship to the West became of crucial importance.

1. For a list of English translations of this and other primary sources, cf. the bibliography appended to Volume II. [Editor's note].

2. A. Bruckner, for example, *A Literary History of Russia* (London, 1908).

3. Unfortunately we do not know why the third brother, Sviatoslav, who was murdered at the same time, was not accorded the same honor.

4. In Russian (and sometimes other) secondary literature we occasionally find the assertion that it is typical of the "Russian soul" that *pravda* means both "truth" and "justice"; unfortunately this is the case not only in Russian but in several other languages (primarily Indoeuropean ones). "Right" has somewhat the same meanings in English ("to be right" and "to have rights"), as does "veritas" in Latin (cf. the topos "truth in exile"—*veritas exsul*).

5. I refer the reader to my *History of Russian Literature* (The Hague, 1960), where a list of the literary monuments of the eleventh, twelfth, and thirteenth centuries will be found.

6. A "patericon" is a collection of didactic tales about pious men, usually monks or anchorites.

7. The empire of the "Golden Horde" should not be called "Mongolian." Among the troops which overran Eastern Europe in 1237 and during the following years there were certainly some Mongols, but it should be emphasized that the Tatars, with whom the Russians remained in contact for centuries, were *not* Mongols but Caucasians. The Russians did not come into contact with genuine Mongols until the sixteenth century when they encountered them on the lower Volga (as M. Vasmer has shown).

8. Among the Tatars there were Christians—mostly "heretics," to be sure; Mohammedanism did not become widespread among them until after the subjugation of Russia and did not affect their tolerant attitude toward Christians.

9. The khan of the Golden Horde was now called "emperor," as the ruler of Byzantium formerly had been; not until later was the khan occasionally referred to as the "false emperor."

10. The New Testament had been translated in the ninth century, but from the Old Testament translations had been made only of the Pentateuch, the books of Joshua, of Judges, and of Ruth, the Psalms, and the books of the prophets. The translations of these Old Testament books had been made from a Greek text, a fact which could have made the Judaizers doubt their accuracy; of course, the Judaizers also wanted to become familiar with those parts of the Old Testament which had not yet been translated into Russian.

11. Recent attempts to "justify" the actions of Tsar Ivan cannot disguise the fact that his reign of terror was immoral in character. We have detailed accounts not only by enemies of the Tsar but by two of his non-Russian collaborators. Some German scholars are now attempting to tone down even Ivan's well-deserved epithet—"the Terrible"—by referring to him as "Ivan the Severe" (in one Russian anecdote he is even called "Ivan the Good," an appellation which I personally would consider a valuable stimulus to those who wish to venerate Tsar Ivan). I have chosen to call him "Ivan the Terrible" because that is the name which has been traditionally given to him. Besides, it is to be hoped that his contemporaries judged him according to his moral qualities. In my own opinion, anyone who believes that the Russian people thought of *such* a tsar as no more than a *severe* ruler is depriving the Russian people of all claim to even the most elementary moral and human qualities.

12. Works of an unknown author who claimed to be Dionysios Areopagitica (cf. *Acta apost.* 17:34) but who in fact wrote after 500 A.D. and combined neoplatonic and Christian ideas in his writings.

13. Quoted from Giles Fletcher, *Of the Rus Commonwealth,* ed. A.F. Schmidt

(Ithaca, New York, 1966), pp. 122 and 124. [Editor's note.]

14. The most recent portrayal of the *Domostroi*-type can be found in a poem written by A. Blok in 1914, shortly after the outbreak of World War I:*"Greshit'besstydno, neprobudno . . ."*

15. Siegmund Freiherr von Herberstein (1486-1566), an Austrian diplomat who traveled through Europe on orders of the Emperor and wrote a famous report about Moscow.

16. Adam Ölschläger, Latinized as Olearius (1603-1671), a writer who gained fame as the author of *New Oriental Travels* (1647), a report of the results of two trade expeditions to Russia (1633-1635) in which he took part at the behest of Duke Friedrich III of Holstein-Gottorp; it is one of the most important sources for conditions in Russia at that time.

17. The old legend that the tsarevich was murdered at the command of Boris Godunov can now be considered refuted once and for all. It did form the basis of several literary works, among them works by Pushkin and Count A.K. Tolstoy.

18. During the period we find only a few insignificant works of literature, such as the biography of Feodor which is written in the style of the saints' lives.

19. One should bear in mind that the high point of interest in astrology in Europe was not the Middle Ages but the Renaissance.

CHRONOLOGICAL OVERVIEW

862	Summoning of the Varangian princes and founding of the Russian state according to the *Nestor Chronicle*
978-1015	Reign of Vladimir
988	The Christianization of Russia
1019-1054	Reign of Yaroslav the Wise
1113-1125	Reign of Vladimir Monomakh
Beginning of 12th century	The so-called *Nestor Chronicle* is finished
1185-1187	*The Lay of the Host of Igor*
12th century	The so-called *Kievan Chronicle* (a part of the *Hypatius Chronicle*)
13th century	*The so-called Galician-Volynian Chronicle* (a part of the *Hypatius Chronicle*)
1223 and 1237	Tatar invasions
1325-1341	Reign of Ivan I
1359-1389	Reign of Dimitrii Donskoi
1380	Victory of Dimitrii Donskoi over the Tatars led by Khan Mamai
1391	Death of St. Sergii of Radonezh
1462-1505	Reign of Grand Prince Ivan III
1480	Overthrow of the Tatars by Ivan III
1505-1533	Reign of Vasilii III
1508	Death of Nil Sorskii
1515	Death of Josif Volotskii
1533-1584	Reign of Grand Prince Ivan IV (Ivan the Terrible)
1542-1563	Makarii, Metropolitan of Moscow
1547	Coronation of Ivan IV as Tsar
1584-1598	Reign of Feodor I, last ruler of the Riurik dynasty
1598-1605	Reign of Boris Godunov
1605-1613	Interregnum (The Time of Troubles)
1613	Election of the new Romanov dynasty
1613-1645	Reign of Mikhail, first ruler of the Romanov dynasty
1645-1676	Reign of Aleksei
1652-1666	Nikon, Patriarch of Moscow
1666-1667	Schism in the Church
1676-1682	Reign of Feodor III
1681	Archpriest Avvakum burned at the stake
1682-1696	Reign of Ivan V, co-tsar
1682-1725	Reign of Peter I (Peter the Great)

Bogoliubovo. Church of the Intercession-on-the-Nerl, 1165.

Cap of Vladimir Monomakh. According to legend, Greek Emperor Mono-
machus invited Vladimir to share rule over the Greek Empire, sending him
his own royal cap as a symbol. Since Ivan III all of the Tsars were crowned
with it.

St. Sergei of Radonezh, from a 16th-century manuscript.

Bell Tower of Ivan the Great, the Kremlin, 1505-1508.

*An early map of Russia, made in the year 1562 by English merchant
Anthony Jenkinson.*

Maksim Grek, from a copy of a 16th-century icon.

Josif Volotskii, 17th-century drawing.

An oprichnik *engraved on a candlestick, with the symbols of these first secret police: the broomstick and the dog.*

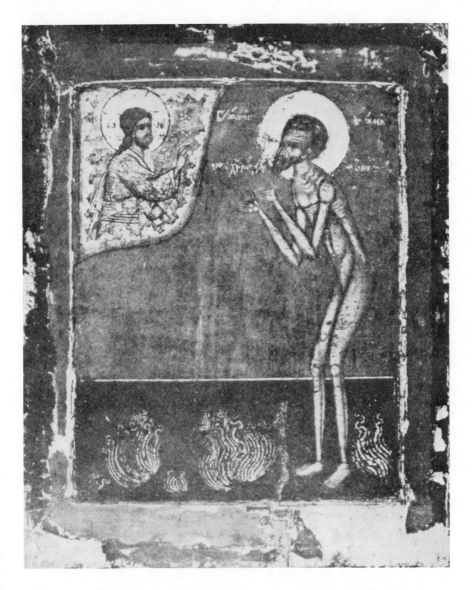

St. Vasilii Blazhenii (the Blessed), Fool in Christ. From a 16th-century icon.

Patriarch Nikon, whose reforms led to the schism.

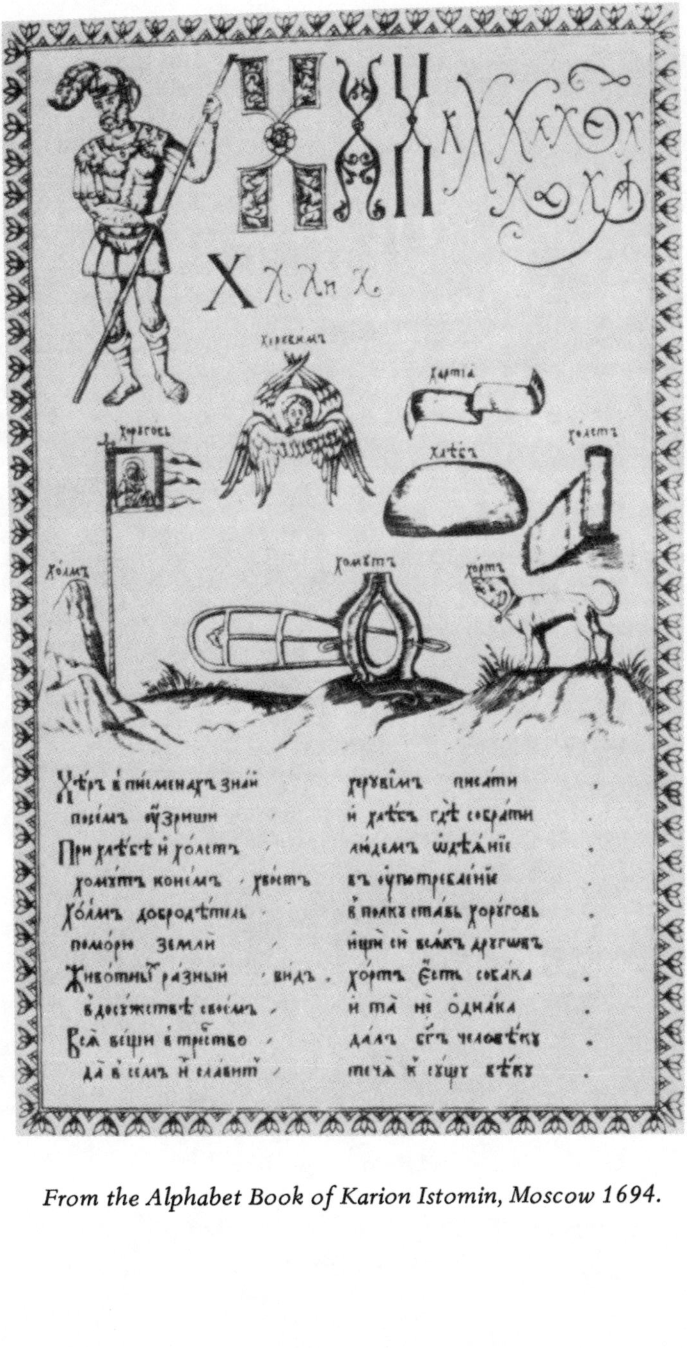

From the Alphabet Book of Karion Istomin, Moscow 1694.

Mikhailo Lomonosov

Alexander Radishchev

Nikolai Karamzin

Pushkin's drawing of Chaadaev on a manuscript page from Chapter IV of Eugene Onegin.

Ivan Kireevsky

Vissarion Belinsky

Alexander Herzen

The writers for the journal The Contemporary *(1856). Standing - Lev Tolstoy, D. Grigorovich. Seated - Ivan Goncharov, Ivan Turgenev, Alexander Druzhinin, Alexander Ostrovsky.*

Caricature from the 1860s over polemics between the nihilists and others on such questions as the "emancipation of women," "Communism," "Nihilism," "Progress," involving the journals The Contemporary *and* The Russian Word.

Fyodor Dostoevsky

БѢСЫ

РОМАНЪ.

Хоть убей, слѣда не видно,
Сбились мы, что дѣлать намъ?
Въ полѣ бѣсъ насъ водитъ видно
Да кружитъ по сторонамъ.
. . . .
Сколько ихъ, куда ихъ гонятъ,
Что такъ жалобно поютъ?
Домового ли хоронятъ,
Вѣдьму ль замужъ выдаютъ?

А. Пушкинъ.

Тутъ на горѣ паслось большое стадо свиней, и они просили Его чтобы позволилъ имъ войти въ нихъ. Онъ позволилъ имъ. Бѣсы, вышедши изъ человѣка, вошли въ свиней; и бросилось стадо съ крутизны въ озеро, и потонуло. Пастухи, увидя случившееся, побѣжали и разсказали въ городѣ и по деревнямъ. И вышли жители смотрѣть случившееся, и пришедши къ Іисусу, нашли человѣка изъ котораго вышли бѣсы сидящаго у ногъ Іисусовыхъ, одѣтаго и въ здравомъ умѣ; и ужаснулись. Видѣвшіе же разсказали имъ какъ исцѣлился бѣсновавшійся.

Евангеліе отъ Луки. Глава VIII, 32—37.

ЧАСТЬ ПЕРВАЯ.

ГЛАВА ПЕРВАЯ.

Вмѣсто введенія: нѣсколько подробностей изъ біографіи многочтимаго Степана Трофимовича Верховенскаго.

I.

Приступая къ описанію недавнихъ и столь странныхъ событій происшедшихъ въ нашемъ, доселѣ ничѣмъ не отличавшемся городѣ, я принужденъ, по неумѣнію моему, начать нѣ-

A page from Dostoevsky's manuscript of The Possessed.

Vladimir Solovyov

PART II: *RUSSIA BETWEEN EAST AND WEST, 1700-1905*

Peter the Great

INTRODUCTION

Fundamental Problems

The most important problem which faced Russian thought in the eighteenth and nineteenth centuries was the relationship of Russia to the West. Russia lies between East and West. To be sure, since the earth is round, every country lies between East and West and has relations with its eastern and western neighbors, but very special cultures lie to the east and west of Russia: the Occident and the Orient, the European West and the Asiatic East. In order to put these relations in proper perspective we shall briefly examine Russia's relations to East and West before the time of Peter the Great.

Russia and the East

During the course of the centuries the relations of the East Slavs to the East and the West were subject to many viscissitudes. The first contact with the West was with the "Varangians" (Scandinavians), but they could not be considered typical of Europe between the ninth and eleventh centuries. The relationship of the East Slavs to Byzantium, which fulfilled an important cultural mission for the East Slavs, was much closer: it brought the East Slavs the Eastern variant of Christianity. Relations with the European West and the Christian peoples of the Near East—the Georgians, the Armenians, the Syrians—were more modest and more incidental, and those with the "real" Orient were of no significance at all, consisting as they did of military confrontations. Some of the areas settled by the East Slavs did of course belong to the Khazar Empire, but that realm was destroyed in the tenth century. Struggles of the East Slavs against the Turko-Tataric Volga Bulgars and especially against the nomadic peoples (likewise Turko-Tataric) who dominated one after another the southern steppes continued until the thirteenth century. The East Slavs did entertain semi-cordial relations with the last of these nomadic peoples, the Polovtsy. There were even marriages between East Slavic noblemen and ladies of the Polovtsian nobility, and this is how it came about that some East Slavic princes were related to the Polovtsy by marriage—in *The Lay of the Host of Prince Igor* the Polovtsy are called "cousins" *(svaty);* but one can hardly speak of any cultural influence of these nomads on the East Slavs. To the north and northeast were situated the primitive Finno-Ugric peoples, who had no organized state, who without resistance permitted the Slavs to assimilate them, and from whom their

135

Slavic neighbors adopted certain "technical" customs of everyday life, in hunting and fishing, for example; but the Finno-Ugric influence on later generations of these assimilated peoples can be demonstrated at most in the area of folklore and skilled handicraft. For the East Slavs trade relationships with the Persians and the Arabians were doubtless of greater cultural significance than the contacts with their nearest neighbors, but even the impact of the intellectual culture of these distant peoples was by no means able to supplant the decisive influence of Byzantium.

Closer relations with the Orient did not begin until the middle of the thirteenth century after the invasions of the Tatars, who for over two centuries ruled over the Russian principalities. Even the contact with the Tatars, however, was only temporary, and one can scarcely ascribe to them any decisive intellectual influence, for they either laid waste to the land with their military forces or were represented in the larger Russian cities only by small groups of supervisors and tax collectors.

All the peoples whom we have mentioned thus far belonged to the Caucasian race. The Tatar dominion is erroneously termed the "Mongolian yoke" only because the Tatars were part of the large Asiatic empire which can be accurately described as Mongolian because its leaders were in fact Mongols. Actually, it is doubtful that there were many Mongols in the armies which invaded Eastern Europe.

There is no doubt, however, that the dominion of the Tatars to some extent ruptured Russia's connections with the West, and it certainly did limit them to a considerable degree, but there was no close contact between the Tatars and the Russians until the sixteenth century. Ivan the Terrible's victory over the two Tatar states of Khazan on the middle and Astrakhan on the lower Volga and the subsequent incorporation into Muscovy of other territories which had been settled mainly by Tatars actually resulted in a considerable increase in Tatar and therefore "Eastern" influence on Russia. The Russification of the Tatars proceeded only very slowly, and even in the twentieth century it has not been completed. Members of the Tatar nobility were taken into the Russian ruling class, a fact attested to by many family names of noble and royal Russian families. Whereas Simeon Bekbulatovich, who was named "tsar" by Ivan the Terrible in the latter's sinister game, was only a straw man, Boris Godunov, who was legally elected tsar in 1698, was from a noble Tatar family, although the family by that time, of course, had been completely Russified. Characteristically, Boris turned out to be the tsar who sought to expand relations with Western Europe.

In the sixteenth century the Russians encountered genuine Mongol nomadic tribes—the Buryates and the Kalmucks—who were then located on the lower Volga and in the western part of Central Asia, and they also became acquainted with the primitive peoples of Siberia. Here no cultural influence from either side was to be expected; besides, there were only few Russian settlers in these areas until the nineteenth century. It is interesting that the only Turko-Tataric people of Siberia, the Yakutes, were able to exert considerable influence on the Russian settlers, a fact which should be emphasized because it is a rare exception. Russia did not establish relations with China until the end of the sixteenth century.

It is important that we focus attention on two things: we must determine Russia's actual relations with the Orient and her "subjective" attitude toward the East, and we must assess the importance of the Orient for Russia in the past and in the future.

Oriental Influences on the Russian Language

In the course of time numerous words of Oriental origin have become part of the Russian language. In the twentieth century the linguist can without difficulty pick out from the vocabulary of spoken Russian numerous elements which are of Oriental origin. If we examine a list of these lexical items we notice immediately that they are almost exclusively words which designate objects—household items, articles of clothing, foodstuffs, etc. (for example, *sunduk*—"chest," *divan*—"couch," *khalat*—"housecoat," *chai*—"tea," *izium*—"raisins," *chesucha*— "raw silk"). Aside from such lexical items there are some words for the color of horses, the names of weapons, but only rarely do we find words for concepts related to social and economic life, such as *iamshchik*—"drayman," *tamozhnia*—"tax office," and *tolmach*—"interpreter." It should be noted that these words of Oriental origin, like the numerous words taken over from Byzantine and Western European languages, are not felt by native speakers of Russian to be foreign. Of course, words borrowed by Russian from other Indo-European languages, especially the numerous scientific and technical terms which were taken over from the West during the eighteenth and nineteenth centuries, are of far greater importance for Russian intellectual history.

The Russian Attitude toward the East

The question of the Russian subjective attitude toward the East is answered by the fact that the Russians, with the exception of a few isolated cases in the twentieth century, have never thought of themselves as Orientals. Of course, they had the notion that in India there was a Christian realm of the emperor-priest John, but this idea was also prevalent in the West. Some Russians also believed that somewhere in the East, Paradise, now forbidden to man, still existed, but this idea, like that of emperor-priest John's realm, amounted to no more than a vague longing for the ideal.

Many a work of literature from the Orient came into Russian literature, such as the old Indian animal fables, which appeared in Russian as parts of a didactic novel,[1] and a story about Buddha, which was likewise made into a novel; but these works, like many others, were transmitted to Russia via Greece in Christianized form. The life story of Buddha, for example, appeared in Russia in a novel entitled *Varlaam and Ioasaf;* in the West the same story was entitled *Barlaam and Josephat.* The Orient presented to the Russian reader in such works was an imaginary Christian Orient, or at least an Orient which behaved in Christian fashion.

By contrast, the Russians always thought of the real peoples of the Orient as "infidels," and the generally used Russian name for them, *basurman,* never had any positive connotations and was occasionally also applied to Westerners who were not Greek Orthodox.

The Russian—A Tatar?

How and why was it possible then that as late as the nineteenth century people in the West felt the "Europeanized" Russians to be "Tatars in European clothing" whose patina of European culture, as Napoleon asserted, could easily be scratched off to reveal the Tatar underneath it? This Western European view of the Russian was based in part on observations which were quite correct and in part on widespread but wholly incorrect notions. There was, for example, the Western conception of the Russian state and the Russian Church. To Western Europeans both institutions seemed to be based on the enslavement of the masses, on the absolute power of the authorities as embodied in the person of the tsar. This is how Hegel portrayed the despotic regimes of the old Orient, and this is how Herodotus, the father of historiography, had imagined the Persian monarchy to be. And this trait can in fact be observed in the general consciousness of Russians in the sixteenth and seventeenth centuries. The fact that Peter the Great's destruction of the old ways of life met with no real resistance did much to strengthen this conception of Russia and the Russians. Even in the time immediately before the Revolution of 1917 the notion of the blind allegiance of the Russian people to the tsar was still quite widespread.

Another trait regarded by Europeans as typical of the Tatars was the "lack of polish" in the Russian character, which manifested itself in crudity, in violent impetuousity, and in extreme immoderation. On his travels the Russian threw his money around like a prince, and in drinking he often went beyond all limits conceivable to Western Europeans. He was capable of losing thousands upon thousands at cards or at roulette. He could not travel without a large retinue, without which he was simply helpless, and if he brought his slave-servants along from Russia, he would frequently treat them in what can only be described as an inhuman fashion. To some extent, the Russian abroad in the nineteenth century reminds one of the Russian ambassadors to the West in the seventeenth; the Europeans, for the very same reasons, had regarded them as "Tatars." Of course, this judgment, arrived at on the basis of isolated examples, was wrong: Europeans saw only the wealthy Russian sybarite and overlooked the modest and industrious Russian student. The main thing which some Russians in foreign countries revealed was the way in which their character had been influenced by serfdom, which actually prevented the Russian landowner from learning to be frugal, industrious, and persistent.

Sometimes people in the West regarded the Russian revolutionaries who later emigrated to Europe as "Oriental" or almost "Oriental" in character, but there were other reasons for this view. The emigration of the revolutionaries, like every emigration, was inclined to indulge in internal quarrels which were not always settled by moral means, and the nature and significance of these quarrels often remained incomprehensible to foreigners and of course seemed senseless to them.

In any event, as time passed the term "Tatars" came to be applied less and less frequently to politically radical Russian emigres, and it seemed that the people in the West were about to relinquish the view of the Russians which had so long prevailed in favor of a different and more accurate assessment of them: of course the Russians were not "Tatars," Russians—even the wealthy and distinguished ones, and indeed often precisely these—were simply on a relatively lower level of culture, provided culture is equated not with clothing and externalia but with intellectual and moral stature.

"Oriental" Influences

If we wish to trace the ways in which "Tatar" influence crept into Russian life, we must think, as noted above, not of the "Tatar yoke" of the thirteenth and fourteenth centuries but of the development of Russian absolutism in the fifteenth, sixteenth, and part of the seventeenth. In a certain sense the Muscovite tsar considered himself the successor to the deposed Tatar khans. He was opposed by an independent, strong, and self-assured bourgeiosie only in a few cities like Novgorod and Pskov, and Ivan the Terrible destroyed the power of these cities for once and for all. The nobility's claims to independence were crushed at the same time, and for the most part hereditary nobility was supplanted by service nobility. The beginnings of class consciousness could not possibly further develop in the gloomy atmosphere of the sixteenth century. The warning voices of Ivan the Terrible's opponents as well as the unsolicited advice of his allies fell on deaf ears.

Tatar administrative practices had a strong influence on the structure of the Muscovite Empire. They were more rigid than those of the appanage principalities, which were growing ever more numerous and ever smaller. In the vast empire of the Golden Horde good organization of the tax-collecting system, of the entire administration of finances, and of the postal system was especially important, and we can scarcely inveigh against the influence of this organization on Russia.

In the past it was quite common to speak of the influence of the Tatars on Russian customs and usages, but we can identify only a few phenomena which in fact reflect such an influence. Formerly it was assumed that the life of women in old Russia, spent in the narow confines of the women's quarters, was one result of Tatar influence, but it should be pointed out that it was only the women of the *upper* classes who passed their lives in this manner and that such a life for a peasant woman would have been completely out of the question. The fact that the Russians adopted some Tatar foods, or became acquainted through the Tatars with various Oriental fabrics and articles of clothing, or followed Oriental models in breeding horses was of no significance for Russian intellectual and spiritual life. And so there remains only that most important characteristic of the old Russian *Weltanschauung*, the one which does in fact stem in part from the tatars: the idea of the absolute power of the tsar.

The old Russian idea that the power of the princes (later tsars) was subject to the laws of neither God nor man certainly does seem to be distinctly "Oriental." It was believed that this phenomenon could also be traced back to Byzantine influence, a contention which has been disputed, and not without good reason. Some have claimed to see in the marriage of Grand Prince Ivan III to a Byzantine princess in the fifteenth century the decisive turning point, but the notion that the power of the sovereign is absolute can scarcely be attributed to the changes in court etiquette and ceremony which occurred at that time. Here various forces were working in concert. The Tatar traditions surely played no small role. There was also the fact that the population of the appanage principalities ,conquered by Muscovy felt Muscovite rule and power to be absolute. And, finally, for a great part of the population it was of fundamental importance that Muscovite rulers functioned as representatives of the Christian state and in the fifteenth century gradually achieved independence from the Tatars. Moreover, these rulers themselves, strengthened in their views by literary works (usually of poor quality), also came to be aware of and proud of their absolute power.

Russia and the West

Not all the East Slavs had the same relationship with the West. There were still Catholic churches and monks in Kiev when the Tatars invaded; after the Tatars had destroyed the city, Irish monks returned home by way of Regensburg. As early as the thirteenth century German merchants and craftsmen were invited to come to Vladimir (Volynia). There were factories of the Hansa in Novgorod and Pskov, and in these cities foreigners had their own churches. Although non-Russians were legally prohibited from participating in the community life of these cities, the citizens at least had the opportunity to see foreigners and to realize that "Germans"—*nemets,* as all Western Europeans were called—were human beings just like the Slavs.[2] That intellectual relationships between foreigners and East Slavs were possible is demonstrated by the fact that some "Germans" converted to Greek Orthodoxy, and this point is in no way weakened by the fact that these Western Europeans, among them clergymen and even saints, may have been West Slavs. At the end of the fifteenth century, as we have seen, foreigners in Novgorod participated in the translation of the Bible.

In the sixteenth century European merchants found their way to Moscow—the English by way of the Arctic Ocean—and concluded trade agreements with the tsar. From that time on, Russian ambassadors were sent to foreign lands and foreign emissaries were received in Moscow. Whereas in Novgorod and Pskov the Hansa factories were situated within the city, in Moscow a so-called "German village" *(sloboda)* was established outside the city limits, and the Western Europeans lived there completely apart from the citizenry of Moscow. Foreign ambassadors did reside within the city limits, but they were strictly isolated from the local populace. This situation in no way changed when at the end of the sixteenth century the tsars hired and brought to Moscow foreign mercenaries under the command of foreign officers. All foreigners were considered "infidels," as were the Polish Catholic and even the Ukrainian Greek Orthodox troops who set up camp near Moscow during the Interregnum, at the beginning of the seventeenth century.

In the seventeenth century attempts were made to translate the popular scientific and even the belletristic literature of Western Europe. The translations were made by Poles and Ukrainians, but of all of the works rendered into Russian almost none were published. Around the middle of the century there appeared in Russia new advances of Western culture which were of no practical importance: illustrated books, copper etchings, musical instruments, and the like. At first they were considered curiosities, and the tsar and his family and secular and church dignitaries were the only ones who possessed them.

The Russian Assessment of Western Culture

The invitation extended to foreigners to come to Russia was also tantamount to the recognition of Western culture, but Russians regarded this culture as of exclusively practical value. When the products of Western technology were imported the producers of these products were sometimes invited to come along. Ivan the Terrible wanted to have European technicians teach their skills to the Russians, but he did not succeed in bringing a large enough number of such teachers to his land.

For a Muscovite of that time, every foreigner was a dangerous "infidel."

For a person who had grown up in the tradition of "ritual Christianity" the essence of religion consisted in those external forms which he took to be the substance of Christian doctrine, but foreigners—most of them Protestants, at that—had quite different churches, they did not worship icons, they crossed themselves differently or not at all, they did not fast, or they ate butter and eggs on fast days. Clearly people who behaved in such a manner were "heretical," non-Christian, or even "godless."

Russia, however, needed these godless people because they possessed technical ability, and for the Russians technology and the West were synonomous. Technology as it applied to military matters was something the Russians could learn, but in other important fields, such as medicine, they were unable to master Western technology because they lacked the necessary background.

At that time the Russians conceived of this Western technology which was so useful as something static, that is, they did not realize that technology develops and changes and that it therefore does not suffice merely to import a certain level of technological achievement. If a technology is taken over but its scientific basis is ignored, it is soon necessary to turn again to the foreign source from which the technology was first borrowed, and if technology is taken over but no attention is paid to the cultural matrix (the general education and training) from which it grew, then for the borrower this technology can be no more than an epiphenomenon of a foreign culture, and the borrower is doomed to remain forever a passive pupil. Peter the Great was the first to dimly perceive that the Russians would have to adopt the general cultural foundations which were the basis of the practical and useful knowledge of the West, but he by no means succeeded in achieving this goal.

For a long time the attitude of the Russians toward elements of culture and technology which they borrowed from the West remained unchanged: in everything which came from the "infidels" they detected some sort of threat to the fundamentals of Russian life and the Christian faith. Unless we keep this constant suspiciousness and caution in mind, we cannot understand many of the episodes in the history of Russia's later relationship with the West. How frequently this attitude is discernible in trifling things! In Russia it was necessary to produce not only beet sugar but also "fast sugar," because the Russian people considered sugar a foreign product—the Chinese made it and "sprayed it with snake oil." And the poet N. A. Nekrasov, who certainly cannot be accused of making fun of the common people, describes a conversation between peasant women at a fair in about 1865 in which there was talk of recent increases in illness and a ready answer as to why this was the case: people were wearing clothes made of French cotton, "and this French cotton (sitec) is dyed with dog's blood. Now do you understand why there is more illness nowadays?" When we become acquainted with some Russian opinions of foreign culture, even modern opinions, we get the feeling that the

142

Russians are still convinced that all culture which is not Russian is, metaphorically speaking, "dyed in dog's blood."

Plan and Organization

In this volume we shall examine Russia's confrontation with the West in the eighteenth and nineteenth centuries, a confrontation which is most closely linked to other main themes of Russian intellectual history and especially with questions concerning Russia's future. We cannot pursue all the lines of development; instead we shall limit ourselves to the five most important epochs of Russian spiritual and intellectual life: *the age of the reforms of Peter the Great* (1700-1725), which might be termed the *external Europeanization of Russia* (Chapter I); *the age of Catherine the Great* (1762-1796), in which Russia comes to grips with European intellectual life in a different way (Chapter II); the rise of independent Russian views of Russian culture and its relationship to the West (*Slavophiles and Westerners*— 1815-1850) (Chapter III); the rise and spread of *Russian political radicalism* between 1850 and 1880 (Chapter IV); and the *change in the Russian concept of culture* and the rise of "modern" intellectual and political Russia between 1890 and 1905 (Chapter V).

CHAPTER I. THE AGE OF PETER THE GREAT

Peter's Early Years

Peter the Great's near fantastic story, so like a romance, is quite well known. Peter–tsar, carpenter, and sailor–completely changed his Asiatic country. He "Europeanized" it. Out of nothing he created a "new Russia." We are interested here primarily in what is generally considered his main achievement, the "Europeanization" of Russia, and in its consequences for Russian intellectual history.

Peter was born in 1672, the fourteenth child of Tsar Aleksei. His father died in 1676 and was succeeded by Peter's oldest brother, Feodor, who died in 1682. Because Peter's somewhat older brother, Ivan, was sickly both in mind and body, Peter, a lad of ten, was proclaimed tsar–after a revolt by the old Russian guard, the *streltsy*. A short time later, however, the restless *streltsy* changed their minds, and Ivan was made tsar along with Peter. Their older sister, the energetic Sofia, became regent. She was supported in this by her favorite, Prince V. V. Golitsyn. Peter and his mother were sent into a sort of exile at a summer castle near Moscow. In this connection it is important that Peter's father (Tsar Aleksei), Feodor, one of Peter's maternal uncles, Sofia, and especially Golitsyn were all moderate members of the group which desired closer cultural ties with the West. Peter, who had enjoyed a rather old-fashioned schooling in Moscow, thus at least had the opportunity to see in his home various "curiosities" from the West.

In the country Peter grew up without the strictures of the royal ceremonial traditions of old Russia, and his interest in Western "curiosities" and in military affairs soon led him to establish contact with some foreigners from the "German village" who were able to teach him the fundamentals of mathematics and technology and to acquaint him with the Western European life of the "German village." At the age of sixteen Peter married and fathered a son, Aleksei, but paid little attention to his wife and later rejected her completely. He was less interested in family life than in his "military games," which he began to take more and more seriously, and in his acquaintanceship with the "Germans," who unfortunately inculcated in him a taste for crude pastimes and drinking bouts. In point of fact, almost none of the members of his circle of foreign acquaintances were people of any intellectual stature.

The *streltsy* rebelled again in 1689, this time with the intent to make Sofia the absolute monarch. The revolt was unsuccessful, and now Peter's mother was made the regent for the two young tsars. She turned the affairs of state over to the boyars, and Peter devoted himself to his former pastimes and to the "German village." His newly organized military forces and the fleet which had been built under his supervision did not remain inactive. Peter successfully tested their strength on the Turkish fortress of Azov on the lower Don. The conquest of Azov was the first indication of the goals of Peter's foreign policy, which aimed at opening up for Russia access to the oceanic trade routes, and these led to Europe.

Peter's Trip to Europe

In 1697 Peter did something which no one would have expected of a reigning prince, least of all a Russian tsar. He travelled incognito to Europe with an official Russian delegation. Two of the tasks of the delegation were to recruit European technicians to work in Russia and to study foreign military and naval establishments.

After visits to royal courts where his incognito was compromised and both his good and bad traits were equally admired, Peter went to Saardam in Holland and there had himself trained to be a "carpenter"—actually a boatbuilder—and acquired practical facility in all the techniques required of this profession, from the simplest to the most complex.

After visiting England and Vienna the Tsar was forced to break off his fifteen-month trip and hasten back to Moscow where the *streltsy* were again rebelling, with the idea of finally making Sofia the absolute monarch of Russia.

Peter's Life and Career in Russia

By the time Peter arrived in Moscow the revolt had already been put down, and there was nothing left for him to do but to punish the rebels. This he did with unparalleled cruelty, acting as both judge and executioner. His cruelty awakened memories of the time of Ivan the Terrible, whose exploits had already become legendary, but there was something else which frightened Muscovite society even more.

After his return Peter did none of the things which were expected of a "Christian sovereign." He neither went to church, nor did he order that divine services of thanks be held. Paying a visit to the "German village" was more important for him. Moreover, at his first court reception he cut off some of the boyars' long beards with his own hands and made them shorten their long court clothes. Soon afterwards official orders followed which prescribed that Peter's subjects should "look like Europeans" and forbade them, under pain of severe punishment, to wear beards or to sell "Russian garb." The Tsar surrounded himself with foreigners. He smoked and drank and demanded that all at his court do likewise. People were probably less shocked by the fact that the Tsar engaged in manual labor than they were by his other pastimes, which he all too often was wont to pursue outside the walls of the palace. Even before his trip to Europe Peter had led a dissolute life, but now people's hair stood on end at the sight of some of Peter's ways of amusing himself, particularly at the activities of the "All Fools' Synod," which he had founded. The members of this group bore titles borrowed from the Church hierarchy, and their meetings, which were often public, were blasphemous parodies of the divine service.

In 1721 the marriage of "the Pope" of the "Synod," one of the most extreme travesties on Christian feasts, was held in a church. Since Peter was actually pious in a certain sense, even if he did insist that he could see no difference between Greek Orthodoxy and Protestantism, the psychological reason behind this public affront to the religious sensibility of his subjects can be understood only if we assume that Peter had the traditional Russian view that the power of the tsar was unlimited.

Other aspects of the Tsar's personal conduct were also scandalous. For no apparent reason he abandoned his wife and then lived with a servant girl who had been taken prisoner in the Baltic and who had formerly been the mistress of his friend Menshikov. He later married this girl and even had her crowned empress; she also became his successor to the throne. His "disrespectful" son, Crown Prince Aleksei, died while under investigation; he probably died as the result of torture or was simply murdered.

In 1703 the Tsar left Moscow and founded a new capital city in a swampy area along the Finnish gulf: St. Petersburg. Peter also developed a comprehensive domestic and foreign policy which in part changed the shape of Russia and in part merely threw it into upheaval without achieving any lasting results.

Wars and Reforms

Since we are not concerned with political history, we are able to do no more than touch on Peter's foreign policy in general terms. His prolonged war with the then powerful Swedes and their talented general, King Carl XII, at first met with some frightening failures but eventually led to a decisive victory in 1709 at Poltava. The war nevertheless dragged on, and Peter was not able to conclude a peace treaty with the Swedes until 1721. He had gained access to the sea in the north. His war in the south, against Turkey, met with less success.

The wars forced Peter to institute reforms. He may have planned to undertake them anyway, but they became a matter of dire necessity if he was to be able to finance the wars. Some of his measures were later amended in many respects, and some of them were rescinded, but almost always they were carried out precipitously and never pursued to conclusion. Details about

146

Peter's internal reforms cannot be given here. They concerned administration, finance, the Church, and the armed forces. Kliuchevsky's assertion that Peter "acted first and then thought things over" is perhaps no more than a *bon mot,* but it seems to be confirmed by the absence of any planning and the signs of great haste which characterize many of Peter's measures. Almost all of them were in response to the exigencies of the moment.

Only one thing is of importance: Peter built, reorganized, and equipped a great army; he created a fleet which was not without its imperfections; and the victories which he won assured Russia a position of respect among the countries of Europe. In reorganizing the administration of the country Peter introduced the principle of collective leadership. It is characteristic that he took particular pains to change the names of administrative positions and the titles of those who held them: he "Europeanized" the language of officialdom. He was particularly concerned with financial problems, and he resorted to numerous measures, some of them only temporary and promulgated by force. Besides the head tax he introduced various lesser taxes; for example, he taxed markets and public baths. He also decreed that various products were state monopolies—for example, honey, potash, tobacco, tar, cod liver oil, and even oak coffins. He also had some plans for taxation which did not succeed or proved impossible to promulgate.

These unbearable burdens and the unbelievable waste of human life, not only in the wars but also in the construction of St. Petersburg and of canals, determined in large measure his subjects' opinion of him.

The Church

Peter saw in Church circles the enemies of his innovations. Patriarch Yoakim, a confirmed adherent to the old values and an opponent of foreigners, died in 1690. When his insignificant successor, Adrian, died in 1701, Peter chose not to have a successor elected but to appoint a Ukrainian bishop, Stefan Yavorskii, "temporary holder of the patriarchal throne." Meanwhile Peter appointed Ukrainian churchmen to various ecclesiastical posts. Because of their Western education and their readiness to accept Western culture, the Ukrainians seemed more acceptable to Peter than the Great Russians, who clung to the old Russian tradition. In choosing these candidates Peter did in fact sometimes make mistakes. Not even Yavorskii accepted all Peter's innovations without a murmur. Metropolitan Dimitrii Tuptalo of Rostov, who was the most important of these Ukrainian appointees and who was later canonized, likewise expressed grave doubts about the way things were going. Peter did find a faithful co-worker, however, in Feofan Prokopovich, who was also Ukrainian and was strongly influenced by Protestantism.

When Yavorskii died in 1721 the patriarchate was abolished. It was supplanted by a collegium, the "Holy Synod," which had besides bishops a secular representative—later called the "Over Procurator"—on whom the Synod's decisions in large measure depended. This was the most severe blow which had ever been dealt the Russian Church by the secular authorities.

The commentaries on the Synod's statutes were written by Prokopovich in a tone which was polemical and in many instances offensive to the clergy, and this and other measures were of no less importance. The Tsar was visibly striving to secularize the Church completely. The state had no need of monks; Peter believed that they stirred up unrest among the people. His plan was to re-educate them gradually and train them for "more practical" work, such as caring for the sick. What the monks wrote had to be submitted for inspection. With a radicalism which is typical of Russian legislative action, monks were even forbidden to have paper and ink in their cells. Even the secrecy of the confessional was abolished insofar as the interests of the state were concerned. Peter regarded the Synod as an instrument of political power. This is the impression which is given by the oath sworn by members of the Synod, who were to recognize the tsar as the "highest judge of this clerical collegium."

As a result of such measures and of the above-mentioned official commentaries on the statutes of the Synod, the clergy was reduced to the level of state officials, not merely *sui generis* but socially and politically as well. The reason for abolishing the patriarchate had been expressed clearly: "The state does not expect from a collegial administrative body the revolts and troubles which can come from a single spiritual leader." In the police state, which Peter considered the ideal one, the Church could not remain outside the state system.

The Police State

In Russia the ideological sources of the police state surely antedated the Petrine reforms. Even before they were put into effect, the Church led only an apparently independent existence. The state, in the person of the tsar, comprised all areas of life, and only the very restricted sphere of private affairs was not subject to its control. Now the state also assumed responsibility for the intellectual and spiritual life of the people. Tsar Peter was too energetic, too capricious and too cautious to leave anything in Russia not subject to the inspection and the control of the state. Every aspect of the life of his subjects was intended to serve the state and could be guided by the state alone. All of this, to be sure, was for "the general welfare of Russia," but the state did not permit its subjects to ponder about what constituted this "general welfare."

It was therefore no accident that Peter's reforms concerned such external things as beards, clothing, and social life. Deviation from the old Russian customs was not only permitted, it was prescribed; and most important of all, old customs and values were expressly prohibited. Peter required his subjects to participate in balls *(assambleia)*, where they were *forced* to dance, smoke, and even drink vodka.

The character of this police state was expressed unequivocally in 1711 when inspectors *(fiskal)* were introduced. They were supposed to conduct *secret* inspections of law courts, government offices, and finances and then report their findings. The inspector received half the fine imposed on those found guilty. This inspection system, in which false reports by inspectors went unpunished, became more and more extensive. There were even plans to have "spiritual inspectors," and the Holy Synod installed some who were at first even called "inquisitors"; monks were to be used in these positions. We should note that this system of inspection had nothing at all in common with the normal system, in which higher offices had the right to supervise and inspect those subordinate to them; it was instead a sort of "internal espionage organization" which was above the official administrative unit.

Since that time the police state has been more or less consistently maintained in Russia. Life in an ideally organized and flawlessly operating police state is unbearable; it may even be "biologically" impossible. The severity of the burdens imposed upon the individual in a police state is therefore eased by various factors. The most important of these is the fact that government officials are inefficient and can be bribed. Characteristically, almost all inside observers maintained repeatedly that Peter's reforms led to an increase in the corruptibility of government officials. It is possible that various causes were at work here; for example, now the new governmental officials came from all rungs of the administrative ladder, and unlike the old families they were poor and "hungry," so to speak. But the proverbial susceptibility of Russian officialdom and particularly of the police to bribery and corruption is inherent in the police state.

"Europeanization" of Life?

We must not forget that the purely external "Europeanization" of life affected only a thin upper layer of the Russian population. Forcing the officers' corps and government officialdom, in fact the entire nobility, to shave off their beards and wear European clothing—actions carried out with a ruthlessness, crudeness, and disregard for human dignity which is characteristic of Peter—also made a strong, probably even overpowering impression on those social classes which were not affected by this reform. The impression made by the unhindered social intercourse of the Russian upper class with foreigners, i.e. with "infidels," was just as strong.

The goals which the Tsar set for himself and achieved through this external "Europeanization" are important. He had noticed—and he was probably right—that for Russians of that time "external things" were of prime importance. External things were not merely symptoms of what lay beneath them; exterior and interior were in large measure felt to be identical. And to Peter this exterior was surely not very important. Rather, by changing the exterior he wanted to change what was inside Russian humanity. He was not completely wrong in looking at the matter this way. Even though this "Europeanization" was only superficial, it nevertheless gave Russians a psychological shock, debased them, and "softened them up" so that like wax they could be easily molded into new forms. Peter, a captive of the tradition of Russian absolutism and of his consciousness of his own absolute power, failed to recognize that as a result a lack of character was developing which could be of little or no use in establishing new values and traditions.

Even though this external "Europeanization" was only apparent, Peter took a step toward "inner Europeanization" which his predecessors had never considered. Whereas in earlier times it had been thought sufficient to import finished products from the West, or at least have them made in Russia by foreigners, Peter wanted the Russians themselves to learn to make these products. He was no longer satisfied to import to Russia the products of Western technology; he wanted to import the technology itself. The technologists were now to be Russians. Peter had probably already realized that technology is based on certain scientific achievements. Either Peter did not understand that this scientific basis is of greater importance than finished technology and that for this reason schools are more important than factories, or else in the haste of waging his wars he simply could not wait so long—setting up technological production takes less time than training a new generation which can further develop the new culture, even if that new culture be one of technology. And so it happened that the schools were the most unsuccessful of all of Peter's innovations.

Education and the Educational System

Peter never understood that culture is an entity and that one cannot appropriate whatever individual parts of a culture one deems best; he wanted to mold his co-workers—and that included all his civil servants and indeed all his subjects—in his own "image and likeness." This meant that they were to adopt "European" customs (i.e. what the Tsar thought were European customs) and European technological knowledge, particularly in the fields of navigation and marine construction—precisely the fields in which Peter himself had rather accidentally become interested. Peter, and we must keep this in mind, "needed Europe for only a few decades; then it could be ignored," as he himself once remarked. This is why Peter, as a matter of precaution, always put foreigners in subordinate positions while reserving the top positions for Russians; but since the Russians were mostly incompetent, the Tsar was obliged to give foreigners the top positions after all. In his later years Peter did occasionally refuse to import foreigners and ordered his officials "to look for Russians for the jobs." Such Russians were not to be found, however, for they first had to be trained. Peter underestimated the difficulties which he faced. He thought he could simply "import" culture (in the narrow sense in which he understood the term), just as his father had imported various "curiosities." That was a mistake!

At first he sent young people to Europe and had them trained there, mostly in navigation and shipbuilding. These people were there, however, without sufficient guidance, without supervision, primarily because they had been forced to go. Frequently the first thing with which they became acquainted was European pleasure spots, often of the basest sort. Some of them became acquainted with the fashions and customs of more distinguished society. Sometime they even studied the subjects they had been assigned to learn. When they returned home they were at best merely trained naval officers and marine engineers, but then they were often assigned to work in other areas. If they were close to the court of the Tsar they had to adapt themselves to the manners of taverns frequented by soldiers and sailors; if they went out into the country, then after a few years nothing was left of the European education. Often they even let their beards grow and led a life which could hardly be distinguished from that of their parents and grandparents.

It was not possible, however, to send all young Russians to foreign countries to study. The Russian schools which had existed as early as the end of the seventeenth century were drected by Ukrainians and Greeks and provided a general education despite their predominate "clerical" character, but they did not satisfy Peter's practical needs. He therefore established technical schools, again primarily for training maritime technicians. The problem of teachers was at first solved by appointing a Scot (in 1701) to establish a professional school "of mathematics and the science of navigation." A few students enrolled voluntarily, but it was also necessary to recruit students by force. In 1716 a dozen schools were founded in provincial cities, and the students of the school for navigation were sent to them as teachers. Knowledge of "geometry and geography" were the main requirements. The twelve schools were called "mathematicals" *(tsifirnyi)*. By 1722 there were 42 schools with a total enrollment of nearly 2,000. Almost half the students were the children of churchmen; the burghers soon managed to have their children exempted from required education (on the grounds that they ought to learn a trade or business). By the end of Peter's reign 46 more parochial schools had been established with an enrollment of almost 3,000. Children of the nobility were of course required to attend school, but most of them continued to be educated outside Russia.

All the schools, however, suffered from an abrupt decrease in enrollment, and gradually a whole series or them were obliged to close. At the end
of Peter's reign only 28 of the 42 "mathematical" schools were still in opera-
tion, and by 1744 only eight. The parochial schools fared better, even though
many of their pupils did no more than learn to read and write.[3] This does
not mean, of course, that the country was populated with analphabets, for
many people were taught to read and write by the clergyman in the nearest
village with a church.

The parochial schools also developed a network of other schools, but
we really know only very little about them. For example, from 1706 on,
fifteen lower schools were established by the episcopal school of Novgorod.
Since in Moscow and especially in Kiev the "parochial academies," which
had various names at that time and were similar to colleges, were devoted
to general education and particularly to the study of Latin, they could have
been institutions of higher general education. This is the case especially with
the Kievan Academy, which at that time drew more than two-thirds of its
students from the laity. If this and other "parochial academies" did not function as centers of higher learning, then it was partly because Peter regarded
with a certain mistrust anything of a religious nature, but also partly because
the highly developed class consciousness prevalent in old Russia in many
instances prevented members of the nobility from attending parochial
schools. Until the early nineteenth century, however, the parochial colleges
furnished students to the universities and other colleges which were founded
later, and as a result two educated classes developed in Russia. The one consisted of those who came from the clergy, attended parochial schools, and
often became professors, journalists, and even leading civil officials. The other
was made up of members of the nobility, who after the crisis and the decline
of the maritime schools learned first and foremost good manners *(polites)*
and less often acquired a certain amount of general education from foreign
tutors at home or abroad. This second class nevertheless occasionally remained uneducated.

Members of these two classes frequently could not understand each
other or despised and even detested each other until they were later united,
at least partially, in the so-called intelligentsia *(intelligentsiia),* a new class
which was of importance for Russian intellectual history and which will
be treated below.

Sources of Intellectual History

The Petrine era offers few good sources which can acquaint us with
the spiritual and intellectual life of the period, and the most important ones
remained inaccessible to the reader of that age. There are the writings of
Antiokh Kantemir (1708-1744), a gifted poet of Rumanian extraction who

portrayed, particularly in his satires, various human types; of course, in sketching these types he for the most part followed not Russian models but Western European literary traditions. There are also works of Ivan Pososhkov (1652-1726), a farmer and merchant who on the basis of his practical experience gave his opinions of Peter's reforms (by and large he approved of them).[4] There are also the writings of V. Tatishchev (1686-1750), a nobleman who was a proponent of the reforms. And finally there are the reminiscences of a few contemporaries. None of these works were published until later. Kantemir's satires did not appear in print until 1762, and some of the other works were not published until the nineteenth century.

While we cannot examine in detail the sources which we are using here, we should note that they give the impression that the Russian population was divided into several groups, each of which judged its age differently and diverged from the other groups even more radically in its views of what was to come. Several of these groups deserve our consideration. First of all there are the convinced opponents of the reform, among them the "Old Believers," who form a group unto themselves. Among the supporters of the reforms we can differentiate those who represented "secular life" and those who were proponents of "evangelical life." By and large, this classification of the people of the time follows the one arrived at by Pososhkov.

Opponents of the Reform

A good deal can be learned about the opponents of the reforms from the political trials of the time. One striking fact is that the opponents of the reform belonged to various social classes and that the trials for the most part concerned the spreading of various rumors about Tsar Peter. It was believed, for example, that the Tsar, who immediately upon his return from traveling abroad had promulgated such shocking and objectionable changes in Russian life, was not the genuine successor to the throne and the son of pious Tsar Aleksei at all. There were various versions of the rumors which were spread about this. According to one, the Tsar had been exchanged for another child immediately after birth. According to another, he had disappeared abroad and "another person" had returned to Russia in his place. According to yet another, he was supposed to have been fried in a frying pan in Stockholm by the "Swedish queen" or thrown into a barrel into which sharp nails had been hammered, and the barrel had then been thrown into the sea. Instead of him, a "German" had been sent back to Russia. Even Peter's wife and the mother of the unfortunate successor to the throne, Aleksei, is said to have maintained that Tsar Peter was "not *her* tsar."

It was really not difficult to find proof for these allegations. Peter simply did not correspond to the ideal tsar as the people imagined him.

153

He imposed on the people unbearable burdens and by inducting soldiers into the army made "women into widows and children into orphans." He had "gobbled up the entire world." He executed the *streltsy* in a cruel fashion; he divorced his wife; he incarcerated one of his sisters in a nunnery; he consorted only with foreigners and refused to recognize the Orthodox Church; he had church bells melted down and turned into cannon. "He is simply a German; perhaps the son of Lefort" (a foreign friend of Peter). In other words, Peter was a "usurper," a type which the Russian people had known several times during the seventeenth century. "Perhaps," it was whispered, "the true tsar had been rescued even after his Stockholm adventure and was merely hiding somewhere." And so the people expected that after the death of the "usurper" the true tsar would reappear.

The other view was even more radical: Peter was the Antichrist! An old Ukrainian pamphlet which was directed against Rome was interpreted to mean that the Antichrist would appear "in the name of Peter." This indeed fitted the name of the Tsar. There was even talk of several Antichrists who were to follow one another. Peter, it was thought, was merely one of them, perhaps a forerunner of the last and "genuine" Antichrist. Peter showed himself to be the Antichrist not only by melting down the church bells but also by destroying the old customs. He also had people branded with the "seal of the Antichrist." This is the way people looked on the branding of recruits with a mark of identification; the stamps on passports and on other papers were also thought to be nothing more than "signs of the Antichrist." In the bargain, Peter publicly ridiculed religious customs with his "All Fools' Synod." Moreover, he established "mathematical schools and academies condemned by God," and he had astrological calendars printed. The question of the calendars was more serious than one might assume. According to the old reckoning of time (from the beginning of the world), the new century was to begin in the year 7400 (1692); in the new calendar, however, the new century began in the year 1700. The result was that "the Tsar had stolen eight years from God." Moreover, the new year did not begin on September 1, as did the Church year, but on January 1. There were rumors of yet other imminent decrees, decrees which to be sure were never promulgated. For example, the Great Festival of the Fast was supposed to be "reduced by one week," and later fasting on Wednesdays and Fridays was to be abolished.

There was also the fact that Peter's birth had not been a blessed one. He was the son of widowed Tsar Aleksei's *second* wife, and that "was indeed already a sinful origin." The tsar's mother was reputed to be a heretic because "she bore only girls." It was well known that Peter suffered from a facial tic, and in this people saw a sign that he was possessed by the evil spirit. And finally, or so it was maintained, his imperial title of "Emperor" (Russian *imperator*) was the clearest sign that he was the Antichrist, because the word *"imperator,"* which should really be *"iperator"* (the "m" was merely introduced in order to lead people astray) was in fact the "number of the Antichrist," 666, when the numerical value of the Church Slavic letters of the word was calculated.

Many of Peter's enemies were arrested, tried, and condemned, but the legends about the tsar-usurper and the tsar-Antichrist lived on, particularly among the Old Believers, who lived in constant expectation of the end of the world.

The "Old Believers"

Tsar Peter surely cared little about the religious views of the Old Believers, but in his eyes the Old Believers themselves were adherents of "old Russia." Moreover, as a result of their persecution under earlier tsars they had become an anti-government force which offered perhaps the most dangerous sort of resistance to the state, passive resistance. And it was among the Old Believers that the view of Peter as the Antichrist was most widespread. One of the several eschatological prophecies set 1699 as the year in which the Antichrist would appear; and then, it was asserted, the end of the world was to be expected in the near future. Once again the northern forests were lit by the flames of the self-immolators who hoped to escape the power of the Antichrist by burning themselves to death. In this way these people also escaped the obligations which Peter wished to impose on all his subjects, and thus their very deaths were in fact acts of treason. This was why the Old Believers were persecuted during Peter's reign. To be sure, the measures which Peter took against them were less severe than those employed by his predecessors. He was satisfied with making the Old Believers a source of additional revenue for the state, and the increased taxes which he levied on them demonstrated to the followers of the "true faith" that the Antichristian world did not intend to eliminate them by direct action.

As a result, the Old Believers gradually regained their composure to some extent and adapted themselves better to the "hostile world." They were faced with two problems. First of all, since they had no bishops there was no one available to consecrate priests, and they either had to make do without them or find somewhere a bishop who was in the apostolic succession. They actually did look for a theological argument in favor of a church without a priesthood. Secondly, the Old Believers were quite concerned about the spiritual and intellectual basis of their congregations, which were now without state support and left to their own devices. The solution to this serious problem led finally to the division of the Old Believers into various sects and religious movements.

Of course, the Old Believers did make efforts to create a spiritual and intellectual culture of their own. This they did by continuing the old literary tradition, the copying of old manuscripts. The often posed question of whether more people read the printed works of the Petrine era or the manuscripts of the Old Believers is not as silly as it may sound. Some of the Old Believers' manuscripts of eschatological works were especially popular. Among these were the saint's life of "Basil the New," a work by Palladius about the end of the world, the old works about the Antichrist which had been written by Hypolit, and other writings in this vein. This literature in manuscript form lived on until recent times. In the Old Believers' manuscripts, it might be noted in passing, book illumination developed to great richness. The art of painting icons was also preserved and continued.

The most important cultural achievement of the Old Believers was the establishment of an "Academy," a college far in the north which was under the direction of Andrei Denisov and which was devoted to theology. Strange though it may seem, Denisov, who had studied at the Kievan Academy, combined with theology an interest in Baroque poetics and chose as the basic philosophical text for the Academy the works of Raimundus Lullus. These had been borrowed by Kiev from Spain, where there was still in the eighteenth century a copy of Lullus' *Ars magna et ultima.*[5]

The theology of the Old Believers was "pseudomorphous," that is, while it appeared on the surface to be old Orthodoxy, it nevertheless contained views which were by no means old. It is characteristic, for example, that several Kievan works were especially popular reading among the Old Believers. These works were probably chosen because they were *not* printed in Moscow and because some of them did appear in print *before* the Church schism of 1666; they dealt with eschatological questions which played a role of some importance around 1600 in the Ukraine in connection with efforts to form a union with Rome.

The Old Believers pursued several quite serious and genuine religious aims. They were proponents of the independence of the Church from the state, and they believed that man should seek his way to God through his own decision. In addition, they became defenders of freedom of conscience, even though this role was forced on them. The members of the Old Believers' circle were in any event people inwardly dedicated to religion, not those who were "lukewarm" and indifferent, and when in the eighteenth century the Old Believers realized that they would have to keep on living in the Antichristian world, they attempted to fashion for themselves a genuinely Christian life, a life completely in the spirit of the early Christian community. They were unsuccessful in these efforts because, misled by Russian tradition, they equated "Christian life" with the fulfillment of certain forms and rites which were allegedly early Christian in origin. Their genuinely Christian emotions were ineffective because their conception of the essence of Christianity was wrong. It was a tragic misunderstanding.

When we read the writings of the Old Believers we are again and again amazed that they were unable to give expression to their real aims and were concerned solely with external matters. Later a popular work by one Evfimii portrays the "catastrophe" of the Church during Peter's reign as follows:

"This tsar planned to introduce pagan (!) Greek and Latin laws, for example, shaving beards, wearing German clothes, letting hair grow long and braiding it in pigtails tied with a ribbon, wearing cloth around the neck,[6] tying up the hair and putting grease on the pigtail, powdering the hair with flour and smoking and drinking tobacco in the mouth and nostrils,[7] eating from the same dishes used by dogs and eating meat dogs have already chewed or meat from animals that have been choked to death, and practicing other such pagan customs and eliminating the last vestiges of the old and pious ways." This is a far cry from the expressions of principle by the first polemicists of the Old Believers. It is to be hoped that historians may consider the truly Christian aims of the Old Believers and forgive them their pettiness and narrow-mindedness. In any event, a culture peculiar to the Old Believers still existed in the nineteenth century. It was portrayed in a highly idealized but impressive way in two long novels by P. Melnikov-Pecherskii (1819-1883), *In the Forests* and *In the Mountains*. Participants in Russian spiritual and intellectual life took almost no notice of this culture, however, except for misguided atempts to interest the Old Believers, because they opposed the government, in joining forces with the revolutionary movement.

It is significant that even Pososhkov regarded the Old Believers as people outside of public life and advocated strict and cruel persecution of these schismatics: "The weeds should be destroyed so that they do not strangle the good wheat." The Old Believers, according to Pososhkov, turned a deaf ear to all attempts to enlighten them *(nauka),* and "Twenty years of enlightenment could not achieve as much as a single year of cruelty." Adherents to the old faith, he said, ought to be identified, using torture during the investigations, and those found guilty as well as the Orthodox priests who were tolerant of the Old Believers ought to be burned at the stake. But the persecution of the Old Believers was never this cruel, and the Old Believers, many of whom were rich merchants and large farmers and were thus among the positive and constructive forces at work in society, were often able to moderate the strictness of the laws by employing means which we have already mentioned, foremost among them bribery.

The "Evangelical" and the "Secular" Life

Pososhkov draws a sharp distinction between the "people today" who lead a "secular" life and those who lead an "evangelical" one. Typically, he considered the "secular life" to be useful to the state. Such people can be successful in the pursuit of economic activity or "the useful sciences" (Pososhkov rejects such "useless sciences" as astronomy!). For this reason Pososhkov wanted to permit the upper classes, who were called upon to govern the country, to lead such lives. Tatishchev went even further. In the spirit of moderate Enlightenment he sees in "worldly life" on the one hand

157

the satisfaction of man's natural needs, even though he tries, on the other hand, to defend some regulations of the Church as "demands of nature," claiming, for example that fasting is healthful. For Tatishchev "worldly life" was primarily cultural life, even though he had a different conception of "culture"–"education," as he called it–than the educated farmer Pososhkov had.

For Pososhkov, and certainly for many members of the most diverse social classes at this time, the ideal life was the "evangelical" life, which was conceived of as a strictly *ascetic* way of life. Pososhkov was not as narrowminded as the Old Believers, whom he detested, and he even finds some good in the way of life of foreigners (these "good institutions" date from the time "before Luther"); but for his Greek-Orthodox countrymen he set forth a higher ideal, one which was actually monastic. He defines this ideal *per negationem:* adherents to "evangelical life drank water instead of Rhine wine, wore poor clothes instead of garments embroidered in gold, slept not on feather beds but on the floor, lived in caves instead of beautiful houses, spent their nights not in dancing French dances but in wakeful contemplation, had instead of much money many lice, and instead of enjoying music and amusements they wept for their sins day and night." Return to such a life, of course, would have completely nullified all of Peter's reforms. Pososhkov did not realize this and developed his "utopia of the past" in the paradoxical form of a philosophy of society in which the passive majority leads the "evangelical life" while the minority, in the interest of the state, is permitted to deviate in every way from this ideal. He also failed to realize that in real life there were no representatives of the "evangelical life,'" that they belonged to a utopian realm, a "Nowhere."

There were no small number of contemporaries who severely condemned "worldly life" as it existed at the time, among them several religious writers, including Ukrainian bishops whom Peter had invited to come to Russia and who, like St. Dimitrii of Rostov, condemned in the "worldly life" of the Russian upper classes of the time not so much Western or pseudo-Western forms but rather the unchristian substance of the police state. Characteristically, some adherents of the "evangelical life" sought this life among members of other confessions, particularly among protestants.

Protestantism

In his own way Peter was pious, but the confessional point of view remained alien to him. Moreover, he regarded not only the Old Believers but also the clergy of the official Church as at least potential enemies. From his own utterances we are acquainted with his supra-confessional point of view: Protestantism and Greek Orthodoxy, as he understood them, taught essen-

158

tially the same thing.

It is worth noting that at this time people came under the influence of Protestantism. I do not refer to Feofan Prokopovich, who had studied Catholic and Protestant theology abroad and strove to effect a synthesis of Protestant and Greek Orthodox theology. For a long time his system of Orthodox theology in the Latin language, composed on the model of Protestant handbooks, remained the basis for theological instruction in Russian religious schools and kept this instruction separate from the tradition of the Eastern Church fathers. Prokopovich also maintained relations with German Pietists and encouraged the translation, publication, and dissemination of pietistic literature.

I refer to the much more interesting "Tveretinov case." Dimitrii Tveretinov was the offspring of a burgher family in Tver (now called Kalinin). By working as an assistant to a German physician in Moscow he acquired some knowledge of medicine, which at that time entitled one to practice medicine. Tveretinov is of interest not only because he was one of the first Russian doctors but also because he was a "heretic" of a new type. He may have heard a good deal about the teachings of Protestantism from the physician for whom he had worked and from whom he had learned medicine, but then, on the basis of independent study of the Bible, he drew up a list of those doctrines and particularly those rites of the Greek Orthodox Church which are not supported by the Bible *(argumentum a silentio)* or are in direct contradiction to what is stated in the Bible. This list of "dubious" church doctrines contained several points which were in agreement with Protestant views—rejection of the worship of icons, of prayers for the deceased, of prayers addressed to saints, etc. He was so lacking in caution as to show his "notebooks" to various acquaintances and even to discuss his doubts with monks. He was arrested, and even though Peter held a protecting hand over him, he was placed under indictment. His position was rendered even more tenuous when, during the investigation of his case, one of his "followers," moved by desperation to take action, damaged an icon in a church in Moscow by plunging a knife into it. The follower was burned at the stake, but after being under indictment for years Tveretinov escaped with a mild punishment.

Results

After Peter there was no way to avoid coming to grips with the West. People wavered between uncritical adoption of everything that was foreign and the caution with which formerly everything foreign, especially foreigners themselves, had been regarded. Here again Pososhkov's views are typical. He was prepared to exploit foreigners. For him the technical supremacy of the West was indisputable. But he also wanted the masters from foreign countries sent back home after they had taught their skills to Russians. He said that in acuity *(ostrotoiu)* the Russians were in no way inferior to foreigners. The extent of Western technical ability was explained as the result of habitual practice and good organization *(rasprava)*. According to Pososhkov, foreigners did not wish Russia well and did not tell Russia "the real truth," that is, they did not reveal the secrets of their success. Pososhkov's observations, then, are profoundly pessimistic. He did not comprehend that the "real truth" about Western culture was that it was necessary to adopt not mere results but rather the bases and prerequisites for these results, that it was necessary to build further on these bases, to renew them, and to make new discoveries. It can be assumed as certain that at this time there were already a number of men in Russia who recognized this and everything it implied but who simply were paid no heed because, especially after Peter's death, they played no significant role in Russian cultural life. Only the Old Believers rejected Western culture in its totality, but even they were forced to borrow from the West, even though what they borrowed—the philosophy of Raimundus Lullus, for example—was often quite out of date.

With the death of Peter there began an epoch in which the influence of the West spread more and more through Russia. The time was ripe for coming to grips with the culture of the Occident, although several decades passed before this conflict became serious.

Peter's Successors (1725-1762)

There is no more remarkable period in modern Russian political history than the four decades following Peter's death. The death of the great reformer was as paradoxical and contradictory as his whole life had been. At the age of only 53 he died of a cold (he caught it rescuing some people from drowning) and of the consequences of a venereal disease which had not been cured. In his law regulating succession to the throne, a law for which Prokopovich wrote the commentary, Peter had made succession to the throne a decision subject to the arbitrary and sole will of whoever happened to be tsar, but when Peter himself died unexpectedly he had made no such decision and there was no legal heir to the throne. On his death bed Peter was able to whisper only the words "Give everything to . . ." before death prevented his listeners from finding out whom the Tsar had in mind.

At first the crown of Russia, an empire which already occupied an important position in the European system of states, fell into the hands of Peter's closest collaborators, but it became evident that Peter had neither trained nor surrounded himself with competent and worthy co-workers. Thus it happened that for forty years "occasional rulers" disposed over the throne of Russia, first those who had belonged to Peter's circle during the last years of his life. In fact, of these men only Prokopovich can be considered a true follower of Peter. Menshikov, Peter's closest friend, was an ambitious, egotistical, and perfidious man. Other members of Peter's circle were simply insignificant. Later several Germans joined the circle of the most influential personages: Biron was a selfish parvenu and the newly appointed Duke of Kurland; Ostermann, the son of a Westphalian pastor, received a patent of nobility in Russia and was, it seems, a gifted diplomat and politician; and Münnich was an engineer who rose through the ranks to become field marshal general. Some of these men did devote themselves to the welfare of their adopted country, but the bad thing was that as a group they also pursued their own interests, let themselves be guided in policy-making by egotistical motives, and frequently attempted to achieve their ends by dishonest means. In doing so they, like the pretenders to the throne, relied on a new power base, the royal guard, which was composed of young noblemen (later its composition became much more heterogeneous). The actions of this royal guard, like those of all military cliques, were always motivated by factors which were obscure and incalculable.

The throne was occupied in rapid succession by three women who were more or less incompetent to rule. Peter's widow, Catherine, whose origins and past life were equally obscure, ruled from 1725 to 1727; Peter's niece, Anna Ioannovna, reigned from 1730 to 1740; and Elizabeth, the daughter of Peter and Catherine, was tsarina from 1741 to 1762. Interspersed between these three tsarinas were tsars who were sovereigns in name only. Peter II, Peter the Great's infant grandson, was nominal ruler from 1727 to 1730 when he died at the age of fifteen. From October 1740 until November 1741 the tsar was Ioann Antonovich,[8] a babe in arms. During this period Biron, the favorite of the previous Tsarina, Anna, functioned as regent for three weeks until he was deposed by the royal guard. Then the regency passed to the mother of the Tsar, Anna Leopoldovna; in an atmosphere of intrigue and hostility and in constant fear and confusion she became, as Kliuchevsky put it, "a quite wild princess." Elizabeth, who was at least the daughter of Peter the Great, deposed Anna with the help of the royal guard. Ioann Antonovich, the unfortunate infant tsar, died years later in a Russian prison.

The twenty years of Elizabeth's reign which followed the turbulent year between 1740 and 1741 were calmer times, but Elizabeth could decide on no more lawful successor than the Prince of Holstein-Gottorp, whom Elizabeth herself referred to as "my nephew, that monster, and may the devil take him." After Elizabeth's death the Prince, under the name Peter III, ruled for only a short time, from December 25, 1761 to June 28, 1762. He was not "taken by the devil"; he was deposed (again with the help of the royal guard) by his own wife, Sophie-Auguste, former Princess of Anhalt-Zerbst, and a few days later he was murdered by conspirators. Sophie-Auguste, under the name of Catherine II (the Great), enjoyed a long and brilliant reign, from 1762 to 1796, a reign which deserves the close attention of intellectual historians.

Politics

Strange as it may seem, the improbable history of the Russian throne from Peter the Great to Catherine did not result in catastrophe and did not even essentially weaken the position of Russia in Europe. This might be regarded as proof that a state which is adrift like a ship without a helmsman is not necessarily doomed to sink immediately, providing, of course, that no storms arise on the political seas. And Russia was in quiet waters: Poland represented no threat to it; the Tatars in the Crimea were satisfied with raids on the Ukraine; and in the north, in those years Sweden was preoccupied with domestic problems. The European states were squabbling among themselves. Russia participated in the Seven Years War and occupied not only East Prussia but Berlin—we might note as a curiosity the fact that it was Tsarina Elizabeth who appointed Kant to his professorship at the University of Königsberg. As so often happens, it was not the war but the peace which Russia lost. Peter III, an admirer of his enemy, Frederick the Great, simply withdrew his troops from Prussia. Other wars in which Russia was involved were no less inconclusive, and great victories over the Tatars and the Turks also ended in 1739 with a peace which sanctioned only minor territorial gains on the Black Sea and the Sea of Azov.

Russian domestic policy was also aimless, although no essential aspects of Peter the Great's reforms were given up—the law concerning the shaving off of beards was, in fact, repeatedly reaffirmed. Legislation was overshadowed by the struggles between magnates and royal favorites, and the only measures which are of interest to the intellectual historian are those which concerned the legal status and relationship of the landed aristocracy and the serfs. Decisive steps in domestic policy were not taken until the reign of Catherine II.

Spiritual and Intellectual Developments

Stagnation, rather than movement in any given direction, was the hallmark of the spiritual and intellectual life of this period. Whereas Peter the Great's court was the center of a specific, though by no means "courtly" culture, after Peter's death the court of the tsar was of no cultural significance whatsoever. Elizabeth did indeed have some intellectual interests. For example, she loved a good sermon and attracted many a preacher to her court. She was interested in music and cultivated good religious and secular music. Even the folksong found acceptance at her court, and it seems probable that she did indeed compose the poems, written in a popular tone, which are attributed to her. And the thousands of dresses in her wardrobe attest to her aesthetic inclinations.

Of much more importance for the "microscopic" processes which

162

paved the way for a later blossoming of cultural life was the simple fact that between 1725 and 1760 a new generation was born and grew up, one which was forced to concern itself with Western technology and in the process gradually to come into contact with the intellectual culture of the West. The measures taken by Peter and his successors, on the other hand, were for the most part ineffectual and fruitless. This was true of the Russian Academy of Sciences, which Peter founded shortly before his death and which until the middle of the nineteenth century functioned as an agency for propagating Western European science in a land which was indifferent to it. There were no Russian members of the Academy until the 1740's, and the work of the most gifted of them, M. Lomonosov (1711-1765), aroused hardly any interest in Russia at that time.

Students by the hundreds fled from Peter's schools; in 1727 alone 322 of the 2000 students enrolled fled because they "feared the abyss of wisdom." In a preparatory school which was opened in conjunction with the Academy the students were for the most part non-Russians; the only Russians who enrolled were those who wanted to learn foreign languages. When university lectures of the Academy began in 1747 there were 24 students, but by 1753 the lectures were abandoned because there were not enough students enrolled. In 1755 the University of Moscow opened with an enrollment of 100; in 1785 the enrollment was only 82, and in some of the departments there was sometimes only one student. Lectures were usually held in languages other than Russian.

In the schools for the nobility which were founded in 1731 and 1750 students were permitted free choice of subjects. In 1733, 237 of the 245 students enrolled elected to study French, and 110 took dancing, but only 36 were studying geometry, 28 history, seventeen geography, and fifteen Latin.

Literature

Modern Russian literature begins during the reign of Elizabeth. The older poets still adhered to the Baroque tradition, but quite unexpectedly a wave of poetic enthusiasm came over the noble youths in a military school. As early as the 1750's they were writing and publishing numerous poems of various kinds and varying quality, many of them in the spirit of the new literary fashion, neoclassicism.

But what literature was there between 1725 and this time? Unfortunately it must be recorded that during Peter's time literature ceased to exist. There were still religious writers, primarily Ukrainians, but the only secular author of importance, A. Kantemir, remained almost unknown. The Old Believers copied works of old religious literature, and other readers, as in the past, found edification in works circulated in manuscript form. Of the books printed during the Petrine epoch only very few were widely circulated, and these were usually religious or "old-fashioned" works. It was not until after 1740 that more important authors, such as Lomonosov and V. K. Trediakovskii (1703-1769), began to appear, and, as we have noted, they cultivated the Baroque style.

In the few remnants of Russian literature from the time between 1700 and 1740 one will seek in vain the "new man" who was supposed to emerge during the Petrine era. As P. Berkov has proved, the novels in manuscript form which are often called "literature of the Petrine age" date from the period after 1730, and the most remarkable thing about these works is that not the slightest trace of "the new man" can be found in them.

Soviet Russian scholars, to be sure, have found "the new man" in seventeenth-century novels in manuscript form; they have even discovered "lyrical motifs" and "delicate eroticism" in a novel which employs over and over again one stock phrase as a circumlocution for love: "and he wallowed in the filth of lewdness." In the three novels typical of the post-Petrine era we find heroes of various social classes: a sailor, Vasilii; a nobleman, Aleksandr; and a merchant, Ioann.[9] The only thing new about these works is the view that every man can climb up every rung of the social ladder, a view which became popular as a result of the era of court favorites. This is, after all, an indication that the old social order was breaking down, but perhaps this attitude was merely taken over from old fairy tales. The three heroes are the most primitive sort of "Westerners." Even the plots of the novels are laid in Western Europe (the authors, of course, have no clear idea of Western Europe; they have characters travel from Vienna to Florence by ship and on foot from Paris to Africa). The three heroes, born in Russia, go to Western Europe and there find their fortune in the form of foreign ladies with such non-Russian names as Eleonora, Hedwig, and Dorothee. One of these ladies is even a princess of undefineable nationality named Irakliia. The character who is meant to represent the "new man" has left Russia forever and completely forgotten it; only Ioann, the merchant, returns to Russia, but once there "he could never forget Eleonora." The authors of these novels had at their disposal no colors with which to paint Russian life, but for European life they employed all the hues familiar from the fairy tale.

Most of the other novels of this time have heroes of unknown nationality, with such names as Doltorn, Frantsel-Ventsian, Princess Berfa, etc. Does this mean that the half-educated author who had some vague notions of the West felt Russian life to be a complete void and deemed it impossible to portray it in a literary work? Whether this was the case or not, we can find no "new man" in Petrine and post-Petrine literature, however hard we try. "New men" appear for the first time in the literature of the 1760's and later, but they are not always attractive men, nor can they always be taken seriously.

From other sources we learn of the existence of men who brought to

Russia their own image of Europe, usually a distorted one, and who arranged their lives in Russia to conform with this image. These men were not in the least interested in Russia either, and with them begins the long line of "foreigners of Russian birth" who ignore or even despise their native land.

CHAPTER II. THE AGE OF CATHERINE II

Significance of the Age

During the 1740's and 1750's independent stirrings of the Russian spirit are evident only occasionally, but the 1760's make it clear that there already were small circles which had achieved some intellectual prominence, however modest. This is evident most of all in the way in which literature developed. This literature, however, was to some extent stilted; ceremonious odes and heroic tragedies were the genres which could best legitimate a poet as a creative spirit. There were even Russians who were interested in knowledge, which only goes to show that they were not the exceptions to Aristotle's rule that every human being by his very nature strives to know. What was remarkable was the fact that the religious interests of the upper classes were only vaguely delineated and often required foreign stimulus to achieve a certain degree of definitude: now the idea of "Holy Russia," which had dominated the pre-Petrine epoch, no longer seemed right. The years between 1760 and 1800 are full of intellectual and spiritual movements striving to express themselves which may seem primitive to us today, but which for their own time may be considered signs of increasing maturity.

The Empress

There is considerable dispute about Catherine, the princess from the tiny German kingdom of Anhalt-Zerbst who became the empress of a vast realm. She has been criticized both for her politics and her morals.

Having come to power over the corpse of her spouse, she kept the throne for herself by a twofold usurpation. Two people were still alive who had more right to the crown than she did: Ioann Antonovich, who had been deposed earlier by Elizabeth and was still languishing in prison; and Catherine's own son, Paul, whom she banished from court and sent to spend his life in his private residence. Scholars who are interested in court gossip can find more than enough material in the private life of the Empress. In choosing lovers she employed purely physiological standards, and she changed lovers the way other women change gloves. Of all her lovers only Potyomkin, whose "villages" have earned him dubious fame, was a man of real stature. The Empress was in the habit of bestowing on her favorites enormous wealth, usually in the form of thousands and thousands of serfs.

It is here that the criticism of political historians begins. Catherine expanded and strengthened serfdom, which even at that time was an antiquated institution. One of the things she did in this regard was to reduce the free Ukrainian peasants to serfdom. Moreover, she deprived serfdom of its last vestiges of a rationale when she did away with the principle that noble landowners were obliged to serve the crown. Whereas the compulsory service of the serfs was considered until this time a sort of recompense to the landowners for the services they were obliged to render to the state, now owning serfs was a privilege which was in no way justified. Nor did the Empress make any effort to limit in any way the powers which the landowner held over their serfs.

The Empress has also been branded a "hypocrite." At the beginning of her reign she convened a sort of advisory legislative assembly, the "Commission," and she herself worked out a set of guidelines *(nakaz)* which it was to follow—a compilation made with the help of works written by Montesquieu, Beccaria, and others on politics and law. Then, when the various estates expressed their wishes all too emphatically in the Commission, the Empress simply dissolved it. One political sin which has been correctly ascribed to Catherine was her initiative in partitioning Poland, a state which was under her "protection." And in doing so she did not give even a moment's thought to her legal obligations to the Poles.

So much for the negative view of Catherine. In her defense it must be said that she witnessed both the rebellion of Pugachev in Russia (1773) and the French Revolution (1789). These events probably forced her to change the liberal views which she held in 1762. In spite of this, the accusation has been leveled at Catherine that in her correspondence with representatives of the French Enlightenment she concealed her true views and attempted to imitate the literature of the Enlightenment but at the same time persecuted Russian enlighteners and independent thinkers.

A long list of such accusations could be compiled, and yet it should not be forgotten that Catherine's reign was marked by political successes and cultural advances. The final liberation of the Crimea from Tatar dominion must be accounted one of the political successes. Although the Empress was not born a Russian, she never offended the newly awakened feeling of nationalism among the Russians. She may even have been the first "Russian imperialist." The poet G. R. Derzhavin (1743-1816), who was her secretary for a time, related that she once said: "If my reign could last two centuries all Europe would be subject to the crown of Russia." In her own time, and later in memory of her, many of her contemporaries were wont to sing the battle hymn "Resound, O Thunder of Victory" *(Grom pobedy razdavaisia).*

Intellectual Culture

The advances in culture were also significant. The beginnings of the cultural movement were already present in the 1750's. The Empress had the knack of finding not only lovers but also gifted men who could work with her, and the social class to which these men belonged was of little concern to her. The impoverished nobleman Derzhavin was one of them. He became famous through his poetry, was appointed to high administrative posts, and was for a time, as already noted, secretary to the Empress. The fact that the Empress herself tried her hand at literature (regardless of how bad her works may be) and the fact that for a time she published a satirical journal and engaged in polemics with other writers removed the stigma which had been attached to intellectual labors. And even though she was fickle in bestowing her favor on poets, she did make literature a profession which was permissible and even held in esteem.

The publishing business, however, would have developed even without the support of the Empress. Before Catherine's time, annual book production amounted to only around five to twenty-five titles, and only a part of these were written in Russian. In the 1770's and 1780's the number of published titles rose to between 100 and 300 per year. An important contributing factor was that since Peter's time two generations had been born, and the imperceptible "microscopic" processes of intellectual development had been proceeding quietly during the decades between 1725 and 1760, which were apparently so intellectually barren. The years following Peter's reign, or so it seems, were a "culturally creative pause."

The age of Catherine, however, by no means produced literary works which were important, "eternal," and of consequence beyond the boundaries of Russia. There were, of course, several gifted poets, but only one of them, Derzhavin, was clearly superior to the rest. He did achieve prominence outside Russia through his ode "God." In the sciences it was still foreigners— except for Lomonosov, who continued to be ignored in Russia—who investigated the history and geography of Russia. But the intellectual movement which began during the reign of Catherine gained such momentum that it could no longer be stopped.

The Enlightenment

The eighteenth century has been characterized as the Age of Enlightenment, that is, the age dominated by rationalistic and sceptical enlightened philosophy. This is not completely accurate, for it is difficult to make Rousseau fit this description and even more difficult to make other groups fit it: the Pietists, the mystics, and the members of "Storm and Stress" and of the "preromanticism" so typical of this age. The same was true in Russia. In some respects the Enlightenment had been spreading in Russia since the time of Peter the Great. It had in common with the Enlightenment in France the struggle against traditions which could not be defended rationally. During the reign of Catherine II philosophical ideas of the Enlightenment also gained currency in Russia, though in an oversimplified form, and because of their very oversimplification these ideas could be radical, sometimes more radical than in the West.

In the West criticism of religious tradition developed from quarrels between the faiths, and acquaintanceship with non-Christian religions sharpened this criticism until it became religious scepticism and occasionally even atheism. In Russia this criticism was simply adopted without question. The spread of religious scepticism was due more to religious indifference than to serious independent thought. The Russians first adopted the thoughts of so-called "deism";[10] but by the end of the century we are encountering atheists. It was easier to be an atheist in Russia than it was in the West. The story is told that Voltaire interrupted a guest in the middle of an atheistic statement with the remark: "Let us not speak of this matter, for our servants will hear it and they will butcher us like steers." Russian freethinkers of the eighteenth century, by contrast, could deny the existence of God in the presence of their servants without any qualms. Of course, Voltaire and his guest were speaking French, and the servants too were Frenchmen, whereas the Russian atheists conversed in French and their Russian servants could not understand a word of French. We must not assume that the number of atheists in Russia was very large. The less educated the "critic" was, the more radical was his criticism of religious traditions. And it was certainly not necessary to import criticism of the clergy from the West when Peter had already called monasticism "gangrene" and had even expressed doubts that prayer was of importance: "Everyone prays. What good does that do for society?" Immediately after his arrival in Petersburg young D. I. Fonvizin (1745-1792), who later became a famous writer, was informed by a chance acquaintance that there is no God, and one anecdote portrays an Over Procurator of the Holy Synod as a propagandist for atheistic views.

Catherine was cautious enough not to offend the feelings of her devout subjects. In outer appearance, at least, she was a faithful daughter of the Orthodox Church, although she regarded the Church as no more than a source of potential hostility. She also chose not to insist that the Holy Synod take a position on the suggestions made by the Over Procurator under her husband Peter III. These proposals are most indicative: the period of fasting should be shortened; "superfluous" festival days should be abolished, and the church service should also be shortened; celibacy should no longer be required of bishops; the garb of the priests should be modernized; and divorce should be made less difficult to obtain. Attention was devoted, however, not exclusively to primarily external matters. The reformers wanted to have the worship of icons restricted, "false miracles" extirpated from Church tradition, and the Church itself purged of all "superstition." Many of Catherine's enlightened contemporaries would certainly have agreed to such a "church reform," but not one of these proposals was accepted; characteristically, not a single one of them was explicitly rejected either—the Holy

Synod acted as if these proposals did not exist. Unfortunately the suggestion that the Old Believers be permitted to practice their religion without interference or restraint was not considered either.

Natural law was another field where the Russians imitated the Enlightenment in the West. In 1764 a description of theories of natural law was published in the Russian language, and ultimately natural law became a required subject in the study of jurisprudence. Man's natural rights, such as the right "to defend his person and his property," take precedence over "acquired rights," which entitle the sovereign to rule over his subjects, the master over his slaves, the husband over his wife, etc. The idea that the power of the tsar was an arrangement arrived at by society and that it was based on a sort of contract between the tsar and his subjects was significant enough.

Religious scepticism and the new concept of the power of the tsar reflected the philosophical attitudes of men who at that time and later were termed "Voltairians." Such men could still be found in Russia at the beginning of the nineteenth century, and slight traces of "Voltairianism" can be discerned in some of the Russian romanticists.

Some Orthodox theologians also succumbed to the spirit of the Enlightenment. At that time a German translation of the catechism written by the famous preacher and metropolitan Platon was published. Protestants too agreed in large measure with Platon, with the sole reservation that his catechism, like others, contained sections on the veneration of saints and of icons. At this time some of the old saints' lives were revised and "purified" in the spirit of the Enlightenment; some of them, as noted above, were even destroyed.

The Old Believers and the Religious Sects

The Old Believers' spiritual resistance to the "Antichristian world" had abated somewhat. Instances of direct persecution of Old Believers became less frequent and under Catherine ceased almost completely. People were adapting to a world which had changed. The eschatological motif, however, persisted: the Old Believers were of the opinion that Peter III, Prince of Holstein-Gottorp, like Peter the Great, bore in his name the number 666, the number of the Antichrist (the number was arrived at by adding up the numerical values of the letters in his name when Holstein was misspelled "Golstin").

The "Apocalypse" *(Apokalipsii)* of the Old Believers, written sometime after 1764, discovered in Russian politics and culture of the time portents of the end of the world. After Peter the Great the next ruler was a "Roman woman," Catherine I, who was alleged to be Roman Catholic—in fact, the religious affiliation of this woman of obscure origins was so uncertain that Peter the Great, as a precautionary measure, deemed it necessary to have her baptized Greek Orthodox. Catherine, "the Roman woman," was succeeded by "the new Venus"—Elizabeth, who loved pretty clothes, music, and dancing but was also devout. During the reign of Catherine the Great the "portents" increased in number. Poems were published in which Peter the Great was called "God," as in a work by Sumarokov; literary works were written about the "Golden Age," which the learned author of the *Apocalypse* considered worship of Saturn, a pagan god; and, finally, a monument to Peter the Great was erected on which the satanic snake was portrayed—the snake, crushed under the hoofs of Peter's horse symbolized Peter's enemies. With harsh words the Old Believers attacked the "loose living" which was now tolerated by the "Jewish Synod" (they identified "synod" with the "synedrion," which was familiar from the Gospels— Matthew 5:22 and Mark 13:9).

The inner life of the Old Believers was full of cares and quarrelings. Catherine's relative tolerance did not prevent the authorities from using military force in 1764 to destroy Vetka, the center of the Old Believers' movement. The greatest problem of the Old Believers concerned the restoration of the priesthood, for a legally consecrated bishop who could ordain priests had still not been found. This is why a split occurred between the moderate adherents to the "old faith" and various "theoreticians," such as those who, often with specious reasoning, denied that a priesthood was necessary or even that marriage was sacramental in character. Among these "theoreticians" were several groups of fanatics who, like the "Runners" *(Beguny)* for example, attempted to avoid the traps and snares of this world by keeping constantly on the move. There were also various groups which joined forces with sects that had arisen in the seventeenth century. The two most important of these were the *"Khlysty,"* an ecstatic sect, the name of which might be roughly translated "flagellants," and the *"Skoptsy,"* or castrati, who attempted to save their souls in the fashion indicated by the name of their sect.

The emergence of further rationalistic sects resulted from the turmoil in the congregations of the Old Believers and the dissatisfaction with the officially recognized church. Two of these rationalistic sects were the *"Dukhobory,"* which might be translated as "spiritual-intellectual Christians," and the *"Molokane,"* a sect which arose at the end of the eighteenth century, to some extent as a result of the influence of German Pietists who had immigrated to Russia, and whose members were called *Molokane,* or "Milk Drinkers," because they ignored the rules for fasting. These sects too attracted new members from among Old Believers.

The Russian religious sects, with their numerous "prophets," ecstatics, and frauds, some of whom claimed to be Christ reincarnate, are an important aspect of Russian spiritual and intellectual life in the nineteenth century. The harsh and senseless persecution of these sects by the police succeeded only in creating numerous martyrs and in transforming even politically apathetic congregations of sectarians and Old Believers into close-knit groups which were a constant source of unrest, groups which often joined in any rebellion, whatever its cause. Catherine the Great found this out on the occasion of the Pugachev revolt (1773).

Intellectuals

At the end of the eighteenth century, as we have seen, there were numerous social, national, and ideological groups. They owed their existence to the complex history of the Russian empire, and in view of the size of the country the presence of these groups is quite understandable. Then, as later, they were able neither to fuse together to form a homogenous society nor to reconcile themselves in the least to one another. For almost a century after Catherine's unsuccessful attempt to convene an advisory legislative assembly there was no basis on which a reconciliation of these groups could take place. No one but the government had any voice in social and political life, and the efforts of the government, strange as it may sound, were devoted for the most part to perpetuating wherever possible the boundaries which separated the groups from each other.

There was, of course, one group which arose in the eighteenth century and which, at least in the sphere of ideology, was able to transcend all these social and political boundaries. These men were the so-called "intellectuals," a group which is called in Russia the *"Intelligentsia."* It is very difficult to define this extremely important sociological term, because in the course of the decades the meaning of the term *"Intelligentsia"* changed several times. For this same reason it is difficult to write a history of this group. Since the beginning of the nineteenth century the *"Intelligentsia"* has played a decisive role in the spiritual and intellectual history of Russia, and for that reason the portrayal of Russian intellectual history between 1840 and 1917 can be limited almost exclusively to a history of the intellectuals; the other strata of society were really on the periphery of Russian spiritual and intellectual life.

For a long time "intellectuals" were considered to be identical with "the well-educated"—Turgenev was still using the word "intellectuals" in this sense in 1860—but in retrospect not every well-educated person can be designated an "intellectual" or an intelligent person. In the Russian absolutistic state the most important characteristic of the "intellectual" was his intellectual independence, primarily his independence in respect to the political interests of the state, to the political and economic interests of individual groups and social classes, and to the government in power and the policies of that government. It is clear that by definition most government officials could not qualify as members of the intelligentsia and that the

172

persons most likely to be intellectuals were those who pursued independent professions, but it is simply impossible to give hard and fast rules—for a long time intellectuals were in no way forbidden to serve in the government or the military.

More important than these external criteria is the subjective attitude of the intellectuals, who not only strove to be "intellectually independent" but also believed that they represented the *true* interests of the Russian people— of Russia. As Fedotov has noted, they wanted to join the Russian people in opposing the government. But because these "true interests" can be viewed in so many different ways, there occasionally arose among the intellectuals quite different philosophies and even opposing ideological camps which attacked each other bitterly but nevertheless preserved a certain awareness that they were essentially of one mind. The "Westerners" and the "Slavophiles," who will be treated below, are an example.

When at the end of the nineteenth century the intellectuals were given the chance to fight for their ideas, a crisis for the intellectuals began and with it violent arguments about the nature of this peculiar class of the Russian people. The weightiest accusation almost always hurled at the intellectuals at this time was that they "did not have their feet on the ground," that they were incapable of adapting their goals and ideals to reality. They were accused of espousing an ideology which was primarily utopian. This is just as one-sided and wrong as the other view, which overemphasizes the inner uniformity and cohesiveness of the Russian intellectuals as a group and calls them a sort of "order," a term which F. Stepun has used of late. The phrase "an order without written statutes" is in itself a contradiction in terms, for the most important characteristic of an order is the existence of precisely determined rules which govern it. Moreover, one can speak of an inner cohesiveness of the intelligentsia only in respect to a few short periods between 1860 and 1890 and even then only with important reservations.

The two one-sided views are merely inadequate attempts to express the true characteristics of the Russian intelligentsia. That intellectuals "did not have their feet on the ground" was often the result of intellectual independence, and that they were "like an order" was occasionally only exaggerated awareness of their inner unity, increased at some periods by the inner discipline and intolerance which prevailed in individual groups of intellectuals. But the intelligentsia always consisted of groups quite different in ideology and of numerous individualists whose status as intellectuals certainly no one would deny.

It is difficult to determine precisely when the intelligentsia originated as a class. During the reign of Catherine the Great, there were two ideological groups, the Freemasons and the independent (and mostly radical) politicians, whose members had all the earmarks of the later intelligentsia. While adherents of the Enlightenment as such could be found among *all* educated and semi-educated segments of the population, the Freemasons and the independent politicans emerged as members of autonomous intellectual movements. Both movements were stimulated by ideas from the West, but neither of them ignored problems peculiar to Russia.

The Freemasons

As far as Russian Freemasons of the eighteenth century are concerned, the term "Freemasons," even if one is speaking of "mystic Freemasons," must be taken with a grain of salt. They were intellectuals who banded together in the masonic lodges which had been founded somewhat earlier and who sought to satisfy their intellectual needs in these "lodges." Unlike the best students of the Petrine epoch, such as the historian Tatishchev, they were no longer satisfied by scholarly study. They rejected firmly contemporary "Voltairianism" and the Enlightenment in general. What they basically wanted was the same as what pre-Enlightenment Russian Christians had wanted: knowledge of God and His commandments, and personal intellectual perfection. To be sure, these goals were now interpreted differently than they had been in pre-Petrine Russia. It was no longer a matter of of "ritualistic Christianity"; these truly "new men" were interested not in external forms but in the intellectual and spiritual content of the Christian religion. They were more or less committed representatives of *intellectual Christianity* and faced the same problems as intellectual Christians in other times and in other countries. As. G. Florovsky has noted, there can be no doubt that this return to the old Russian tradition of Christian piety wore new garments and was stimulated by the West.

We possess several sources, unfortunately not unambiguous ones, from which it is possible to form a judgment concerning the ideology of the Freemasons: their letters, manuscripts of the lectures which they held, and, most important, the works which they translated, which are preserved in manuscripts and in numerous printed books. There was not complete ideological uniformity in these circles, but their members did conceive of their "work" as self-education through reading and through a sort of inner asceticism. Soon there were also dependable leaders who instructed their disciples personally and through correspondence in the ways to achieve this perfection. The way to do this was to observe oneself, to gain knowledge about oneself, and to practice intellectual self-discipline, which sought to extirpate the "root of evil" from the soul or at least to prevent evil from gaining the upper hand. This meant that the individual was struggling against his own "willfulness." It was the ideology of the "inner monastery," of a life which rejected participation in the "vanity of the world." This education in moral responsibility, self-control, and moderation agreed in many respects with the demands of Christian morality, but the requirement that one actively love one's neighbor, which was meant to lead to the establishment of the

174

"kingdom of Christ in the soul," led even further in this direction.

The Freemasons had already developed, in fact, widespread philanthropic activity, and from this era and somewhat later times we are familiar with people who were educated in masonic circles and who revealed no small amount of inner independence, moral strength, firmness, and loyalty in fulfilling the duties (including service to the state) which they took upon themselves; for they believed that man should bear his "cross," which is imposed on him without any regard for his personal desires. To be sure, they did not always find suitable activity in a society in which there were so many things one could achieve only by immoral means and in which one could defend only with difficulty one's moral purity, not only against inner temptation but against the pressures and constraints of one's environment.

It is worth noting that these circles attributed to knowledge a very great role, perhaps too great a role, in achieving inner perfection. They strove to achieve a sort of "gnosis," and one way in which they obtained this knowledge was from the readings recommended to them. The readings themselves were remarkable.

Russian Freemasons made many translations, which were circulated both in manuscript and in printed form. They translated especially works of Western European mysticism—works by Valentin Weigel (1533-1588), Mme du Guyon (1648-1717), and particularly by Jacob Böhme—as well as works by Pietists—particularly the Suabian Pietists—and even individual works by the Church fathers. Johann Arndt (1555-1621) and his *Four Books on the True Christianity* (1609) occupied a special position in this literature. It is interesting that a small "Handbook," a short commentary on Paul's Epistle to the Colossians which was written by the Suabian Pietist Philipp Matthäus Hahn and which was a sort of Christian utopia, marks, despite its vagueness, the beginning of Russian utopianism.

The spread of the works of Louis Claude,Marquis de St. Martin, who was a disciple of Jacob Bohme, proved to be fateful for the Freemasons, for St. Martin's political tendencies, however unclear, together with the tense political situation, moved the Empress to order, immediately before the French Revolution, that Freemasons be severely persecuted. Nikolai I. Novikov (1744-1818), the leader of the Freemasons' philanthropic and publishing activities, was arrested, and the publications of his press were confiscated and for the most part destroyed. It is worth noting that the metropolitan who was charged to investigate Novikov found him to be a "model Christian."

The action of the Empress, however, did not seal the fate of Russian Freemasonry. At the beginning of the nineteenth century it was revived, only to be prohibited again in the twenties. Never again did it play a significant role in the intellectual history of Russia.

The writer who represents the beginning of that type of Russian literature which—with reservations, it is true—can be termed "political" was none
other than Novikov. He was the editor of satirical journals which were
modeled on the moral weeklies of Addison and Steele and of their imitators
in other European countries; journals of this sort had increased in number in
Russia since 1769. Their life span, of course, was often quite short; Novikov's
journals continued to appear until 1773. It was not until after 1789 that I. A.
Krylov (1769-1844), who later gained fame as a writer of fables, began to
publish similar and equally short-lived periodicals.

The first Russian satirical journal was published anonymously in 1769
by the Empress herself, and other writers followed her example. Two types of
satirical literature soon developed. The one, represented by Catherine's journal, strove to "improve human affairs" through education and to improve and
perfect the individual citizen; the other demanded social and political reforms. Novikov's journal was of the second type. These periodicals directed
their attacks against abuses in public life, primarily against serfdom, which
meant "poverty and slavery" for the people, as it was phrased in Novikov's
journal as early as 1772 by an as yet unidentified author who signed his
article with the initials "I. T." The landowners, who are portrayed in the
satires of both types of journals as uneducated, selfish, and often cruel, have
no right to possess unlimited authority over their serfs, who are usually depicted as primitive but noble in spirit. The themes of literature attacking
serfdom have remained by and large the same. They are still found in the
works of Turgenev (in the *A Hunter's Sketches*) and in those of other authors
who were writing in the 1840's and 1850's.

The Serfs

We know very little about the intellectual life of the serfs, and what
we do know is only at second hand. In the 1760's and 1770's a few
"laments" were written by peasants. Typical works are the "Lament of
the Slaves" *(Plach kholopov),* which was written sometime after 1767, and
the "Petitions to Heaven's Chancellory," composed at the end of the century
by peasants owned by the state, whose lot was in any event better than that
of the serfs owned by private citizens. There are also several short stories
which have been preserved in manuscript form. We have no reason to doubt
that at about the same time songs about serfdom originated, although we can
date exactly only those songs which were written in the Ukraine, for serfdom
was first introduced there by Catherine. These works, however, are either
hopelessly pessimistic portrayals of "poverty and slavery," with the main
emphasis on poverty, or satires on the stupidity of public officials and land-

owners who are duped by sly peasants. Neither of these two types of literature gives much concrete information about the conditions which prevailed
at the time.

We should have every reason to expect that the Pugachev revolt would
provide us with material on which to base a characterization of the ideology
of the lower classes. This revolt, actually a "peasant war" which extended
over large areas, primarily along and beyond the Volga, involved Cossacks,
serfs, Old Believers, and nomadic tribes. The rebels were able to take a number of cities and fortresses and hold them for weeks, even months. Unfortunately, we can draw only one conclusion from their indiscriminate
slaughter of members of the upper classes, public officials, officers, and often
priests: various and extensive segments of the Russian population found their
lot "unbearable." But the leader of the revolt, the Cossack Emil Pugachev,
was a mere usurper who pretended to be Tsar Peter III, Empress Catherine's
husband, who had been murdered ten years before. Numerous written appeals
made by him and his generals to the civilian population have been preserved,
in which Pugachev usually threatens to punish the "traitors" who oppose
him and promises to all who will join his forces vaguely defined "proofs of
his gratitude." Only infrequently, and then in equally vague terms, do these
appeals speak of serfdom. The promise to do away with the landowners, and
indeed the upper classes as a whole, can scarcely be regarded as a political
program. The enunciation of a political program came from another
quarter.[11]

A. N. Radishchev

The political program, naturally, came from one of the intellectuals,
the forefather of the opposition movement, both liberal and radical, Aleksandr Radishchev (1749-1802). The son of a wealthy landowner, he and a few
other young noblemen went to Leipzig in 1766 to study law. These young
students became acquainted not only with representatives of the moderate
German Enlightenment but also with such French enlighteners as Helvetius
and such British economists as Adam Smith. After his return to Russia in
1771 Radishchev kept abreast of foreign literature and read Herder's works
as they appeared. Because his official duties required only little of his time
Radishchev remained primarily a freelance writer. As a poet, journalist,
and translator he by no means ranks as one of the best authors of his time.
His works owe their great significance to their content.

One of his works was the point of departure for and the source of
the intellectual development of the intelligentsia for years to come. It was
devoted to serfdom, and its effect is all the more astonishing when one considers that for decades it was difficult to procure and was known only by
word of mouth. This work is *Journey from Petersburg to Moscow*. Radi-

shchev published it semi-legally, for astonishing as it may seem, an office of the government gave him permission to print it. He sent several copies to acquaintances and delivered 25 copies to a bookstore. The Empress read the book and was horrified: its author, she thought, was "worse than Pugachev" or "worse than George Washington." Her reaction, of course, settled the matter. Radishchev barely had time to burn the some 600 copies which he still had at home. He was arrested and treated as a fomentor of rebellion. Condemned to death, he was pardoned and sent to Siberia, for even in Russia there were ways to temper the severity of absolutism. Radishchev was saved by one of these ways—friends in high places; and as a result the trip to Siberia took longer than a year, and a lady friend was permitted to join him and bring along his two children. In Siberia Radishchev was permitted to continue his literary pursuits. After the death of the Empress in 1796 Emperor Paul, who undid everything his mother had done, permitted Radishchev to return to his estate. In 1801 he was completely "rehabilitated" by Emperor Alexander I, but in 1802 he took his own life.

Radishchev on Serfdom

As a writer Radishchev is a representative of late neoclassicism, which under the influence of Western literature usually took as its point of departure the portrayal of human emotions. His work belongs to a favorite genre of that time, the "sentimental journey" (a number of such works were written in imitation of Laurence Sterne's work of that title). The individual stages of the journey from Petersburg to Moscow are the stages of Radishchev's experiences. We hear almost nothing of the villages and towns where he stopped, but we learn a great deal about the fates of the people whom he met at these stops. Radishchev's *Journey,* of course, is a literary work, but even if the individual episodes are invented, they nevertheless are most accurate in spirit, for they portray typical examples of what was going on at that time and had always gone on in Russia.

The main theme of the *Journey* is serfdom. Radishchev builds up his description from chapter to chapter: the depiction of a peasant working industriously in his own field on Sunday because he has to spend all the other days of the week working in the fields of his master is followed by a discussion of the normal corporal punishments and of the mistreatment of peasant women by landowners, and then by the description of the auction of serfs which led to the separation of families and by the portrayal of the induction of recruits into the army which at that time was tantamount to permanent separation of the recruit from his family (the period of service was 25 years). Next came a story about the sad fate of a serf who by order of his master had received the same education as his master's son and was then treated like a serf. And finally there were descriptions of the unhappy marriages which took place at the command of the master. By way of contrast Radishchev showed his readers the noble peasants: "I was repeatedly astonished to find so much highmindedness in the attitude of the villagers." Remarks about that most talented scholar-poet, Lomonosov, who was the son of a state-owned serf, conclude the work and were probably intended to emphasize by example the importance of the peasants for society and the state. The portrayal of a folksinger served the same purpose. Landowners, of course, were not presented in person to the reader, but by their deeds and the condition of their serfs the reader could form an opinion about them.

Peripherally Radishchev treated government officialdom. The characteristics of this class were its preoccupation with formalities, its lust for power, its abuse of the law, and, most prominent of all, its susceptibility to bribery. Radishchev deals the bourgeoisie a few blows in passing: in describing two merchants, a father and a son, he paints burghers in the gloomiest colors imaginable. Their main characteristic is their involvement in dishonest business transactions; next most prominent is their complete lack of culture.

Radishchev attempted to demonstrate on the basis of a few examples that Russian life was rotten to the core. The Russians in some cases even considered misfortune to be good luck—military service, harsh as it was, was considered escape from a cruel landowner. This shocking picture of Russian reality is supported by theoretical reflections. Radishchev proves that serfdom is unprofitable because slave labor is less productive than free labor. He excoriates censorship and stresses the importance of education for all social classes.

Such a description of her state was the primary reason for Catherine the Great's indignation. She paid no heed to the really moderate plan for a gradual liberation of the serfs which Radishchev elaborated.

Monarchy and Serfdom

We can only presume that Radishchev regarded the republic as the only acceptable form of government; as far as Russia was concerned, he considered monarchy to be the source of all the abuses found in Russian life. Certainly he believed that in Russia monarchy was most intimately connected with serfdom and the privileged position of the nobility and that the Russian monarch, as a matter of principle, was incapable *(nemoshchen)* of abolishing serfdom. These views earned Radishchev the title of founding father of Russian republicanism.

In point of fact, open rebellion was the only way to destroy serfdom. Radishchev considered such an action possible and even probable, and he portrayed it as vengeance taken on the "scoundrels," the serfowners. "Fire and death will be the way we are repaid for our cruelty and inhumanity." He did not call on the serfs to rebel, but instead exhorted "those who bear the name of the protectors of the public welfare" to rise up against serfdom: "Destroy the tools of his agricultural economy (the "scoundrel," i.e. the cruel landowner is meant); burn his granaries, his barns, and his silos and strew the ashes on the fields which witnessed his tyranny; brand him a public criminal so that all who meet him will not only despise him but avoid his company."

In his book Radishchev cited the ode "To Freedom" which he had written in 1781. This poem makes it perfectly clear that Radishchev was a confirmed opponent of Russian absolutism. And succeeding generations of intellectuals all too often believed, whether independently or under the influence of Radishchev, that without revolution no improvement was possible.

Russia and the West

During the last third of the eighteenth century the upper classes in Russian society continued to move closer to the West. This movement was fostered not only by numerous journeys to the West but also by the increased use of French, which supplanted German, formerly more widespread, as the language in which "polite society" conversed. European dress and European customs became more and more widespread, even though the minor landed gentry of noble birth, now no longer obliged to enter the service of the state, were at the same time returning to a way of life which was almost pre-Petrine. The merchant class, which showed no signs of developing into a "third estate" conscious of its place in the social hierarchy, clung to the old way of life even more tenaciously; in the nineteenth century it represented the patriarchal life-style, and as a result it became not only the butt of satire, as in the works of the dramatist A. N. Ostrovskii (1823-1886), but also, strange to say, the object of enthusiastic praise by some traditionalists, such as the critic and poet Apollon Grigoriev (1822-1864).

In the eighteenth century most of those who blindly imitated or scorned the West gave no thought to their attitudes. There were primitive worshippers of the West who had only a superficial knowledge of its culture. At that time there were such people in all of Europe, most of them mere "fools of fashion" *(shchegoli)* of the sort depicted by Holberg in his comedies. In a comedy by Fonvizin, a Russian imitator of Holberg, one such fool of fashion says: "To my misfortune I was born in Russia, but my heart belongs to the crown of France." In this instance the "crown of France" was French fashion. Because the Russian fools of fashion were members of the wealthiest and most prominent families, they often rejected the "narrowness" and "stinginess" of European life, and that was a form of criticism of the West. It is indeed a fact that whereas gambling debts were paid in the West with coin, many of Catherine's favorites gambled with

180

diamonds which they spooned out of little chests placed on the gaming tables. Serfdom had made it impossible for the Russian nobility to learn to be thrifty, and thus there originated the "open-handed Russian nature" which was later so admired.

Another group was made up of "Voltairians" who acquired at least something from the *intellectual* culture of Europe and perceived in this culture the light which might dispel Russian "prejudices." To these men it was clear that Russia was lagging far behind the West and that they had to close this gap. The optimistic Tsarina believed that the cultural development of Russia had in earlier times kept pace with that of Europe and had fallen somewhat behind only in the seventeenth century, a loss, to be sure, which Peter's reforms had made good almost completely. The differences between Russia and Europe, to her way of thinking, were only quantitative, not qualitative. People of her sort simply considered themselves "Europeans," and only few of them realized that the quantitative differences had become too great and had already become qualitative differences.

Strange as it may seem, however, many of them found that Russia, in spite of—or precisely because of—the fact that it had fallen behind, surpassed Europe in some respects. This was the view of the adherents of primitive "Slavophilism," which was for the most part based on an underestimation of European culture. Fonvizin, the above-mentioned writer of comedies, was sharply critical of European culture. In France he had become acquainted with journalists, authors, and scholars, among them truly outstanding men like d'Alembert, but because he was quite unable to comprehend the true nature of intellectual work and ideological polemics, he thought all these men vain idlers, swindlers, and parasites. His judgment of the French as a nation shows how inaccessible the intrinsic intellectual value of French culture was for him: "A Frenchman possesses no understanding, and if he did he would consider it the greatest possible misfortune," for all Frenchmen strive only for cheap pleasures. The thought of Prince M. M. Shcherbatov (1733-1790), who in 1786/1787 wrote a work *On the Corruption of Morals in Russia* (not published until the nineteenth century), was somewhat more complex. He recognized, in part correctly, that not European culture but the way in which it was imitated was responsible for the "corruption of morals," but he was able to produce as a rival to European culture no native Russian cultural value except Greek Orthodoxy.

It is important, however, that Russians now understood that Peter's "Europeanization" of Russia had been primarily "external" in nature. Catherine's activities were regarded not as a continuation of Peter's reforms but as an effort to make them more profoundly meaningful for Russia. Hardly anyone in Catherine's time would have denied that "Europeanization" of Russia was necessary; doubts arose only concerning the extent to which "Europeanization" should be pursued and the way in which it should be carried out. In the meantime people in the West—such as Mably,

181

Condillac, etc.—had also realized this. The criticism leveled at the "Westernism" of the time was directed primarily at superficial Gallomania, at the folly of slavishly imitating foreign fashions, and at the exclusive use of the French language. Critics demanded the right of literature to depict Russian life and simple Russian people. Even religious authors were in large measure "Westerners."

N. M. Karamzin

The most important representative of early Westernism at the end of the eighteenth century was the poet and historian, Nikolai M. Karamzin (1766-1826). Karamzin was one of the first Russians who during his tour of Europe was interested almost exclusively in the intellectual values of the West and who spoke to Russian readers about these values. During his youth, from 1785 to 1789, he was allied with the Freemasons. In 1789-90 he made an eighteen-month tour through Germany, Switzerland, France, and England and reported on it in his *Letters of a Russian Traveller* (1791/92), a work of the same genre as Radishchev's *Journey*. Everywhere Karamzin went he visited famous men—Kant, Herder, and Lavater, to name only three, but his characterizations of them were not always accurate. In addition, he described the life of the common people, the political institutions, and sometimes even the natural beauties of the places he visited. In his *Letters* Karamzin is more than a "Westerner"; he is simply a Western European. Russians, having been treated somewhat badly by nature and history, could only envy the Western Europeans. On the bank of the Rhine, in the vicinity of Schaffhausen, Karamzin fell to his knees, kissed the earth, and exclaimed: "O happy Swiss!" He could not imagine that people could live so happily in Russia. Karamzin's further development led him away from this enthusiastic Westernism.

When he tried to describe Russian life in his short stories, however, it turned out that he did not know the realities of Russian life at all. His pictures of it are often merely taken over from Western European literature—his portrayal of a monastery is a noteworthy example. As a poet Karamzin was a representative of that form of late neoclassicism which is called "sentimentalism" in Russia and which places great value on rather naive portrayals of man's emotional life.

CHAPTER III. SLAVOPHILES AND WESTERNERS

The Period of Transition—Alexander I

Catherine the Great's son, who as Paul I ascended the throne in 1796, tried in vain to undo as many of his mother's reforms as possible. His reign, considered by contemporaries a time of insane despotism, was brought to an end in 1801 by the last Russian palace revolution and the assassination of the Tsar. Paul's son, Alexander I, who ruled from 1801 to 1825, lived through the rise of Napoleon and played a decisive part in the "Wars of Liberation," which ended with the defeat of Napoleon and the formation of the "Holy Alliance."

From the point of view of intellectual history it was a very agitated age, and traditions of the late eighteenth century played a great role in it. The Freemasonic movement again became a force to be reckoned with. Now to be sure, the mystical literature of the eighteenth century was augmented by new Pietism (the works of Jung-Stilling, for example), which played a part even in Russian foreign policy when the "Holy Alliance" was established. For a time ecstatic mysticism thrived at the Russian court. In the so-called "Bible Society," groups which were close to Western European Pietism joined forces. With time the enlightened liberalism which characterized the opening years of Alexander's reign disappeared. In the last years of his life he turned away from pietistic mysticism, prohibited Freemason lodges, dissolved the "Bible Society," and banished from his court and even from Russia the Pietists whom he had for a long time patronized.

Alexander's personal development is typical of that of the men of his time. It was an age of "inwardness" which found expression in the literature of the "sentimental school" and in that of early Russian romanticism. In Napoleon both the Old Believers and the people as a whole were able to find once more a living "Antichrist": in numerology his name, when rather fantastically spelled "Napoleontii," made a total of 666, the number of the "Antichrist"!

The Decembrists

To some extent, however, the younger generation of intellectuals took up again the tradition of Radishchev. Young Russian officers who had been able to observe Europe at first hand during the military campaigns began to doubt Russia's political and social constitution; and when, after the Wars of Liberation, Russia took a central position in Europe's political system, these

183

doubts were intensified and became manifest as a purely negative attitude toward the Russian monarchistic constitution and toward serfdom.

The second half of Alexander's reign was a time of political secret societies which, of course, worked out programs which were quite different from each other. Every conceivable solution to Russia's problems was proposed, from purely fantastic ones, such as resettling the inhabitants of Greenland in Siberia, to thoroughly realistic plans for liberating the serfs and introducing a constitutional form of government, either constitutional monarchy or a republic. Most members of secret societies were still greatly influenced by the Enlightenment, but some romantic influences can also be discerned.

After Alexander's unexpected death, the revolutionary movement ended abruptly. In December, 1825, a group of conspirators attempted to take advantage of some ambiguities in the policies for choosing a successor to the throne and, with the help of regiments loyal to them, tried to overthrow the Romanov dynasty. The rebellion in St. Petersburg and in the southern provinces was soon suppressed because it had been badly organized and the conspirators were indecisive. The conspirators have gone down in history as the "Decembrists," and their revolt set an example for later ages.

Nicholas I

The Tsar who now ascended the throne and ruled from 1825 to 1855 was Alexander's second oldest brother, Nicholas I. His reign had most serious consequences for the future of Russia, mainly because of his personality and his imposing but sinister appearance. He had been educated to be a military leader, and he was completely unprepared to assume the leadership of the government. Before he was named Tsar he had been commanding general of a brigade, and as Tsar he attempted to rule Russia the same way he had commanded his brigade. The manner in which he treated the Decembrist rebels aroused some hostility among the upper classes. He had five of the rebels executed, among them an important poet K. F. Ryleev (1795-1826), and he sent more than a hundred as convicts to Siberia; for the most part those punished were members of the upper nobility. The candor with which the rebels expressed their opinions during their hearings led Nicholas to beleve that they were the sworn enemies of him and his dynasty. He then tried to rule with the assistance of government officials who were not of Russian birth, many of them Germans. Because they were creatures of his own making they were indeed loyal to him, but they were not always faithful public servants. Nicholas made every effort to avoid making any changes, even those changes which he recognized as necessary, and thus he took no decisive measures to abolish or at least alleviate serfdom.

The new tsar hated and despised intellectuals, and he himself had no intellectual interests. Intellectual culture seemed to him to be a dangerous cancer in the body politic. He held Goethe and Schiller in part responsible for the March Revolution of 1848, and he persecuted individual Russian poets and scholars with a tenacity which seems all the more incomprehensible when we consider that there were not many of them in Russia at that time anyway and that for this very reason the activities of each of them were of all the more value to Russia. His political ideal was the police state. Peter the Great before him had had a similar political ideal, but he had not been able to place all of Russian life under police control to the extent that Nicholas did. Moreover, Peter's state had been "dynamic." The police state of Nicholas I, however, was destined to remain unmoving and static. All too often the Tsar considered it his duty to preserve the status quo. Some of his pronouncements are particularly characteristic of this attitude. In one argument he remarked: "I think so too, because I learned that as a youth." Nicholas simply could not conceive the possibility that what he had learned thirty or forty years earlier might no longer necessarily be regarded as true. Perhaps we ought to be happy that as a youth Nicholas had not learned very much and was thus not often in a position to appeal to "what he had learned in his youth." In the realm of politics Tsar Nicholas was an odd sort of "Old Believer" who would have liked most of all to see everything in Russia and in Europe kept in the same "magnificent" state that had obtained in about 1815. This attitude brought down a terrible vengeance not only on him but on his state and his people as well. The resounding defeat of Russia in 1855 in the Crimean War finally made the Tsar aware of his mistakes. That his sudden death was actually suicide must remain no more than unproved speculation.

The Police State

It cannot be denied that some innovations were made during the reign of Nicholas I. Among other things, Russian law was finally codified. On the orders of the Tsar, M. M. Speranskii (1772-1839) published in forty-five volumes innumerable old Russian laws—more than 30,000 ordinances! Speranskii, a gifted statesman and mystic, had renounced his earlier plans for reform and had become the preserver and perpetrator of things old and out of date. Then, in 1833, the great collection of laws in fifteen volumes appeared; it contained only those laws which were still in effect, and by and large it remained in force until the Revolution of 1917. For us the "style" of this collection of laws is of particular interest, especially the "style" of those sections which are for the most part the work of the codifier, for in them the concept of the state held at that time is most clearly reflected. One volume contains, among other things, a compilation of "Measures for Prevention of Crimes." These "Measures" are no more than a collection of the moral regulations of the police state which are proclaimed without sanctions, that is, no punishments for violations of them are prescribed.

What, then, is the content of these regulations? "All must live together in peace, harmony, and sinless love," or "Drunkenness *(pianstvo)* is forbidden to one and all," or "It is forbidden to rush to the scene of a fire out of mere curiosity," "Males of more than seven years of age are prohibited from entering women's bathhouses when women are bathing there," and so on. The "finicalness" of formulation should be noted. If "love" had not been further restricted by the adjective "sinless," God only knows how it might have been interpreted, or if entering women's bathhouses had been prohibited to all males without further qualification, then workmen could not have entered them to make repairs.

Even though most of these regulations may never have been enforced, as were others not included in the books of law, the written regulations do reveal the mentality of their author: the state was to regulate the *entire* life of its subjects, and the individual was to be granted no "sphere of freedom," however restricted. The ideal state was the ant or termite colony. Moreover, the philosophy on which the "Measures for the Prevention of Crimes" was based is paradoxical and self-contradicting: on the one hand, it was assumed that the subject was so "good" that he would obey all these petty regulations even if not threatened with punishment should he violate them, and on the other hand it was believed that this very same subject was so inclined to evil that it was necessary to formulate as laws the most primitive moral precepts. In practice the police state demonstrated that every man was expected to be evil rather than good. The activities of the censors of the time are the clearest proof of this.

Censorship

By their actions the censors showed that the universal and all-encompassing supervision of the police state was meant not only to prevent subjects from committing certain acts but also to suppress "harmful" or even merely "undesirable" *thoughts* and *opinions,* and some censorship measures give the decided impression that in fact *all* thoughts and opinions were in and of themselves "undesirable." Truly, thinking *(rassuzhdenie),* in contrast to blind obedience *(povinovenie),* seemed to be the most dangerous thing. Even though some of the anecdotes about Russian censorship are undoubtedly apocryphal, there are enough documented cases to show what narrow limits the Tsar wished to set for the thoughts of his subjects.

One example may suffice. A poem by the Slavophile A. S. Khomiakov was suppressed by the censor on the grounds that even though it "contained nothing objectionable it could give rise to interpretations *(istolkovaniia).*" It must be admitted that this way of putting it certainly does accurately characterize the nature of every linguistic utterance, for it is in the very nature of language that it can and should be interpreted. Thus it was not the content which was found objectionable but the possibility that someone might read into a harmless statement a meaning which was "criminal" or merely "undesirable." Not only punishable acts, suspect views and thoughts were prosecuted. A state in which mere suspicion can justify punishment cannot be a state which functions according to law. Since that time, of course, the world has seen a number of states established on the same principles.

The word and the thought, by their very nature, had aleady become suspect. Victor Hehn has called attention to one of the Tsar's resolutions which best epitomizes his attitude: in commenting on the decree of the Minister of Education to introduce geometry into the curriculum, Nicholas wrote, "Yes, but *without proofs.*" But that was tantamount to saying that intellectual activity was "undesirable," for when a person learns to prove, he also soon learns to refute.

The Intellectuals

It was in this atmosphere, which became more and more oppressive as the reign of Nicholas progressed, that Russian intellectuals were obliged to live. And it was inevitable that intellectual movements could flourish only in the narrow circles of private groups. The only social institutions where Russian intellectual life could possibly survive were young people's groups and the salons of the "better families." There were also, of course, some literary journals—the Tsar had refused to grant permission to found any more of them on the grounds that "there are already enough of them"—but their continued existence depended on the whim of the censors, and their activity was all too often restricted or curtailed completely by police measures.

The existence of intellectual circles, especially when they had the slightest political tinge, was always threatened. Young people's groups, including as members such personalities as Alexander Herzen, Dostoevsky, and the Ukrainian poet Shevchenko, were not only forced to dissolve; their members, without formal sentence, were subjected to severe punishments, ranging from banishment to imprisonment or forced military service as enlisted men. It was precisely within these groups that those questions were discussed and those philosophies elaborated which are of interest to the intellectual historian.

One of the most important topics of discussion was the problem of the relationship between Russia and Europe. After the Napoleonic wars this problem was a particularly pressing one for the simple reason that Russians had to reach an understanding of why Russia was playing a role in

European politics and what entitled it to do so. These very questions were central to Russian thought between 1820 and 1860. Let us first give a survey of the views of those who believed that Russia's position of political power in Europe at that time and in the future was justified. These are the men who are called Slavophiles, in the broadest sense of the word, and who in part referred to themselves as Slavophiles.

The Thought of the Slavophiles

The general term "Slavophilism" is not completely defensible. The views of the so-called Slavophiles differed greatly. Moreover, the term "Russophilism" would really be more accurate, simply because most of the so-called Slavophiles took no interest in other, non-Russian Slavs and were often rather negative in their assessments of the culture of the other Slavic peoples, particularly of the Poles.

Where Russia was concerned, the Slavophiles held greatly divergent views . Perhaps we may sum up these views in a few succinct formulas: "Russia has a culture equal to that of Europe," "Russian culture is a complement to European culture, which is one-sided," "Russia is destined to save Europe, which is on the decline," "Russia is destined to succeed Europe in the development of culture" or "Russia is to be the heir of European culture," and, finally, "Russia will push Europe back" or even "Russia will destroy Europe."

The Decembrists

Only in a few of the works of the Decembrists do we find Slavophile ideas. Even immediately after the War of 1812 we can scarcely discern in Russia any genuine Francophobia, while at the same time we do find, as might be expected after a victorious war, a rejection of foreign cultural influences, especially French influence, and a strong rejection of foreign customs and fashions and of the use of a foreign language for everyday conversation. Chauvinism was also rare. In a very few years Napoleon was thought of as "a great man" and a "hero" burdened with tragic fate. The authors of some revolutionary plans regarded the "oppressed" Slavic people, the Poles and the Ukrainians, as natural allies in the struggle for the liberation of the Russian people. In the absence of any number of pronouncements in favor of Slavophilism, the fact that some Decembrists—Ryleev, for example—foregathered for "Russian breakfasts" of black bread and sauerkraut should be noted.

The "Liubomudry"

At the same time the Decembrists were engaged in their activities, intellectually committed members of the much younger generation born around 1800 were gathering together in Moscow to hear lectures on philosophy and to engage in philosophical discussions. There were among them several young men who were later to play significant roles in Russian intellectual life. Vladimir F. Odoevskii (1804-1869) in particular should be mentioned. His circle called itself the "Liubomudry," a Slavic translation of the word "philosophers."

The "Liubomudry" were preoccupied with romantic philosophy among other things, especially with the philosophy of Schelling, whom Odoevskii praised as the "Columbus of the soul," as the founder of the new psychology.[12] The members of this circle took upon themselves the task of "getting to know our fatherland." Russia had already demonstrated that it constituted an important "complement" to Europe. Europe, the circle thought, was awaiting its "Peter the Great" who would graft Russian (or Slavic) elements onto European culture, and one could already see Europe "turning unconsciously" to the northeast. Russia, the circle was convinced, was destined to bring unity out of the "chaos of European cultural developments," and this would constitute Russia's "intellectual conquest of Europe."

In later times the views of various members of the "Liubomudry" differed. One member of this circle, A. Titov, witnessed during his European tour in 1836 the one-sidedness of Europe and believed that Russia was to be "the mediator between East and West" and would be able to come to the aid of Europe—what he meant by "the East" is not clear. Odoevskii himself, however, gradually abandoned his anti-European position. One of the characters who appears in the discussions which frame his collection of short stories *Russian Nights* is an opponent of European culture who laments the loss of cultural unity in Europe and the decline of "living knowledge" there; in his lament this character frequently repeats the statements of the German romanticists. Odoevskii finds the words of this character— "Europe is perishing" *(Europa gibnet)*—too strong and asserts: "I see no signs of an impending decline." He goes on to contend that Russia, "which stands on the border of two worlds," is in a position "to save the soul of Europe" and to bring to its fragmented culture a new unity. This thought we shall hear repeated later by Dostoevsky. In later life Odoevskii became a confirmed enemy of the "Slavophiles," whose overestimation of "old Russia" he found quite misguided.

The Slavophiles

Not until the 1830's do we again find lively discussion of intellectual history in student groups and literary salons. The discussions were stimulated by the new philosophical ideas of the time, the ideas of Hegel and, to a lesser extent, by those of Schelling. And now, from the ferment of minds in search of truth, the philosophies of the Westerners and the Slavophiles crystallized. In the thought of the Slavophiles, of whom some were close to Hegel and others to Schelling, we can also discern an internal relationship to the philosophy of history and government propounded by the German romanticists. Whether these ideas were the result of the direct influence of the German romanticists has still not been established.

The two most important representatives of the older Slavophile movement were A. S. Khomiakov (1804-1860) and Ivan V. Kireevsky (1806-1856); among their younger comrades the most prominent were Konstantin S. Aksakov (1817-1860) and Yurii F. Samarin (1819-1876).

The most important theses of the "classical" Slavophile movement which now arose were roughly as follows:

1) Russia has its own unique spirit and ought to go its own historical way—one quite different from that of the West.

2) The unique character of Russia was imprinted upon it in "old Russia" (for some this meant Russia before Peter the Great, i.e. before the eighteenth century; for others it meant Russia before Ivan the Terrible, i.e. before the sixteenth century). Developments after Peter constitute deviations from Russia's unique path.

3) One of the essential elements of Russia's unique character is Greek Orthodoxy.

4) The Slavs, or at least some of the Slavic peoples, are intellectually and spiritually closely related to the Russians.

To be sure, this last thesis was not stated by all Slavophiles. Many of them knew really very little about the other Slavic peoples. For this reason, there is usually no justification for calling the Slavophiles of this time "Panslavists." In other respects, too, the thought of the Slavophiles was far from homogeneous. Moreover, in the unparalleled lack of intellectual freedom which prevailed in these decades, not all of the Slavophiles had the opportunity to develop their thoughts systematically in writing. Some of these ideas were expressed only in fragmentary form in occasional publications which appeared at intervals of a number of years. For example, Kireevsky's important essays appeared in 1829, 1845, and from 1850 to 1856.

The Slavophiles by no means represented the official Russian point of view. On the contrary, Tsar Nicholas considered them to be dangerous political dreamers and even "revolutionaries." The censors dealt harshly with their works and periodicals and often banned them without even subjecting them to close scrutiny. Konstantin Aksakov and Samarin possessed all the qualifications necessary at that time to receive professorships—in fact, Samarin's dissertation is even today not without relevance—but both were denied permission to teach at the university. Because Nicholas was determined to maintain the status quo in Europe, he viewed the relationships of the Slavophiles with members of other Slavic peoples as improper

190

meddling in the internal affairs of other states and in the prerogatives of other monarchs. Even after the death of Nicholas the censors treated the periodicals of the Slavophiles rather ungently. Fines were assessed repeatedly against Ivan Aksakov's monarchistic and conservative newspapers, and on occasion he had to suspend their publication. The best way to become acquainted with the views of the Slavophiles is to examine the philosophies of a few of them in isolation.

Ivan Kireevsky

Kireevsky believed philosophy to be his calling. In Berlin he had heard the lectures of Hegel and in Munich those of Schelling, and early in his career he is said to have been an ardent disciple of Schelling's philosophy. In 1829 he founded in Moscow *The European,* a periodical which was banned after its first issue because Kireevsky's philosophy was interpreted in political terms—a method employed repeatedly by Russian censors. It was not until fifteen years later that Kireevsky found another opportunity to express his thoughts in a periodical, and it was not until the last year of his life that such an opportunity occurred again.

Kireevsky's main theme is the contrast between European and Russian culture. His thought, it is true, never advanced beyond tentative speculation, and we have scarcely any reason to designate him an "important thinker." Nevertheless, we can summarize his contrast of Europe and Russia in a series of clearly formulated (though not always well founded) antitheses. Let us enumerate a few of them:

1) In Europe there is only *abstract-rational* science, and European theology is no exception to this rule; in Russia there is a *total* philosophy of life.

2) In Europe science is the province of scholastic and *juridical universities* (K. Aksakov makes it clear that "juridical" is a pejorative term—see below); in Russia sciences are cultivated in the *monasteries,* and they "unite higher knowledge."

3) The socio-political order of Europe is based on "separate and *mutually hostile classes";* Russia's socio-political order is based on the *"unanimity of the people." (edinodushnaia sovokupnost').*

4) In the West "*external* justice" reigns supreme; Russian cling to the ideal of "*inner* justice."

5) In Europe there are "artificially created laws"; Russian law developed on the basis of the simple life-styles *(byt)* of the people.

6) In Europe improvements in the socio-political order are always accompanied by *violent upheavals* (revolutions); in Russia reforms are the result of *natural growth* (Peter's reforms must be considered one of the exceptions to this rule).

7) The "*luxury* and artificality" of Western life is in stark contrast to the "*simplicity* of the needs" of the Russian people.

8) In the West personality is based on "wavering *egocentricism*"; in Russia it is based on "firm *family and community relationships*."

9) The experience of the Westerner can be characterized as "*pampered* dreaming"; the spiritual life of the Russian is "a *healthy* totality of the powers of the individual."

10) The Western European lives in a state of "*spiritual and intellectual restlessness*"; the dominant factor in Russian spiritual and intellectual life is "*profound peace and quiet.*"

11) The European is "convinced of his moral perfection," and his moral consciousness can be characterized as conscious *pride;* for the Russian, "constant mistrust in himself" is characteristic, and this is a sort of *humility.*

This list of antitheses could be expanded, but even as it stands it shows clearly that vague dislike and half-conscious hatred for the West has been replaced by an effort to comprehend in concepts the differences between Russia and the West. The boldness of these contrasts should not obscure the fact that some of the antitheses are vague and that others are either incorrect or highly exaggerated. Such basic concepts as "unity" and "totality" are never clarified, and the idea of an idyllic, patriarchal, and static life of the Russian people is certainly untrue, even when we take into account the fact that Kireevsky was speaking of Russians who had not yet been affected by the reforms of Peter the Great, the moral upheavals of Ivan the Terrible's reign of terror in the sixteenth century, or the Interregnum of the seventeenth century, and that he falsely conceived of "old Russia," i.e. Russia from prehistoric times down to at least the middle of the sixteenth century, as a unified land in which cultural development and cultural change were unknown. In Kireevsky's time not nearly enough was known about the Russian past. Even if Kireevsky's characterization is conceded to be valid for a certain select stratum of the simple Russian folk, his picture of spiritual and intellectual Europe still requires major corrections. He forgets that the West had not only abstract-rational theology but also occidental mysticism (Point 1). He forgets that change ("improvement") in European life was by no means always accompanied by revolution (Point 6). In characterizing the European he often combines the traits of individual social groups from different historical epochs—traits of the old nobility and of the modern petite bourgeoisie, and so on (Points 5, 7, and 11). Kireevsky ignores such essential aspects of the Russian past as the "intellectual unrest" of the Old Believer movement and of the old sects of the fourteenth and fifteenth centuries, the class struggles in Novgorod since the twelfth century (with which Kireevsky was quite familiar), and not only the revolts of the Interregnum or of Stenka Razin but also those of the eleventh and twelfth centuries. Finally, he sees in the past of Russia features which were not present at all: the "higher knowledge" of the monasteries, which in his opinion was superior to the knowledge of European universities; and Russian law allegedly born of the life-style of the people—he was able to cite in support of this only the law of custom. And he forgets that European universities created the intellectual tradition of which he was a part and that "external justice" afforded the very guarantees of human life with dignity and the very protection against evil which the Slavophiles looked for in vain from the Russian sovereigns of their time.

Kireevsky believed, of course, that since Peter the Great Russia had deviated from its historical path—indeed, even under Ivan the Terrible there had developed the false esteem of "external forms of tradition" which he condemned. In other words, since the sixteenth century Russia had been travelling the wrong path. Kireevsky was overly optimistic in his belief that the old traditions still lived on among the simple people, but he was perceptive enough to realize that it was impossible to return to the spiritual and intellectual state which had prevailed from the eleventh through the fifteenth century. That would have been a miracle; in fact, the mere re-institution of ways of life which had already died out would have been, to his mind, the "greatest misfortune" *(velichaishee bedstvie)*. He recognized, moreover, that he and his contemporaries had already become so "European" that they could no longer dissociate themselves from the West. He writes: "If I had sometime or other dreamed that any aspect which was peculiar to our former life and had long since died out had suddenly become effective in our life in its former form *(vmeshalas' v zhizn' nashu)*, a vision of that sort would have terrified me." And thus Kireevsky immediately gives up again the "utopia of the past" which he had portrayed in such vivid colors in his set of antitheses; or, rather, he does not wish to regard this utopia as a goal for the future but as a guiding light, a "regulative principle" which should be given primary consideration when the longed-for creative rejuvenation of Russian life is undertaken. In Kireevsky's writings we find only very vague hints of how he imagined such a rejuvenation to be.

The Concrete Goals of the Slavophiles According to Kireevsky

The goals of the Slavophiles according to Kireevsky may be described as follows: Russians ought to retain the "healthy" elements of European culture (or Culture—with a capital C, as Kireevsky usually phrases it), and one ought to revive the old elements of Russian culture and bring them to bear in a new and intensified way.

And how was it possible to revive true Russian culture? Kireevsky believed that "the roots of Russian culture were alive" in the simple folk "as well as in the holy Church." These roots—it would be more accurate to call them seeds—could be stimulated to grow and develop if that group of men who had achieved "the self-consciousness of the people," i.e. the intelligentsia, would finally become aware of the "one-sidedness of European culture" *(Kultur)*.

The easiest way to overcome the one-sidedness of European culture, in Kireevsky's opinion, was to bring about in Russians an inner transformation, to stimulate Russians to reeducate themselves. The inner turmoil of European culture, the preeminence of reason, which had at its disposal only the tool of analysis, this "self-propelled knife of autocratic reason" which "recognized nothing beyond itself," had to be overcome. It was necessary to "concentrate all the parts of the soul into a single power . . . and to find that center of being where the entire scope of the spirit becomes a living unity." Kireevsky set up faith in opposition to reason, for he believed that faith alone could provide "the spirit with a unified power of vision" (by which he meant intuition).

Expressed in this form Kireevsky's ideal still remains a utopia. His thesis, "revival," is less than a program, it is a sterile thesis. It would have been necessary to clarify and elaborate the concept of the new "living," "total" knowledge, a concept inspired in part at least by German romanticism; and it would have been necessary to do the same for the positive content of the moral and social ideal. But Kireevsky did not do this, and there is indeed reason to doubt whether an elaborated philosophical system could have immediately formed the basis for a program of action. What was really needed was to find the *real* elements of Russian life which could help change the ponderous realities of Russia—elements which, in the spirit of the Slavophile ideal, deserved to be "revived." It was for such elements that A. S. Khomiakov and Konstantin Aksakov were searching.

Khomiakov and the Doctrine of the Church

Khomiakov did not agree with all of Kireevsky's views. He was especially critical of the optimism with which Kireevsky asserted that in old Russia "Christian doctrine was expressed in private and public life in complete purity and to the fullest extent"; "There is not a single people of whom that can be said." Khomiakov discerned all sorts of foreign influences on Russian life of the distant past—Scandinavian, Tatar, etc. He saw in the *Domostroi*, the community life of old Russia, signs of vulgar "moral sentiments." True Christianity could be found only among the saints, in the monasteries, and in" individuals," but even in these instances Khomiakov saw a "lack of consciousness," or, as he put it, nothing but "synthesis without analysis," for he considered "analysis," by which he meant the rational comprehension of religious and moral ideas, the prerequisite for more profound and more elevated stages of knowledge and faith.

Khomiakov, in comparison to Kireevsky, made significant new contributions in the area of religion. Khomiakov was a comprehensively educated, very well-read and extremely versatile man, and an acute dialectician, and he developed his thoughts in the literary salons. His essays, some of which were published posthumously, almost always seem to be collections of aphorisms. Nevertheless, theologians are certainly right in regarding him as one of the most important Russian thinkers.

Khomiakov saw in the philosophy of Hegel, to whom not only some Westerners but even Khomiakov's partisans, Konstantin Aksakov and Yurii Samarin, paid homage, the *typically* negative features of the Western mind. His criticism of Hegel's philosophy is linked with his criticism of Western rationalism itself. The results of this criticism are the same as those found in the works of Kireevsky: "We place the European world above our own and acknowledge its incomparable superiority." But if Russians are to avoid the shortcomings of European culture, they must not "neglect any of the spiritual-intellectual or material achievements of Europe," and they must also not strive simply to restore the life-style of old Russia, for that would be laziness *(nepodvizhnost'),* and "there is something ridiculous and even immoral in the fanaticism of laziness."

The discord and rationalism of Western culture, Khomiakov believed, could be overcome only by practicing the principles which are found in the Greek Orthodox Church. The foremost of these principles is *"sobornost',"* a term for which there is no adequate translation and which is familiar to every Western theologian. *"Sobornost'"* characterizes the true nature of the Church. It is its *unifying* principle and is based on faith. Whereas the rational powers of the mind (pure and practical reason) separate men from each other, for every man thinks "from within himself and for himself," in the Church, knowledge corroborated by faith is imparted to every man solely by virtue of his being a member of the Church. Here man does not find himself "in the impotence of spiritual-intellectual isolation but in the power of his spiritual-intellectual union . . . with his fellow men and with the Savior." *Sobornost'* is not a human but a divine characteristic of the Church. In the Church all members are united in a *mystic* and "supra-conscious" community with each other and with the head of the Church, Christ. To be sure, Khomiakov was not thinking of the Church as it existed as an institution at his time but of "the true Church." Thus, we find again in the *Weltanschauung* of this leading Slavophile a utopian note.

The "wisdom" over which the Church disposes can serve only as the *basis* for a *Weltanschauung;* it cannot be a concrete philosophical or scientific doctrine. This philosophy, however, will necessarily be all-embracing and unified, while the spiritual and intellectual culture of the West is characterized by its inner turmoil and divisiveness. But, Khomiakov thought, that cannot satisfy us, for man's soul is not like a mosaic, and its "true life" must be a unity and totality. Khomiakov's point of departure, then, was Greek Orthodoxy. His interest in non-Orthodox Slavs was therefore not very great or profound.

195

Khomiakov felt that the contrast between Europe and Russia was the result of historical developments, and he determined with a certain amount of astonishment that even in his time, around 1845, Europeans without exception regarded Russia with distrust and contempt and occasionally with hatred. The reason for these feelings was on the one hand that Europeans correctly felt that the two areas had developed differently and on the other that Europeans were irked that Russia, so different from Europe, had now become the political equal of the Western European countries. The attitude of the Russians was quite the opposite: they regarded European culture with something akin to veneration and their own Russian culture with humility. Khomiakov's judgments concerning Russian culture were really for the most part inappropriately modest. As late as 1845 he wrote: "Our literature is poor in content"; and in 1849 he expressed the opinion that Russian science was also insignificant *(nichtozhna)* and that even Russian music and art were still not Russian in character. In 1855 he wrote a poem which is a flaming condemnation of the entire Russian past and in which he enumerated its "sins."[13] For him the West was still the "land of holy miracles," which, to be sure, was being enveloped by impenetrable darkness. These "miracles" were the cultural achievements of the past, but even in the present Khomiakov looked upon England as an exception. He can certainly not be accused of isolating himself from European culture.

For Khomiakov Russian life in the past was not totally "dark." In contrast to Kireevsky, he discerned in Russian history epochs in which the spiritual and intellectual life of the country was "fire and light . . . filled with new forces." This was the case even after the time of Ivan the Terrible, during the reign of Ivan's son Feodor in the sixteenth century, during that of Aleksei Mikhailovich in the seventeenth, and during that of Elizabeth in the eighteenth. His own time, Khomiakov believed, was suffering because the intellectuals were separated from the simple people, among whom the bases for genuine Russian spiritual and intellectual culture were still alive. The two basic elements of this culture, he thought, were the Christian faith and the social structure of the Russian village community (the *mir*). Perhaps Khomiakov called the organization of the Russian village to the attention of Baron A. von Haxthausen, a German traveller from Westphalia; perhaps Baron von Haxthausen became aware of the peculiarity and significance of this village system of government on his own. Whatever the case, not until after the appearance in 1847 of Haxthausen's account of his travels did the *mir* begin to play a central role in Russian socio-political thought.

Khomiakov believed that the village system of government was originally Slavic and went back to the earliest times. Not every single peasant had statutory rights to the land tilled by the peasants. The land, after all, belonged to the owner of the estate; but the serfs cultivated part of it for themselves, and this part was disposed over by the *entire community*. The fields which were placed at the disposal of every individual family were redistributed from time to time, because the number of families grew or their composition changed in other ways, and because this arrangement prevented some members of the community from receiving preferential treatment by retaining permanent tenure of better land or more conveniently situated fields.

This means of land distribution was considered proof not only that each individual felt himself to be socio-economically a member of a collective pesonality but also that in law and economics the individualistic principle had not yet become prevalent. Later the *mir* was viewed as the first stage of socialism.

We should note at this juncture, however, that in actual practice there were a number of negative aspects to this village system of government, that it hindered agricultural progress, and that, as will be seen later, it was by no means in accord with the wishes of those peasants who much preferred to own their fields as their private property. Moreover, in the 1850's Russian historiographers and historians of law presented convincing proof that the *mir* was not of Slavic origin but was rather a system which had been introduced by the authorities for fiscal reasons, namely to guarantee the collection of the taxes, for which the whole community stood warranty. The Slavophiles, like the so-called *narodniki* later on, were unwilling to draw any conclusions from the findings made by the historians.

Konstantin Aksakov and the State

Konstantin Aksakov, an enthusiast who had been a Hegelian in his youth and remained an admirer of Schiller his whole life, took the tenets of the Slavophiles to such extremes that their one-sidedness became especially manifest, but because of their extreme form these views attracted more adherents and defenders, among them Konstantin's brother Ivan (1823-1886), who was for many years an energetic publicist of Slavophile ideas. In Konstantin Aksakov's works we occasionally find rather profound insights on linguistics, history, and folklore presented with the same force of conviction as are all manner of fantastic ideas.

Konstantin Aksakov generalized the thesis of the *mir* and provided this generalization with an ideological foundation, which consisted of restricting the positive significance of the law and the state. Every man and every people, so Aksakov argued, can construct the community (and the community in which the individual lives is identical with the people) on the principle of either "external" or "internal" justice. For these two concepts Aksakov uses the terms *pravo* and *pravda*. Law—"external justice"—is regulated, determined, and guaranteed by the state; "inner justice" is a matter for the people, or, as Aksakov often said, a matter "for the country" *(zemlia)*, to which he contrasted the state. The state can require that the law be obeyed and can force men to obey it. The rules and regulations of "inner justice" are acknowledged and obeyed voluntarily and "sincerely." Restriction of freedom is the way of the state, freedom is the way of inner justice.[14] Only the second way is worthy of man. "Blessed is the people which preserves its faith in inner justice." Among the Slavs, Aksakov believed, the *mir,* the village community, originated as a result of the quest for inner justice.[15]

Aksakov believed that the state necessarily puts an end to freedom, the individual conscience, and inner conviction, in short to "true life." It lulls to sleep man's "moral alertness," and therefore "the state by its nature is the principle of evil" or "the lie." The Slavs, and foremost among them the Russians, are "stateless peoples," in Aksakov's opinion, but as early as the ninth and tenth centuries they had "invented" the *mir,* and that was a great "human achievement" of universal historical significance.

The Slavophiles on Western Europe

There were adherents to the Slavophile doctrines who could find in European culture not a scintilla of goodness, truth, and beauty. Often these men knew hardly anything about Europe. Some of them considered Russia to be the only fixed pole in European politics. Some spoke of the West as "dying," "dead," or "rotten " and "rotting" *(gniloi zapad).*

The Slavophiles, characteristically, paid almost no attention to Russia's position as the land between the East and the West. This generation regarded the East, greater and greater parts of which fell to the Russian empire during the nineteenth century, merely as the passive object of Russian and European policy. When Russia is contrasted with the West, then Russia is, after all, "the East." "What sort of East do you wish to be?" Khomiakov asked, "the East of Xerxes or the East of Christ?" The answer to this question was obvious: Russia was the East of Christianity, and in this respect essentially it had much in common with the West.

The thought of the Slavophiles was also strongly influenced by the thought of the West, primarily by the ideas of the German romanticists. Khomiakov in his doctrine of the Church seems to be dependent on the German Catholic theologian Johann Adam Moehler (1796-1838), the most important member of the so-called "Tubingen School" of Catholic theology and later a professor at Munich. The views of the French "traditionalists"— de Maistre, Bonald, and Lamennais (in his early period)—were even more important for the Slavophiles. As we have seen, the first person to examine the *mir* scientifically was a German, Baron von Haxthausen. In fact, even the words "rotting Europe" seem to have been coined by a European who was dubious about the future of the West. As P. Struve has ascertained, S. P. Shevyrev, a reactionary Slavophile who was the first to use the expression in the journal *Moskvitianin* in 1841, took it from an article by Philarete Chasles which had appeared in the *Revue des deux mondes* in November, 1840.

At the "Slavic Congresses" of the 1860's and later, one sarcastic observer remarked, the delegates conducted their business in German, drank Rhine wine, and spent their time cursing the Germans. This caricature is even more accurate for the older Slavophiles, who were basically "anti-European" Europeans.

The tone for the polemics against the West was the result of reading the "negative" European literature written between 1830 and 1848, works by such men as Feuerbach, D. F. Strauss, Max Stirner, Marx, and Engels. At that time even F. Tiutchev (1803-1873), who was a serious political thinker, a diplomat, and a poet, thought that only Russia could save Europe from social revolution. That he, like Dostoevsky after him, was wrong did not become evident until much later.

The Westerners

In the beginning the ideas of the Slavophiles were of limited effectiveness. Most people of the time, even the thoughtful ones, were actually "unconscious Westerners" or "Russian-speaking Europeans" who at best recognized that Russia would have to "catch up" with the West culturally and politically. Even Tsar Nicholas I was a Westerner *sui generis*. To be sure, he was forced by circumstances to devote his attention to European politics and in so doing, as his critics have pointed out, he did indeed too often neglect the real interests of Russia. He did not realize the peculiarities of Russia, nor did he by any means consider it a "retarded" country.

The conscious Westerners constituted even less a unified coherent group than did the Slavophiles. We must therefore now examine a few representatives of the various types of Westernism.

P. Ya. Chaadaev

One of the more isolated Westerners was Piotr Chaadaev (1793-1856), who had been a member of the Decembrists but made no lasting impression on either Slavophiles or Westerners until he participated in the discussions of the 1840's. The scion of a wealthy and distinguished family, he served as an officer in the Russian army and after the Wars of Liberation spent years in Europe, even longer than Karamzin before him, with the result that he became more thoroughly familiar with European intellectual life than Karamzin had. In Europe he moved primarily in Catholic circles. The first of these was probably the group of the Baron d'Eckstein in Paris, and it was presumably through this group that he became acquainted with the works of the French traditionalists. He also studied German philosophy—Kant—and had the opportunity to meet Schelling personally. Later he wrote a few letters to Schelling, but like Khomiakov he had only a vague notion of Schelling's religious development. In 1826 Chaadaev returned to Moscow, but only after several years of isolation did he gain access to the salons frequented by the intellectuals. In 1836 he published in a newspaper a "Philosophical Letter to a Lady," the addressee of whom was perhaps a literary fiction. The "Letter" affected its readers like "a pistol shot in the night" and spurred the authorities to take drastic action: the newspaper was forced to cease publication, its editor was banished, and Chaadaev was declared legally insane and placed in medical and police custody. Soon, however, he was permitted to appear in society again. His other "Philosophical Letters" did not become known until later, the last of them not until after 1917, and even today not all of them have been published in the original French version.

What enraged the censors and the Tsar was the description of Russia as a historical "void." After the early pagan barbarism, Chaadaev wrote, Russia had experienced, under Byzantine influence, an epoch of crude ignorance, then the alien influence of the Tatars, and, after Peter the Great, Russia had blindly and slavishly imitated the West. Chaadaev regarded the Russia of his day as a country devoid of tradition, and he condemned the Decembrist movement, with which he had probably formerly sympathized. He painted his pessimistic picture of Russia, it should be noted, with the same colors which some of the traditionalists were using to sketch their pessimistic pictures of Europe.

Chaadaev probably did not write his letters for the sole purpose of drawing this hopelessly pessimistic picture. Russia, he believed, could be saved if it allied itself with Western culture, which Chaadaev saw in a Catholic light—whether or not he was actually converted to Roman Catholicism is unimportant. He believed that alliance with Western culture would constitute the true Christianization of Russia—and here too it is immaterial whether he was thinking of an alliance of the Russian Church with Roman Catholicism or of some sort of transformation of Russian Christianity. In my opinion the recently discovered "Philosophical Letters" of Chaadaev[16] reveal that he had some sort of pastoral intention; he certainly entertained the idea that the individual Russian could find a way out of the intellectual turmoil of his time by joining the Roman Catholic church.

Chaadaev's *Apology of a Madman,* which was written later and never completed, does not prove with certainty that he changed his views, but in it we do find the assertion that Russia, precisely because it has not developed any fixed tradition, represents the ideal soil for further positive development. That sounds like a sincere expression of opinion for the very reason that we find other Russian thinkers saying approximately the same thing.

V. G. Belinsky and Early Russian Socialism

Belinsky (1811-1848), the most famous of all Russian critics, has been canonized in the Soviet Union and occupies a place alongside "the classical writers of Marxism and Leninism," but it is possible to judge his activity differently. A man with little education, without any real knowledge of Western European philosophy, and without consistency in his literary aesthetic judgments, Belinsky achieved his fame primarily because he had the knack of presenting both true and false ideas to his readers in a form which was simple and easily comprehended and remembered.

Belinsky, however, was one of the men who turned Russian Westernism toward political radicalism, and the significance of this feat should not be underestimated. Both his personal philosophy and his political views changed frequently. After a period of "reconciliation with reality," when Belinsky based his thought on a misunderstanding of Hegel's doctrine that "all reality is rational," there followed a period when he vigorously opposed the "horrible Russian reality" of his time. He probably believed that the struggle against this reality would have to proceed along the line of the revolutions in France of 1789 and 1830. The primary objective was to eliminate dynasties, to abolish monarchy, and to put an end to serfdom. Then, gradually, he rebelled more and more against the Russian Church, indeed against religion in general. Belinsky's impressive polemics against theoretical philosophy, which allegedly justified completely the status quo, were developed in his personal correspondence and were based on the conviction that every human being has a right to happiness in *this* world, a point of view also found in Europe during the years before the Revolution of 1848. Of course, Belinsky was prepared to sacrifice thousands of members of the "older generation" in order to achieve this happiness—political and social "liberation," and he believed that this happiness could be brought about by socialism, of which he had rather vague notions.

It is understandable that there was a need to define the socialist ideal more precisely and more concretely. The socialism with which Russians were familiar was primarily the French "Utopian Socialism" of Charles Fourier (1772-1837). After 1845 we hear from all sides how Russians were studying the socialistic literature of Western Europe. One of the best known groups was located in St. Petersburg and consisted of young men who had

201

gathered about M. Petrashevskii. Several young authors, among them Dostoevsky, were members of this circle, and some of them were sentenced to death for reading about and discussing socialism but were subsequently "pardoned" (Dostoevsky was sentenced to four years in prison in Siberia). In Russia "Fourierism," which held that socialist "phalanges" could infiltrate Russian society, soon became generally connected with the mood of revolt to which conditions in Russia had given rise. Abolition of monarchy became the axiom of every socialistic and radical liberal movement.

As far as Belinsky was concerned, Peter the Great remained the greatest hero in Russian history. What Belinsky admired was the Tsar's struggle against old Russia and his turn to the West. Belinsky was not, however, a blind admirer of the West; in fact, during the last years of his life he became convinced that perhaps Russia was better endowed than the West and closer to achieving the final goal of socialism. Here we find enunciated again his old idea that Russia was destined to become the heir to the other peoples of Europe or to comprise within itself the spiritual and intellectual culture of the West.[17]

Alexander Herzen

Belinsky owed his knowledge of philosophy mainly to well-read members of a student group in Moscow around 1835 which was led by a talented young Hegelian, N. Stankevich (1813-1840). Even earlier, around 1830, there were student groups in Moscow which were more interested in French socialism than in German philosophy. One of the members of such a group was Alexander Herzen (1812-1870). His father was a Russian nobleman and his mother a Suabian, and in accordance with his father's wishes he retained in the spelling of his name the initial "H," a letter which does not exist in the Russian alphabet.[18] Herzen's group was soon broken up, and he himself was banished to the northeast of Russia. In 1843 he was finally permitted to return to St. Petersburg and later to Moscow, where he was in close contact with the Stankevich circle. In 1846 he received permission to travel abroad, and he remained in the West as an emigrant until his death in 1870.

Several factors combined to make Herzen one of the central figures in Russian intellectual movements during the 1840's, 1850's, and 1860's, even though he was not enough of a fanatic to formulate a clear program for revolutionary activity. He was a brilliant and talented political journalist; his knowledge of the West was based on first-hand experience and on his personal contact with Western European radical circles; and in the West he published not only Russian periodicals but also brilliantly written memoirs, *My Past and Thoughts (Byloe i dumy)*, and important political works, the most significant of which was *From the Other Shore* (published in German in Hamburg in 1850 and eight years later in Russian).

To characterize Herzen's unbelievably broad, many-faceted, and not always consistent political writings, it is necessary first to emphasize the direct effect which his London periodical, *The Bell (Kolokol)*, had on the corruption prevalent in Russia. Through *The Bell* the people of Russia, who were forbidden to buy and read the journal, learned how effective freedom of speech is. Later, unfortunately, Russian intellectuals often granted freedom of speech only to the political opposition, and just as often they overlooked the fact that Herzen considered it absolutely necessary to apply moral standards in politics. Herzen's political ideal was a combination of democracy and socialism. The failure of the Revolution of 1848 led him to judge Western European liberalism harshly, although he continued to hold England's liberal constitution and liberal traditions in very high esteem. After 1848 he saw only "victims" and "the oppressed." In time he became convinced that Russia, like America, was a country with few traditions and thus best suited for socio-political reforms, all the more so since in Russia there were also the psychological beginnings of socialistic consciousness, namely in the *mir,* which Herzen regarded not as a happily preserved vestige of the patriarchal and idyllic past, but as the germ of a future political order.

Of course Herzen, who developed gradually from Hegelianism to atheism and sceptical positivism, could not wax enthusiastic about old Russian cultural values the way the Slavophiles had. He placed more value on the reforms of Peter the Great, which he almost equated with the founding of Russia. He recognized more and more clearly, of course, the negative aspects of Peter's reforms, but he still considered the past of Europe to be the highest cultural achievement of mankind. The Europe of his own time, however, was to his mind consumed by the struggle of socialism against the "decrepit," "rotten" civilization of the bourgeoisie. The future, he thought, belonged to the Russian peasant and the European working man, both of whom had the same goals and tasks—socialism.

Boris Chicherin

The Russian liberal camp consisted at that time of isolated thinkers and, of course, the Westerners. The most typical of them was Boris Chicherin (1828-1903), who was a philosopher and historian of law, a Hegelian, and a scholar in the European sense of the word. For a short time he was also a university professor. Because his political ideal demanded freedom for the individual and because he was in favor of only gradual change in the Russian political system, he was regarded as an enemy both by the authorities and by the political radicals. His ideas seemed strange to his contemporaries: his high regard for the state and for private ownership ran counter to the philosophy of socialism, and when in the 1860's and later he supported idealistic philosophy and "even" religion, this "conservative liberal," as P. Struve has called him, was branded a "reactionary" by the political radicals.

He rejected the ideas of the Slavophiles, but he also realized that the Russian "socialism" of the Westerners was not based on the cultural traditions of Western Europe. His Westernism was a species of English liberalism, and from this point of view he too presented a negative characterization of the Russian way of thinking: "The specific characteristic of Russian thought is the lack of the concept of limitation. It almost seems as if the vast immeasurable expanse of our fatherland has been impressed upon our brains. Every concept appears to us in unconditional form. For us all boundaries which separate it [this concept] from other neighboring areas disappear; we recognize neither the place it occupies in a series of other concepts nor its relationship to concepts which touch upon it." The culture of Western Europe arose from the struggle of various forces which became clearly differentiated as opposites and which prescribed limits to each other. In Russia "as among the peoples of the Orient, everything disintegrates into the infinite." "A Russian wants all or nothing." "With us there is no golden mean."

Like Chicherin, other Russian liberals of the time also remained isolated. The era of Nicholas I contributed in many ways to the fact that the traits of Russian thought emphasized by Chicherin emerged even more strongly in the following decades. Besides, in the Russian world there was no place for liberal Westerners anyway.

The Effects of the Era of Nicholas I

The following epoch, which is usually referred to as "the sixties" but which comprises at least three decades of Russian spiritual and intellectual history, from 1855 to 1885, rose from foundations established during the era of Nicholas I. The "sixties" was the age of Russian "Enlightenment," but through his cultural policies Nicholas had already established a firm basis for this spiritual and intellectual style.

The primary characteristic of the official ideology of the age of Nicholas was "utilitarianism." Every person, every deed, and every event was judged only in terms of its usefulness to the state. As a criterion, however, usefulness obliterated all boundaries, rendered everything and everyone comparable, and forced everything in the world onto the same plane. In the "sixties" profit for the state was replaced by profitability for the people. Autonomous independent values were not recognized in either case. A judgment of utility, when all other values are ignored, can only be subjective and arbitrary. The "sixties" had their own authoritarian judges, but the era of Nicholas I had only one—the Tsar himself. The "sixties" were interested in "benefiting the people"; Nicholas was preoccupied with "the interests of the state."

If we keep in mind this basic standpoint of the political philosophy of Nicholas, we can understand the "incomprehensible" aspects of his character. When Nicholas got word that M. Yu. Lermontov (1814-1841), the most important Russian poet of his time, had fallen in a duel, that this man whom the Tsar had persecuted with a tenacity impossible to understand was now dead, all that Nicholas could say was: "He was a dog—and he died like a dog." The Ukrainian poet Shevchenko, who was a painter by profession, was banished to Central Asia as a common soldier and was forbidden "to paint and to write." The Tsar turned the first work of the new Russian drama, Pushkin's *Boris Godunov,* over to the dismal, petty, but faithful journalist Bulgarin to criticize, and Nicholas, probably at Bulgarin's advice, suggested to Pushkin that he turn his drama into a novel. As is well-known, Dostoevsky was sent to prison because he was a member of a circle which studied Fourier and engaged in liberal discussions. Even the novelist I. S. Turgenev (1818-1883) was banished to his estate, simply because of an obituary of Gogol which he had written. We could expand the martyrology of Russian literature by numerous other instances. Among the Decembrists who were banished to Siberia were such important writers as Prince Alexander Odoevskii (1802-1839), A. Bestuzhev-Marlinskii (1797-1837), and W. Küchelbecker (1797-1846), and all of them died early deaths.

The Tsar's faithful servants acted in accordance with his views, and because it was always difficult to tell what was useful and what was harmful, their suppression of publications was even more capricious than that of the Tsar and their actions even more unpredictable and unwarranted. We have already noted that literary works were forbidden merely on the grounds that they "might" be harmful. Even the publication of folksongs was prohibited, and for this reason the publication of the collection of folksongs made by Ivan Kireevsky's brother, Peter, was not completed until shortly before the Revolution of 1917. The Slavophiles—the Aksakov brothers, Ivan Kireevsky, and Prince Cherkasskii—were not only forbidden to have their works printed, they were even forbidden to submit them to the censors for approval. S. T. Aksakov, a well-known poet who by no means shared the Slavophilic views of his sons, Konstantin and Ivan Aksakov, was refused permission to publish a collection of writings on hunting on the grounds that he was related to subversives. All these decisions were made on the basis of the principle of utility. Unfortunately, these views were later adopted by those who were diametrically opposed to Nicholas I.

It is no wonder that scholarship, especially such branches of learning as philosophy and theology, found itself in a particularly difficult position. Since every word seemed to be dangerous, words which conveyed thought could not help seeming much more dangerous. The persecution of philosophy, which had begun during the reign of Alexander I, ended in 1850 with an edict forbidding the teaching of philosophy at Russian universities. The reason given was that "there is no proof that philosophy is useful, and it is quite possible that is is harmful." The official legal opinion on the matter contains the following characteristic passage: "Because of the uncertainty of its basic principles and the unsatisfactory nature of its results and its lack of clearly definable scope and precise boundaries," philosophy can lead to "dangerous experiments." The word used is *popolznovenie*, which means the intention to commit a crime, and the imprecision of this term makes it possible to justify all sorts of prohibitive laws. The fear of "anyone who thought differently" *(inakomysliashchii)* was particularly great. Russian satire of the time takes note of "a project to introduce into Russia a single way of thinking *(edinomislie)*." This satire would have hit the mark completely, were it not for the fact that the Tsar and his servants would have liked it best if no one thought at all. This goal was, in fact, achieved in part, as the following decades showed.

CHAPTER IV. THE RUSSIAN ENLIGHTENMENT

The Age of Reforms

The death of Nicholas I was greeted with a sigh of relief by those of his subjects who still were thinking men—not merely by the political radicals, whose numbers had grown "underground" in spite of all the persecutions to which they were subjected, but even by monarchists and conservatives, such as the Aksakov family and the poet Tiutchev, who was a chamberlain, a court official.

The successor to Nicholas I, his son Alexander II (1855-1881), had at least overcome the inertia with which his father had clung to old traditions, but the necessary reforms were carried out too late. The first reform undertaken was the liberation of the serfs, and it met with enthusiastic approval from members of the older generation, Slavophiles and Westerners alike— even "leftists" like Herzen approved of it. Only one leading prelate raised his voice to warn against the abolition of serfdom. Some of the landowners, of course, wanted to water down the reform as much as possible, but in 1861 the emancipation of the serfs was proclaimed.

Of other important reforms the revision of the courts must be singled out. Trials were declared open to the public, and the jury system and the separation of functions (grand jury, judge, state attorney, lawyer) were adopted from the West. The reform of the courts was perhaps the most liberal, and there were numerous men who devoted their energies to the new courts, which had replaced the old justice-of-the-peace system. Autonomous local administration within rather narrow limits *(zemstvo)* and the introduction of universal military service were other important reforms promulgated at this time.

The inertia of the reign of Nicholas I was also overcome in many other areas. The resounding defeat suffered by Russia in the Crimean War showed that Russia could no longer match the technology of the Western European nations. In the war Russia's lack of railroads had had catastrophic consequences. No efforts had been made to modernize the Russian army. For example, no modern rifles had been adopted by the army (the "beauty" of operating the ramrod etc., had been preserved). Now Russia had to catch up.

And so in Russia the age of modern capitalism arrived. To be sure, early capitalism assumed repulsive forms among government officials who were corrupt and workers who had no legal protection and who only yesterday had been serfs, and as a result it was less attractive to thoughtful and morally sensitive people in Russia than elsewhere.

207

The Enlightenment of the "Sixties"

Enlightenment is a phenomenon which can assume varying forms in the intellectual history of different countries and different epochs. The thought of the Greek Sophists and the philosophy of the French Enlightenment in the eighteenth century are the forms most familiar to us. In Russia in the "sixties" we find a form of enlightenment which, granted, is of little importance philosophically but is extraordinarily radical.

One characteristic of the ideology of the time is perhaps difficult to comprehend because in its intellectual content the Russian Enlightenment, in contradistinction to other forms of enlightenment, was extremely primitive and impoverished. Negation was the essence of the Russian Enlightenment, a type of negation which was never really completely developed and delineated because the adherents of the Russian Enlightenment, who are sometimes called "nihilists," did not strive to do this and were not capable of doing it.

There are some, not many, autobiographical reminiscences by "men of the sixties." Even the ideological enemies of the "men of the sixties" find the basic characteristic of the age to be "restlessness," "inconstancy," "movement." Sometimes this "movement" is characterized as "intellectual and spiritual," or mention is made of "restlessness of thought." Such characterizations are inaccurate because at this time we do not detect the slightest bit of thinking. The era of Nicholas I had been a time when thought gradually fell asleep, and now thought was replaced by a simple categorizing activity. Everywhere evaluations and revaluations were undertaken on the basis of certain principles which were accepted as "axioms." Of course, the values of the time did not recognize degrees or gradations; hierarchy as such was rejected, and "yes" and "no" were the only answers which were recognized as valid. Florovsky has termed this sort of evaluation predominantly "moralistic," but this assessment is not completely accurate; the illness which had befallen Russian thought was in part the result of the state of Russian morals, but the illness, not the state of morality, was characteristic of the times.

Thought which accepted only "yes" and "no" answers could not come to grips with the great reforms of the time, because even these reforms did not satisfy absolute demands. The "limited" and realistic reforms were supplanted by programs for total revolution which were more consistent but totally unrealistic. Socialism, not the emancipation of the serfs, was seen as the task at hand. The goals were not constitutional government, but "the social republic" or even anarchy; not the solution of the nationality problem, which had become acute and had confronted both Russia and the Russians in the Polish rebellion of 1863, but cosmopolitanism and the victory over "national narrowness"; not freedom of conscience but atheism. This was the very tendency "to ignore all limitations" (and also all gradations, phases, transitions) of which B. Chicherin had spoken.

208

This trait of the philosophy of the Russian Enlightenment is based on a metaphysical hypothesis, namely the assumption that *being* is "a one-story house," "only one stratum"; that there are no higher or lower stages of being; that there is no hierarchy of "spheres of being" or "levels of being." It was presumed that higher stages of being could be derived from lower ones, and it was usually presumed—not without strong influence by the materialism and positivism which then dominated Western Europe—that matter was a lower stage of being, allegedly the simplest stage and the basis for all higher stages. "Egoism," the drive for self-preservation, and the like were regarded as the simplest form of morality on which altruism and society were based.

The Russian Enlightenment is one of the first examples of the way in which the Russians, in adopting some elements of Western culture, were able to intensify these elements and "raise them to a higher power" (the very process which later occurred with Marxism). At the same time, in the "sixties" the adoption of Western premises rested on blind faith, and Russian enlighteners did not attempt to "derive" higher forms of being from lower ones. They were satisfied with the belief that this was possible, indeed easy, and that someone or other had already done it or was going to do it.

It is important that all traditions which could not be obviously "derived" and "grounded" were rejected. The unhistorical and anti-historical character of the Russian Enlightenment is particularly striking. Proponents of the Russian Enlightenment did not merely reject everything which could not be easily comprehended and easily derived, they denied that it existed at all; and as a result the Russian Enlightenment fell into a strange sort of illusionism. Reality was displaced by mere thought and by whatever the philosophy of the Enlightenment demanded. This can be seen most clearly in politics, where enlighteners were convinced that the socialistic peasants were ready to revolt immediately. This same illusionism, which was really no more than self-delusion, also prevailed in Russian intellectual culture.

Judgment of Intellectual-Spiritual Values

This life in the sphere of primitive and arbitrary constructs—of things merely thought, of illusion—this break with all concrete reality, and this rejection of all "prejudices," accompanied by the firm conviction that people who thought this way were "realists," could end only in tragedy and catastrophy. In the field of intellectual and spiritual culture it was for a long time possible to treat illusion like reality. Typical of this attitude are such "classical" sayings as "Boots are greater than Shakespeare," or "A real apple is more beautiful than a painted one," because boots were more useful than Shakespeare, and a real apple could be eaten, which was hardly possible in the case of a painted one.

With this belief in the objective character of their judgments and evaluations, the proponents of the Russian Enlightenment lived in an atmosphere of subjectivity and arbitrary caprice. They were supported by the *communis opinio* (general agreement with their views) in the illusion that their judgments were universally valid, and this general assent (by intellectuals, it should be emphasized) can usually be explained as the result of opposition to the status quo, an attitude which so successfully bred a class of Russian intellectuals during the time of Nicholas I. The portrayal of this moral and intellectual subjectivism found in the works of Turgenev *(Fathers and Sons)* and especially of Dostoevsky *(The Possessed)* may be exaggerated in many respects, but in terms of basic characteristics at least, it is accurate.

It is easy to discern the effect of this subjectivism in the writings of all the leading "enlightened" journalists of the time. Every problem, insofar as it did not pertain to real life in Russia, was solved quite arbitrarily but in a "materialistic" and "progressive" way (for those questions which did deal with Russian reality there was a fixed political program). This is why the influential critic D. I. Pisarev (1840-1868) attacked Pasteur, because Pasteur's discoveries (the founding of bacteriology) contradicted the materialistic belief that living matter developed from dead matter. Another writer, V. Zaitsev, proved "materialistically" the "inequality of the races" and defended the enslavement of blacks (but not Russian serfdom). He was of the opinion that a proper diet was the answer to all social questions: "The root of all evil is lack of education and development, and the cure for it is the development of the natural sciences and the recognition of the effect of various nutrients on the human organism." This view may not have been widespread, but no objections to this "theory" were raised. Many more such examples of enlightened subjectivism could be cited.

Literature

For many years this ideology created a barrier between the intellectuals and those creative minds who were devoting themselves to science, art, and literature. As a result, many an artistic talent was probably stifled. At the time when the new school of painting was flourishing in France, Russia was dominated by the most primitive sort of art, almost photographic realism. The value of works of plastic art was determined almost exclusively by their "ideological merit." But critics went even further. Pisarev wrote: "When confident youths follow in the footsteps of someone like Glinka, Briulov, and Mochalov[19] they'll acquire nothing but the regrettable habits of mooching and boozing." Or: "To gape *(skalit' zuby)* at a marble statue with joy is a very stupid, useless, and unrewarding way to pass the time.... And two sorts of people, aesthetes and artists, occupy themselves completely that way and think that they are achieving something" *(delaiut delo)*. Pisarev could find in aesthetic pleasure nothing more than sexual gratification.

Literature was better able to resist such attacks. People read the works of good writers, at least those of Tolstoy, Turgenev, and Dostoevsky, and the writings of some recognized classicists—Pushkin, for example. Perhaps they even read the plays of Shakespeare, despite the fact that they were considered less useful than a pair of boots. But Pisarev totally "destroyed" Pushkin, and Zaitsev did the same to Lermontov. One enlightened and influential critic, Skabichevskii, summarized Tolstoy's *War and Peace* as follows: "A simple but garrulous noncommissioned officer relates his war experiences in a remote village." *Anna Karenina* was called "melodramatic nonsense *(drebeden')* in the style of the old French novels; here the writer expatiates on the trite flirtations between a fop from high society and a Petersburg official's wife who has a weakness for military uniforms *(aksel'-banty)*." This same literary authority of the Russian Englishtenment wrote the following about Tiutchev, one of Russia's outstanding lyric poets: "He is difficult to read and esteemed only by particularly avid and incorrigible aesthetes." There was not a single favorable review of Dostoevsky's works from 1860, when they began to reappear, until the author's death. Even the enlightened satirist M. E. Saltykov-Shchedrin (1826-1889) was advised to devote himself to popularizing the natural sciences instead of writing literary works. And in the late 1880's, when Chekhov's works began to appear, the critic Skabichevskii prophesied that Chekhov would die dead drunk in a ditch—the absence of political tendencies in Chekhov's words indicated that nothing of value could be expected of him.

It was a struggle of non-culture against cultural values. Of course, the basis of the struggle was quite different from what it had been during the reign of Nicholas I. Now the fight was led by "good" socio-political intentions, by the Enlightenment, and by the desire to serve the common good.

Philosophy

Philosophy suffered more than any other discipline. Here the struggle was intensified by the crisis in idealistic philosophy, a crisis which was also occurring in the West. The Russian Enlightenment regarded its own metaphysical *Weltanschauung,* be it materialism or positivism, not as philosophy but as a rigorous science.

Pisarev wrote: "Philosophy has lost its prestige in the eyes of every sensible person; no one believes its charlatan's promises *(sharlatanskii),* no one devotes himself to it with passionate enthusiasm. . . . If sensible people do pay attention to philosophy, then they do so only to make fun of it or to reproach people for their stupidity and their astonishing gullibility." We should bear in mind that the greatest authority of the enlighteners, Belinsky, and the whole generation of the forties were indebted to philosophy for their own *Weltanschauung*. In this instance, the new generation broke with their own intellectual and spiritual fathers.

The arguments advanced against philosophy mainly emphasize its "inadequacy" for the "common man." Pisarev asserts that only the sciences, which are accessible and intelligible to everyone, have the right to exist.[20] In 1864 an anonymous writer went even further and claimed that the time had come to popularize already existing ideas. "Pose new questions and solve them? What questions?" he asked ironically, not realizing that he was preaching complete intellectual stagnation. Paradoxically, that statement was made one year before the appearance of Karl Marx's *Das Kapital*, a book which was to lead radical Russian thought down quite new paths.

The Revolutionary Movement

After the death of Nicholas I the underground revolutionary currents came to the surface, at first in the press in the form of discreet declarations and intimations of their ideological premises, then in the form of organized movements. This did not happen all at once, nor was there immediately a definite, fixed political program. Even earlier there had been some who admired "utopian socialism," primarily that advocated by Fourier and his followers. Russians could not long be satisfied with the idea of the gradual "growth and development" of socialistic communities into modern society, even though the echoes of Fourier are still quite strong in *What Is to Be Done?*, the famous novel by N. G. Chernyshevsky (1828-1889), who was one of the ideologists of Russian "peasant" or "popular" socialism. Fourier's dreamy and fantastic plans could not evoke enthusiasm for long from citizens of a police state who were confronted by very real problems.[21]

We have already noted the "enlightened" ideological premises from which the generation of the "sixties" proceeded. From this point of view men of that generation attempted to judge the facts of real life in Russia, but this reality was very complicated, and thus the revolutionary movement could not develop in a straight line. The revolutionaries, and even wider circles of intellectuals, had not the slightest doubt that the social order envisioned by socialism was the ideal one. Precisely what sort of society this would be was not clear, however, and the prevailing view was that after the revolution this social order would develop of itself because, after all, the bases and germs of socialism already existed among the Russian people in the form of the village commune, the *mir*.[22] The only clear idea which was generally agreed on was that it was necessary to change the conditions which existed in Russia; *how* this was to be done was by no means clear. During the last decade of the reign of Nicholas I, conflicts between serfs and landowners had occurred more and more frequently and had often taken on the character of genuine insurrections, and the new tsar, Alexander II, had made public his intention to abolish serfdom. The preparatory work for the reform, in which public officials and landowners participated, was such that doubts often arose concerning the nature of the reform and even concerning its ultimate promulgation; and the reform itself, which was officially dated February 19, 1861, had all sorts of shortcomings, primarily concessions to the landowners, whose opposition to reform had gained strength.

We cannot describe in this book the history of the Russian revolutionary movement; rather we can offer only a typology of the most important revolutionary trends. Because the revolutionary movement ran underground, it was hardly possible to work out a single political program acceptable to all revolutionary groups, and thus we find a large number of individual groups which were known in the West by such misleading names as "nihilists" (from Turgenev's novel *Fathers and Sons*) or "anarchists."[23] Assassinations and acts of terrorism in Russia were what attracted the most attention in the West, but terrorism was by no means practiced by all Russian revolutionary groups. At that time even the name of the "peasant socialists," *"narodniki"* (literally "populist," or "friend of the people"), which is what the revolutionaries called themselves, cannot be regarded as absolutely accurate.

"Typology" of the Revolutionary Movement

One idea which was shared by all revolutionaries and which probably did correspond to the situation that really obtained was the conviction that profound dissatisfaction prevailed among the "working people," i.e. the serfs. The revolutionaries knew from experience that the intellectuals opposed the government solely because the police state afforded them scarcely any opportunity to exert their powers in a way which could give them inner satisfaction. The conclusion which was often drawn, however, namely that a general revolt of the people could begin "any day," was wrong. The revolutionaries soon learned from their participation in individual peasant uprisings that such *local* movements do not tend to spread to the entire population. They thought, however, that they could actually start a revolution through the activity of rather small groups and through individual acts of terrorism. It was this hope which gave rise to the first attempts on the life of the Tsar, for example, the one in 1866 by Karakozov.

The revolutionaries also believed that they would first have to "enlighten" the people, that is, engage in agitation and propaganda. In Russia, to be sure, circumstances were such that there was little room for widespread agitation. However, socialist agitation, carried out by word of mouth or through literature published abroad or illegally in Russia, soon showed that the Russian people, most of whom in fact could not read, were not ready for agitation. Turgenev shows the failure of such efforts in his novel *Virgin*

213

Soil (1877). It was possible to educate only individuals, not the people as a whole in the spirit of revolution. The revolutionaries were able to mount a more extensive movement only when they practiced deceit and called on the people to revolt in the name of the Tsar against the authorities, basing their action on the spurious "Golden Document," which public officials and landowners were allegedly keeping secret from the people. But this was only an isolated case. It is characteristic that not all revolutionary circles condemned this fraud.

In the 1870's—and this is the main topic of Turgenev's *Virgin Soil*—these failures led to attempts to get closer to the populace by "going out among the people" *(khozhdenie v narod)*. This particular movement succeeded in attracting many young intellectuals. The revolutionary settled in a village or went to work in a factory, and by living together with the people he attempted to win their confidence. He attempted to adapt himself completely to their environment, wearing the same clothes and living in the same fashion. But when the revolutionary began to "enlighten" the people, he attracted the attention of either the police or the rich peasants and merchants in the village who were rubbed the wrong way by propaganda in favor of revolution. And so this attempt to bridge the gap between the intellectuals and the common people, perhaps the most important such attempt, ended in failure. The authorities treated this new type of revolutionary almost the same way they did the terrorist. They attempted to hold a show trial, but they could lodge plausible charges against only 193 of the 1000 whom they had arrested. After several years in investigative custody and after trial, only fourteen of the accused were condemned to penal labor in Siberia, and many were completely acquitted.

There were, of course, voices in the wilderness crying out that the fight for socialism could be fought only in a land which had political freedom and that for this reason the first step should be to achieve political freedom in Russia, but these voices were ignored, and their proposals were generally considered by the revolutionaries to constitute an unacceptable "minimalization" of the political program, a renunciation of the social goals of the movement, and even a betrayal of socialism.

The young revolutionaries who had "gone out among the people" had learned from the investigative custody, the trials, and the sentences a bitter lesson: they had learned that it was impossible for them to remain at peace with the tsarist regime. Besides the "Trial of the 193" there were several other trials in which the authorities did not always attempt to determine guilt or innocence but instead set out to make a frightening example of the accused. Forced labor in Siberian prisons, sentences to the penitentiary, banishment to the Siberian wasteland, several death sentences, and isolated cases in which the courts went so far as to employ manufactured evidence provided the revolutionaries with martyrs but by no means frightened them; instead, such actions aroused in large parts of the population sympathy for the martyrs. The attitude of society is best shown by the trial of Vera Zasulich (1849-1919), the girl who shot and slightly wounded the chief of police of Petersburg because without any good reason he had had a condemned student whipped. In 1878 Vera was acquitted by the jury which heard her case—and jury trials were an exception to the general rule.[24]

Two cases in particular were not forgotten. In 1861 the well-known poet M. L. Mikhailov (1826-1865) was sentenced to six years of hard labor in the Siberian mines because he admitted writing a revolutionary proclamation (which in fact he had not written); he died in exile. In 1864 the popular political journalist N. Chernyshevsky, also accused of writing a revolutionary proclamation, was found guilty on the basis of forged evidence and the testimony of a spy; he was sentenced to fourteen years of hard labor in Siberia. The sentences imposed on participants in a demonstration in front of the St. Petersburg cathedral in 1876 were among those noteworthy for their severity. The demonstration itself was unsuccessful, and it was by no means proved in all cases that the accused had participated in it, but three of them were condemned to fifteen years of hard labor in Siberian prisons, two (one a nineteen-year-old) to ten years of hard labor in military fortresses, a sixteen-year-old to six years and eight months imprisonment, and twelve (one an eighteen-year-old) to exile to Siberia. Sentences like these speak for themselves!

The Terrorists

After the disappointing failure of peaceful agitation and after the numerous trials of the seventies, a relatively small group of leaders of the *narodniki* decided to use outright terroristic methods and to assassinate the Tsar himself. There were a number of reasons for this decision. The terrorists made no secret of the fact that they wanted to avenge the large number of people who had fallen victim to the state. Some terrorists also still clung to the belief that acts of terror could trigger a popular revolution. Others held the view that by using terror tactics they could extract from the government some political concessions which would make the further fight for socialism easier.

In the late seventies preparations began for the attempt on the Tsar's life. Some acts of terrorism were perpetrated by individuals acting on their own initiative and were usually aimed at those persecutors of revolutionaries who were particularly hated. The group which was called *Narodnaia volia,* or "The People's Will," made one attempt after another on the Tsar's life. They planned to blow up the Tsar by mining streets and railroad lines, but sometimes the Tsar traveled by a different route and sometimes the bombs failed to function properly. One worker got a job in the Winter Palace at St. Petersburg and planted dynamite there, but the only victims of this

215

assassination attempt were soldiers of the palace guard—ten were killed and 53 wounded. Finally, on March 13, 1881 (March 1 on the old Russian calendar) the terrorists succeeded in killing the Tsar with a bomb. The Tsar had just signed a law which created a popular representative assembly (a quite limited one to be sure).

Even before the assassination the police had picked up the trail of the terrorist organization; and afterwards the leaders were sentenced to death and executed, and in the course of the next few years the rest of the organization was destroyed.

The new Tsar, Alexander III (1881-1894), was an adamant opponent of reform. During his reign even some of the reforms of his father were modified or nullified. The revolutionary movement grew weaker and weaker, even though new revolutionary groups, all of them short lived, continued to spring up. Lenin's older brother, who was a member of one of the groups which were plotting to assassinate Alexander III, was executed in 1887 along with his fellow conspirators. After 1881, however, essential changes in revolutionary ideology took place, and to some extent this ideology came to be greatly influenced by the West.

The Psychology of the Revolutionary Movement

The revolutionary movement of the 1860's and 1870's was an important stage in the intellectual development of Russia. In some respects the movement reminds one of the schism of the seventeenth century. Here too, large numbers of people, most of them young and enthusiastic, fled "the world," renouncing the ordered life of Russian society and the prospects which this life offered them. As early as the 1860's the "underground" (podpol'e) originated. In the "underground," men and women equipped with forged identity papers lived for years in constant danger, without permanent homes, without any possibility of settling down, of pursuing a profession, and of raising a family; and they often ended their lives in prisons, in penitentiaries, or in the wastes of Siberia, unless they were fortunate enough to survive their flight from Russia and safely reach a foreign country. But even these fortunate ones often returned to Russia where they then shared the fate of those who had not managed to escape. Later particularly dismal prisons were established, like the one in the Schlüsselburg fortress, where until 1905 political prisoners were held in solitary confinement. The cases of suicide and insanity there indicate how harsh this imprisonment was.

The history of the revolutionary movement as a whole, not merely the fantastic and adventurous history of the terrorist groups, shows how ready and willing these men and women were to sacrifice themselves for their cause, and in this respect too they resemble the old schismatics. We can also see that in a differently constituted society these energetic people could have played a constructive role, but that in Russia as it was at that time they felt it their duty only to disrupt and destroy.

It is indeed true that these revolutionaries possessed heroism and ethical enthusiasm. The biographies of individual revolutionaries afford sufficient proof. The revolutionaries of the sixties and seventies, unlike the schismatics of the seventeenth century, at least included members of the "oppressed classes," serfs and workers, as well as sons and daughters of priests, noblemen, landowners, and military officers. Some of them were very wealthy: for example, Prince Kropotkin (from impoverished nobility, to be sure), and S. Perovskaia, the daughter of an influential dignitary during the reign of Nicholas I, who was executed after the assassination of 1881.

The enlightenment ideology of the "sixties" exerted considerable influence on the revolutionaries, but their ethical enthusiasm and their willingness to sacrifice themselves for a cause can hardly be derived logically from the materialistic philosophy of the Russian Enlightenment. Later the philosopher Vladimir Solovyov parodied their point of view as follows: "Man is descended from the ape; *therefore* we should sacrifice ourselves for our fellow man." Among the active revolutionaries, however, there were also other types of people. Some even revealed unabashed interest in religion, but as a general rule we certainly ought not to characterize them as representatives of "the Russian religious type," as some scholars—Berdyaev, for example— have done. The personal philosophy of the Enlightenment was widespread, and it soon came to be accepted as unassailable dogma.

Among the revolutionaries there were occasionally, though infrequently, some who preached and advocated amoralism. Even these phenomena were merely the result of the life of illegal activity which put blinders on the people who lived "underground," prevented them from gaining insight into the world about them, and transformed them into people "possessed." Dostoevsky's portrayal of the "Nechaev case" in *The Possessed* corresponded by and large to the actual facts, but this case and a very few others were unusual.

Literary treatments of the revolutionaries usually reveal that the authors had no real knowledge of the "underground," and therefore the negative portrayals of revolutionaries found in the works of Dostoevsky and in a few other less famous novels had no lasting affect. For a long time Russian society remembered the revolutionary of the 1860's and 1870's as a model human being and as the prototype of the Russian intellectual.

The Liberals and the Political Slavophiles

Moderate political groups were of much less importance for Russian intellectual history. The majority of thoughtful Russians welcomed the reforms of Alexander II, and many idealistic people cooperated in liberating the serfs or took an active part in the newly established local self-governing councils *(zemstvo)*. Now, it appears, the "superfluous men" *(lishnie liudi)* of earlier decades had found their place in public life.

With the passage of time, however, it became apparent that the old authorities were reluctant to step aside, and soon liberals who were cooperating in the reforms found that they had no choice but to join the opposition forces. As a result of this petty warfare which old officialdom waged against the public, valuable men who had worked for reform chose to retire from public life. It is also significant that some important scholars saw themselves forced to emigrate and found only outside Russia the opportunity to carry on their work without interference. One of these, I. Mechnikov (1845-1916), was for a long time director of the Louis-Pasteur-Institute in Paris and won the Nobel Prize for physiology and medicine in 1908.

The importance of the liberals was also diminished by the fact that they had not only no uniform political program but also no common philosophy of life. Among the liberals were men of every possible philosophy, from religious thinkers and idealists to outright "enlighteners." The liberals, moreover, were unable to delineate any ideal man to whom the younger generation could have look as a model.

The Slavophiles exerted even less influence. The old Slavophiles either wanted to stay out of politics (the stance of K. Aksakov, who died in 1860) or presented as an alternative to the "revolutionary utopia" of the radicals their own "patriarchial utopias," which were equally far removed from the realities of Russian life. Moreover, at this time genuine Panslavism came to the fore among the Slavophiles, and it was soon being abused by official political circles to achieve their own goals. It is true, the Slavophiles were able to attract to their banner adherents of other movements in 1877, when the Russo-Turkish War broke out and the fight for the independence of the South Slavs—the Serbs and the Bulgars—was carried to its successful conclusion. It soon became clear, however, that Russian officialdom did not wish the cooperation of Russian society. Ivan Aksakov, the active political journalist of the old Slavophile movement, died in 1886, and from that point on, the younger members of the movement played no important role of any sort in the intellectual history of Russia.

Dostoevsky and the "Pochvenniki"

The small circle which worked between 1861 and 1863 on *Vremia* and *Epokha*, the two newspapers published by the Dostoevsky brothers, was to a certain extent spiritually related to the Slavophiles. This group called itself the *pochvenniki* (enthusiasts of the soil) so as to differentiate itself from the Slavophiles even in its name, for it rejected the Slavophile "utopia of the past," and the "soil" on which it wished to stand was the simple Russian folk of the time. The Dostoevsky circle acknowledged that Peter the Great had remade Russia, and its members believed that Russia should not be separated from Europe by a "Great Wall of China." Instead, they, like Vladimir Odoevskii and his friends earlier, believed that the "Russian idea" ought to be a "panhuman idea," that is, the *synthesis* of the ideas advanced by the peoples of Europe. Of course, it was not clear *what* ideas these were to be. These men, naturally, rejected the "Enlightenment" of the time, and we can discern in them no sympathy for the two Christian confessions of the West. Among the most active co-workers on the Dostoevskys' journals we find one follower of Schelling and one of Hegel. Dostoevsky himself was dependent on some of Schiller's ideas (and, some scholars believe, on the thought of Schelling and Hegel too, but this seems doubtful). At that time Dostoevsky was struggling to find a coherent philosophy of life. For the *pochvenniki* the European ideas which were to be synthesized in Russia were probably merely the cultural achievements of the West. They not only thought that Russia was destined to "unite" the cultural achievements of the Europeans—a point of view which Dostoevsky expounded in particularly impressive fashion shortly before his death in his "Pushkin Speech"; they also believed that in the future Russia would "utter a new word" which would become the word of *all European culture.* This "new word" would be the universal Christian culture, the culture of Greek Orthodoxy. Later, particularly in *The Brothers Karamazov*, Dostoevsky attempted to formulate at least some of the elements which should go to make up this Russian synthesis. These elements, however, reflect for the most part efforts to overcome European cultural ideals. Dostoevsky's ideas are polemical and are directed against Western individualism and the Western secularization of culture.

Dostoevsky also paid more and more attention to Russian expansion into Asia and considered Russia an independent middle link between Asia and Europe. In the last years of his life he referred to himself occasionally as a Slavophile, but he never established a vital relationship with the Slavic world beyond the borders of Russia, and the *pochvenniki* had little interest in social questions (and in the village commune). The main problems which preoccupied them were not the social organization of Russia but the moral character of the people and the ideas which the people could produce.

One of the men who worked with the Dostoevsky brothers on their journals was the Hegelian N. N. Strakhov (1828-1896). He believed that Russia must resist the influence of the West. He regarded the philosophy of life of Russian Westerners like Herzen and of modern Western thinkers like Feuerbach and Renan as a sort of "nihilism"—that is, disbelief in the intellectual and spiritual foundations of the old European culture. These men,

Strakhov felt, also doubted the value and dignity of the human personality, the universal validity of scientific knowledge, and the absolute character of ethical norms and aesthetic judgments. Belief in "truth, beauty, and goodness" was being destroyed not only in Russia but in the West. "We ought to respect the West and even venerate with all our hearts *(blagogovet')* the greatness of the West's intellectual accomplishments," Strakhov thought, but at the same time, in the name of intellectual values Russians ought to fight against modern Western ideologies. Strakhov, like Dostoevsky, foresaw the advent of philosophical ideas which would reach the height of nihilism: the doctrine of the "superman," which would negate the value of human existence; and the doctrine of "eternal recurrence," which would destroy completely the meaning of being. A few years later both ideas were, in fact, formulated by Nietzsche.

The *pochvenniki* were able to provide neither the comprehensive synthesis nor the "new word." In the seventies and eighties there did appear several ideological "loners" whose philosophies of life were in fact complete and systematic, but they attracted few followers. The most important of these were the diplomat, poet, and monk Konstantin Leontiev (1831-1891), who was called "the Russian Nietzsche," and the philosopher Vladimir Solovyov (1853-1900). Both were bright stars, but they cannot be linked together to form a coherent philosophical constellation. Two other equally solitary figures, N. Ya. Danilevskii and K. Pobedonostsev, are of special interest to us.

Nikolai Yakovlevich Danilevskii, Russia and Europe

Danilevskii (1822-1885), a natural scientist by profession, was known for his criticism of Darwinism and was active as a political journalist, explorer, and economist. His book *Russia and Europe,* which appeared in 1869, presented a completely new view of the problem. The work influenced only a very small circle and did not gain wide currency—and even then more in the West than in Russia—until after the appearance of Spengler's *Decline of the West* when Danilevskii came to be regarded as a "forerunner of Spengler."

Danilevskii's view is the antithesis Russia-Europe taken to its extreme, and his prognosis is that "Russia will supplant Europe in world history." By this he did not mean that Russia would effect a synthesis of Russian and European intellectual culture, or that Russia would become the new dominant cultural force which would compete with a West grown old, or even that Russia was to fall heir to the cultural contributions of Europe. He meant that Russia would supplant Europe because European culture would be completely displaced or would disappear and die away. Danilevskii, without giving any particular reasons for it, thought of "Russia" as the Slavophiles did, as "Russia and the Slavic world."

The basis for Danilevskii's prediction is the theory of "cultures," "cultural spheres," or "cultural areas."[25] He saw these cultural areas as analogous to living organisms, to creatures which are born, grow and develop, and then grow old and die. According to him, world history had already witnessed ten cultures; the new Russian culture would be completely different from any of its predecessors, and the future would belong to it after Europe had finally expired.

Besides these theses, the erroneousness of which is apparent at first glance, his ideological program, which was to be realized in the future, was simply that there existed the "idea of the Slavic world" which was above and beyond political ideals and rational comprehension. Europe, he contended, was not merely alien to Russia (and the Slavic world generally); it was hostile to them. Russia ought to remain completely aloof from all European interests; and all the successes of Europe—political balance of power, peace, scientific and technological progress, etc.—could be only harmful and dangerous for Russia. Danilevskii, however, is able to describe the nature of "the Slavic idea" only in vague terms. It is clear that he does follow the older Slavophile movement in asserting that Greek Orthodoxy and the village commune (mir) are elements of "the Slavic idea." The political goal he had in mind was a Slavic federation, which, in fact, would also include Greeks, Rumanians, and Hungarians and which would have Constantinople as its capitol.[26]

In his book Danilevskii combines with his theory of biological cultures two ideas, that of the Slavophile utopia and that of imperialistic power. The second of these ideas did find some degree of support in a few small Panslavist circles.

The Reaction: K. P. Pobedonostsev

There were conservatives and reactionaries in Russia after the death of Nicholas I, but they were hardly in a position to strive to nullify Alexander's reforms. They could only grumble about them and try to obstruct work on the new organizations, and to some extent they did manage to place some limitations on the reforms. The only important ideologist of reaction was Konstantin Petrovich Pobedonostsev (1827-1907), who for almost a quarter of a century, from 1881 to 1904, actually did exert almost unlimited influence on both Alexander III and Nicholas II (1894-1917).

The offspring of a family of jurists, Pobedonostsev was first a professor, and from 1881 on the Over Procurator of the Holy Synod. Although he influenced and sometimes even formulated policy, he always remained in the background. He did not write much, and we are acquainted with his ideas for the most part only from his correspondence and from the recollections of his contemporaries. He had no connections with any of the Slavophile groups.

221

In his opinion the educated, the intellectuals, and the spokesmen for intellectual powers played only a slight role or no role at all in Russian life. He completely ignored the political radicals, who were of course being persecuted; he despised the liberals; and he even failed to show any interest in the conservatives, who were to become his cohorts. For him Russia consisted only of the Tsar and the Russian people; all other classes were insubstantial and illusory. As the highest Church official in Russia he believed that the main duty of the Church was to serve the state.

Pobedonostsev believed in the soul of the people, inert, patriarchal, and bound by tradition. The naive faith of the people, who placed God and the Tsar on the same level, had to be preserved and perpetuated. Education of any kind, he thought, might disrupt and destroy this strength, for it would lead to freedom of thought. Unmediated feeling, the "semi-darkness" of the simple untutored soul, subconsciousness—these were to continue to form the basis of the Russian state. It appears that Pobedonostsev's own soul felt no affinity for the simple folk and their naive beliefs and that Pobedonostsev was in fact, as G. Florovsky has contended, a rationalist and a sceptic.

From his point of view theology, which could satisfy only the intellectual needs of the intelligentsia, was useless, perhaps even harmful. He believed that only external forms and norms rooted in tradition were of importance. Pobedonostsev was therefore an enemy not only of independent religious thinkers but also of orthodox thinkers and teachers who might have "too much" effect on the people.

In Pobedonostsev we see once again an embodiment of the old Russian fear of creative change. If culture is called on only "to protect the holy traditions of our ancestors," it would be best to bring all of life to a standstill. This is precisely what Pobedonostsev attempted to do, and thanks to his influence on the two Tsars, he was in large part successful. The period from 1881 to 1900 might accurately be termed the "Age of Pobedonostsev."

Literature, Art, and Science

In the absence of a free political arena, literature had attained since the end of the eighteenth century a greater significance in Russia than in other countries because only in literary works was it possible to break the law of silence. At the time of Nicholas I, such works as Turgenev's *A Hunter's Sketches* were of great importance in the struggle against serfdom. Later, in the "sixties," works of literature could at least allude to socialistic ideals and to the shortcomings of Russian life.

This meant two things for literary works: for one thing, usually attention was focused on content and external form was for the most part ignored; for another, the poet was expected to present authoritative instruction and guidance. We have already seen how this attitude led to distorted criticism.

222

But in spite of unjust criticism, readers heard the message not only of poets who were attuned to the spirit of the times but also of men like Dostoevsky and Tolstoy. Of course, second-rate realists and, of the important writers, Turgenev were more popular.

The appearance of several talented writers may be considered one of fate's chance favors. At the same time Russian music was also attracting world attention. Tchaikovsky and Borodin enjoyed great popularity, as did Musorgsky, a bold innovator whose true significance did not become clear until later decades.

The fine arts, it must be admitted, were in a state of decline. This was true not only of the completely dead "academic art" but also of the realistic art of the *Peredvizhniki*, a group which arose in opposition to academic art and set ideological tasks for itself but neglected purely artistic goals. This sort of art was of hardly any importance at all in either Russian or European art history.

Despite the unfavorable conditions, Russian culture did develop in various areas. Russian science began to attract as much attention in Europe as did Russian literature and music. Only now did N. I. Lobachevsky (1792-1856), the founder of non-Euclidian geometry, become widely known. Whereas until the 1870's foreign scholars generally played leading roles in the St. Petersburg Academy, now more and more Russian scientists, particularly mathematicians and natural scientists (chemists, astronomers, etc.), were becoming well known in Europe. Some of them even did their work in Europe. The director of the Louis-Pasteur-Institute, I. I. Mechnikov has already been mentioned. Others included the surgeon N. I. Pirogov (1810-1881), the social historian M. M. Kovalevskii (1851-1916), and the mathematician (and first lady professor in the world) Sofia V. Kovalevskaia (1850-1891). In Russia itself scholars were merely an isolated group scarcely known to the public at large. For example, as late as the 1870's Dostoevsky dared state only that there were already scholars in Russia whose work "could be useful to European science." Even for that time this was surely too modest a statement.

Religious Life

There can be no doubt that during the Enlightenment religious life in Russia underwent a crisis, but it is difficult to tell how serious this crisis was. It is characteristic that for the most part those who represented enlightenment, materialism, and atheism came from the families of clergymen, were the sons of priests, and had received their education in seminaries. Clearly, both the Church and religious education had somehow failed. Religious indifference and particularly indifference to the Church was more widespread than atheism. Parents limited their religious duties to attending church more or less irregularly, and their children stopped going at all. The Church, for its part, had grown indifferent to the intellectual and spiritual interests of the intelligentsia and "had nothing to say to them."After the death of Dostoevsky, whose Christian message the intellectuals at least still heeded, the metropolitan of St. Petersburg expressed his opinion of the deceased novelist as follows: he was really just a novelist who had not written "anything special."

The situation of the Church under the leadership of the Holy Synod, in which the secular Over Procurator held the top position, contributed in no small measure to the ever widening gap which separated Church and intelligentsia. The situation became particularly grave under Pobedonostsev, who considered every religious movement, even within the framework of the Orthodox Church, to be superfluous and indeed dangerous. In the nineties theological periodicals which attracted readers from educated circles had to suspend publication. Religious censorship became particularly harsh. Now, for example, it was not permissible to treat the most important episodes in the history of the Russian Church, from the Christianization of Russia to the schism of the seventeenth century and the reforms of Peter the Great. Theologians who were more cautious saw themselves forced to remain silent and to conceal their views. Whether the spread of the Enlightenment or this ecclesiastical policy of the Church authorities was of more crucial importance for Russian religious life is a moot question.

This chasm separating intellectuals from Church circles explains the success of Protestant preachers who were occasionally effective in various small circles. The spirit of the Orthodox Church was kept alive in the monasteries and among individual monks, who were usually called "elders" *(startsy)* and who were regarded as "knowers of the soul." Among those who turned to these men were such important figures in Russian intellectual and spiritual life as Gogol, Dostoevsky, the Slavophiles, and even L. Tolstoy. The Optina Hermitage *(Optina pustyn')* was the real center of the "elder" movement. Dostoevsky attempted to portray in the elder Zosima, a character in *The Brothers Karamazov,* the effect of the *startsy.* Of the works which originated in these circles the writings of the hermit Feofan (Feofan Zatvornik) deserve attention. It is significant that K. Leontiev, the talented writer and original thinker who has been termed, inaccurately, "the Russian Nietzsche," ended his life as a monk.

The People, the Old Believers, and the Sects

Pobedonostsev wanted to use the religiosity of the Russian people as a foundation on which to build a Russian empire. He was well aware that some measures had to be taken to cultivate this religiosity, which consisted primarily in the preservation of the customs and usages of the Church. The most important of these measures was the improvement of elementary religious instruction and of the economic position of the village priest. The village priests were poor; they had to farm their land, and to meet their material needs they often had to depend on the patronage of rich farmers and village merchants. The main obstacle to improving the economic status of the priests was the shortage of state finances. In order to improve religious instruction Pobedonostsev tried to place the grammar schools in the hands of the priests, but here too he was confronted with material difficulties.

It became clear in the "Age of Pobedonostsev," however, that the people were no longer satisfied with religious ritual and religious "semi-darkness." This is sufficiently proved by the stubbornness with which the Old Believers maintained themselves against the official Church and even more by the spread of old and new rationalistic and mystic sects. We cannot describe here the life of these sects in all its complexity, but there can be no doubt that millions of peasants and townsmen were members of them or were Old Believers.

The most characteristic phenomenon is the rise and spread of so-called "stundism," the very name of which indicates that the movement originated under the influence of German immigrants who settled in Russia, and particularly under the influence of German Pietism. Russian peasants read the Bible on their own, particularly the Gospels, and they also observed the way in which these German settlers lived. These two factors led to the rise of stundism among some Russian peasants. Reading the Bible led them to rationalistic conclusions: to neglect ritual, the worship of icons, and fasting, and sometimes even to refuse to take oaths and to enter military service. Because the stundists neglected to attend church, to go to confession, and to take communion, usually they soon attracted attention to themselves and were subjected to persecution which included the harshest and most senseless police measures. It can hardly be denied that the interpretations of the Gospel which were offered by the well-read laymen of these groups were often questionable, but the life and teachings of the mystic sects, who believed their leaders to be the reincarnation of Christ or the Virgin Mary and whose meetings often ended with ecstatic dances, were much more questionable.[27]

The sects had no contact with the intellectual and spiritual life of the intelligentsia except for misguided attempts by intellectuals to recruit persecuted Old Believers and sectarians for the revolutionary movement. Some revolutionaries, by virtue of their moralism (developed on different bases, to be sure) and their ascetic way of life, were able to make friends with Old Believers and sectarians. Even in Church circles the persecution of the sects by the police aroused dissatisfaction with official Church policy.

CHAPTER V. THE RISE OF MODERN RUSSIA

Politics

Both contemporaries and later generations felt the age of Alexander III (1881-1894) to be a time of decline in the traditions of Russian intellectuals. The revolutionary movement was broken up and was paralyzed by an internal crisis when the old programs for action proved to be ineffective. Literature was subjected to more and more extensive censorship, and the older generation of writers died off. Even the activity of the liberals—in local self-governing bodies, for example—became more and more limited. The universities and even the middle and upper schools came under the administration of people who were more concerned with combating political "unreliability" than with educating the youth. They attempted to keep the lower classes from entering them. Church policy was primarily intent on "protecting" old established practices.

Alexander III was not prepared for the task of governing—the actual successor to the throne was his older brother Nicholas, but he died in 1865. During Alexander's reign Pobedonostsev was almost omnipotent. When Alexander III died in 1894 at the age of fifty, his son Nicholas II, who was the last tsar and reigned from 1894 to 1917, was twenty-six years old, but he had taken scarcely any part in the affairs of government. Nicholas, moreover, had no definite political views and at first left the conduct of government to "tried and true" Pobedonostsev. Any hopes for a relaxation of the conservative policies of the government were destroyed soon after Nicholas' accession to the throne by the new tsar's initial words and deeds. But political life could not come to a standstill. In the meanwhile a younger generation, those born between 1865 and 1875, had emerged, and although this generation grew up in the stagnation of the "Age of Pobedonostsev," it was by no means imbued with the spirit of that age. Moreover, little was done to educate the elite in the official ideology. More attention was devoted to seeing to it that the younger generation should not achieve any intellectual mobility, but this proved to be an impossible task.

The Awakening

We can detect the beginnings of the new intellectual movement as early as the late 1880's. It arose first of all as a reaction of profound disappointment in the philosophy of the "sixties,"the intellectual standpoint of the fathers of the younger generation, and its beginnings might best be described as an "awakening." This awakening was initially a series of impulses and movements which might be called more "spiritual" than "intellectual." The "mind," the clear light of consciousness, at first played a less important role than vague moods and vague longings. The *Weltanschauung* of the "sixties"—materialistic, postivistic, and even "nihilistic" scepticism—afforded a point of departure which with the new generation developed certain "repulsive forces," i.e. the rejection of the old *Weltanschauung*. Because the philosophy of the Enlightenment was primitive and simple, it became a clearly defined target.

It was maintained that the older generation had failed and that the revolutionary wave had dissipated without visible results. Even those members of the older generation who were liberals were no longer active in political life. The schools, which endeavored first and foremost to drive ideas "dangerous to the state" out of the minds of young people but offered no attractive substitute for them, actually achieved the opposite of what they intended and were primarily responsible for the disappearance of all sympathy for the *ancien régime*. As a result, the youth at first were baffled by the realities of Russian life, which presented few enticements. Public life offered only very few opportunities, and the career of the public official was no more attractive than it had been during the reign of Nicholas I.

This bafflement, however, was in fact the reason for the "awakening." Vague longing and pessimistic despair were in many instances succeeded by reflection on the nature and basis of the despair. Was not the older generation, "the men of the 'sixties' " *(shestidesiatniki)*, to blame for this situation? The eyes of the intellectuals were opened, and the first thing they saw was the illusory character of the allegedly "sober" and "positive" basic premises of the philosophy of the Enlightenment. Firm foundations, not empty illusions, were what was needed. This meant that men were no longer satisfied to draw up lists of desiderata (the ideal state, ideal art, ideal politics, etc.) but rather made an effort to find an *ontological* basis for achieveing the things they desired.

The quest for fundamentals preoccupied Russian intellectual life between 1890 and 1910. Only through study was it possible to determine and to "discover" these fundamentals—social realities, principles of aesthetics in art and literature which were realized in Russian and world art and literature, and, finally, philosophical and religious theories. These two decades were a time of "discoveries." First of all men discovered continents which had long since been known or dug out the values which the older generation through its inattentiveness had forgotten. Only gradually did they press on further into the past and the present and find genuinely existent forces, principles, and laws which made it possible to build in one area or the other habitable homes instead of the "castles in the air" of the "sixties." Of course, they too sometimes followed false trails and came to dead ends, and they too made illusory discoveries which vanished into air in the same way that the intellectual culture of the "sixties" had. The most difficult and complex problem was to find new ways in politics, the simplest was probably to find new paths in art.

Political Regroupings

In politics the new age had to find the real social forces which could be relied upon in political struggles and which could serve as points of orientation. After the political crisis of the 1880's the mood of the nation was first expressed in the "recognition of the reality" in which people were forced to live and work. In political journalism there is suffiient evidence of the above-mentioned "sceptical" attitude toward ideals and goals which are "set too high." It is not true, of course, that members of the younger generation were "born sceptics," as one political journalist asserted in 1886. The realities of life in Russia had taught the younger generation to be sceptical. The same writer continued his characterization with the following words: "They [the people of this generation] could not be dominated by the ideals of their fathers and grandfathers. They feel no hatred and no contempt for everyday life, they recognize no obligation to be heroes, they do not believe that the ideal man exists. All these ideals are arid logical products of individual thought, and for the younger generation the only thing that exists is the reality in which they have to live and which they therefore recognize as valid." In Russian political journalism various "substitute words" were used for "impermissible" concepts—"ideals" for "socialism," "hero" and "ideal man" for "revolutionary," "subjective thinking" for "individual thinking." With the clumsiness in the use of philosophical terminology which is characteristic of the age, the author clothed his rejection of materialism in the statement, "We are returning to a pantheistic philosophy."

The old socialists judged these attitudes quite differently. For them it was an "age of terror and of near universal stultification." "What is there to hope for? to believe in? to desire? to strive for? Everything has been smashed to pieces," wrote N. K. Mikhailovskii (1842-1904), the ideologist of agrarian socialism. "You can't trust anyone, you can't believe anything anymore; everywhere the world is tottering," wrote the satirist Saltykov-Shchedrin and created the shocking picture of a "triumphant swine" which devoured helpless justice *(pravda)*.

But people could not live for long without thought of the future, and very soon new socialistic and liberal movements arose. The central question which these movements faced was once again the old one of the relationship of Russia to Europe, more precisely of whether the development of Russia and Europe followed the same or different paths.

228

The Tradition of the Old Revolutionaries. The "Narodniki"

For the older generation of revolutionaries it went without saying that Russia, in contrast to the West, had a "straight and easy path" to socialism. This axiom was formulated as "the possibility of a direct transition to a better state, without having to go through the intermediate stage, the stage of the "bourgeois state" (and "bourgeois" meant "capitalistic").

As early as the late seventies, however, it became clear that "Europe" and "chumazyi" (the filthy one)–a "substitute word" for "capitalism"[28]– had already come to Russia and were beginning to spread there. Factories attracted peasants to the cities, and capitalism invaded the villages in the form of the kulak, the well-to-do peasant who operated within a money economy and made small peasants dependent on him. This was the favorite theme of writers who sympathized with the "narodniki." The socialists were particularly upset by the fact that the "small-scale capitalism" of the kulaki was the only new and vital element in village life. Whereas the mir (the village commune), which was thought to contain the seeds of socialism, showed no signs of development and did not bring about anything "new" and "essential," the kulaki often exhibited "truly brilliant capacities." As G. Uspenskii remarked, there were no other similar signs "of reason, of talent, of power of observation, and of general giftedness" in village life. The mir seemed to be having the rug pulled out from under it. That constituted a capitulation to Europe, i.e. to capitalism.

Whereas in 1883 people were still saying that Russian capitalism was "in an embryonic stage of development" and that they could still protect themselves from it, by the early 1890's they saw capitalism in Russia strong and constantly growing. The old traditions of the village commune, by contrast, were in a state of decline. Some "popular agrarian" socialists began to doubt that it was possible to achieve socialism in Russia through the mir.

These doubts led some to acknowledge "small deeds" (malye dela) in everyday life. "Breathtaking idealistic prospects" could no longer be reconciled "with real down-to-earth labor." At most, people thought of the possibility of creating in ordinary labor new elements of socialism, perhaps in the form of labor cooperatives (artel'). Some even hoped that the government would help in the struggle against capitalism. All this amounted to no more than idle dreams and utopias.

The catastrophic famine of 1891, which affected large areas of Russia, put to a test the ideals of "agrarian socialism." The public attempted to alleviate the need because the measures taken by the government were by no means sufficient. Often the authorities obstructed the aid projects of the intellectuals, whose motives were always deemed "suspect." (We learn a great deal about this situation from the biography of L. Tolstoy, who participated in this aid program). The peasants, however, remained passive at a time when they might have been expected to rebel or to offer resistance to the government.

One important prerequisite for the further development of the "agrarian socialism" of the *narodniki* was a specific historico-philosophical *Weltanschauung* which became the ideological basis of agrarian socialism. The philosophy in question was developed chiefly by two theoreticians, P. Lavrov and N. Mikhailovskii.

Lavrov and Mikhailovskii

Piotr Lavrov (1823-1900), who emigrated in 1870, exerted the most influence on the *narodniki* with his book *Historical Letters* (1870), while the political journalist N.K. Mikhailovskii (1842-1904) was largely able to present his views only by implication. Both men developed ideas which agree only in general principles. One of these was the moral rationale that the intellectuals were obliged to fight in the interest of the exploited masses to whom they and the propertied classes were indebted; another was the idea that "critical thinkers," the elite, play a leading role in the historical process. Neither idea was really new, but each nevertheless had the effect of a revelation. The fact that these simple ideas were propagated primarily by Lavrov's dry, unemotional book demonstrates that they satisfied some of the needs of the age.

The New Socialist Party

From this theoretical basis for socialism it was deduced that an organized and functioning *political party* ought to be established. This "social-revolutionary" party, which was abbreviated "SR," set up a new program. Through a democratic reshaping of the Russian state the foundation was to be laid for expropriating the lands of large landowners and for building up a socialistic agrarian economy on the basis of the *mir*. Political agitation and propaganda as well as terrorism and revolutionary uprisings were regarded as the ways in which the reshaping of the Russian state could be effected.

While the idea of democratizing Russia constituted a transition to political realism, the *naraodniki* nevertheless retained in their new program utopian elements, the most important of them the belief that the seeds of socialistic views were already firmly rooted in the minds of the masses and only needed to be "activated."

Besides the *naraodniki* there was another new revolutionary movement, the social democratic movement, which was abbreviated "SD" or "SDek." Members of this movement had become acquainted with the type of socialist movement found in Germany and Switzerland, the labor movement, and with the "scientific theory" of socialism, Marxism. Russian socialists, and even some Russian liberals, were impressed by the Marxist idea that there are within capitalistic society forces which of necessity will lead to the rise of a socialistic society. Some of the *narodniki,* such as Lavrov, adopted some elements of Marxism, while others became Marxists outright. The free labor organizations also seemed to be worth imitating. Now Russians saw the "essential foundations" on which socialistic politics could be built.

Socialistic politics, of course, presupposes the existence of one real force, the proletariat, and no matter how broadly one chooses to define the term, the proletariat in Russia, even in the 1890's, amounted to at most six to seven per cent of the population. Moreover, legal labor organizations were hardly possible in Russia. The necessary presupposition, therefore, on which the acitivity of the early Russian social democrats was based was the belief that in the future capitalism would develop in Russia and also that the type of organization created by the old illegal revolutionary movement must be adopted by Russian social democrats.

The belief that Russia would soon develop into a capitalistic country proved to be true. Whereas in the sixties and seventies individual workers became members of revolutionary groups, in the eighties and nineties there arose an unorganized labor movement which at first pursued only concrete economic objectives. This was the strike movement, which was directed against poor working conditions. In 1895 and in the years following the number of strikers rose from 50,000 to 100,000.

As early as the 1880's emigres had formed small "Marxist" groups. In 1895 the "Militant Union *(Soiuz bor'by)* for the Liberation of the Working Classes" arose in St. Petersburg, and in 1898 at an illegal convention in Minsk the "Social-Democratic Party of Russia" was founded, with a program influenced by that of the German social democrats.

The Polemics of the Narodniki and the Marxists

The ineffectuality of the strict censorship of the time is demonstrated by the fact that it was possible for several Marxist works to appear in Russia. The censors paid no heed to the political threat of books devoted to questions of national economics and the philosophy of history, and so P. Struve (1870-1944), who was later one of the leaders of Russian liberalism, was able to publish in 1894 his *Critical Notes on the Economic Development of*

Russia, a book which dealt with the significance of the development of capitalism in Russia. In 1895 the emigrant G. Plekhanov (1857-1918) published under the pseudonym N. Beltov a book entitled *Concerning the Question of the Development of the Monistic Views of History,* a work devoted primarily to questions of the Marxist philosophy of history. In 1897 *The New Word (Novoe Slovo),* a major periodical with a Marxist orientation, was published. These works achieved popularity despite the fact that they were dry and ponderous. Even Lenin's *The Development of Capitalism in Russia* (written under the pseudonym N. Ilyin), which was in large measure a statistical work, was eagerly read, and its readers were able to discern behind the dry columns of figures and the theoretical discussions Lenin's socio-political views.[29]

Marxist works written by emigres were accessible only to limited circles and were of less importance. They also contained some theses which were, from the Marxist point of view, very questionable. For example, the role of personality in history was denied almost completely, and the conception of historical development was almost fatalistic. The *narodniki,* the adherents of "agrarian socialism," attacked the new political tendencies in violent polemics. They mainly accused the Marxists of judging capitalism favorably and also of neglecting the interests of the peasantry. The *narodniki* were especially incensed that the Marxists asserted that the Russian peasants were at heart altogether indifferent toward socialism and were basically merely small property-owners. Moreover, the Marxists' complete rejection of terror as a political weapon was contrary to the attitude of the *narodniki,* who still venerated the terrorists of the 1860's and 1870's. It was significant, in any event, that both sides were equally positive in their assessment of the importance of fighting for democratic freedoms.

The successes of Marxism were also regarded as a sort of "intellectual epidemic" *(povetrie).* The rapidity with which Marxism spread can be explained primarily by the fact that the Russian Marxists found in the proletariat a force which was real and effective in the political struggle and which provided that struggle, as it were, with an "ontological basis." It is, in fact, characteristic of the times that the revolutionary parties made an effort to join, to influence, and to direct the real movements of specific strata of the population.

The Liberals

The position of the liberals was a far more difficult one. Of course, among the educated classes their numbers grew larger and larger, and the liberal camp included professional men such as doctors and lawyers, and members of the local self-governing bodies; but the liberals did not have the support of those groups which were fighting for concrete objectives. The Russian bourgeoisie, the middle class, was too weak and too fragmented, and more-over it was in part still almost without culture (the merchants, for example) and in part quite satisfied with the living and working conditions as they were.

Thus Russian liberals were from various rather powerless strata of the population. Among them there were even socialists who refused to take an active part in the struggle; there were participants in local self-governing bodies who saw their activities frustrated by the arbitrary actions of the authorities; there were, finally, a few theoreticians, like B. B. Chicherin, who were the only genuine representatives of liberalism. The liberals were unable to win the youth over to their side. Students who were interested in politics were generally socialists, with the possible exception of those who were studying to be teachers of law.

The philosophy of the liberals was not as uniform as it had been in the past. Probably most of them were still committed to an ill-defined positivism, but there were among them those who espoused an idealistic philosophy, and some of them were even primitive materialists and "unpolitical" Marxists.

The liberals also lacked a clearly formulated political program, and for that reason it was possible in the twentieth century for some of them to join with the revolutionary parties in advocating one demand or another. It is quite significant that in 1905 the liberals almost without exception sup-ported the demand for universal suffrage, a demand which from their own point of view was unreasonable in a country whose population consisted for the most part of people who could not read or write.

At the turn of the century the liberals too decided to publish their political writings outside Russia. The man who played the most important role in that activity was P. Struve, a former Marxist and author of the first program for Russian social democracy.

Literature and Art

New movements in literature and the arts were also stimulated by disappointment in the ideals of the "sixties" and by the quest for principles for artistic creativity completely peculiar to Russia. The literature of the *narodniki,* which was "noble" but "impoverished" from an artistic point of view, could not long inspire readers and young poets. The unjust and con-temptuous treatment of such great writers as Dostoevsky, Tolstoy, and the great lyric poets alienated the younger generation. In 1893 D.S. Merezhkov-skii (1865-1941) went so far as to publish a brochure on "the reasons for the decline of Russian literature." It was written in a very mild tone, but it nevertheless provoked a storm of protest. There were already innovators who wished to lead literature in new directions. Merezhkovskii, his wife Zinaida Gippius (1867-1945), F. Sologub (Teternikov 1863-1927), and

233

K. D. Balmont (1867-1943) were already publishing their works in the little-read periodical *Severnyi Vestnik*. From 1894 on, K. Balmont, V. Briusov (1873-1924), and several other young poets presented their works to the reading public in a series of anthologies entitled *The Russian Symbolists*. The title was reminiscent of the French symbolist poets, but the Russian poets were actually not in the French tradition. Of this group Briusov succeeded in attracting attention and arousing universal indignation by taking the tendencies of these new "symbolists" to extremes. This, indeed, was what he had set out to do, and he made no effort to deny the accuracy of the name "decadents" which was applied to the movement. Such writers as the impressionist Chekhov (1860-1904), the lyricist Bunin (1870-1953), and the poet of the vagabonds *(bosiaki)* and the dregs of society Gorky (A. M. Peshkov 1868-1936), none of whom belonged to this group of literary rebels, met with less resistance, even though the complete absence of socio-political tendencies in their works did appear to be unusual.

The attention of the symbolists of this "first generation" was overwhelmingly focused on poetic technique, on the discovery of new poetic themes, and on the "up-dating" of the poetic vocabulary. After 1900, however, younger and more important adherents of symbolism appeared. The most significant of these were A. Blok (1880-1921) and Andrei Bely (B. N. Bugaev 1880-1934). From the very beginning they treat philosophical topics and are moved by problems of philosophy and religion.

At about the same time yet another new artistic movement began, but it must be conceded that in the establishment and development of this movement the influence of the West played an important role. Russians now learned about modern art, first of all impressionism, in Paris and Munich, the cities to which young artists gravitated to pursue their studies. The first Russian impressionists, however—Somov is an example—enjoyed little popularity with the Russian public because of the ideological "emptiness" of their works. Significantly, the most outstanding talents—V. Kandinsky, A. V. Yavlenskii, and Marianne von Wereffkin (M. Verevkina)—remained as good as unknown in Russia during their early impressionistic phase and remained "permanently" outside Russia, mostly in Germany, where they were able to influence others in turn.

Philosophy and Religion

Symbolist poetry implied a philosophy of life which can be termed with some justification "neoromantic." The central thought of this philosophy was that being and truth cannot be found on the "surface" of the world but rather lie mysteriously hidden far beneath the surface. The men of the 1890's attempted to penetrate to these depths, but since their eyes lacked spiritual and intellectual training, they stood little chance of success.

The first attempts to determine the foundations of this philosophy ended in failure, for those engaged in these efforts confined themselves to vague assertions, the most important of which was that there are, outside of the directly accessible world, powers and forces which determine this world and our existence. The world, they thought, was a labyrinth in which blind fate predominated.

Two aspects of this philosophy were even more significant. Its adherents turned away from the principle of utilitarianism, and in taking this attitude to an extreme they also turned away from moralism and cultivated an amoralism which they occasionally flaunted. Ethics was replaced by aesthetics, by an aesthetics which was prepared to place beauty above truth and goodness.

The philosophical quest proceeded aimlessly, and while in poetry a renaissance, a reawakening of Russian literary traditions going back to Pushkin, Gogol, Tiutchev, and Dostoevsky was possible, Russian philosophy, except for programs and intimations, was unable to produce anything of the like. As a result Russian philosophers turned to the West and borrowed there from the most varied sources—from Spinoza, Schopenhauer, and Nietzsche, and somewhat later from Bergson, the Neokantians, and the phenomenologists. The symbolists became acquainted with the ideas of Vladimir Solovyov (1853-1900), a Russian philosopher of their own age, almost by accident.

Up until that time Solovyov had followed the path which was typical for the isolated thinker of the time. A well educated man and brilliant writer, he was ignored by all but a few in the 1870s and 1880's, partly because he was opposed to materialism and positivism, but mainly because his philosophy was based on religion. The first people to turn to him were those who became interested in philosophy directly, not through aesthetics. By 1900, however, Solovyov's system, which was complex and was often organized and presented in a rather unproductive way, achieved wider effectiveness. His influence also led to a revival of interest in religion. In 1903 there appeared a collection of essays entitled *Problems of Idealism* in which the contributors, some of them former Marxists, attested that they had turned to idealistic philosophy and to religion.

Various poets, for various reasons, also turned to religious questions. Some acted on the basis of personal ties to Church tradition, others were influenced by the ideas of Dostoevsky and Tolstoy, and some were following the model of the West where both confessions were still vigorous and vital after the age of "new Enlightenment," which was far more moderate in the West than the Enlightenment had been in Russia.

The founding of the "Religious and Philosophical Society" in 1901 was a remarkable phenomenon. At its conferences certain groups of Russian intellectuals, for whom D. Merezhkovskii often served as spokesman, met with representatives of the Church, theologians, and bishops to discuss religious questions. The "Society" existed for only sixteen months, from 1901 to 1903, and was then prohibited. Reports on its discussions were published, but they were censored and incomplete. The main question raised by the intellectuals was how Christianity could become a vital force in everyday life. The intellectuals reached some measure of understanding only with the educated theologians; most of the prelates considered the "Society" merely an opportunity for a sort of "inner mission." The intellectuals desired some reforms in Church life, for the official Church seemed to have little to offer them, and to their way of thinking had become inert and unyielding. Members of the ecclesiastical hierarchy saw the Church with optimistic eyes; after all, the simple people were generally faithful and orthodox. On the one hand we can discern echoes of the "sixties," in "ennobled" form, and on the other we can detect the spirit of Pobedonostsev's Church policy, though somewhat adulterated. The Church had absolutely no premonition of the upheavals which were approaching, while the intellectuals expected them, looked forward to them, and were firmly convinced that they were necessary. These expectations, when placed in the context of religion, could not help taking on an eschatological, "apocalyptic" character.

It is evident that on both sides there was actually a disposition toward further rapprochement, and this was perhaps the real reason why the "Society" was abolished. The authorities regarded the intellectual movement within the Church as a tremor which might shake one of the most important pillars of the status quo. Even if the discussions had not been prohibited, however, they would probably not have produced any tangible results, for the Church apparently had no ready means to satisfy the wishes of the intellectuals, who expected from Christianity not only the answer to questions of individual religious life but also answers which could establish standards for "art and science" and even for "public life" and politics.[30]

The Revolution of 1905

The tremor which was caused by the "Religious and Philosophical Society" and which rocked the "pillars" of Russian society was quite insignificant in comparison to the tremors which were soon to be caused by the social forces of Russian life. We cannot pursue the history of the revolutionary movement in detail, but we should note that several factors were of importance. One, of course, was the labor movement. Another was the growing need which had arisen in the Russian countryside when the increasing agricultural population could no longer find any use for its resources—"overpopulation of the peasantry"—and wanted to increase its land-holdings. And, finally, there was the unfortunate war with Japan, which remained incomprehensible to the people and exposed to public view the weaknesses of the government. All these led to a drastic rise in public dissatisfaction and to the outbreak of a popular movement, with the result that on October 17, 1905 (by the older calendar) the Tsar published a manifesto in which he promised his subjects civil liberties and a constitution, perhaps with the intention of later reneging on these promises.

In point of fact, the Revolution of 1905 was suppressed, and the laws governing election to the legislative assembly, the *Duma,* were weakened after the opposition had twice achieved a majority in the *Duma.* The year 1905 nevertheless marks the beginning of a new era in Russian political life, an era which, to be sure, lasted only twelve years, until November, 1917. During this period important spiritual-intellectual processes were at work.

After the Revolution. Political Groups

In the now rising, now falling waves of reaction and opposition the philosophical-political parties which arose in the 1890's—the *narodniki,* the Social Democrats, and the liberals—continued to exist, but they were no longer the only parties, for new parties were founded. The first to emerge as a coherent group was made up of "reactionaries." They were now in a position to be of service in defending the monarchy. It must be conceded that their services were in part as clumsy and stupid as possible. When we speak of an "ideology" of the Russian reactionaries of the time, we must put the word "ideology" in quotation marks, for the activity of the reactionaries actually to some extent compromised the monarchy by plotting the assassination of members of the democratic parties and by organizing secret bands, the so-called "Black Hundreds," to carry out resistance against revolution.

One of the new liberal groups exerted little influence. Its foremost representative was the former Marxist, P. Struve, who was able to attract only a few followers to his cause. To him it seemed only natural that liberalism, based on an ideologically supported theory, was to become the political representative of specific interests and that these interests, as in the West, could be those of capitalism. In Russia there were indeed "modern" capitalists who were prepared to support economic interests through political action. Moreover, the ideology of imperialistic Russia *(velikoderzhavnaia Rossiia)* attracted some supporters. Struve's journalistic attempts to convince Russian youth to abandon their socialistic tendencies in favor of his new brand of liberalism had little success, it seems. Nor did the liberals who were organized into political parties adopt his "capitalistic-imperialistic" ideology. The liberal party organizations, of course, were still not permitted by law and had been formally approved only in the *Duma* (parliament).

The most important development, it later turned out, was the split of the Social Democratic Party, even before the Revolution of 1905, into two factions. One of the factions, the Bolsheviks *(bol'sheviki),* was led by V. I. Lenin; the other, the Mensheviks *(men'sheviki),* included in its leadership not only the old ideologist Plekhanov but also Yu. Martov. Both factions remained faithful to the Social Democratic Party. The true nature of Bolshevism cannot be comprehended if this faction is dismissed as nothing more than "the more radical" wing of the party. The peculiarity of Bolshevism lies in its approach to party organization and to political tactics. Bolshevism emerged as a movement with a centralized leadership, which remained in the hands of Lenin, and with a strong penchant for the old conspiratorial tradition of the revolutionaries.

The Social Democrats at first regarded the impending Russian revolution as a "middle-class" revolt which would do no more than create the climate for the further struggle of the working class. Lenin, on the other hand, was already writing as follows in 1897: "Only the proletariat is capable of fighting on the front lines for political freedom," for "only the proletariat is capable of carrying through to its conclucsion the democratization of the political and social system." These words were written at a time when the proletariat made up less than ten per cent of the Russian population and had as yet scarcely been organized. During the Revolution of 1905 Lenin went even further in his prophecies: "The bourgeoisie, the landowners, the manufacturers," and "society" cannot accomplish "a decisive victory over tsarism"; "They do not even want a decisive victory"; "The decisive victory can lie only in the *revolutionary democratic dictatorship of the proletariat and the peasantry."* This paradoxical concept of "democratic dictatorship" signified a return to the ideas of the revolutionary conspirators of the "sixties," and here the trail was already blazed which Bolshevism was to follow in the Revolution of 1917, all the more so since Lenin, in contrast to the party program, came out in favor of terrorism: "We have never rejected terror on principle, and we cannot reject it. It is one of those weapons which are quite useful and even necessary at a certain point in the struggle."[31]

After the Revolution of 1905 Lenin attempted to build up the Bolshevik organization from rather small illegal groups which were to provide underground direction for the workers' movement. Bolshevism had genuine successes, particularly after 1912, but these lie beyond the scope of this study.

The twentieth century brought significant changes in all fields of intellectual endeavor. This can be seen best in university life. Whereas before 1910 there had been at all universities chairs which were unoccupied or occuped by temporary appointments, several new universities which were founded after 1910 were immediately able to hire as many professors as needed from the older universities. Scientific book production also underwent rapid growth.

Philosophical studies are particularly important for intellectual history. In this field we find original schools which at first were under the influence of Western philosophy. One particularly remarkable movement was "intuitivism," which began by examining epistemological problems and developed into a sort of "New Realism." The main figures in this school were, after 1904, N. Losskii (1870-1965), somewhat later S. Frank (1877-1950),and A. Askoldov.

A new school of the philosophy of religion was far more important for Russian intellectual development. Taking as a point of departure Schelling on the one hand and Vladimir Solovyov on the other, thinkers of this school attempted to find a new philosophical posture and the solution to basic questions of theology. Among the leaders of this school were N. Berdyaev (1874-1948) and S. Bulgakov (1871-1944), both of whom were formerly Marxists and the publishers of *Problems of Idealism.* Two other important figures were Prince S. Trubetskoy (1862-1905) and his brother, E. Trubetskoy (1863-1920). Several significant works on the philosophy of history were also published, among them works concerning Greek and Roman philosophy, St. Augustine, Leibniz, Fichte, and Hegel. There were also original thinkers who do not fit into any particular school. The most important such independent philosophers were V. Rozanov (1856-1919) and Viacheslav Ivanov (1866-1949), an important symbolist poet. Gradually the West too began to pay attention to Russian philosophical literature. For Russian intellectual history it is of particular importance that philosophers questioned the basic religious and confessional premises of Russian culture. As yet, to be sure, no one made any effort to give definitive answers. Particular emphasis was usually placed on the relationship of "Russian philosophy" to patristic thought on the one hand and to German mysticism on the other.[32]

Two men already mentioned, Rozanov and V. Ivanov, were also members of symbolist circles. After 1900 the problematic aspects of the ideology of the symbolists were extended beyond the sphere of aesthetics. V. Ivanov strove to achieve a universal cultural synthesis, the same goal on which the program of romanticism and the ideals of the Slavophiles were focused, but Ivanov's cultural synthesis was quite different in appearance. It was to be the union of classical antiquity and Christianity, the revival of all life in beauty, and beauty was to be as holy for the "new man" as it was presumed to have been in classical antiquity.

The first generation of symbolists fought for a "good" Russian literature, concentrating their attention, for example, on verse techniques, and they demanded that literary themes go beyond the narrow confines of sociopolitical questions. The second generation had more extensive goals and ideals. Members of this generation believed that they were the argonauts who were destined to find and take possession of the Golden Fleece of a revived Russian culture. Their goal was to reshape all aspects of life. Their ideals, it is true, were not uniform or precise, and their efforts were misunderstood— at first ignored, and later attacked—by the majority of the intellectuals. For many people the symbolists were never anything more than "decadent writers." Here again the old primacy of social criteria in poetry became the standard. Resistance to the new poetry stiffened after 1905 when the revolutionary movements subsided and when sultry eroticism, primitive amoralism, and morbid themes became predominant in the works of some symbolists, and especially in the works of some hangers-on who had only adopted the new style and bits and pieces of "neoromantic ideology" because that was the fashionable thing to do. There were still a sufficient number of writers who espoused realism, and some authors, Gorky and Bunin among others, returned to their ranks.

The years around 1910 brought victory for the new art and literature in several areas. As a direct result of symbolism, the aesthetic level was raised in various areas. Russian books now looked better: care was taken to produce beautiful type, bindings, and book illustrations; theatre directing and stage settings underwent a revival; the modern Russian ballet was developed; and the role of arts and crafts grew considerably. Of much more importance, of course, was the fact that it was now permissible to read and praise older and contemporary non-realistic literature of Russia and of other countries—works by Poe, Ibsen, Oscar Wilde, and "the moderns." Even more important, however, was the fact that the symbolists and the members of the older and younger generation of thinkers and scholars, who around 1900 had manifested no understanding for or interest in the new literature, now were united. Viacheslav Ivanov and Berdyaev could discuss things with each other: Andrei Bely, who was then studying Kant and the Kantian philosophers, was permitted to become a co-worker on a philosophical periodical; Briusov became the literary editor of the major periodical which P. Struve published; and the scholarly establishment took notice of the symbolists' works on the history and theory of literature.

As so often happens with intellectual trends, however, these successes and victories signaled the end of the symbolist movement. To the generation which emerged around 1910 the literature and the aesthetic views of the symbolists seemed "out-of-date." Symbolist literature was too bound by tradition, too "sweet," indeed "sickeningly sweet," and not bold enough. The new literary movement at first confined itself to a purely literary "revolution." Its members were the futurists, who in some respects resembled the German expressionists. The most important of the futurists was V. Mayakovsky (1893-1930); young Boris Pasternak (1890-1960) joined their ranks shortly after 1910.

The Crisis of the Intellectuals

The meaningful accomplishment of the age was the overcoming of the spirit of the "sixties," but most intellectual circles were hardly conscious of this. Berdyaev later noted: "Marxism was in itself a crisis of consciousness for intellectuals. . . . It contained intellectual and cultural interests which were alien to earlier Russian intellectuals." As we have just seen, however, orthodox Marxists of all sorts were no more able to properly evaluate the new literature than were the *narodniki* and the positivistic liberals. The collection of essays entitled *Signposts (Vekhi),* which appeared in 1908 and in which Berdyaev, Bulgakov, P. Struve, and S. Frank among others subjected the traditions of the intellectuals to penetrating criticism, enjoyed only little success. The authors level a number of charges. The goals of the intellectuals, they said, were utopian, which at the time was no longer justifiable; the intellectuals were neglecting cultural questions, which was right only in part; moreover, the intellectuals were inclined toward an enlightened *Weltanschauung,* manifested religious indifference, were removed from the down-to-earth tasks of "the people," and had cut their ties with genuine "Russian tradition."

At about the same time the revolutionary organizations underwent an inner crisis of quite a different sort. It turned out that Asef, who was a member of the Central Committee of the Social Democratic Party and was responsible for organizing that party's partially unsuccessful assassination attempts, was in fact a police agent who was working for both sides. Even Malinovskii, the most talented Bolshevist labor representative in the *Duma,* was a police spy. After the Revolution of 1917 the revolutionaries discovered in the state archives considerable evidence that tsarist agents had infiltrated the revolutionary movement. The illegal underground organization of the revolutionary party proved to be by no means a practical and safe fighting group. This inner crisis even found expression in literature, particularly in Andrei Bely's novel *Petersburg,* the most important prose work of the time. In this novel patricide is made the symbol of the Revolution.

While the new literary movements were at least able to prevail in Russia to some extent, the position of painters and sculptors was far more difficult. After 1900 the rather moderate Russian impressionists did achieve some success, but it is highly significant that the most important Russian artists, the very ones who belonged to the avantgarde, simply emigrated. They left Russia, and most of them never returned—that is, they did not return as artists, even though some occasionally paid visits to their native land. We have already mentioned V. Kandinsky (1866-1944), A. V. Yavlenskii (1864-1941), and M. V. Wereffkin (1860-1938). Now many Russian artists emigrated to Paris: the sculptor A. Arkhipenko went there in 1908: Serge Charchoune (Sharshun), who was also a poet, in 1912; Antoine Pevsner and Puni (Jean Pougny) in 1910: and Ossip Zadkine in 1909. Naum Pevsner, whose pseudonym was Gabo, went to Munich in 1909, and Chagall, perhaps the best known of the group, emigrated in 1910. Several recent studies have attempted to show that the work of at least some of these artists is intimately connected with Russian intellectual-historical and artistic traditions (icons, popular Russian art).

In 1910 and later, some of these artists attempted to participate in various exhibitions in Russia, but what was considered good modern art in Western Europe merely caused a scandal in Russia. A few of them—Kandinsky, for example—were able to work in Russia after the Revolution for only a short time; then they were driven away again forever by the "nonart" of "socialist realism." The fate of those artists who stayed in Russia was tragic. Kasimier Malewich (1878-1935), whose works dating from before World War I even today strike us as quite modern, died in Russia in complete obscurity.[33]

Lev Tolstoy

From the 1880's on, the views of Lev Tolstoy concerning ways to reform life became a matter of intense and universal interest. Tolstoy's decision to give up his literary career, his new theology as articulated in *A Short Description of the Gospel* in 1880 and *The Kingdom of God in Us* in 1893, and particularly his views on ethics and social philosophy presented in the *Confession* of 1879 appeared to be outside all Russian intellectual traditions. It was characteristic of the age that in some circles Tolstoy's program for living was put into practice, or at least attempts were made to put it into practice. A sort of "sect" arose which included not only prominent intellectuals, such as N. Strakhov and the writer N. Leskov, but also numerous half-educated and uneducated people. For Russian life Tolstoy's doctrine was certainly a very significant attempt to bridge the gap between the intellectuals and the people. This is somewhat reminiscent of the work of the revolutionaries during the 1870's, but the premises on which Tolstoy proceeded were entirely different, for he ignored politics completely. Politically his doctrine was "anarchism," because he completely rejected the state and the law. Although Tolstoy's religious views may be regarded as "specifically Russian," they were in point of fact very strongly influenced by the "liberal theology" of Protestantism.

Tolstoy himself described his inner development. The meaninglessness of life, which ends with death—the destroyer of all life—apparently first stimulated Tolstoy to seek a "meaning of life." He first arrived at an apparently religious solution: "To know God and to live is one and the same thing;" therefore "live in quest of God." For Tolstoy, however, this quest was a rational activity, and Tolstoy was one of the most complete rationalists in Russian intellectual history. For this reason he ended by contructing a rationalistic Christianity which was an abstract religion "purified" of everything that was "unintelligible." His thoughts sound strangely like those of the French Enlightenment in the eighteenth century.

Tolstoy presented his views in an intentionally "primitivizing" form. Man's life, he believed, should be based on reason, and the authentic teachings of Christ constituted "the strictest, purest, and most complete expression of the laws of reason." All metaphysical aspects of Church doctrine— Christ's assumption of human form, the Trinity, the immortality of the soul, etc.—and all church ritual in particular were in Tolstoy's opinion no more than a falsification of the true teachings of Christ. These teachings, according to Tolstoy, are moral precepts and are based primarily on reason. The highest law of life is the type of love which can demand that man ignore his own interests and his own welfare whenever the welfare of others requires him to do so; in other words, man must reject all use of force and even "refuse to resist evil," or at least refuse to use force to combat evil. But all culture, Tolstoy thought, is based on power, and it is power alone which preserves the state and the law. The law requires punishment, but every punishment merely magnifies evil.

In Tolstoy's view, the state is merely an "aggregate of people who do violence to other people." Laws are "the product of self-interest, of deceit, and of partisan struggles; they cannot serve genuine justice." Not even the socialist state represents a better form of government; in fact, such a state, which "will control all aspects of private life," will be much worse—"the most cruel and horrible band of robbers is not so frightful as that sort of state."

Reason demands, said Tolstoy, that all men should be equal. Equality ought to be achieved by simplifying the life of the upper classes. Tolstoy demands first what he calls *oproshchenie,* a term which almost defies translation. The word, which I have rendered as "simplifying life," means that people should refrain from satisfying their "superfluous" and "unnatural" needs, and by this Tolstoy meant everything which the Russian peasant has to do without. Tolstoy, even in his literary works, attempted to "unmask" the meaninglessness of so-called "cultural" needs, such things as the clothing worn by the upper classes, their food and servants, their doctors, and even their midwives, as well as all other things which serve only the wealthy: the theater, the ballet, the opera, art, and science. All these things, according to Tolstoy, were "superfluous" and ought to be eliminated. If people would do without these things, then private property would cease to exist, especially the property rights to land, which ought to be at the disposal of those who work on that land. When all men become equal in this sense, Tolstoy believed, then the desire for power *(vlastoliubie)* will also disappear and with it "deceit, hypocrisy, humiliation of people, prisons, citadels, executions, and murders," police, armies, wars; and, consequently, the state too; and the kingdom of Heaven will exist on earth.

Tolstoy believed that the kingdom of Heaven is in us, not in another world, and that it is easy to attain: "Everyone should do what he ought to do," and when all men who "have recognized the truth" are also willing to proclaim it publicly, then no armies of millions of soldiers, no state attorneys, no revolutions, and no wars will be able to withstand it. True Christian faith, said Tolstoy, requires man to refuse to obey the power of the state, and when that happens "Christianity will destroy from within all the foundations of governmental power," because no government can do anything to people who practice only passive resistance.

This idea of the path to "the kingdom of God" was utopian, of course, and was contrary to all the other movements in Russian intellectual history at the time in that it hoped to achieve the ideal state not by engaging in political warfare but by having every single person turn within and practice passive resistance against force and power.

Some of Tolstoy's theses are certainly important. All too often they are considered "genuine Russian" components in his philosophy and occasionally occur in the writings of rationalistic and pietistic sects and of individual Russian thinkers and poets. These theses are "resisting evil without resorting to force," the demand for personal moral reform, and the yearning for *oproshchenie*.[34] The maximalism and utopianism of Tolstoy's practical suggestions were also long since familiar to Russian intellectuals, who were also quite sympathetic to his criticism of culture, especially in so far as it was directed against the state.

The Orient

In the nineteenth century the Orient disappeared almost completely from Russian thought. L. Tolstoy esteemed Buddhism and Confucius particularly as "wisdom of the East," but his attention was probably drawn to

Buddhism by Schopenhauer. In Solovyov the idea of an eventual westward move of the East, the "yellow peril," aroused only visions of anxiety. He probably intended to give admirers of Buddhism a warning in his portrayal of "Buddhistic atheism." As we have seen, Russian thinkers conceived of Russia as an "Orient *sui generis*" opposed to the West, and the real Orient thus went unheeded. Besides, Christian Russia could not be a part of the pagan or Islamic Orient.

At the same time Russia, as a result of a policy of conquest and colonization, was moving eastward.[35] The uncultured primitive peoples of Siberia and also the nomads beyond the lower Volga were looked upon as subjects of the state. Christian missionaries who worked among these peoples paid hardly any attention to the peculiar aspects of their culture. Russians fought the mountain tribes of the Caucasus for years without every giving any serious thought to their cultural relations with them. The motifs which Russian literature took from this "Russian Orient" are significant. The peoples and territories of these lands furnished romanticist and realist alike either with exotic themes or with the raw material for portraying "the good and noble savage." Less frequently we hear complaints about the inhuman way in which these noble savages were treated both by the merchants who were exploiting them and by the Russian authorities who were governing them.

At the beginning of the eighteenth-century Leibniz had harbored the hope that Russia would play the role of mediator between Europe and the Orient, but Oriental studies in Russia developed only slowly and merely because foreign scholars, most of them of German origin, took part in them. When Russians pushed forward into Central Asia in the second half of the nineteenth century, they came into contact with new and more highly developed Oriental cultures, some of which were in fact already in a state of decline, and this encounter was destined to arouse more serious interest in the Orient. Via Siberia Russia came to the Pacific Ocean and to America— to Alaska and to California. These colonies in America were given up in return for modest payment. There were good reasons for this action: these distant colonies could hardly be defended; England was far more of a threat than the United States; and Russia could not have prevented by force the expansion of England in Canada.

At the turn of the century unscrupulous Russian entrepreneurs, with the protection of the Russian government, moved into Manchuria and Korea and there came into contact with Japan, which was then becoming Europeanized. The ensuing conflict between the economic interests of Russia and Japan ended with the resounding defeat of Russia in the Russo-Japanese War of 1904-1905, but even this defeat was able to draw to the Orient the attention of only an insignificant part of the general Russian public.

Again we find interest in the "wisdom of the Orient" stimulated by *Western* influences. England was the source of so-called "theosophy," which, of course, owed its origin to the Ukrainian landowner H. Blavatskaya. Even instruction in Oriental languages and culture, however, remained the provice of extremely exclusive universities, the Oriental Department of the University of St. Petersburg and the Oriental College in Vladivostok.

Visions and Prognoses

Nevertheless, in conjunction with the Russian Revolution, the Orient began to achieve a certain importance in the eyes of Russian intellectuals. This interest manifested itself in the form of visions and prognoses which generally went unheeded. As early as the 1870's Dostoevsky was speaking with serious pathos about the "great tasks" which faced Russia in Asia. He even went so far as to term Russians in this connection "Asiatics." As so often, however, his words were ignored.

It was surprising that the poet V. Briusov, who otherwise always spoke of European culture with great respect, published in 1905 a poem entitled "The Coming of the Huns" in which he asserted that new waves of peoples would come from the unknown depths of Asia, would inundate Europe, and would destroy European culture. The poet envisioned wild hordes who would dance around a bonfire to which books and art treasures had been consigned. This vision was surely suggested to him by the "anti-bourgeois" feelings which arose in him during the Revolution of 1905.

In 1908 Andrei Bely wrote his novel *Petersburg*. Here old and new Russia alike are troubled partly by the boiling up of "Tatar blood" (the hero's father, modeled on Pobedonostsev, is of Tatar origin) and partly by sinister visions of the Orient invading Russia. Awake or in a delirium Dudkin, the revolutionary who is hiding underground, sees Japanese and Persians pass before his eyes. The heroine is surrounded by articles fashionable in Japan—fans, kimonos, etc. The tenacity with which "Oriental" motifs appear again and again, like leitmotifs, indicates that Bely, the representative of the younger symbolist generation, also regarded the "Oriental danger" as a real one. In revisions of the novel Bely did nothing to weaken these motifs.

A long poem entitled *The Scythians*, which appeared ten years later, was much more impressive. It was the work of another representative of the second generation of symbolists, A. Blok. In the name of the Russians, who are here called Scythians, the poet utters terrible threats against Europe. Because the West, which the Russians understood so profoundly and loved so intensely, abandoned Russia in her hour of need (he means the Revolution of 1917), the "Scythians" will remain neutral in the coming struggle of the technical culture of Europe against the "wild Mongolian hordes." If the West rejects Russia's last offer of friendship, then Russia will turn her Asiatic force to the West. The "Scythians" will no longer protect Europe from the East, they will make no move when "the cruel Huns rob graves, burn cities, drive herds of horses into the churches, and waste the flesh of our white brothers." The "Scythians," the "Asiatics," and the "barbarians," it is clear, are the Russians! Anyone familiar with the strength of Westernism in Russia at the beginning of the twentieth century cannot help being astonished at this outburst of feeling directed against the West. Notes in Blok's diary show that this feeling on his part did exist.

After 1917 a Russian emigre movement arose whose members were called "Eurasians" (it held no public meetings after World War II). The ideologists of this movement (at first Prince N. S. Trubetskoy (1850-1938), the important Russian linguist and Slavist at the University of Vienna, was one of them) contended that Russia was outside the sphere of European culture, that it belonged to a "special" world which was made up of Eastern Europe and Northern Asia, i.e. Eurasia, and which formed a geographic, economic, and linguistic unit, and that, most significant of all, it was a cultural entity. According to this view, Russian culture was not European but "Turanic," and in the Russian mind the following characteristic traits of the "Turanic" type could be discerned: the union of life style and religious faith; the tendency toward contemplativeness; the preference for the ceremonial; bold jingoism; and schematizing primitivism in thought and philosophy. We need not take into consideration here the fact that some of the "Eurasians" considered the blood relationship of the Russians with the Turko-Tataric and the Ural-Altaic peoples to be the basis of this affiliation and that they particularly emphasized the "spiritual," not the intellectual bases of this "Eurasian type." The "Eurasians" were certainly the first to make an effort to pose the question of "Russia, Europe, and the Orient" and to answer it in a new way. For more than two decades now, proponents of this view, if such there still be, have been silent, but we should emphasize this new ideology here at the conclusion of this study.

We break off our description of the intellectual and spiritual development of Russia with the great catastrophe which befell old Russia as a result of the War of 1914 and the Revolution of 1917. We have been able to do no more than show what led up to this situation. Further developments in Russia have posed new questions for which at present there can hardly be definitive answers.

NOTES

1. *Stefanit i Ichnilat (The Crowned and the Tracer)*—According to Professor Tschiževsky "a translation of this reached the East Slavs probably in the twelfth to thirteenth centuries." (*History of Russian Literature,* the Hague, 1960, p. 27). [Editor's note.]

2. The word *nemech* did not originally mean "the mute one" as popular literature sometimes would have it, but "one who speaks in an unintelligible way," which corresponds roughly to the meaning of the Greek *barbaros.*

3. It must be emphasized, however, that ten of the 46 clerical schools were located in Ukrainian bishoprics, which at that time were part of Russia, and that nearly half of the students attended these ten schools. To be sure, the Great Russian students often studied in the Ukraine too in order to complete their education—Lomonosov is a case in point.

4. Pososhkov was a "state farmer,'" which meant that he was under a governmental administrative unit and with its consent was permitted to engage in trade and commerce in return for payment of certain fees *(obrok)* to the official treasury. His life ended tragically. He died in the prison to which he had been sent in 1725 for reasons unknown to us—a bad omen for free thinkers and writers in later times.

5. Raimundus Lullus (1232/34-1316) was a Catalan Franciscan and Mohammedan missionary, mystic, poet, and author who influenced Nicolas Cusanus. His work on logic, *Ars magna et ultima,* was famous during his time. How a copy of this work got to Kiev is not clear, although it is known that a Kievan scholar, Bohomodlevskii, studied in Spain and composed a philosophical work in the vein of Lullus' disciples.

6. Collars or "jabots" are meant.

7. "Drinking tobacco" was an expression also common in English (cf. Ben Jonson, *Every Man in his Humour, III,* ii—"The most divine tobacco I have ever drunk.")

8. Known as Ivan VI [Editor's note.]

9. These three famous tales *(povesti')* of the early eighteenth century are known as *The Tale of the Russian Sailor Vasilii, The Tale of the Russian Gentleman (Kavaler) Aleksandr,* and *The Tale of the Russian Merchant Ioann.* All three are anonymous. [Editor's note.]

10. Deism was the belief, widespread in the eighteenth century, that after creating the world God has refrained from intervening personally in nature and in history.

11. A. S. Pushkin's beautiful novel, *The Captain's Daughter,* which was written sixty years later, offers little which could contribute to a better understanding of the Pugachev revolt. [In 1834 Pushkin published a work in two parts entitled *A History of the Pugachev Revolt;* the second part contains various documents, memoirs, and other materials such as manifestoes and reports which all pertain to the revolt. Editor's note.]

12. The interest of the group was not so much in the works of Schelling himself as in those of some of his disciples in the West, such as G. H. Schubert, but it is even more characteristic of the mood of the Russian intellectuals of the time.

13. Khomiakov, who was not always consistent, occasionally writes in a different tone; strange as it may seem, he terms Russian painters and sculptors "the best in Europe with the sole exception of Germany," but he regards Glinka and Gogol (who as a Ukrainian was not, to Khomiakov's way of thinking, a true Russian) as "great models" for future Russian composers and writers; it never occurred to Khomiakov that Europe might show interest in them or that their works might be successful in the West.

14. These distinctions are most likely based on the terms *Legalität, Moralität,* and *Sittlichkeit* as used by Hegel where *Sittlichkeit* refers to a general, public morality and *Moralität* to the ethical behavior of the individual, i.e., a personal morality. [Editor's note.]

15. Aksakov shared the conviction of the Slavophiles and of even some scholars of the time that the Slavic peoples, in their original state, had been patriarchal, pastoral, and peaceful. This was the view of Western Slavists and Slavophiles like Kollar and Shafarik, whose views influenced Russian Slavists.

16. The major part of the recently discovered letters consists of a history of philosophy compiled mainly from a work which Lamennais had written while he was still a traditionalist.

17. The immediate source of this idea is a now forgotten work written by Belinsky's colleague K. Zelenechkyi, who was later a professor in Odessa.

18. Herzen's father was a wealthy Moscow aristocrat, Ivan Alekseivich Yakovlev; his mother's name was Henrietta Wilhelmina Lousia Haag. His own name, Herzen, from the German word for "heart," was selected by his father, perhaps in connection with the German euphemism for an illegitimate child "ein Kind des Herzens" (a child of the heart). [Editor's note.]

19. Mochalov was a tragedian who also enjoyed great acclaim during the pre-Enlightenment, the age of Belinsky.

20. Cf. Shigalev's speech in Dostoevsky's *The Possessed.*

21. Several facts should be kept in mind. Fourier had predicted that with the advent of socialism nature would be completely transformed: salty sea water would turn into a sort of lemonade; new species such as the "anti-tiger" and the "anti-lion" would arise; 300 new planets, now already approaching our solar system, would appear; and so forth. He wanted to put members of socialistic society into a complicated system of ranks (echoes of the plan are discernible in Dostoevsky's works, particularly in the parody of socialist programs which Shigalev develops in *The Possessed*). Fourier painted life in the new society as a series of festivals and celebrations. He wanted to put even love and marriage under strict controls.

22. Among those who were sceptical about the *mir* was the old revolutionary and anarchist Mikhail Bakunin (1814-1876). He had been a Hegelian in the 1840's and had taken part in the Revolution of 1848 in Europe. In 1861 he emigrated to Europe (he had been in exile in Siberia). He had only limited influence on the ideology of the revolutionary movement in Russia.

23. Neither Bakunin's anarchistic ideas nor the thought of Prince P. Kropotkin (1842-1921), an early participant in the Russian revolutionary movement who only later presented his ideas in a systematic form, had much influence in Russia. The anti-traditionalism of these two anarchists, who were much more influential in the West, was characteristic of Russian intellectual history, however.

24. Vera Zasulich avoided immediate arrest after her acquittal by fleeing the country. As an emigree she later became a member of the moderate wing of the social democrats.

25. Vladimir Solovyov, the most interesting critic of Danilevskii, maintains that Danilevskii's theories were taken from a book by the German historian Heinrich Rückert (1823-1875) entitled *Lehrbuch der Weltgeschichte in organischer Darstellung (World History Portrayed Organically);* this assertion is certainly not completely accurate, although it is possible that Danilevskii was inspired by Rückert's work.

26. He does foresee, however, the complete "destruction" of the Poles as a result of their too intimate relationship with the West and with Rome.

27. A description of such a mystic sect can be found in Andrei Bely's novel *The Silver Dove.*

28. The word was probably at first an allusion to factory workers who were grimy with soot and machine oil.

29. This book advanced, on the basis of inadequate statistical arguments, the thesis that in Russia small agricultural enterprises were being displaced by large ones, that is, that the same process of concentration was taking place in agriculture as was

occurring in industry.

30. The fact that Merezhkovskii was occasionally called "the Russian Luther" shows how exaggerated these expectations of Church reform were.

31. Compare these statements with the following made by Martov: "Terror is unnecessary when the organized masses vanquish absolutism; it is useless when this task exceeds the powers of the popular movement; and it is harmful because it prevents the development and organization of this movement."

32. This is the approach taken by S. Frank, for example.

33. Russian theatre and ballet aroused particular interest in the West. The emigration of Igor Stravinsky, the most important modern Russian composer, seems to be less symptomatic of the cultural situation in Russia than was the emigration of Russian painters and sculptors.

34. In the arguments in favor of *oproshchenie* reminiscences of stoicism can be clearly discerned.

35. Tsar Paul I (1796-1801) planned a military expedition to India, but his plan was prompted more by the enmity he felt toward England than by any interest in eastward expansion.

862	Summoning of the Varangian princes and founding of the Russian state according to the *Nestor Chronicle*
978-1015	Reign of Vladimir
988	The Christianization of Russia
1019-1054	Reign of Yaroslav the Wise
1113-1125	Reign of Vladimir Monomakh
Beginning of 12th century	The so-called *Nestor Chronicle* is finished
1185-1187	*The Lay of the Host of Igor*
12th century	The so-called *Kievan Chronicle* (a part of the *Hypatius Chronicle*)
13th century	The so-called *Galician-Volynian Chronicle* (a part of the *Hypatius Chronicle*)
1223 and 1237	Tatar invasions
1325-1341	Reign of Ivan I
1359-1389	Reign of Dmitrii Donskoi
1380	Victory of Dmitrii Donskoi over the Tatars led by Khan Mamai
1391	Death of St. Sergii of Radonezh
1462-1505	Reign of Gand Prince Ivan III
1480	Overthrow of the Tatars by Ivan III
1505-1533	Reign of Vasilii III
1508	Death of Nil Sorskii
1515	Death of Josif Volotskii
1533-1584	Reign of Grand Prince Ivan IV (Ivan the Terrible)
1542-1563	Makarii, Metropolitan of Moscow
1547	Coronation of Ivan IV as Tsar
1584-1598	Reign of Feodor I, last ruler of the Riurik dynasty.
1598-1605	Reign of Boris Godunov
1605-1613	Interregnum (The Time of Troubles)
1613	Election of the new Romanov dynasty
1613-1645	Reign of Mikhail, first ruler of the Romanov dynasty
1645-1676	Reign of Aleksei
1652-1666	Nikon, Patriarch of Moscow
1666-1667	Schism in the Church
1676-1682	Reign of Feodor III
1681	Archpriest Avvakum burned at the stake
1682-1696	Reign of Ivan V, co-tsar
1682-1725	Reign of Peter I (Peter the Great)
1703	Founding of St. Petersburg
1721	Abolition of the Patriarchate
1725	Founding of the Academy of Sciences
1725-1727	Reign of Catherine I
1727-1730	Reign of Peter II
1730-1740	Reign of Anna
1740-1741	Reign of Ivan VI
1741-1762	Reign of Elizabeth
1755	Founding of the University of Moscow

1757	Founding of the Academy of Arts
1762	Reign of Peter III
1762-1796	Reign of Catherine II (Catherine the Great)
1764	Secularization of Church lands
1773-1775	Pugachev Revolt
1786	Publication of program for educational system
1796-1801	Reign of Paul
1801-1825	Reign of Alexander I
1809	Speranskii's constitutional project
1819	Founding of the University of St. Petersburg
Dec. 14, 1825	Decembrist Revolt
1825-1855	Reign of Nicholas I
1833	Publication of revised Code of Laws
1855-1881	Reign of Alexander II
1855-1856	Crimean War
1861	Emancipation of the serfs
1866	Attempted assassination of Alexander II
1880	Dostoevsky's "Pushkin Speech"
1881	Assassination of Alexander II
1881-1894	Reign of Alexander III
1894-1917	Reign of Nicholas II, last tsar of the Romanov dynasty
1898	Formation of the Russian Social Democratic Labor Party
1903	Strike movement in southern Russia
1905	Russo-Japanese War and Revolution of 1905

SELECTED BIBLIOGRAPHY

I Sources in English

A *Anthologies*

1. Edie, J. M. et al., eds. *Russian Philosophy*. 3 vols. Chicago, 1965; reprinted, Tennessee, 1976.
2. Fedotov, G. P., ed. *A Treasury of Russian Spirituality*. New York, 1948.
3. Matlaw, Ralph M., ed. *Belinsky, Chernyshevsky, and Dobrolyubov: Selected Criticism*. New York, 1962.
4. Raeff, Marc, ed. *Russian Intellectual History: An Anthology*. New York, 1966.
5. Reeder, Roberta, ed. and trans. *Down Along the Mother Volga: An Anthology of Russian Folk Lyrics*. Philadelphia, 1975.
6. Riha, Thomas, ed. *Readings in Russian Civilization*. 3 vols. 2nd ed. Chicago, 1969.
7. Segel, Harold. *The Literature of Eighteenth-Century Russia: A History and Anthology*. 2 vols. New York, 1967.
8. Vernadsky, George, senior ed. *A Source Book for Russian History from Early Times to 1917*. 3 vols. New Haven, Conn., 1972.
9. Zenkovsky, Serge, ed. *Medieval Russia's Epics, Chronicles, and Tales*. New York, 1963. 2nd ed., 1974.

B *Individual Works* (chronologically arranged)

Cross, Samual Hazzard, and O. P. Sherbowitz-Wetzor, eds. *The Russian Primary Chronicle: Laurentian Text*. Cambridge, Mass., 1953.

Perfecky, George A., trans. *The Hypatian Codex, Part Two: The Galician-Volynian Chronicle*. Vol. 2. Munich, 1973.

Kantor, Marvin, and Richard S. White, trans. and commentaries. *The "Vita" of Constantine* and *The "Vita" of Methodius*. Ann Arbor, 1976.

Nabokov, V., trans. *The Song of Igor's Campaign*. New York, 1960.

Nestor. "A Life of St. Theodosius" and "From St. Theodosius' *Sermon On Patience and Love,"* in number 2, above.

St. Nilus Sorsky. "The Tradition to the Disciples," "The Monastic Rule," and "St. Nilus' Last Will," in number 2, above.

Kleimola, Ann M. *Justice in Medieval Russia: Muscovite Judgment Charters (Pravye Gramoty) of the Fifteenth and Sixteenth Centuries*. Philadelphia, 1975.

Dewey, Horace W., and Ann Kleimola, trans. and eds., with commentary. *Russian Private Law in the XIV-XVII Centuries: An Anthology of Documents*. Ann Arbor, 1973.

Fennell, J. L. I., ed. *The Correspondence between Prince A. M. Kurbsky and Tsar Ivan IV of Russia 1564-1579*. Cambridge, 1963.

Fletcher, Giles. *Of the Rus Commonwealth*. New York, 1966.

Avvakum. *The Life of Archpriest Avvakum by Himself,* in number 2, above.

Shafirov, P. *A Discourse Concerning the Just Causes of the War Between Sweden and Russia: 1700-1721*. Dobbs Ferry, N.Y., 1973.

Shcherbatov, Prince M. M. *On the Corruption of Morals in Russia*. Trans. A. Lentin. Cambridge, 1969.

"The Polemics Between Catherine II and Novikov," in number 7, above.

Skovoroda, Gregory. *Socrates in Russia,* in number 1, above.

Fonvizin, Denis I. "Letters from my Second Journey Abroad (1777-1778)" and "Letters from my Third Journey Abroad" (1784-1785)," in number 7, above.

Radishchev, A. N. *A Journey from St. Petersburg to Moscow.* Trans. L. Wiener, Cambridge, 1958.
Chaadaev, P. Ya. *Philosophical Letters and An Apology of a Madman.* Trans. Mary-Barbara Zeldin. Knoxville, Tenn., 1969.
Karamzin, N. M. *Memoir on Ancient and Modern Russia.* Trans. Richard Pipes. Cambridge, Mass., 1959.
Khomyakov, Alexis S. *The Church is One.* London, 1948.
―――. "On Recent Developments in Philosophy," in number 1, above.
Kireyevsky, Ivan. "On the Necessity and Possibility of New Principles in Philosophy," in number 1, above.
―――. "On the Nature of European Culture and Its Relation to the Culture of Russia," in number 4, above.
Aksakov, S. T. *The Family Chronicle.* Trans. M. C. Beverley. New York, 1961.
Belinsky, V. G. *Selected Philosophical Works.* Moscow, 1956.
Herzen, A. *Selected Philosophical Works.* Moscow, 1956.
―――. *My Past and Thoughts.* 5 vols. Trans C. Garnett. London, 1924-1926.
Bakunin, Michael. *God and the State.* Boston, 1885.
―――. *The Political Philosophy of Bakunin: Scientific Anarchism.* Compiled and edited by G. P. Maximoff, Glencoe, Ill., 1953.
Confino, Michael, ed. *Daughter of a Revolutionary: Natalie Herzen and the Bakunin-Nechayev Circle.* La Salle, Ill., 1973.
Chernyshevsky, Nicholas G. *Selected Philosophical Essays.* Moscow, 1958.
―――. *What is to be Done?* New York, 1961.
Pisarev, Dmitry. *Selected Philosophical, Social, and Political Essays.* Moscow, 1958.
von Haxthausen, Baron August. *Studies on the Interior of Russia.* Ed. S. Frederick Starr, trans. E. L. M. Schmidt. Chicago, 1972.
Lavrov, Peter. *Historical Letters.* Trans. J. P. Scanlan. Berkeley, 1967.
Plekhanov, G. V. *History of Russian Social Thought.* Trans. B. M. Bekkar et al. New York, 1967.
Leontiev, Konstantin. *Against the Current: Selected Writings.* Ed. George Ivask, trans. G. Reavey. New York, 1969.
Solovyov, Vladimir. "Lectures on Godmanhood," in number 1, above.
Berdyaev, Nicholas. *The Russian Idea.* Boston, 1962.

II Secondary Sources

Abraham, G. *On Russian Music: Critical and Historical Studies.* New York, 1939.
Alexander, John T. *Autocratic Politics in a National Crisis: The Imperial Russian Government and Pugachev's Revolt: 1773-1775.* Bloomington, 1969.
―――. *Emperor of the Cossacks: Pugachev and the Frontier Jacquerie of 1773-1775.* Lawrence, Kans., 1973.
Almedingen, E. M. *The Emperor Alexander II.* London, 1962.
Alpatov, M. V. *The Russian Impact on Art.* Trans. I. Litvinov. New York, 1950.
―――. *Art Treasures of Russia.* New York, 1967.
Altenhoff, Herbert T. *Catherine the Great: Art, Sex, Politics.* New York, 1975.
Alston, Patrick L. *Education and the State in Tsarist Russia.* Stanford, 1969.
Annenkov, P. V. *The Extraordinary Decade.* Ann Arbor, 1968.
Arseniev, Nicholas. *Holy Moscow.* London, 1940.
Bain, R. Nesbet. *The Daughter of Peter the Great.* New York and Westminster, 1900.
―――. Peter III Emperor of Russia: *The Story of a Crisis and a Crime.* Westminster, 1902. AMS Press reprint, New York, 1971.
Barratt, G. R. V. Voices in Exile: *The Decembrist Memoirs.* Montreal and London, 1974.
Benz, E. *The Eastern Orthodox Church: Its Thoughts and Life.* New York, 1963.

Berdyaev, Nicholas. *Dostoevsky.* Cleveland, 1957.
———. *The Russian Idea.* Boston, 1962.
Bergamini, John D. *The Tragic Dynasty: A History of the Romanovs.* New York, 1969.
Billington, James H. *The Icon and the Axe: An Interpretive History of Russian Culture.* New York, 1966.
———. *Mikhailovsky and Russian Populism.* New York, 1958.
Black, J. L. *Nicholas Karamzin and Russian Society in the Nineteenth Century: A Study in Russian Political and Historical Thought.* Toronto and Buffalo, 1975.
Blinoff, Marthe, ed. and trans. *Life and Thought in Old Russia.* University Park, Penna., 1961.
Blum, Jerome. *Lord and Peasant in Russia.* Princeton, N.J., 1961.
Bohachevsky-Chomiak, M. *S. N. Trubetskoi: An Intellectual Among the Intelligentsia in Prerevolutionary Russia.* Belmont, Mass., 1976.
Bolshakoff, S. *Russian Nonconformity.* Philadelphia, 1950.
———. *The Doctrine of the Unity of the Church in the Works of Komyakov and Moehler.* London, 1946.
Bowman, H. E. *Vissarion Belinskii 1811-1848: A Study in the Origins of Social Criticism in Russia.* Cambridge, Mass., 1954.
Brower, Daniel R. *Training the Nihilists: Education and Radicalism in Tsarist Russia.* Ithaca, N.Y., 1975.
Bulgakov, S. N. *The Orthodox Church.* London, 1935.
Cant, C. B. H. "Avvakum and his Scottish Contemporaries." *Slavonic Review,* 44(1966), 381-403.
Carmichael, Joel. *A Cultural History of Russia.* New York, 1968.
Carr, E. H. *Michael Bakunin.* New York, 1937.
———. *The Romantic Exiles: A Nineteenth-Century Portrait Gallery.* London, 1933.
Charques, R. D. *A Short History of Russia.* New York, 1956.
Cherniavsky, M. "The Old Believers and the New Religion." *Slavic Review* (1966), 1-39.
———. *Tsar and People.* New Haven, Conn., 1961.
Chmielewski, E. *Tribune of the Slavophiles: Konstantin Aksakov.* Gainesville, Fla., 1962.
Christoff, P. K. *An Introduction to Nineteenth-Century Russian Slavophilism.* Vol. I: *A. S. Xomjakov.* The Hague, 1961.
———. *The Third Heart: Some Intellectual-ideological Currents and Cross Currents in Russia: 1800-1830.* The Hague, 1970.
———. *An Introduction to Nineteenth-Century Russian Slavophilism.* Vol. II: *I. V. Kireevskij.* The Hague, 1972.
Čiževskij, Dmitrij. *History of Russian Literature from the Eleventh Century to the End of the Baroque.* The Hague, 1960.
Clardy, Jesse V. *The Philosophical Ideas of Alexander Radishchev.* New York, 1964.
Cohen, Stephen F. *Bukharin and the Bolshevik Revolution: A Political Biography, 1888-1938.* New York, 1973.
Conybeare, F. *Russian Dissenters.* New York, 1962.
Cross, A. G., ed. and introd. *Russian Literature in the Age of Catherine the Great. A Collection of Essays.* Oxford, 1976.
Crummy, R. O. *The Old Believers and the World of Anti-Christ.* Wisconsin, 1970.
Cracraft, James. *The Church Reform of Peter the Great.* Stanford, 1971.
Curtiss, J. S. *Church and State in Russia: The Last Years of the Empire (1900-1917).* New York, 1940.
Curtiss, Mina. *A Forgotten Empress: Anna Ivanovna and Her Era, 1730-1740.* New York, 1974.
Danzas, J. *The Russian Church.* London, 1936.

Dewey, H. W., ed. *Muscovite Judicial Texts:* 1488-1556. Ann Arbor, 1968.

Dorosh, H. *Russian Constitutionalism.* New York, 1944.

Dukes, Sir Paul. *Catherine the Great and the Russian Nobility.* Cambridge, 1967.

———. *A History of Russia: Medieval, Modern and Contemporary.* New York, 1974.

Dvornik, Francis. *Byzantine Missions Among the Slavs.* New Brunswick, N. J., 1970.

———. *The Slavs in European History and Civilization.* New Brunswick, N. J., 1970. Reprint 1975.

Engel, Barbara Alpern et al., eds. and trans. *Five Sisters: Women Against the Tsar.* New York, 1975.

Evans, John L. *The Petraševskij Circle.* The Hague and Paris, 1974.

Fedotov, G. P. "Religious Backgrounds in Russian Culture." *Church History* (Mar, 1943), 35-51.

———. *The Russian Religious Mind.* Vol. I: *Kievan Christianity: The Tenth to the Thirteenth Centuries.* Vol. II: *The Middle Ages: The Thirteenth to the Fifteenth Centuries.* Cambridge, Mass., 1966.

Fennell, J. L. I. *Ivan the Great of Moscow.* New York, 1961.

Fennell, John, and Antony Stokes. *Early Russian Literature.* Berkeley and Los Angeles, 1974.

Fischer, G. *Russian Liberalism.* Cambridge, Mass., 1958.

Florinsky, M. T. *Russia: A History and an Interpretation.* 2 vols. New York, 1953.

———. *Russia: A Short History.* 2nd ed. London, 1969.

Frank, Joseph. *Dostoevsky: The Seeds of Revolt 1821-1849.* Princeton, 1976.

French, R. *The Eastern Orthodox Church.* London, 1951.

Fulop-Miller, R. *Rasputin: The Holy Devil.* New York, 1928.

Fuhrmann, Joseph T., ed. *Essays on Russian Intellectual History.* Austin, Texas, 1971.

———. *The Origins of Capitalism in Russia: Industry and Progress in the Sixteenth and Seventeenth Centuries.* Chicago, 1972.

Gerstein, Linda. *Nikolai Strakhov.* Cambridge, Mass., 1971.

Gleason, Abbott. *European and Muscovite: Ivan Kireevsky and the Origins of Slavophilism.* Cambridge, Mass., 1972.

Gribble, F. *Emperor and Mystic: The Life of Alexander I of Russia.* New York, 1931.

Grunwald, C. *The Saints of Russia.* London, 1960.

———. *Peter the Great.* Trans. V. Garvin. London, 1956.

Gudzii, N. K. *History of Old Russian Literature.* 2nd ed. Trans. S. Wilbur. New York, 1949.

Hamilton, G. *The Art and Architecture of Russia.* London, 1954.

Hamm, Michael F., ed. *The City in Russian History.* Lexington, Ky., 1976.

Haney, Jack V. *From Italy to Muscovy: The Life and Works of Maxim the Greek.* Munich, 1973.

Harcave, Sidney. *Russia: A History.* 4th ed. New York, 1959.

———. *Years of the Golden Cockerel: The Last Romanov Tsars 1814-1917.* New York, 1968.

———. *The Russian Revolution of 1905.* London, 1970.

Hare, Richard. *Pioneers of Russian Social Thought.* London, 1951.

———. *Portraits of Russian Personalities between Reform and Revolution.* London, 1959.

Hindus, M. *The Cossacks.* Westport, Conn., 1970.

Hingley, Ronald. *The Tsars 1533-1917.* New York, 1968.

Hunczak, Taras, ed. *Russian Imperialism from Ivan the Great to the Revolution.* New Brunswick, N. J., 1974.

Jakobson, R. O. "The Puzzles of the Igor Tale." *Speculum,* 27(1952), 43-66.

Jelavich, Barbara. *St. Petersburg and Moscow: Tsarist and Soviet Foreign Policy, 1814-1974.* Bloomington and London, 1974.

Jones, Robert E. *The Emancipation of the Russian Nobility, 1762-1785*. Princeton, 1973.

Kennan, George, F. *The Marquis de Custine and His Russia in 1839*. Princeton, N. J., 1971.

Kerner, R. *The Urge to the Sea: The Course of Russian History*. Berkeley, 1942.

Klyuchevsky, V. O. *A History of Russia*. 5 vols. New York, 1911-1931.

———. *The Rise of the Romanovs*. Trans. L. Archibald. New York, 1970.

Kmietowicz, Frank A. *Ancient Slavs*. Stevens Point, Wisc., 1976.

Kochan, M. *Life in Russia Under Catherine the Great*. London, 1969.

Kohn, Hans. *The Mind of Modern Russia*. New Brunswick, N. J., 1955.

Kondrakov, N. *The Russian Icon*, Oxford, 1927.

Koslow, Jules. *Ivan the Terrible*. New York, 1961.

———. *The Kremlin, Symbol of Russia*. London, 1960.

Kostka, Edmund K. *Schiller in Russian Literature*. Phila., 1965.

Lampert, E. *Studies in Rebellion*. New York, 1957.

———. *Sons Against Fathers: Studies in Russian Radicalism and Revolution*. London, 1965.

Lang, D. M. "Boileau and Sumarokov, the Manifesto of Russian Classicism." *Modern Language Review*, XLIII (1948), 500-506.

———. *The First Russian Radical: Alexander Radishchev, 1749-1802*. London, 1959.

Lantzeff, George V., and Richard A. Pierce. *Eastward to Empire: Exploration and Conquest on the Russian Open Frontier, to 1750*. Montreal and London, 1973.

Lentin, A. *Russia in the Eighteenth Century: From Peter the Great to Catherine the Great*. (1696-1796). New York, 1973.

Leonard, R. *A History of Russian Music*. New York, 1957.

Lipski, Alexander. "A Re-examination of the 'Dark Era' of Anna Ioannovna." *The American Slavic and East European Review*, 15 (1956), 477-488.

Longworth, Philip. *The Three Empresses: Catherine I, Anne and Elizabeth of Russia*. London, 1972.

Lossky, N. O. *History of Russian Philosophy*. New York, 1951.

Lukashevich, S. *Ivan Aksakov, 1923-1886: A Study in Russian Thought and Politics*. Cambridge, 1965.

Lyons, Marvin. *Nicholas II: The Last Tsar*. Wheatcroft, N.Y., 1974.

MacMaster, Robert E. *Danilevsky: A Russian Totalitarian Philosopher*. Cambridge, Mass., 1967.

McNally, Raymond. *Chaadayev and his Friends: An Intellectual History of P. Chaadayev and his Russian Contemporaries*. Tallahassee, Fla., 1971.

Macha, Josef, S.J. *Ecclesiastical Unification: A Theoretical Framework Together with Case Studies from the History of Latin-Byzantine Relations*. Rome, 1974.

Malia, Martin. *Alexander Herzen and the Birth of Russian Socialism (1812-1855)*. Cambridge, Mass., 1961.

Maloney, George A., S. J. *Russian Hesychasm: The Spirituality of Nil Sorskij*. The Hague and Paris, 1973.

Masaryk, Thomas G. *The Spirit of Russia: Studies in History, Literature and Philosophy*. 2 vols. New York, 1955.

Mathewson, Rufus W., Jr. *The Positive Hero in Russian Literature*. 2nd ed. Stanford, Cal., 1975.

Mazour, A. G. *Modern Russian Historiography*. Princeton, N. J., 1958.

———. *The First Russian Revolution, 1825*. Stanford, 1961.

———. *Women in Exile: Wives of the Decembrists*, Tallahassee, Fla., 1975.

Menshutkin, B. M. *Russia's Lomonosov: Chemist, Courtier, Physicist, Poet*. Princeton, N.J., 1952.

Miliukov, Paul. *Outlines of Russian Culture*. 3 vols. Phila., 1942; reprinted, Gulf Breeze,

Fla., 1975.

Mirsky, Dmitri S. *A History of Russian Literature.* New York, 1955.

Mochulsky, K. *Dostoevsky: His Life and Work.* Princeton, 1967.

Muller, Alexander V. *The Spiritual Regulation of Peter the Great.* Seattle, 1972.

Nerhood, Harry W., comp. *To Russia and Return: An Annotated Bibliography of Travelers' English-Language Accounts of Russia from the Ninth Century to the Present.* Columbus, Ohio, 1968.

Oldenbourg, Zoe. *Catherine the Great.* Trans. A. Carter. New York, 1965.

Oliva, L. Jay. *Russia in the Era of Peter the Great.* Englewood Cliffs, N.J., 1969.

–––. *Catherine the Great.* Englewood Cliffs, N. J., 1971.

Payne, Robert. *The Holy Fire: The Story of the Eastern Church.* London, 1958.

–––, and Nikita Romanoff. *Ivan the Terrible.* New York, 1975.

Pelenski, Jaroslaw. *Russia and Kazan: Conquest and Imperial Ideology* (1438-1560's). The Hague and Paris, 1974.

Pipes, Richard, ed. *The Russian Intelligentsia.* New York, 1961.

–––. *Struve. Liberal on the Left, 1870-1905.* Cambridge, Mass., 1970.

–––. *Russia Under the Old Regime.* New York, 1974.

Platonov, S. F. *A History of Russia.* New York, 1925.

–––. The Time of Troubles: *A Historical Study of the Internal Crisis and Social Struggle in Sixteenth- and Seventeenth-Century Moscovy.* Trans. J. Alexander. Lawrence, Kansas, 1970.

–––. *Moscow and the West.* Trans. J. L. Wieczynski. Hattiesburg, Miss., 1972.

–––. *Boris Godinov: Tsar in Russia.* Gulf Breeze, Fla., 1973.

–––. *Ivan the Terrible.* Gulf Breeze, Fla., 1974.

Poggioli, R. "Vyacheslav Ivanov." Oxford Slavonic Papers, V (1954), 41-55.

–––. *The Poets of Russia: 1890-1930.* Cambridge, Mass., 1960.

Pronin, Alexander, and Barbara Pronin. *Russian Folk Arts.* South Brunswick and New York, 1975.

Raeff, M. M. *Speranskij, a Statesman of Russia.* Den Haag, 1957.

Riasanovsky, V. V. *Russia and the West in the Teaching of the Slavophiles.* Cambridge, Mass., 1952.

–––. *Nicholas I and Official Nationality in Russia: 1825-1855.* Berkeley and Los Angeles, 1961.

–––. *A History of Russia.* New York, 1969.

Rice, David, and Tamar Tolbot Rice. *Icons and Their History.* Woodstock, N.Y., 1974.

Rice, Tamara Tolbot. *A Concise History of Russian Art.* New York, 1963.

–––. *Elizabeth: Empress of Russia.* London, 1970.

Rogger, Hans. *National Consciousness in Eighteenth-Century Russia.* Cambridge, Mass., 1960.

Rosenthal, Bernice Glatzer. *Dmitri Sergeevich Merezhkovsky: The Development of a Revolutionary Mentality.* The Hague, 1975.

Sablinsky, Walter. *The Road to Bloody Sunday.* Princeton, 1976.

Schneiderman, Jeremiah. *Sergei Zubatov and Revolutionary Marxism: The Struggle for the Working Class in Tsarist Russia.* Ithaca, N.Y., 1976.

Setchkarev, Vsevolod. *Gogol: His Life and Works.* New York, 1965.

Simmons, E. J. *English Literature and Culture in Russia (1553-1840).* Cambridge, Mass., 1935.

Slonim, M. *Russian Theater from the Empire to the Soviets.* Riverside, N.J., 1961.

Sokolov, Y. M. *Russian Folklore.* Trans. C. R. Smith. New York, 1950.

Spector, Ivar, and Marion Spector, eds. *Readings in Russian History and Culture.* Palo Alto, 1968.

Szamuely, Tibor. *The Russian Tradition.* New York, 1975.

Terras, Victor. *Belinskij and Russian Literary Criticism: The Heritage of Organic*

Aesthetics. Madison, Wisc., 1974.

Tomkins, S. R. *The Russian Mind.* Norman, Oka., 1953.

Uspensky, Boris. *The Semiotics of the Russian Icon.* The Netherlands, 1976.

Utechin, S. V. *Russian Political Thought: A Concise History.* New York, 1964.

Venturi, F. *Roots of Revolution.* New York, 1960.

Vernadsky, G. *Ancient Russia.* New Haven, Conn., 1943.

–––. *The Origins of Russia.* Oxford, 1959.

Vlasto, A. P. *The Entry of the Slavs into Christendom: An Introduction to the Medieval History of the Slavs.* New York, 1970.

von Herberstein, Sigmund. *Description of Moscow and Muscovy 1557.* Ed. Bertold Picard, trans. J. B. C. Grundy. New York, 1969.

Voyce, A. *Russian Architecture: Trends in Nationalism and Modernism.* New York, 1948.

Vucinich, A. *Science in Russian Culture.* Stanford, Cal. 1963.

Walder, David. *The Short Victorious War: The Russo-Japanese Conflict, 1904-5.* London, 1973.

Waliszewski, Kazimierz. *Ivan the Terrible.* Phila., 1904.

–––. *Paul the First of Russia.* London, 1913.

Ware, T. *The Orthodox Church.* Baltimore, 1969.

Weeks, Albert L. *The First Bolshevik: A Political Biography of Peter Tkachev.* New York, 1968.

Aristotle, 101, 126, 166
Arkhipenko, Alexander, 242
Armenia, Armenians, 135
Army, Russian, 34, 97, 145, 147, 154, 207
Arndt, Johann, 175
Ars magna et ultima (Raimundus Lullus), 156, 248
Art, Russian, 38, 127, 196, 210, 222 f., 227, 233 f., 240 ff.
Asceticism, ascetics, 27, 40 ff., 45 ff., 54 ff., 58, 69 ff., 76 ff., 80 ff., 86 f., 107, 158, 174, 225
Asef, Evno, 241
Asia, Asiatics, 63, 219, 244 ff.
Askoldov, A., 239
Assassins, Assassinations, *see* Terrorism, Terrorists
Associationism, 13
Astrakhan, 63 f., 90, 136
Astrology, 92, 129
Astronomy, 68, 157
Atheism, 169, 203, 208, 223, 245
Athos, Mount, 41, 75 f., 99
Augustine, St., 13, 239
Augustus, Emperor of Rome, 93 f., 103
Avraamii Palitsyn (monk), 114
Avraamii of Smolensk, St., 57 f.
Avvakum, Archpriest, 118 ff.
Azov, Sea of, 18, 63, 162
Azov (Turkish fortress), 145

Babylon, Babylonian Empire, 94
Bakunin, Mikhail, 249
Baldwin I, King of Jerusalem (1100-1118), 28
Ballet, 240, 244
Balmont, Konstantin, 234
Baltic Sea, 31
Banishment, 99, 114, 119
Baptism, 18, 21 f., 25, 27
Barlaam and Josephat, 138
Baroque poetics, 156
Baroque poetry, Muscovite, 127, 163 f.
Basil, *see* Vasilii
Basil II, Emperor of Byzantium (976-1025), 21
"Basil the New" (saint's life by Palladius), 156
Basileia (Maksim Grek), 100
Batu [Batyi] (Tatar general, grandson of Ghengis Khan), 63
Beccaria, Cesare Marchese de Bonesana, 167
Bekbulatovich, Simeon [Saint Bulat of Kasimov], 136
Belinsky, Vissarion Grigorievich, 201 f., 211, 249
The Bell (*Kolokol,* edited by Herzen), 203
Bel'tov, N. [pseudonym of Plekhanov], 232
Bely, Andrei [pseudonym of Boris Nikolaievich Bugayev], 234, 240 f., 246, 249
Berdyaev, Nikolai Alexandrovich, 217, 239 ff.
Beregini (demon), 24
Bergson, Henri, 235
Berkeley, George, 13

Expropriation, 97, 230

Family life, 109 f.
Famine of 1601-1603, 111, 113
Famine of 1891, 229
Fasting, 41 ff., 78, 81 f., 107, 142, 154, 158, 169, 225
Fathers and Sons, 210, 213
Fedorov, Ivan, 126
Fedotov, Georgii Petrovich, 33, 81, 105, 173
Feodor (uncle of Peter the Great), 144
Feodor I [Ivanovich], Tsar (1584-1598), 100, 111, 113
Feodor II [son of Boris Godunov], Tsar (1605), 111
Feodor III [Alekseievich], Tsar (1676-1682), 112, 126, 196
Feodosii, Archbishop of Novgorod, 94 f.
Feodosii, St. (abbot of the Kievan Cave Monastery), 34 f., 37, 41 f., 45, 47, 55, 95
Ferapont of Menzen, 74
Feuds, 14 f., 30, 33; among princes 34 ff., 48 ff., 59, 65
Feuerbach, Ludwig, 199, 219
Fichte, Johann Gottlieb, 239
"Fifth Ecumenical Council," 93
Filaret, Patriarch, 112 f., 116
Filipp, St. (metropolitan), 100 f., 105 f., 111, 114
Filofei (monk of Pskov), 92 f.
Finances, 147 (*see also* Taxation)
Fines, 37
Finns, 12, 25, 70
Fletcher, Giles, 108, 111, 128 f.
Florence, 164
Florentine-Ferrara Union, 66, 119
Florovsky, Georgii Vasillievich, 66, 68, 93, 174, 208, 222
Folk songs, Russian, 14, 162, 205
Fonvizin, Denis Ivanovich, 169, 180 f.
Foreign policy, 32, 50 f., 95, 145 ff., 183
Four Books on the True Christianity (Johann Arndt), 175
Fourier, Charles, 201, 205, 212, 249
Fourierism, 201 f., 212 f., 249
France, 182, 210
Frank, Semen, 239, 241, 250
Frederick the Great, King of Prussia, 162
Frederick III of Holstein-Gottorp, 129
Frederick III, Emperor of the Holy Roman Empire (1452-1493), 88
Freemasonry, Freemasons, 173 ff., 183
French Revolution, 167, 175, 201
From the Other Shore (Herzen), 202
Futurists, 241

Gabo [pseudonym of Naum Pevsner], 242
Galen, 68
Galicia, 51, 63
Gallomania, 181 f.
Gauntlet, throwing down of the, 14 f.
Genealogies, false, 93 f., 103

139, 141, 145, 190, 192, 196
Ivan V (co-tsar with Peter the Great, 1682-1696), 112, 114
Ivan VI, Emperor (1740-1741), 161, 166, 248
Ivanov, Viacheslav, 239 f.
Iziaslav I [Yaroslavovich], Grand Prince of Kiev (1054-1078), 36, 41
Iziaslav II [Vsevolodovich], Grand Prince (1146-1154), 59

Japan, Japanese, 237, 245 f.
"Jewish Synod," 171
John (alleged emperor-priest of India), 137
John of Bulgaria, Archbishop, 28
John Chrysostum, St., 34, 45
John Climakos, 77, 79, 93
Josif Volotskii [Volokolamskii], 75 f., 80 ff., 89, 97 ff., 105, 121
Journalism, journalists, 91 ff., 100 ff., 168, 176 f., 187, 191, 198 ff., 202, 218 f., 224,
    228 f., 231 ff., 240 f.
Journey from Petersburg to Moscow (Radishchev), 177 ff., 182
Judaizers *[zhidovstvuiushchie]*, 67 ff., 79 ff., 128
Judicial reform, 207
Juliana, St., 46
Jung-Stilling [i.e. Johann Heinrich Jung (1740-1817)], 183
Justice, 30, 35 ff., 90, 95 f., 101 ff., 113 f., 198
Justinian, Emperor, 39

Kalka River, 63
Kalmucks, 136
Kandinsky, Vasilii, 234, 242
Kant, Immanuel, 162, 182, 200, 240
Kantemir, Antiokh, 152 f., 163
Das Kapital, 212
Karakazov, Dimitrii (would-be assassin of Alexander II), 213
Karamzin, Nikolai Mikhailovich, 182, 200
Karna (demon), 24
Karpov, Fedor, 101 f., 110 f., 116, 126
Kazan, 63, 90, 126, 136
Khazar empire, 20, 30 f., 135
Khlysty (flagellant sect), 171
Khomiakov, Aleksei Stepanovich, 186, 190, 194 ff., 198, 200, 248
Khors (East Slavic god), 23
Khvorostinin, Prince Ivan, 127
Kiev, 15, 18, 20 ff., 27 ff., 30, 34 f., 38 ff., 43, 45, 48, 52, 54, 57, 59, 61 ff., 67,
    127, 140, 152, 156, 248
Kievan Academy, 152, 156
Kievan Cave Monastery, 34 f., 40 ff., 45, 55, 59 f., 70
The Kingdom of God in Us (L. Tolstoy), 242
Kireevsky, Ivan Vasillievich, 190 ff., 196, 205
Kireevsky, Piotr Vasillievich, 205
Kirill, St. (9th century), 122
Kirill of Beloozero, St., 73 ff.
Kirill of Turov, St. (bishop), 37, 56 f., 62
Klim Smoliatich, 37
Kliuchevskii, Vasilii Ossipovich, 90, 103, 120, 147, 161
Kniga o vere [Book of Faith], 123

Knighthood, 19, 49 ff.
Kobiak (Polovtsian chieftain), 48
Kola Peninsula, 73
Kollar, 249
Korea, 245
Kotoschikhin, Grigorii, 127
Kovalevskaya, Sofia, 223
Kovalevskii, Maksim, 223
Križanič, Jurii, 127
Kropotkin, Prince Piotr Alekseievich, 217, 249
Krushchev, Ivan, 86
Krylov, Ivan Andreievich, 176
Küchelbecker, W., 205
Kulaki, 229
Kurbskii, Prince Andrei, 101 ff., 111
Kuritsyn, Fedor, 67
Kursk, 50

Labor movement, 230 f., 236 ff.
Lake Ilmen, 18
Lake Ladoga, 18
Lamennais, Hugues Félicité Robert, 199, 249
"Lament of the Slaves" *(Plach kholopov),* 176
Landowners, 109, 117, 139, 176 f., 178 ff., 207, 212 f., 217, 230, 238
Language, East Slavic, 19, 38
Language, French, 180, 182
Language, German, 68 f., 180, 190
Language, Greek, 61, 84, 118
Language, Old Church Slavic, 27
Language, Old Russian, 12, 15
Language, Russian, borrowings from Scandinavian, West Germanic, and Greek, 19
Language, Russian Oriental influences on, 137
Last Judgment, 57 f., 123
Latin and Armenian heresy, 113
Latin language and literature, 38, 68, 106, 126
Lavater, Johann Kaspar, 182
Lavrov, Piotr, 230f.
Law, 14 (Old Polish); 37(pagan); 101 f. (Russian)
Lay of the Host of Igor, 23 f., 35, 48 ff., 54, 135
Lefort, Francis, 154
Legends, 14, 35, 41 f., 45 ff., 69, 71 f., 74 f., 76 f., 93 ff., 100, 104 ff.
Legends about *yurodivye,* 106 ff.
Leibniz, Gottfried Wilhelm, 239, 245
Lenin, V. I. [pseudonym of Vladimir Ilyich Ulyanov], 216, 232, 238
Leninism, 201
Leontiev, Konstantin, 220, 224
Lermontov, Mikhail Yuryevich, 205, 211
Leshii (wood sprite), 24
Leskov, Nikolai Semyonovich, 242
Letters of a Russian Traveler (Karamzin), 182
Liberalism, liberals, 183, 202 ff., 217 ff., 222, 226 ff., 230 ff., 237 f., 241
Literary salons, 187, 189, 194 f., 200
Literature, ecclesiastical, 36

Literature, European, 101, 153, 174 ff., 199, 201 ff.
Literature, illegal, 213
Literature, Indian, 137 f.
Literature, Latin, 38
Literature, Old Church Slavic, 27, 99, 122
Literature, Pietistic, 159
Literature, Russian, 27, 37, 40, 113, 135, 156, 163 ff., 166, 168 182 f., 196, 205, 209 ff., 222 f., 227, 233 f., 240 f., 242, 245 ff.
Literature, Russian, ornate style of, 48 ff., 54, 56
Literature, Russian, philosophical, 239
Literature, Russian, polemical, 91 f., 100, 113 f., 122., 168
Literature, Russian, political, 176 ff., 220, 233
Literature, Russian, religious, 26 ff., 40 f., 43 f., 54, 56, 60 f., 67 f., 70 f., 76 ff., 124
Lithuania, 102
Liturgy, Slavic, 27
Liubech, 41
Liuboml', Church of St. George, 53
Liubomudry, 189
Lobachevsky, Nikolai Ivanovich, 223
Locke, John, 13
Lomonosov, Mikhail, 163 f., 168, 179, 248
Losskii, Nikolai Onifriyevich, 239
Louis-Pasteur-Institute, 218
Lucidarius, 68f.
Ludmila, St., 28
Lullus, Raimundus, 156, 160, 248
Luther, Martin, 158
Lutheranism, Lutherans, 113

Mably, Gabriel Bonnot de, 181
Maikov, Nikolai, see Nil Sorskii
Maimonides, Moses, 68
Maistre, Joseph Marie Comte de, 199
Makarii, Metropolitan of Moscow, 86, 95, 104
Maksim Grek, 98 ff., 106, 110, 122, 126
Malebranche, Nicole, 13
Malewich, Kasimier, 242
Malinin, Vladimir, 92
Malinovskii (Bolshevik labor leader), 241
Manchuria, 245
Manuscripts, 13 f., 26 f., 61, 155 f., 163 f., 174 f.
Maria of Suzdal, Princess, 54
Martov, Yulius [pseudonym of Yulius Ossipovich Zederbaum], 238, 250
Martyrdom, martyrs, 33 f., 55, 124
Marx, Karl, 199, 212
Marxism, 13, 201, 209, 231 f., 241
Maskiewicz, 110
Mat' syra zemlia [Mother Moist Earth], 24
Materialism, 209, 211 f., 217, 223, 227 f., 233, 235
"Mathematicals" *[tsifirnyi],* 151 f.
Maximus the Confessor, 79, 105
Mayakovsky, Vladimir, 241

"Measures for the Prevention of Crimes" (in the 15-volume collection of Russian laws), 185 f.
Mechnikov, Ilya, 218, 223
Medicine, 142, 159, 218
Mediterranean Sea, 47
Melnikov, Pavel Ivanovich [pseudonym: Andrei Pecherskii], 157
"Men of the Sixties" *[shestidesiatniki]*, 227
Mensheviks, 238
Menshikov, Alexander Daniilovich, 146, 161
Merezhkovskii, Dimitrii, 233, 236, 250
Mestnichestvo [service nobility], 114
Methodius, St., 122
Mikhail of Chernigov, Prince, 64 f.
Mikhail of Klopovo, St., 108
Mikhail Romanov, Tsar (1613-1645), 15, 112 f., 115 f.
Mikhailov, M. L., 215
Mikhailovskii, Nikolai Konstantinovich, 228, 230
Militant Union for the Liberation of the Working Classes *[Soiuz bor'by]*, 231
Military affairs, 142, 145, 153 f., 179, 207, 225
Military service, universal, 207
Minsk, 36, 231
Mir, 196 ff., 203, 212, 219, 221, 229 f., 249
Miscellany [Isbornik], 43 f., 61
Mochalov, 210, 249
Moehler, Johann Adam, 198 f.
Mohammed [the Great], Sultan, 96 f.
Mohammedanism, 20, 128
Mokosh (East Slavic god), 23
Molokane (sect of "castrati"), 171
Monarchy, 179 f., 184, 201 f., 237
Monarchy, constitutional, 184, 237
Monasteries, founding of, 37
Monasteries, rules of, 78, 80 f.
Monasteries, wealth of, 56, 79 f., 84, 98
Monastery of the Caves near Kiev, *see* Kievan Cave Monastery
Monastery on the White Sea, 98
Monasticism, Palestinian, 42
Monasticism, Russian, 41 ff., 54 ff., 60 ff., 75 ff., 79 ff., 98 f., 101 f., 148 f., 169, 224
Mongols, 128, 136
Montesquieu, Charles, 167
Moravia, 63
Moscow, Muscovy, 16, 64, 67, 74, 82 ff., 87 ff., 90 ff., 97, 99, 106 ff, 110 ff., 118 f., 125 ff., 139 f., 144 f., 152, 156, 159, 189, 191, 200, 202
"Moscow–the Third Rome," 91 ff., 96, 104, 111, 123
Moskvitianin (journal), 199
Mother Moist Earth *[mat' syra zemla],* 24
Mstislav, Grand Prince of Kiev (1125-1132), 31, 47
Mstislav, Vladimirovich [the Brave], 34
Munich, 191, 199, 234, 242
Münnich, Burkhard Christoph, 161
Muscovite absolutism, 15, 84, 87 ff., 90 ff., 97 ff., 110, 114 f.
Music, composers, 162, 171, 196, 210, 223
Musorgsky, Modest Petrovich, 223

My Past and Thoughts (Byloe i dumy) (Herzen), 202
Mysticism (Byzantine), 69
Mysticism, in Russia, 79, 174 f., 183, 192, 239
Mythology, low (East Slavic), 23 ff.

Napoleon, 16, 138, 183, 188
Napoleonic Wars, 183, 187 f.
Narodnaia volia ("The People's Will"—a terrorist group), 215
Narodniki, 197, 213, 215, 229 ff., 237, 241
Nastas [Anastasius] (Greek churchman), 28
Nataliia Narishkyna, Tsarina (1689-1694) (mother of Peter the Great), 144, 154
Nationalism, 50, 117, 122
Natural Law, 111, 170
Natural sciences, 210 f., 223
Navy, Russian, 145, 147, 151
Nebuchadnezzar, King, 94
Nechaev, Serge [Jacobin] (terrorist), 217
Nekrasov, Nikolai Alekseievich, 142
Neoclassicism, 163, 178, 182
Neokantians, 235
Neoplatonism, 73 f.
Neoromanticism, 234 f., 240
Nestor (monk and chronicler), 18, 35
Nestor Chronicle, 18 *et passim*
"New man," 164, 174, 240
New Oriental Travels (Oehlenschlager), 129
New Realism, 239
The New Word (*Novoe Slovo,* a Marxist periodical), 232
Nicholas [Alexandrovich] (brother of Alexander III), 226
Nicholas I, Emperor (1825-1855), 184 f., 187, 191, 199, 204 ff., 207, 210 ff., 217,
    221 f., 227
Nicholas II, Emperor (1894-1917), 221, 226
Nicolas Cusanus, 248
Nietzsche, Friedrich, 220, 235
Nihilism, nihilists, 208, 213, 219 f., 227
Nikifor, Metropolitan of Kiev, 43
Nikola of Pskov (holy fool), 108
Nikola Sviatosha, Prince of Chernigov (and monk at the Kievan Cave Monastery), 60
Nikon (monk and author), 81
Nikon, Patriarch of Moscow, 112, 116, 118 ff., 121, 123 f.
"Nikonian church," 122 ff.
"Nikonian Councils," 122
"Nikonian innovations," 122
Nil Sorskii, 71 ff., 75, 77 ff., 86 f., 95, 97 ff., 104, 111, 121
Nizhnii Novgorod, 112
Nobility, ranking of *[mestnichestvo],* 114
Normans, *see* Varangians
Novgorod, 18, 22, 33, 37, 41, 49 ff., 59, 61, 63, 65, 67, 90, 106, 108, 112, 139 ff.,
    152, 192
Novikov, Nikolai Ivanovich, 175 f.

Occident, 26, 47, 68
Odoevskii, Prince Alexander, 205

Odoevskii, Prince Vladimir, 189, 219
Oehlenschlager, Adam [Olearius], 110, 112, 129
Officialdom, government officials, 90, 96 f., 179, 214, 218, 227
Old Believers, 120 ff., 127, 153, 155 ff., 160, 170 ff., 177, 183 185, 192, 225
"Old Church," 119 f.
Olearius [Adam Oehlenschlager], 110, 112
Oleg [Sviatoslavich] (son of Grand Prince Sviatoslav Igorevich of Kiev), 20
Oleg [Sviatoslavich], Prince of Chernigov (son of Grand Prince Sviatoslav Yaroslavich
    of Kiev), 36
Olga, Grand Princess of Kiev (regent 945-962), 20, 54
On the Corruption of Morals in Russia (Prince Shcherbatov), 181
Oproshchenie, 243 f.
Optina Hermitage [Optina pustyn'], 224
Ordeals, 14
Ordyn-Nashchokin, Voin Afsanievich, 127
Orient, 19, 24, 30, 47, 49, 67 f., 135 ff., 204, 244 ff.
Oriental College (Vladivostock), 246
Oriental studies, 244 f.
Orthodoxy, 68 f., 82 f., 115, 117, 123 ff.
Ostermann, Heinrich Johann Friedrich, 161
Ostromirovo Gospel, 27
Ostrovskii, Alexander Nikolaievich, 180
Ovid, 101

Pacific Ocean, 245
Pafnutii Borovskii, St. (abbot), 80
Paganism, 19 ff., 34 ff.
Painting and sculpture, 127, 196, 210, 223, 242
Paisos, Patriarch of Constantinople, 118
Palace Guard, 161 f., 216
Paleologue, Zoe (wife of Grand Prince Ivan III), 140
Palestine, 28
Palladius (bishop), 45 f., 61, 156
Pandecta, 81
Panegyric (to Emperor Justinian), 39
Panslavism, 218, 221
"Papist-Calvinist-Lutheran faith," 113
Paris, 164, 234, 242
Paphnutius (hermit), 46
Pascal, Blaise, 13
Pasternak, Boris, 241
Pasteur, Louis, 210
Patericon of the Kievan Cave Monastery, 55 ff.
Patericon of Palladius *[Historia lauciaca]*, 46, 61
Patericon of Pope Gregory, 28
Patience *[terpenie, dolgoterpenie]*, 101 ff.
Paul I, Emperor (1796-1801), 166, 178, 183, 250
Pavel of Obnora, St., 71, 74
Pechenegs, 31 ff.
"The People's Will" [Narodnaia volia] (terrorist group), 215
Peredvizhniki (artists' group), 223
Peremyshl, 53
Peresvetov, Ivan 95 ff., 102, 104, 111

Periodicals, *see* Journalism
Perovskaia, Sofia (terrorist), 217
Persians, 136, 246
Perun (East Slavic god), 21 ff.
Pessimism, religious, 54, 56 ff., 98 f.
Peter I [the Great], Emperor (1682-1725), 16, 112, 116, 138, 142, 144 ff., 158 ff., 168 f., 170 f., 185, 190, 193, 200, 202 f., 219
Peter II, Emperor (1727-1730), 161
Peter III, Emperor (1762), 161, 166, 170, 177
Peter of Wallachia, Prince, 96
Petersburg (Andrei Bely), 241, 246
"Petitions to Heaven's Chancellory," 176
Petrasheveskii, Mikhail Vasilievich, 202
Petrine reforms, 16, 138, 142 ff., 148 ff., 158, 162, 181 f., 202 f., 224
Petsamo, 73
Pevsner, Antoine, 242
Pevsner, Naum [pseudonym: Gabo], 242
Phenomenology, 13
"Philosophical Letter to a Lady" (Chaadaev), 200
"Philosophical Letters" (Chaadaev), 200
Philosophy, 189, 195, 199, 203 ff., 211 f., 219, 227, 233 f., 239
Philotheos, *see* Filofei
Pietism, pietists, 159, 168, 171, 175, 183, 225, 244
Piety, external, 39 f., 81 f., 87, 119, 142
Piety, lay, 40, 42 ff., 58 ff.
Piety, pseudomorphic, 87
Pirogov, Nikolai Ivanovich, 223
Pisarev, Dimitrii, 210 ff.
Platon, Metropolitan, 170
Platonism, 13
Plekhanov, Georgii Valentinovich, 232, 238
Plotinus, 13
Pobedonostsev, Konstantin Petrovich, 220 ff., 224 ff., 236, 246
Pochvenniki [enthusiasts of the soil], 218 ff.
Poe, Edgar Allen, 240
Poetry, poets, 14, 126 f., 162 f., 168, 171, 176, 180, 185 ff., 196, 199, 205, 222 ff., 233 f., 239 ff.
Poland, Poles, 12, 14, 32, 35, 90, 96, 111 ff., 114 f., 126, 141, 162, 166, 188, 249
Poland-Lithuania, 16, 64, 67, 118
Police state, 148 ff., 158, 185 f., 213 ff.
Polish Rebellion of 1863, 208
Polotskii, Simeon, 127
Polotsk, 30
Polovtsy, (Cumans), 35 f., 48 ff., 52, 58, 63, 135
Poltava, Battle of, 146
Polycarp (abbot), 59 f.
Polycarp (monk), 55
Positivism, 203, 209, 211, 227, 233, 235
Pososhkov, Ivan, 153, 157 ff., 248
The Possessed, 108, 210, 217, 249
Postal service, 139 f.
Potyomkin, Prince Grigorii Alexandrovich, 166
Prayer(s), 26, 42 f., 56, 76, 78, 82, 98

Predanie [Instruction] (Nil Sorskii), 76
Predislava-Evfrosiniia of Polotsk, Princess, 54
Pre-romanticism, 168
Priests, pagan, 26
Primary Chronicle, 18 *et passim*
Prince, the ideal, 35 ff., 42 f., 53, 94 f.
Princes, power of, 88 f., 140
Prince and Churchmen, 35, 42 f., 97, 100 f.
Printing, 126
Problems of Idealism (collection of essays), 235, 239
Prokhor (monk), 55 f.
Prokopii of Ustiug (holy fool), 107
Prokopovich, Feofan (archbishop of Novgorod), 147, 159 ff.
Proletariat, 231, 238
Property, 244
Prosvetitel' [The Enlightener], 81 f.
Protestantism, 67, 106, 142, 146 f., 159, 170, 219, 224, 235, 243
Proverbs, 14
Prus (legendary brother of Emperor Augustus), 93
Prussia, 93, 162
Pseudo-pacifism, 87
Pseudo-socialism, 87
Pskov, 90, 92, 106, 108, 139 ff.
Pskov Chronicle, 108
Publishing, 126, 155 f., 163 f., 175 f., 239
Pugachev, Emil, 167, 172, 177 f., 248
Puni [i.e. Jean Pougny], 242
Pushkin, Alexander, 129, 205, 211, 235, 248
"Pushkin Speech" (Dostoevsky), 219

Radishchev, Alexander, 177 ff., 183
Railroads, 207
Raskol, see Schism of 1666
Raskol'niki [schismatics], 119
Rationalism, 13, 195
Razin, Stepan [Stenka], 112, 192
Reading Menaea, 104 f.
Realism, 210, 223, 240, 242, 245
Reason, 76, 243
Recruitment of foreigners, 125, 145
Reform of the Church, *see* Schism of 1666
Reformation, 120 ff., 125
Reforms of Ivan the Terrible, 90, 104
Reforms of Peter the Great, 16, 138, 142 ff., 148 ff., 158, 162, 181 f., 202 f., 224
Reforms of the Sixties, 207 ff., 212 f., 217 f., 221, 226 f., 233, 236
Reforms of the Sixties, reaction to, 215, 221 f., 224 ff., 236 f.
Regensburg, 140
Reign of Terror, 90 f., 96, 100 f., 108
Religion (in post-Petrine Russia), 194 ff., 223 ff., 234 ff.
Religious and Philosophical Society, 236
Renan, Ernest, 219
Representative government bodies, 114 f.
Republicanism, 179, 184

"Resound, O Thunder of Victory" *[Grom pobedy razdavaisia]*, 167
Revolt, Pugachev, 167, 172, 177 f., 248
Revolts, rebellions, 15, 112, 116 f., 125, 144 f., 184, 192, 212 f., 230
Revolution, 179 f., 208, 213, 215
Revolution of 1830 (in France), 201
Revolution of 1848, 185, 201, 203, 249
Revolution of 1905, 17, 236 ff., 246
Revolution of 1917, 138, 205, 237 f., 241 f., 246 f.
Revolutionary movement, 184, 202, 212 ff., 225 ff., 231, 236 ff., 240 f., 243, 249
Revue des deux mondes, 199
Rhine River, 182
Riazan, 63
Ritualistic piety, 87, 119 f.
Riurik [Roerek], Riurik dynasty, 19, 30 ff., 88, 93, 103
Romanticism, romanticists, 14, 239, 245
Romanticism, German, 189 f., 194, 198 f.
Romanticism, Russian, 170, 183 f.
Rome, 28, 93 f., 119, 154, 156, 249
Roslagen, 19
Rostislav of Smolensk, Prince, 53, 59 f.
Rostov, 107
Rousseau, Jean-Jacques, 168
Rozanov, Vasilii, 239
Rozhenitsy (demons), 24
Ruckert, Heinrich, 249
Rumania, Rumanians, 221
Runners *[Beguny]* (Old Believers' sect), 171
Rus', 19, 30
Rusalki, 25
Russian Academy of Sciences, 163, 223
Russia and Europe (Danilevskii), 220 f.
Russia-Europe antithesis, 191 ff., 196, 220 f.
Russian Justice [Russkaia pravda], 36 f.
Russian Nights (Odoevskii), 189
The Russian Symbolists (anthologies), 234
"Russian synthesis," 219 f.
Russo-Byzantine Treaty of 945, 31
Russo-Japanese War, 237, 245
Russo-Turkish War, 218
Ryleev, Kondratii Feodorovich, 184

Saardam, 145
Sabbas, St., 42
Sacrifice, human, 20, 23
Sagas, 19 (Scandinavian); 19 (Slavic)
Saint-Martin, Louis Claude Marquis de, 175
St. Petersburg, 146 f., 184, 201 f., 215, 223, 231, 246
Saints, 23, 26, 33 f., 67, 74 f., 105 ff., 122, 170
Saloi [holy fools], 105 ff.
Saltykov-Shchedrin, Mikhail Yevgravovich, 211, 228
Samarin, Yurii, 190, 195
Saracens, 53
Savonarola, Giralmo, 99